Professional Mobility in Islamic Societies (700–1750)

Professional Mobility in Islamic Societies (700–1750)

New Concepts and Approaches

Edited by

Mohamad El-Merheb
Mehdi Berriah

TUTA SUB AEGIDE PALLAS · 1683 ·

BRILL

LEIDEN | BOSTON

Originally published in hardback in 2021 as Volume 157 in the series *Handbook of Oriental Studies, Section 1: The Near and Middle East.*

Cover illustration: Interior stairway and arches, Ibn Yūsuf madrasa, 16th century, Marrakesh (photo: Alamy)

Library of Congress Cataloging-in-Publication Data

Names: El-Merheb, Mohamad, editor. | Berriah, Mehdi, editor.
Title: Professional mobility in Islamic societies (700–1750) : new concepts and approaches / edited by Mohamad El-Merheb, Mehdi Berriah.
Description: Leiden ; Boston : Brill, [2021] | Series: Handbook of Oriental studies = Handbuch der Orientalistik. Section One, The Near and Middle East, 0169-9423 ; volume 157 | Includes bibliographical references and index.
Identifiers: LCCN 2021026990 (print) | LCCN 2021026991 (ebook) | ISBN 9789004467620 (hardback ; alk. paper) | ISBN 9789004467637 (ebook)
Subjects: LCSH: Social mobility—Islamic countries—History. | Islamic countries—Civilization.
Classification: LCC HN656.Z9 S677 2021 (print) | LCC HN656.Z9 (ebook) | DDC 305.5/1309176—dc23
LC record available at https://lccn.loc.gov/2021026990
LC ebook record available at https://lccn.loc.gov/2021026991

Typeface for the Latin, Greek, and Cyrillic scripts: "Brill". See and download: brill.com/brill-typeface.

ISSN 0169-9423
ISBN 978-90-04-69595-5 (paperback, 2024)
ISBN 978-90-04-46762-0 (hardback)
ISBN 978-90-04-46763-7 (e-book)

Contents

Foreword VII
Acknowledgments VIII
List of Maps, Figures, Tables IX
Notes on Contributors X

Introduction: Professional Mobility as a Defining Characteristic of Pre-Modern Islamic Societies 1
Mohamad El-Merheb and Mehdi Berriah

PART 1
Networks of Knowledge and Learning

1 Medinan Scholars on the Move: Professional Mobility at the Umayyad Court 15
Mehmetcan Akpınar

2 Professional Mobility and Social Capital: A Note on the *muḥaddithāt* in *Kitāb Tārīkh Baghdād* 40
Nadia Maria El Cheikh

3 The Aqīt Household: Professional Mobility of a Berber Learned Elite in Premodern West Africa 52
Marta G. Novo

PART 2
Social Mobility and Professionalization

4 The Professional Mobility of Qāḍī ʿAbd al-Jabbār between the Quest for Knowledge and the Confluence with Power 79
Amal Belkamel

5 Mobility and Versatility of the *ʿulamāʾ* in the Mamluk Period: The Case of Ibn Taymiyya 98
Mehdi Berriah

6 Mobility among the Andalusī *quḍāt*: Social Advancement and Spatial Displacement in a Professional Context 131
Adday Hernández López

PART 3
Power, Politics, and Mobility

7 Imām al-Ḥaramayn al-Juwaynī's Mobility and the Saljūq's Project of Sunnī Political Unity 159
M. Syifa Amin Widigdo

8 Iran's State Literature under Afghan Rule (1722–1729) 182
M.A.H. Parsa

9 Islamic Political Thought and Professional Mobility: The Intellectual and Empirical Worlds of Ibn Ṭalḥa and Ibn Jamāʿa 207
Mohamad El-Merheb

Index 231

Foreword

It is my great pleasure to introduce this important book by Mohamad El-Merheb and Mehdi Berriah. This volume is based on a two-day workshop that took place in the splendid Paul Webley Wing of the School of Oriental and African Studies (SOAS) and brought together colleagues from numerous countries in Europe, the US, Asia, and the Middle East. The workshop itself was a testament to scholarly mobility – though this was hampered somewhat by strike action on the other side of the Channel. Each contribution to this volume, and the way these contributions speak to one another, is a result of the discussions that we had during those days in London. This is true in particular for the clear chronological and thematic foci of this book that emerged during these exchanges.

Do we really need yet another book on the scholars, the *ʿulamāʾ*, and thus yet another contribution to ulamology, one might ask? Yes, we do, precisely because the scholarly elite is so visible and was so crucial in textualising their recent and distant pasts – texts that form the backbone of how we study Middle Eastern history today and of the analytical categories that we use in this endeavour. It is thus necessary to continue to reflect on individual scholars and the group as a whole, in terms of internal stratification, the social contexts in which scholars were situated, the cultural practices of those belonging to this group, and so on. This is especially the case because the *ʿulamāʾ*, on account of the many sources that we have for them, seem so deceptively transparent and easy to grasp. In consequence, the field of Middle Eastern history has sometimes used the term in a rather common-sensical way to slot practices, objects and attitudes into an ostensibly neat category of 'scholarly'.

One of those clichés that we see re-appearing over and over again when it comes to scholars and scholarly practices is that of medieval globetrotter-scholars steadily crisscrossing the lands in the pursuit of knowledge. This is where this book comes into its own, as it actually reflects on what this cliché meant in practice and thus raises questions on issues such as what social practices mobility entailed and who was mobile within the scholarly communities. It is exactly this kind of scholarship that is needed in order to move the field ahead by coming to a much better understanding of what we mean when talking about 'scholars' and their 'scholarly' practices. This book is a wonderful contribution to this ongoing debate.

Konrad Hirschler

Acknowledgments

In March 2019, the School of Oriental and African Studies (SOAS) University of London hosted a two-day symposium entitled *Professional Mobility in the Islamic Lands (900–1600): ʿulamāʾ, udabāʾ, and administrators*. Twenty-four speakers from twenty-one institutions based in Belgium, France, Germany, Indonesia, Lebanon, Pakistan, Spain, the UK, and the USA met in the inspiring venue of the Paul Webley Wing of Senate House to present their innovative research on this topic.

This is the first project to cover such a wide range of thematic, chronological, and geographical aspects of professional mobility in pre-modern Islam. It was possible thanks to the generosity and support of several institutions and individuals. In particular we are grateful to CNRS-UMR 8167 Orient et Méditerranée in France, the CEFREPA (The French Research Centre of the Arabian Peninsula) in Kuwait, and the Institute of Historical Research (IHR) and the School of Oriental and African Studies (SOAS) in the UK for their generosity. We wish to thank especially Sylvie Denoix, Abbès Zouache, Hugh Kennedy, Jo Fox, and Konrad Hirshler who provided the necessary support and guidance for this symposium to succeed.

We are also grateful to Abdurraouf Oueslati, Roy Fischel, Mattin Biglari, Christopher Bahl, Mat Schofield, Kathy Van Vliet, Nadia Maria El Cheikh, Suzanne Ruggi, and May Farhat who have been most helpful.

Mohamad El-Merheb and Mehdi Berriah

Maps, Figures, Tables

Maps

3.1 Locations for Islamic learning in West Africa ca. 1100–1600 56
3.2 West African scholarly networks ca. 1100–1600 65

Figures

6.1 Judges appointed to several posts 143
6.2 Types of mobility along the different periods 147
6.3 Judges appointed in Andalusī cities 149
6.4 Judges appointed in Maghrebi cities 149

Tables

7.1 The intellectual genealogy of Imām al-Ḥaramayn al-Juwaynī in Shāfiʿī legal school 165
7.2 The scheme of of Imām al-Ḥaramayn's intellectual pedigree in Ashʿarī theology 169

Notes on Contributors

Mehmetcan Akpınar
is a historian of Early Islam. He obtained his PhD in 2016 from the University of Chicago, with a dissertation entitled "Narrative Representations of Abū Bakr (d. 634) in the 2nd/8th Century." He is currently a junior research and teaching fellow at the University of Tübingen.

Amal Belkamel
is a PhD candidate in Islamic Studies at the École Pratique des Hautes Études, Paris. Her work focuses on the articulation of the idea of original human disposition (fiṭra) in relation to the knowledge of God and human acts in the corpus of the Medieval Sunnī theologians of Kalām specifically ʿAbd al-Jabbār al-Hamadhānī and Abū Ḥāmid al-Ghazālī. Her area of works and interest are: Qurʾanic and theological concepts.

Mehdi Berriah
is Assistant Professor of Classical Arabic and Islamic Studies at the Faculty of Religion and Theology and member of the Centre for Islamic Theology (CIT) of the Vrije Universiteit of Amsterdam (VU). He also teaches courses at Sciences Po Paris University and is an editor for SHARIAsource at the Program in Islamic Law of the Harvard Law School. He obtained his PhD in 2019 from Paris Sorbonne University. His research and publications focus on Islamic military history, *furūsiyya*, Islamic thought, jihad ideology, Islamic law of war and ulamology. He is currently leading a research project entitled "The taymiyyan corpus on jihad: reception, decontextualization and use by contemporary jihadist movements" funded by the French Ministry of the Interior – Central office of worship (call for projects 2020 "Islam, religion and society").

Nadia Maria El Cheikh
is Professor of History at the American University of Beirut (AUB). She received her B.A. in History and Archeology at AUB and her Ph.D. degree in History and Middle Eastern Studies from Harvard University in 1992. Her book, *Byzantium Viewed by the Arabs*, was published by the Harvard Middle Eastern Monographs in 2004 and translated into Turkish and Greek. She has co-authored a book entitled *Crisis and Continuity at the Abbasid Court. Formal and Informal Politics in the Caliphate of al-Muqtadir (295–320/908–932)*. Leiden: Brill, 2013. Her most recent book, *Women, Islam and Abbasid Identity* was published in 2015 by

Harvard University Press. In 2016 she was appointed Dean of the Faculty of Arts and Sciences at the American University of Beirut.

Mohamad El-Merheb
is Assistant Professor of Medieval History at the University of Groningen. His main research area is the history of Islamic political thought, especially under the Mamluks, Ayyubids, and Seljuqs. He is interested in the ideal of 'the rule of law' as expressed in Islamic advice literature. His other research interests include the 'Crusader' period, the depiction of Frankish kings such as Louis IX and Frederic II in Islamic historiography, and professional mobility in the premodern Islamic world. Mohamad is currently completing his monograph entitled, *Islamic Political Thought in the Mamluk period.*

Marta G. Novo
is Assistant Professor at the Arabic and Islamic Studies Department at the Universidad Autónoma de Madrid. She is part of the MASYG (Society and Geography of the Maghrib, University of Alcalá) and IEXCUL (Arab Ideologies and Cultural Expressions, UAM) research groups. Her research focuses on the History of the Islamic West (al-Andalus, Maghrib, *bilād al-sūdān*), and more precisely, on premodern West African historiography. She is the author of several articles about slavery and the sociopolitical role of scholars in the works of Aḥmad Bābā al-Tinbuktī, book chapters in collective works about the biographical literature of the Islamic West and prepares a monograph and Spanish translation of al-Tinbuktī's treatise on slavery, *Miʿrāj al-ṣuʿūd.*

Adday Hernández López
(PhD Universidad Complutense de Madrid, European Doctorate, 2014) is Postdoctoral researcher Juan de la Cierva – incorporación (IJCI-2017-31351) at the Institute of Languages and Cultures of the Mediterranean (ILC), CSIC – Madrid. She is a scholar specialized in Islamic law in the premodern Islamic West (economic legal doctrines and practices; religious minorities); in the intellectual history in the same area (circulation of texts and ideas) and in the Arabic literature of the Horn of Africa. She has contributed to three research projects, two of them funded by Advanced grants of the European Research Council (KOHEPOCU: Knowledge, Heresy and Political Culture in the Islamic West (eighth-fifteenth centuries)); IslHornAfr: Islam in the Horn of Africa. A comparative Literary Approach, held at the University of Copenhagen (2015–2019), and a third one funded by the CSIC (Manuscritos fechados en al-Andalus: Repertorio y análisis). Included among her publications are two books on

Islamic Law (*El valor del tiempo. Doctrina jurídica y práctica de la usura* (*ribā*) *en el Occidente islámico medieval*, Helsinki: Academia Scientiarum Fennica, 2016, and *El Kitāb Al-ribā de ʿAbd Al-Malik B. Ḥabīb* (*m. 238/852*)*: La Doctrina Legal Temprana Sobre La Usura*, Fuentes Arábico-hispanas 37, Madrid: CSIC, 2017) and several articles, such as "Qurʾanic studies in al-Andalus: An overview on the state of research on qirāʿāt and tafsīr", Journal of Qurʾanic Studies, 19/3 (2017), 74–102.

M.A.H. Parsa
is studying state formation and fragmentation in eighteenth century Nāderid Iran at the School of Oriental and African Studies (SOAS), University of London. Currently in his last year, his study takes an eclectic approach to the military, fiscal, and politico-cultural trends which gave rise to Iran's last (Nāderid) empire. In conjunction with his doctoral research at SOAS, he is currently working on a paper on 'Nāderid Iran's Imperial Legitimacy in the Central Asian Khanates', to be presented at the annual roundtable held by the British Institute of Persian Studies (BIPS). He is also preparing a talk on the 'Emergence of a Pre-National Iranian Identity in the Eighteenth Century', which he will present at the upcoming Iranian Studies Conference in Salamanca.

M. Syifa A. Widigdo
is a faculty member in the Faculty of Islamic Studies, Universitas Muhammadiyah Yogyakarta (UMY), Indonesia. He completed his doctoral degree in the Department of Religious Studies, Indiana University Bloomington, USA, in 2016 and obtained his bachelor degree in the Department of Arabic Language and Literature, UIN (State Islamic University) Syarif Hidayatullah, Jakarta in 2001. He wrote a number of articles published on topics of Islamic Intellectual History (particularly, in the field of Islamic Philosophy, Theology, Ethics, and Legal Thought), Comparative Religious Ethics, and Islam in Southeast Asia and Middle East.

INTRODUCTION

Professional Mobility as a Defining Characteristic of Pre-Modern Islamic Societies

Mohamad El-Merheb and Mehdi Berriah

The present edited volume presents professional mobility as a defining characteristic of pre-modern Islamic societies. It includes nine case studies from different parts of the Islamic world that examine the professional mobility of Muslim scholars (*ʿulamāʾ*) and literati between the eighth and the eighteenth centuries. From the outset, arriving at this specific theme involved some choices by the project's editors and contributors. The first choice was to limit this study to the pre-modern Islamic period. Patterns of mobility were similar, though not identical, in various parts of the medieval Islamic world and provide an opportunity for comparing social, cultural, and economic conditions that shaped mobility in pre-modern Islamic societies. The second choice was to focus on the professional mobility of the *ʿulamāʾ*, as the nature of pre-modern Islamic sources lend themselves particularly well to such a focus. The study of the mobility of the scholars and literati is best achieved through the genre of biographical literature (*ṭabaqāt*). Unique to Islamic culture, these biographical dictionaries were often authored by the *ʿulamāʾ* to document individual stories of success and failure from within their own social group.[1] The third choice was to treat as many locations as possible from the pre-modern Islamic lands. This decision was grounded in the firm belief that any study of mobility circumscribed to a small geographical area, one language, an imagined historical nation with eternal fixed borders, or one linguistic or tribal group, would fail to capture the social, religious, and cultural mesh of pre-modern Islamic societies.

What is meant by 'defining characteristics' of pre-modern Islamic societies should be clarified before professional mobility is designated as one such characteristic. The work of Chase Robinson, who examined thirty biographies of prominent men and women in order to sketch the first millennium

1 Described as a "unique product of Arab Muslim culture" in Tarif Khalidi, "Islamic Biographical Dictionaries: A Preliminary Assessment," *The Muslim World* 63, no. 1 (1973): 53.

 | DOI:10.1163/9789004467637_002

of Islamic history, is beneficial here.[2] Although his work was intended for a non-specialist readership, it sought to capture the "scale, diversity, and creativity of Islamic civilization".[3] Examining the biographies and legacies of the thirty individuals selected by Robinson is one swift way to identify some of the main characteristics of Islamic civilisation. For instance, Caliph ʿAbd al-Malik (r. 65/685–86/705) stands as a reminder of Islamic architecture and monumental construction, and centralisation attempts; the female Sufi saint and renunciant Rābiʿa al-ʿAdawiyya (d. 185/801) of the emergence of Sufism; the female slave ʿArīb (d. 277/890–91) and vizier Ibn Muqla (d. 328/940) of various flourishing arts such as singing and calligraphy; Caliph al-Maʾmūn (r. 198/813–218/833) of the translation and transmission of Greek texts, theological strife, and succession wars; al-Idrīsī (d. 560/1165) of geography and cartography, cross-cultural contact, and coexistence; sultan Maḥmūd of Ghazna (r. 338/998–421/1030) of patronage, conquest, and the rule of military slaves; al-Ghazālī (d. 505/1111) of philosophical theology, rationalism, and Sufism; and so forth. A list of defining characteristics of Islamic civilisation drawn from these thirty biographies, would include: literature and poetry, translation and transmission of classical knowledge, calligraphy and arts, "iconoclasm", Sufism, philosophical theology and legal diversity, "legalism and dogmatism", medicine and sciences, trade, military slavery, patronage, and charitable endowments.[4] As another main defining characteristic of pre-modern Islamic societies, social mobility deserves a place on this list.

Although not completely absent from scholarly studies, mobility in pre-modern Islamic societies rarely receives the attention it is due.[5] European medievalist Sandro Carocci observed, "In the field of medieval studies, mobility

2 Chase F. Robinson, *Islamic Civilization in Thirty Lives: The First 1,000 Years* (University of California Press, 2016).

3 Ibid., refer to the second page of the book's introduction.

4 Ibid., some of the traits identified by C. Robinson are among those listed here.

5 A notable exception that will be discussed below is the work of Irmeli Perho, "Climbing the Ladder: Social Mobility in the Mamluk Period," *Mamlūk Studies Review* 15 (2011): 19–35. There are other very useful studies covering various parts of the Islamic world from the early modern to contemporary periods including: Afaf Lutfi Al-Sayyid Marsot, "The Political and Economic Functions of the ʿUlamāʾ in the 18th Century," *Journal of the Economic and Social History of the Orient* 16, no. 2/3 (1973): 130–154; Nabil Mouline, "Les oulémas du palais," *Archives de sciences sociales des religions* 149 (2010): 229–253; Sophie Bava, "Al Azhar, scène renouvelée de l'imaginaire religieux sur les routes de la migration africaine au Caire," *L'Année du Maghreb* 11 (2014): 37–55 and "Journeys of African Muslim Elites in Cairo: From Al Azhar to the Bazaar Economy," *Afrique contemporaine* 3, no. 231(2009): 187–207; and Christopher B. Taylor, "Madrasas and Social Mobility in the Religious Economy: The Case of Nadwat al-ʿUlama in Lucknow," *South Asia Multidisciplinary Academic Journal* 11 (2015).

has never, or hardly ever, found itself at centre stage," and this is equally applicable to the discipline of Islamic history.[6] Whenever mobility has been treated in Islamic studies, it was often as a spin-off interest of other subjects such as the study of elites and poetry, to name just two examples.[7] In the case of European studies Carocci attributed the lack of interest in mobility to the nature of medieval sources and the perceived scarcity of data, earlier biased conceptions of medieval European societies, different trends and interests within modern Western national historiographies, and the prevalent ideological prejudice amongst some scholars of European history.[8] The lack of interest in mobility in the case of Islamic history, on the other hand, is rather bewildering given the abundance of pre-modern biographical dictionaries (*ṭabaqāt*).[9] Albeit not on the same scale as modern or contemporary archives, the *ṭabaqāt* literature provides thousands of individual biographies. They even allow quantitative data analysis, as attempted by Richard Bulliet in his seminal study on conversion and by Adday Hernández Lopez in her article on Andalusī scholars in this volume.[10] It is more bewildering still given the fact that biographical dictionaries provide exceptionally valuable information about professional mobility within a specific social segment of the populace, the *ʿulamāʾ*. All this is not to say, however, that mobility has been entirely absent from the purview of scholarly interest.

Our understanding of social mobility in pre-modern Islam has improved thanks to a series of prominent studies that have appeared in the past three to four decades. Benefiting from advances especially in sociology and anthropology that have influenced Islamic studies, these works treated the social and cultural milieus of the *ʿulamāʾ* and their professional training. To name one major

6 Sandro Carocci, "Social mobility and the Middle Ages," *Continuity and Change* 26, no. 3 (2011), 367.

7 For a study focused on elites, refer to Ahmed Khan, "An Empire of Elites: Mobility in the Early Islamic Empire," in *Connecting the Early Islamic Empire: Regional and Transregional Elites*, eds. Hg. Hannah-Lena-Hagemann and Stefan Heidemann (Berlin: de Gruyter, 2020), 147–169. Likewise, Jocelyn Sharlet showed that poets in the medieval Islamic world enjoyed a special identity that provided them with opportunities for social ascension or descent; refer to *Patronage and Poetry in the Islamic World: Social Mobility and Status in the Medieval Middle East and Central Asia* (Tauris, 2011), 204–235.

8 Carocci, "Social mobility and the Middle Ages," 371–375.

9 Richard Bulliet argued that "the number of individual biographies extant must run into the hundreds of thousands and most likely into the millions"; refer to "A Quantitative Approach to Medieval Muslim Biographical Dictionaries," *Journal of the Economic and Social History of the Orient* 13, no. 2 (1970), 195.

10 Richard W. Bulliet, *Conversion to Islam in the Medieval Period* (Cambridge, 2013) is a pioneering work in this form of analysis; refer to the work of Adday Hernández Lopez in Chapter six below.

influence, Pierre Bourdieu's (1930–2002) theory of the forms of economic, cultural, social, and symbolic capital provided historians of Islam, directly or indirectly, with the necessary tools to examine the social and cultural segment of the *ʿulamāʾ*, particularly in medieval Egypt and Syria, and their formation, role in society, and status.[11] In her seminal study, Joan E. Gilbert discussed how Zangid and Ayyubid Damascus witnessed the beginning of the professionalisation and bureaucratisation of the *ʿulamāʾ*.[12] This trend, which only increased under the Mamluks within an Islamic society that was rather open to mobility, attracted the attention of other scholars including Carl F. Petry, Ira M. Lapidus, Anne Broadbridge, and Jonathan P. Berkey, but especially Michael Chamberlain.[13] Their works treated various aspects of the major role played by these professionalised and bureaucratised *ʿulamāʾ* in Islamic societies and their manipulation of knowledge transfer to gain social capital, acquire administrative and political offices and, in some cases, subsequently pass them to their descendants. Moreover, Konrad Hirschler's work on the processes of textualisation and popularisation of knowledge and, accordingly, the spread of written literature has improved our understanding of the social

11 Refer to Pierre Bourdieu, *Raisons pratiques: sur la théorie de l'action* (Paris, 1994); "Les trois états du capital culturel", *Actes de la recherche en sciences sociales*, no. 30 (1979): 3–6 and, in the same publication, "Le capital social. Notes provisoires," no. 31(1980): 2–3; *La Distinction: Critique sociale du jugement* (Paris, 1979), tr. R. Nice, *Distinction: a Social Critique of the Judgement of Taste* (Cambridge, 1984); *Le Sens pratique* (Paris, 1980), tr. R. Nice, *The Logic of Practice* (London and New York, 1990); *Esquisse d'une théorie de la pratique précédée de trois études d'ethnologie kabyle* (Geneva, 1972), tr. R. Nice, *Outline of a Theory of Practice* (Cambridge, 1977); *Choses dites* (Paris, 1987); *Homo academicus* (Paris, 1984).

Bourdieu's influence is most noticeable on the seminal work of Michael Chamberlain, *Knowledge and Social Practice in Medieval Damascus, 1190–1350* (Cambridge, 1995); the fourth chapter of this book is entitled "Social and cultural capital", refer to 108–151.

For a very relevant and useful discussion on the case of European studies, refer to Carocci, "Social mobility and the Middle Ages", 370.

12 Joan E. Gilbert, "Institutionalization of Muslim Scholarship and Professionalization of the ʿUlamāʾ in Medieval Damascus," *Studia Islamica* 52 (1980): 105–134.

13 In addition to Michael Chamberlain's *Knowledge and Social Practice*, refer to Jonathan P. Berkey, *The Transmission of Knowledge in Medieval Cairo: A Social History of Islamic Education* (Princeton: 1992), 95–127 and *The Formation of Islam: Religion and Society in the Near East, 600–1800* (Cambridge, 2002), 224–230; Carl Petry, *Civilian Elite of Cairo in the Later Middle Ages* (Princeton, 1981), 246–268; Ira Lapidus, *Muslim Cities in the Later Middle Ages* (Cambridge, 1984), 107–115, 130–141; and Anne Broadbridge, "Academic Rivalry and the Patronage System in Fifteenth Century Egypt: al-ʿAynī, al-Maqrīzī and Ibn Ḥajar al-ʿAsqalānī," *Mamluk Studies Review* 3 (1999): 85–106. Refer also to Yaacov Lev, "Symbiotic Relations: Ulama and the Mamluk Sultans," *Mamlūk Studies Review* 13, no. 1 (2009): 1–26.

and cultural incubating world of the *ʿulamāʾ* and literati.[14] Irmeli Perho's significant study treated professional mobility head-on, arguing that while individual merits played an important role in the professional mobility of scholars, lineage and networks were also factors in social advancement.[15] In his contribution, Mathieu Eychenne treated the role of personal networks in the social ascension of the *ʿulamāʾ* during the Mamluk period.[16] Similar efforts were carried out in the context of the Islamic West and resulted in a series of influential studies.[17]

The above-mentioned works paved the way for the conception of this project as the first cross-regional and multi-disciplinary study of professional mobility in pre-modern Islam. The intention was to realise this study through the systematic scrutiny of mobility within the literati and, especially, the social-cum-cultural group of the *ʿulamāʾ* based on individual case studies and quantitative mining of biographical dictionaries from different parts of the Islamic world. As such, a principal aim of this project was to understand whether entry into this group of *ʿulamāʾ* was relatively accessible and depended on personal scholarly accomplishment, and whether other considerations like ethnic or geographical origin played a significant role – and if so, how. A second aim was to get a fresh and cross-regional assessment of the influence of social networks and, in some cases, adherence to certain families and legal schools (*madhhab*s), on the professional mobility of the *ʿulamāʾ* and advancement opportunities within this group for religious, judicial, administrative, and political appointments.[18] A third aim was to study how and why the scholarly elite increasingly succeeded in monopolising religious, judicial, and administrative appointments during the period between the spread of

14 Konrad Hirschler, *The Written Word in the Medieval Arabic Lands: A Social and Cultural History of Reading Practices* (Edinburgh, 2012).

15 Perho, "Climbing the Ladder: Social Mobility in the Mamluk Period," 19–35.

16 Mathieu Eychenne, *Liens personnels, clientélisme et réseaux de pouvoir dans le sultanat mamelouk (milieu XIIIe–fin XIVe siècle)* (Presses de l'Ifpo, Damascus-Beirut, 2013), 193–336.

17 The corpus of available studies is rich and we can only cite some titles including: Dominique Urvoy, "The ʿUlamāʾ of Al-Andalus," in *The Legacy of Muslim Spain*, ed. Salma Khadra Jayyusi and Manuela Marín (Leiden, 1994), 849–77; M'hammad Benaboud, "Religious knowledge and political power of the ulama in al-Andalus during the period of the Taifa states," in *Saber religioso y poder político en el Islam: actas del simposio internacional, Granada, 15–18 octubre 1991*, Ediciones mundo árabe e Islam (Madrid: Agencia Española de Cooperación Internacional, 1994), 39–51; Manuela Marin, "Ulemas de Al-Andalus," in *El Saber En Al-Andalus: Textos Y Estudios*, ed. Pedro Cano Avila and Ildefonso Garijo (Seville, 1997), 151–62.

18 As attempted by I. Perho in the Mamluk case.

the *madrasa* under the Seljuqs and the incorporation of the educational system into the Ottoman state. This monopoly was achieved often with the tacit or expressed consent of rulers and political authorities, especially under the Mamluks but similarly under earlier Islamic empires, as will become evident in some of this collection's articles.

These considerations were the focus of a two-day symposium during which some questions were answered as new ones emerged. Consequently, the parameters of the project shifted as it came to address this set of further questions, which include the following: How can our understanding of professional mobility benefit from taking the process of *adab*isation of the *ʿulamāʾ* into account together with their gradual professionalisation and institutionalisation in the long period between the Seljuqs and the Ottomans?[19] How and when did the *madrasas* start to generate bureaucrats who served in different parts of the Islamic world? What did getting close to political authority entail for the professional mobility of the *ʿulamāʾ* and literati? How were offers for higher appointments communicated throughout the Islamic lands across different regimes, societies, and written languages? How did competition between ruling elites and households impact the professional mobility of the *ʿulamāʾ* and literati? To what extent was mobility controlled by these rulers, political elites, and households, or autonomously managed by the *ʿulamāʾ* themselves? Was professional mobility more widespread under certain dynasties and regimes or in certain pre-modern Islamic societies? How did the uniformity or diversity of *madhhab* affect mobility and the opportunities available to the *ʿulamāʾ*? Did certain scholars epitomise professional mobility more than others? How can this project benefit from recent advances in creating databases and digital resources that have benefited scholars of Islamic history and allowed them to conduct quantitative data analysis? How can we begin to study professional mobility from the perspective of gender in a pre-modern Islamic scholarly sphere that was largely dominated by men?

Initially, this project embarked upon an examination of professional mobility along spatial, horizontal, and vertical axes. Vertical mobility is understood in this collection to mean the process by which the *ʿulamāʾ* moved upwards or downwards in various paid jobs, including the positions of *imām* (leader of prayers), *khaṭīb* (preacher), *mudarris*/*shaykh* (professor or teacher), *qāḍī* (judge), *qāḍī al-quḍāt* (chief judge), *shaykh al-shuyūkh* (chief Sufi), *kātib*

19 For more on the process of *adab*isation, refer to Thomas Bauer, "Mamluk Literature: Misunderstandings and New Approaches," *Mamlūk Studies Review* 9, no. 2 (2005): 105–132; refer also to chapter 5 of Konrad Hirschler, *The Written Word*, for a related study on the overlap between popular and high literature.

al-inshāʾ (chancery secretary), and other posts.[20] Typically, this comprises promotions and advancements – or demotions and dismissals – within the same line of proficiency and specialisation, such as from judge to chief judge, from chancery secretary to head of the chancery or even to vizier, and so forth. Horizontal mobility denotes how the *ʿulamāʾ* served in salaried jobs in various branches of the administration and not merely in religious or judicial functions. This includes posts like *muḥtasib* (market inspector), *nāẓir al-awqaf* (supervisor of charitable endowments), and other non-religious administrative jobs including, for instance, *nāẓir bayt al-māl* (superintendent of the treasury), diplomatic emissary, and various appointments in the chancery or the postal service. Horizontal mobility, furthermore, intersects with the notion of *adab*ised scholars since some *ʿulamāʾ* were professional poets and belletrists. Spatial mobility investigates the travels of the *ʿulamāʾ* and literati, not only as émigrés, but also as professionals who, upon receiving work propositions or hearing of chances for new placements, moved both ways between Damascus and Cairo, the *Mashriq* and the Andalus, the *Maghrib* and *bilād al-sūdān*, India and the Ḥijāz, Khurāsān and Anatolia, Central Asia and Syria, Sicily and the Eastern Mediterranean, and various other geographical axes of mobility.[21]

The triple-axis heuristic approach chosen for this project proved to be a beneficial point of departure. Despite some limitations, which will be discussed below, this approach facilitated the conception of nine remarkable studies of professional mobility arranged in three clusters. Part 1 is entitled "Networks of Knowledge and Learning" and contains three contributions. In the first one, Mehmetcan Akpınar explores the fortunes of Medinan scholars who traveled to the capital of the Umayyad Empire, Damascus. He investigates their status and duties within the caliphal court, the subjects taught and discussed in the study circles they ran, and the roles they played in the tutoring of Umayyad princes. Building on existing studies on state administration and scribes (*kuttāb*) of the Umayyad period, Akpınar shows how these Medinan jurists (*fuqahāʾ*) contributed to the administration and assesses their interactions with the *mawālī* who staffed it. The second contribution in this part provides a much-needed gender-based approach to the study of professional mobility. Nadia Maria El Cheikh examines women's education in the ʿAbbāsid context based on al-Khaṭīb al-Baghdādī's (d. 463/1071) biographical work *Tārīkh Baghdād*. She explores the social and geographical mobility of women in Baghdad by shedding light on the branches of knowledge they acquired,

20 The names of these functions may vary in the case of al-Andalus and other parts of the Islamic world. Refer to Chapter six of this volume.

21 Carl F. Petry examined some patterns of related migrations in *Civilian Elite*, 37–127.

in particular the transmission of *ḥadīth*, and their major involvement in the consolidation of this religious science. The status of *muḥadditha* (traditionist) afforded limited spatial mobility to learned women and increased the social capital of their families, thus improving prospects of professional mobility for their male relatives. Marta G. Novo treats the social and spatial mobility of West African *ʿulamāʾ* using biographical works from *bilād al-sūdān*, such as the *tarājim* of Aḥmad Bābā al-Tinbuktī (d. 1036/1627). Her study of scholars from the Aqīt Berber household sketches various aspects of the intellectual life of the *ʿulamāʾ*, the trajectories of their professional mobility, and the roles they played in the public sphere in this understudied part of the Islamic world. Novo notes the *sūdānī ʿulamāʾ*'s emphasis on their academic ties to Cairo, in contradistinction to the *Maghrib*, as a principal differentiator that furthered their status and professional mobility.

Part 2 is entitled "Social Mobility and Professionalisation". It includes three contributions that cover cases of mobility shaped by different tracks of the professionalisation of the *ʿulamāʾ*: in Baghdad and the Islamic East; in the Syro-Egyptian lands; and in the Andalus and the *Maghrib*. Amal Belkamel examines the professional mobility of the Muʿtazilī *qāḍī* ʿAbd al-Jabbār (d. 415/1025). She highlights the impact of his collusion with powerful intellectual and political circles on his professional ascent to the highest juridical post, his scholarly success and acquisition of theological knowledge, and how his influence spread across different provinces. Belkamel, moreover, links ʿAbd al-Jabbār's professional mobility to the Buyyid strategy of adapting some of their policies to existing Sunnī doctrines. Mehdi Berriah provides fresh insights into the biography of Ibn Taymiyya (661/1263–728/1328). To better understand what D. Little termed the "Ibn Taymiyya phenomenon", this contribution highlights new aspects of the mobility of this well-known scholar by analysing his mental world, intellectual interests, dogmatic views, and the reception of his thought.[22] Berriah goes on to show that studying mobility is an important and necessary step towards a better comprehension of the social and intellectual spheres of the *ʿulamāʾ*. In the last article in this part, Adday Hernández López offers a comprehensive overview of the political, cultural, and social context of the Andalus and how it influenced trajectories of professional mobility in the Western lands of Islam. She studies the consequences of the absence of the *madrasa* system on the professionalisation of Andalusī *quḍāt*. Hernández López employs quantitative data analysis that reflects, among other significant findings, attempts made by Umayyad and Almohad rulers to control the *quḍāt*

22 Donald Little, "Did Ibn Taymiyya Have a Screw Loose?," *Studia Islamica*, 41 (1975), 111.

and the judiciary in order to mitigate potential threats posed to central power by established scholarly families.

Entitled "Power, Politics, and Mobility", Part 3 focuses on new trajectories of professional mobility that became available as a result of frequent political changes. This last part examines how service to different or successive rulers and dynasties affected the roles played by the *ʿulamāʾ* and literati in the political sphere and how periods of change impacted state and advice literature produced in places like Isfahan, Damascus, and Cairo. In the first article of this part, M. Syifa A. Widigdo examines the professional career and mobility of the Shāfiʿī jurist and Ashʿarī theologian Imām al-Ḥaramayn al-Juwaynī (d. 478/1085) and his contribution to Islamic intellectual history. He highlights his role in the formation of an eleventh-century Sunnī orthodoxy within the wider intellectual and political project of the Seljuq empire. Widigdo assesses the influence of al-Juwaynī's mobility between Nishapur, Baghdad and the Ḥijāz on his synthesis of law and theology, and his involvement in running the institutions of learning of the Seljuqs and their Shāfiʿī-Ashʿarī vizier Niẓām al-Mulk (d. 486/1093). Subsequently, in the second article, M.A.H. Parsa's contribution covers the largely understudied post-Ṣafavid period of Iran by examining state literature produced under the ruling Afghan Hotakid dynasty. Chancery secretaries relied on Ṣafavid conceptions of ideal Persianate rule to legitimate the new Afghan dynasty. Parsa identifies two novel patterns of professional mobility within the chancery: inter-dynastic mobility (Ṣafavid to Hotakid) by existing staff and the influx of Persian Sunnī administrators, which changed the existing sectarian composition of the chancery. Finally, Mohamad El-Merheb highlights the interrelatedness between professional mobility and the production of Islamic political thought. He links the careers of the two Shāfiʿī jurists Ibn Ṭalḥa (d. 652/1254) and Ibn Jamāʿa (d. 733/1333) under the Artuqids, late Ayyubids, and Mamluks to their original and eclectic styles in authoring advice literature. In so doing, El-Merheb shows how the expansion of Islamic political theory and conceptions of authority were influenced by the thriving careers and professional mobility of the *ʿulamāʾ*.

Despite the opportunities and clear benefits provided by this heuristic approach, professional mobility in pre-modern Islam proved too complex to be envisioned merely along one of three axes. It quickly became clear that this approach, in the cases of several *ʿulamāʾ* and literati, had limitations either because it transpired that the three axes were too enmeshed or simply that they were insufficient. For instance, Chapter six of this collection informs us that spatial mobility among the Andalusī judges was occasionally a form of professional demotion; in this case, spatial mobility is equivalent to downward vertical mobility. Likewise, as treated in Chapter two, spatial modelling is of limited benefit when examining a gendered perspective of mobility as it adds little to our understanding of the accomplishments of female scholars who lived in Baghdad during the second/eighth century and the challenges they faced. Moreover, Chapter nine shows that conceptualising mobility along a vertical axis had its obvious limitations in the case of Ibn Ṭalḥa, the Syrian jurist who voluntarily refused to assume the vizierate and opted instead to spend the rest of his life wandering as a Sufi. The same chapter also shows how Ibn Jamāʿa's professional mobility along horizontal, vertical, and spatial axes was so intertwined that it can only be studied holistically. Nor does the triple-axis model fare well in Chapter five, as Ibn Taymiyya never assumed a prominent judicial or administrative role. Yet the reception of his ideas, at different times and in different locations, provides an interesting case of 'intellectual mobility', which denotes not only the exchange of knowledge and influence between the *ʿulamāʾ*, but also across different theological, legal, and religious or non-religious intellectual currents. Finally, Chapter eight of this volume highlights a case of 'inter-dynastic professional mobility' in the post-Ṣafavid era, for which the vertical, horizontal, and spatial axes alone are inefficient. All these findings and contributions, whether they relied on, benefited from, or eluded the three-axes approach, make this collection all the more valuable and innovative for the study of professional mobility in pre-modern Islam.

A comment is warranted here on the wide chronological and geographical range of this book. The classification of 'pre-modern Islamic societies' fits all the nine articles of this volume and poses no risk of ambiguity to the reader. Nevertheless, pinning down the starting point of modernity in the Islamic world is a standing academic question and a rather difficult one; the absence of scholarly consensus around it is expected to continue for some time. As such Chapter eight, entitled *Iran's State Literature under Afghan Rule* (*1722–1729*) may seem out of place in this collection. This is because some scholars consider the reign of Shāh ʿAbbās (r. 1588–1629) during the Ṣafavid period as the beginning of modernity in Iran.[23] This collection takes the alternative view that the modern period begins after the disintegration of the eighteenth century with the Qajars (1796–1925).[24] No similar concerns related to periodisation can be raised for the remaining articles that cover Islamic Iberia and North Africa,

23 For example, one notable textbook that begins the modern history of Iran with the Ṣafavids is Abbas Amanat, *Iran: A Modern History* (New Haven: Yale University Press, 2017).

24 This is the more conventional narrative, exemplified in the authoritative textbook of modern Iran, Nikkie R. Keddie, *Modern Iran: Roots and Results of Revolution* (New Haven: Yale University Press, 2003).

Umayyad Damascus, ʿAbbāsid Baghdad, Ayyubid and Mamluk Syria and Egypt, and the Seljuq Empire.

The present volume aims merely to initiate a wider discussion on professional mobility by offering a variety of new concepts and approaches. It neither claims to cover all aspects of professional mobility nor propose a unified conception of it. The volume, furthermore, does not intend to suggest that there is a one-size-fits-all approach to the study of mobility that suits all periods and lands of the pre-modern Islamic world. Our contributors approached the theme of professional mobility creatively and in different ways based on the primary sources and tools available to them within their chronological or thematic areas of focus. For instance, the impressive mobility relational database – the "Prosopografía de los Ulemas de al-Andalus" (PUA) – available to historians of Islamic Iberia enabled well-informed data mining and powerful conclusions. Other contributors approached the theme of professional mobility based on: its interconnectivity with Islamic intellectual history, the impact of dynastic changes on administrative jobs, limitations on and contributions of scholarly women, the lives and careers of renowned scholars, and what the absence of professional mobility can teach us about a given setting.

A final note: as mentioned above, the study focuses on the scholars and literati and this is dictated by both the scope of the contributions and the nature of the primary sources. For instance, the editors did not receive contributions that cover the mobility of physicians, although detailed biographical dictionaries focused on physicians do exist. Likewise, we had hoped to include some studies on the professional mobility of Jewish and near-Eastern Christian scholars and literati, as this would have greatly enhanced the thematic coverage of this study given the important role played non-Muslim administrators throughout the history of the Islamic world. Sadly, we did not receive any such submissions. These concerns are at the top of the agenda for phase two of this project, which is already under way.

PART 1

Networks of Knowledge and Learning

CHAPTER 1

Medinan Scholars on the Move: Professional Mobility at the Umayyad Court

Mehmetcan Akpınar

1 Introduction: The Emergence of Scholars as a Professional Class

Medina in the early Islamic period was the center of Muslim scholarship. As the birthplace of the Muslim polity, the town remained the seat of the caliphate until the Umayyads established their rule in Syria in the second half of the 1st/7th century. Thereafter, Damascus emerged as the new political center of the Muslim *umma* and became established as the seat of the caliphate until the demise of the Umayyad dynasty in the middle of the 2nd/8th century. It is during this period that the Umayyad caliphs began to take rigorous measures to create new structures with regard to state administration, finance, the judiciary, and the military.[1] The steps taken to establish a complex but more efficient bureaucracy not only helped the Umayyad state gain a firmer grip over its dominion, but also led the Umayyads to re-establish their relationship(s) with the other centers, including the Hejaz region. In this expanding territory under Muslim rule we observe astonishing social, political, and intellectual transformations. These new forms of interactions between various centers merit closer scrutiny, as they allow us to arrive at a better understanding of this period. By creating new structures, the state presented new opportunities, as well as threats, to people of various backgrounds, facilitating their mobility in various directions, both spatially and socially. In this regard, mobility is a key component in the study of the social, political, and intellectual transformations that took place in this era.

One of the professional classes that began to emerge in the Umayyad period is a group of individuals who devoted themselves to the pursuit and transmission of learning as a vocation, and whom we call scholars (*ʿālim*, pl. *ʿulamāʾ*).[2]

---

1 Fred M. Donner, "The Formation of the Islamic State," *Journal of the American Oriental Society* 106 (1986): 283–296. I use the term "state" as defined in this article.

2 For various terms that apply to scholars and their differentiated uses, see Muhammad Qasim Zaman, *Religion and Politics Under the Early ʿAbbasids: The Emergence of the Proto-Sunni Elite* (Leiden: Brill, 1997), 3–4. Although Muslim scholars are commonly referred to as *ʿulamāʾ*, the term *faqīh* (pl. *fuqahāʾ*) also applies to the scholars of the early Islamic period, denoting not

 | DOI:10.1163/9789004467637_003

These scholars acquired knowledge about a wide variety of aspects vital to the running of the Muslim polity: it encompassed, among others, the exemplary traditions (*sunna*) of the Prophet Muḥammad, his companions and their sayings (*ḥadīth*); Qur'ānic recitation as well as exegesis; the Arabic language and Arabic poetry in particular; the rulings of the early caliphs; expeditions (*maghāzī*); pre-Islamic history; and tribal genealogies. These subjects were not yet self-standing disciplines at the time, but were studied as different aspects of a larger body of traditional learning. Scholars of this era thus often commanded a wide range of topics in varying combinations and on different levels of expertise. A good example is ʿUbaydallāh b. ʿAbdallāh b. ʿUtba (d. 98/715), an expert in legal and prophetic traditions from the generation of successors, who was at the same time an eminent poet, and hence remembered as someone "who combined knowledge" (*jāmiʿ li-l-ʿilm*).[3]

The emergence of this class of scholars and their relationship to the political authorities both in the Umayyad and in the Abbasid period is a topic that has received considerable attention in academic discussions. According to the prevailing paradigm, this relationship has been characterized as an open rivalry or a sharp opposition between state and scholars. I. Goldziher, J. Wellhausen, M. Hodgson and others put forward a view which considered the state, especially under the Umayyads, as a secular or impious entity devoid of any influence on religious life.[4] By contrast, P. Crone and M. Hinds argued that the Umayyads were acting as the sole representative of God's religion, and thus considered themselves the ultimate authority "responsible for the maintenance of the [Muslim] community," ruling out any collaboration with the

only experts in jurisprudence (*fiqh*) but also men of understanding in general. Cf. a statement attributed to Ibn Masʿūd (d. 32/652) about the scholars of his time: "You are in a time when men of understanding (*fuquhā'*) are many and Qur'ān reciters (*qurrā'*) are few ... A time will come upon men when their *fuqahā'* are few but their *qurrā'* are many ..." in Mālik b. Anas, *al-Muwaṭṭa'*, ed. Muḥammad Fu'ād ʿAbd al-Bāqī (Beirut: Dār Iḥyā Turath al-ʿArabī, 1985), 1:173 (book 9, no. 88). See also al-Yaʿqūbī, *Tārīkh*, ed. M.T. Houtsma (Leiden: Brill, 1883), 2:338. Moreover, Ḍirār b. ʿAmr's *Kitāb al-taḥrīsh* (ed. Hüseyin Hansu [Istanbul: Sharikat Dār al-Irshād, 2014]), a 2nd/8th century polemical work, features a scholar who is described as a *faqīh* but remains unnamed throughout the book. This *faqīh* gives answers to hypothetical questions on controversial matters of theology, history, and law.

3 See Ibn Saʿd, *Kitāb al-ṭabaqāt al-kabīr*, ed. ʿAlī Muḥammad ʿUmar (Cairo: Maktabat al-Khānjī, 2001), 7:246; Yūsuf b. ʿAbd al-Raḥmān al-Mizzī, *Tahdhīb al-kamāl fī asmā' al-rijāl*, ed. Bashshār ʿAwwād Maʿrūf (Beirut: al-Mu'assasat al-Risāla, 1992), 19:75; cf. Josef Horovitz: "The Earliest Biographies of the Prophet and Their Authors," trans. M. Pickthall, *Islamic Culture* 1 (1927): 539–540.

4 For a detailed discussion of these views, see Steven C. Judd, *Religious Scholars and the Umayyads: Piety-Minded Supporters of the Marwānid Caliphate* (London; New York: Routledge, 2014), 3–16.

scholars.[5] Both views, although diametrically opposed to each other, agreed that the state and the scholars were antagonists, engaged in a prolonged power struggle over who should become the authority on Islamic doctrine and religion. Moreover, both views considered the *ʿulamāʾ* of the early Islamic period primarily, if not exclusively, as "religious" scholars, suggesting that their intellectual repertoire was confined to knowledge of the items of faith. S.C. Judd convincingly critiqued this model that proposed an opposition between godless rulers and piety-minded scholars, which had prevailed in academic publications for over a century.[6] The intellectual and political spheres of the early Islamic period are too closely intertwined to be forced into a binary model and deserve a more thorough investigation.

The Umayyad state laid the foundations of a functioning system of judiciary that involved not only judges, but also the caliph and the scholars who had a solid command of the legal tradition. There are numerous examples of how Umayyad judges resorted to the caliphs in Damascus, sending them letters inquiring about matters of Islamic law, such as taxes, inheritance, or the manumission of slaves.[7] Countless reports describe how caliphs participated in issuing legal rulings, occasionally asking their counsellors for legal advice.[8] At the same time, there are numerous cases of caliphs sending letters to Medinan scholars, seeking their opinion on legal, doctrinal or other such matters.[9] These letters mentioned in the classical sources are strong testimonies to the lively interaction between agents of the state and members of the intellectual milieus, and paint a different picture than that suggested by earlier research. This interaction is, incidentally, by no means restricted to the Umayyads. It is also characteristic of the early Abbasid era, where there is equally abundant evidence of a continuous interaction between scholars and caliphs.[10]

Quite apart from letters being exchanged, there are indicative cases of a close cooperation between scholars and agents of the state. These are mostly linked to scholars seeking or agreeing to fulfill various administrative tasks within the state bureaucracy or undertaking their scholarly activity under the patronage of rulers. The classical sources offer ample examples of how scholars

5 Patricia Crone and Martin Hinds, *God's Caliph: Religious Authority in the First Centuries of Islam* (Cambridge: Cambridge University Press, 1986), 43–57.

6 S.C. Judd, *Religious Scholars and the Umayyads,* 11–14, 142–146.

7 See, e.g., P. Crone and M. Hinds, God's Caliph, 46–47.

8 Ibid., 48–54.

9 Ibid.

10 Muhammad Qasim Zaman, "The Caliphs, the ʿUlamāʾ, and the Law: Defining the Role and Function of the Caliph in the Early ʿAbbāsid Period," *Islamic Law and Society Islamic Law and Society* 4, no. 1 (1997): 1–36.

both in the Umayyad and early Abbasid period received official appointments as judges, legal advisors, tax collectors, scribes, diplomats, educators, etc., and were invited to serve the caliphate in these capacities. Such positions offered the learned men a welcome opportunity to advance their professional status and to increase their influence and wealth by rising in the hierarchy.

In the following, I will illustrate this with case studies focusing on two scholars from the Umayyad period, Qabīṣa b. Dhuʾayb (d. ca. 86/705) and Ibn Shihāb al-Zuhrī (d. 124/742). I will both track their spatial mobility in the pursuit of a better life and study their professional mobility within the Umayyad state. To illustrate the terms of interaction between these scholars and the political authorities, this paper will assess their motivations in moving to the caliphal court, analyze their initial encounters with the rulers as portrayed in the sources, and examine their scholarly qualifications vis-à-vis the official posts they were entrusted. While absolute certainty cannot be achieved due to the literary quality of the biographical accounts, I will adopt a prosopographical approach and accept the information presented in the sources so long as they form a coherent body of information on the individual's life that is under investigation. I will tackle the question of accuracy only in cases where the information provided conflicts with the rest of the converging data and will tendentially prefer the earlier attested versions of any given information to the later ones.[11]

2 Reception at the Court

Abū Isḥāq Qabīṣa b. Dhuʾayb al-Khuzāʿī was one of the first Medinan scholars to join the Umayyad court in Damascus. Growing up in Medina, he reportedly possessed an extensive knowledge of Prophetic traditions, as he was well acquainted with prominent companions of the Prophet.[12] The details of how he achieved to join the ranks of the Umayyad caliphate require closer scrutiny, as they differ according to source.

The *Kitāb al-aghānī* preserves a report interspersed with literary motifs about how, at a time when several members of their clan decided to leave Hejaz during a drought, Qabīṣa and his sister Nuʿm first moved to Egypt and

11 For a discussion of the biographical sources and their potential utility for the study of the Umayyad period, see S.C. Judd, *Religious Scholars and the Umayyads*, 17–37.

12 Moshe Sharon, *Corpus Inscriptionum Arabicarum Palaestinae* (henceforth *CIAP*) (Leiden: Brill, 1999), 2:212–214.

then to Syria.[13] According to the story, he and his sister continued their migration even when other members of their clan changed their minds and returned to Hejaz on hearing the news of heavy rainfall.[14] One theme that the story emphasizes is the hardship Qabīṣa endured in his early life, which forced him to leave his home. Another tradition likewise stresses the humble origins of Qabīṣa by reporting that he was orphaned at a very young age and lacked family support.[15] As far as the direction of Qabīṣa's travel is concerned, the story in the *Kitāb al-aghānī* designates Egypt as his initial destination and offers no information about why he later travelled on to Syria.

Qabīṣa's forced migration from Medina to Egypt due to a drought contradicts the picture we get from other traditions. According to a report in al-Balādhūrī's *Ansāb* narrated in Qabīṣa's own words, he was resident in Medina at the end of Muʿāwīya's rule (r. 41–60/661–680), where he attended the nightly study circle at the Prophet's mosque together with other Medinan youths.[16] A short report in Ibn ʿAsākir's *Tārīkh madīnat dimashq* further informs us that Qabīṣa lost an eye during the Battle of Ḥarra in 62/683 just in the outskirts of Medina. The battle stands at the onset of the conflict between the Umayyads and the Zubayrids, known as the second *fitna*.[17] If Qabīṣa's participation in the battle is true, then he must have been residing in Medina until the revolt of ʿAbdallāh b. al-Zubayr in 63/683. As for the next episode of his life, the biographical sources tell us that he became a close confidant of the caliph ʿAbd al-Malik (r. 65–86/685–705) at his court in Damascus.[18] These sources are again silent about when exactly Qabīṣa moved from Medina to Syria, but they emphasize that Qabīṣa maintained a close relationship with ʿAbd al-Malik: reportedly, he carried the caliph's signet, was allowed to open the caliph's letters, and could enter his presence unannounced. This intimacy and trust lasted until Qabīṣa's death in approximately 86/705, which coincided with ʿAbd al-Malik's.[19]

---

13 Abū al-Faraj al-Iṣbahānī, *Kitāb al-aghānī*, ed. Aḥmad al-Shinqiṭī (Cairo: Maṭbaʿat al-Taqaddum, 1323/1905), 13:5–6.

14 Ibid.

15 This information is derived from a comment about Qabīṣa attributed to the Prophet; see M. Sharon, *CIAP*, 2:212.

16 Al-Balādhurī, *Ansāb al-ashrāf*, ed. ʿAbd al-ʿAzīz al-Dūrī, ʿIṣām ʿUqla (Beirut, Berlin: Das Arabische Buch, 2001), 4(2):580.

17 Ibn ʿAsākir. *Tārīkh madīnat dimashq* (= *TMD*), ed. Muḥibb al-Dīn ʿUmar b. Gharāma al-ʿAmrawī (Beirut: Dār al-Fikr, 1995–2000), 49:259. For the caliphate of Ibn al-Zubayr over Hejaz in this period, see Chase F. Robinson, ʿAbd al-Malik (Oxford: Oneworld Publications, 2005), 31–48.

18 Ibn Saʿd, *Ṭabaqāt*, 7:174–175.

19 Ibid.; M. Sharon, *CIAP*, 2:213.

The privilege Qabīṣa enjoyed suggests an older confidential relationship between the two, which probably had its roots in their Medinan years.[20] ʿAbd al-Malik, like Qabīṣa, was a first generation born Muslim, who spent the greater portion of his life in Medina, and studied there under the same companions of the Prophet as Qabīṣa did.[21] Qabīṣa mentions ʿAbd al-Malik as one of the attendees of the nightly study circle at the mosque in Medina, which both attended according to the report mentioned earlier.[22] ʿAbd al-Malik moved to Damascus only later in his life, when his father Marwān I (d. 65/685), at the time still governor of Medina, was expelled from the town at the outbreak of the rebellion against Yazīd (I) b. Muʿāwīya (r. 60–64/680–683) in 61/682.[23] This suggests that we can date Qabīṣa's move to Damascus to the period of the second *fitna*. Given the parallelisms between ʿAbd al-Malik's and Qabīṣa's biographies, their likely personal ties, and the political climate in Medina at the time, this account of Qabīṣa's life seems to provide a more plausible explanation of how he came to move to Damascus and pursue a new career as a scholar at the Umayyad court than the romanticized story of brother and sister fleeing from drought.

The other Medinan scholar joining the Umayyad caliph is the renowned expert on Prophetic traditions Ibn Shihāb al-Zuhrī, whose stay at the court extended over the reign of several caliphs.[24] The case of al-Zuhrī is important because he is named as one of the seven representatives of the Medinan

20 Josef Horovitz: "The Earliest Biographies of the Prophet and Their Authors," trans. M. Pickthall, *Islamic Culture* 2 (1928): 37.

21 Jābir b. ʿAbdallāh and Abū Hurayra are reported to be the teachers of both Qabīṣa and ʿAbd al-Malik; see Ibn Saʿd, *Ṭabaqāt*, 7:231.

22 Al-Balādhūrī, *Ansāb*, 4(2):580. Other attendees of the nightly gatherings in Medina are the two Zubayrid brothers ʿUrwa b. al-Zubayr and Muṣʿab b. al-Zubayr, Abū Bakr b. ʿAbd al-Raḥmān b. al-Ḥārith, ʿAbd al-Raḥmān b. Miswar, Ibrāhīm b. ʿAbd al-Raḥmān b. ʿAwf, and ʿUbaydallāh b. ʿAbdallāh b. ʿUtba; cf. J. Horovitz, "The Earliest Biographies," 543.

23 *EI*² s.v. "ʿAbd al-Malik," (H.A.R. Gibb).

24 On al-Zuhrī, see Ignaz Goldziher, *Muslim Studies*, ed. S.M. Stern, trans. C.R. Barber and S.M. Stern (London: Allen and Unwin, 1971), 2:43:49; Josef Horovitz, "The Earliest Biographies of the Prophet and Their Authors II," trans. M. Pickthall, *Islamic Culture* 2 (1928): 33–50; ʿAbd al-ʿAzīz al-Dūrī, "Al-Zuhrī: A Study on the Beginnings of History Writing in Islam," *Bulletin of the School of Oriental and African Studies* 19, no. 1 (1957): 1–12; idem, *The Rise of Historical Writing Among the Arabs*, eds. Lawrence I. Conrad, Fred M. Donner, trans. Lawrence I. Conrad (Princeton: Princeton University Press, 1984), 95–121; Nabia Abbott, *Studies in Arabic Literary Papyri II: Qurʾānic Commentary and Tradition* (Chicago: University of Chicago Oriental Institute Publications, 1967), 166–184; Michael Lecker, "Biographical Notes on Ibn Shihāb al-Zuhrī," *Journal of Semitic Studies* 41, no. 1 (1996): 21–63; *EI*² s.v. "Al-Zuhrī," (Michael Lecker); S.C. Judd, *Religious Scholars and the Umayyads*, 52–61; Sean W. Anthony, *Muhammad and the Empires of Faith: The Making of the Prophet of Islam* (Oakland: University of California Press, 2020), 129–150.

school of law and thus considered one of the founders of the Islamic religious tradition.[25] Contrary to the different traditions of how Qabīṣa entered the Damascene court, we have a detailed autobiographical account of how al-Zuhrī travelled to Syria, achieved to win the caliph's favor and was admitted to the court. This account is uniquely preserved in Ibn Saʿd's *Ṭabaqāt* and was reproduced later in TMD.[26] Because the account presents rare details about a scholar's introduction to the Umayyad court in his own narration, I will examine it more closely.

Al-Zuhrī begins the account of his northward, and socially upward, journey by explaining his financial hardship in Medina due to the suspension of state stipends for his family, and how he travelled to Syria in search for a better life. He establishes his initial contacts at the Umayyad mosque in Damascus, where he first comes across a group of students studying under Qabīṣa:

> When I grew up, I was a young man without any wealth and cut off from the *dīwān* … I then journeyed to Syria and went inside the Mosque of Damascus around dawn and betook myself to a circle with students around the spot where the imam leads the prayers and took a seat there. The group asked me my lineage, and I said [I was] "A man of Quraysh from the inhabitants of Medina." They said, "Do you know any tradition [*ʿilm*] concerning the ruling on slave women who bear their master children [*fī ummahāt al-awlād*]?" I told them what ʿUmar b. al-Khaṭṭāb said concerning such slave women, and the group said to me, "This is the gathering of Qabīṣa b. Dhuʾayb. He's on his way to see you, for ʿAbd al-Malik had asked him about this, and us as well, but he found that none of us knew of a tradition about that …"[27]

Al-Zuhrī finally meets Qabīṣa himself, introduces himself and his family, and names the Medinan scholars with whom he studied, several of which Qabīṣa knew personally.

Their conversation reveals that al-Zuhrī, who was too young to have met Qabīṣa while he still resided in Medina, impresses his senior with his knowledge

25 See Joseph Schacht, *The Origins of Muhammadan Jurisprudence* (Oxford: Clarendon Press, 1950), 243–247; *EI*² s.v. "Al-Zuhrī," (Michael Lecker).

26 Ibn Saʿd, *Ṭabaqāt*, 7:429–432; Ibn ʿAsākir, 55:322–325. For a complete translation of al-Zuhrī's account, see Ibn Saʿd, *The Men of Medina: The Volume II*, trans. Aisha Bewley (London: Ta-Ha Publishers Ltd., 1997), 273–276; S.W. Anthony, *Muhammad and the Empires of Faith*, 132–135. Similar accounts with considerable variations are preserved in TMD 55:297–302.

27 Translation reproduced from S.W. Anthony, *Muhammad and the Empires of Faith*, 132–135.

on a matter of inheritance, which apparently had been discussed among the Damascenes for some time. The young Medinan's expertise prompts Qabīṣa to introduce al-Zuhrī to ʿAbd al-Malik, and the account continues with a description of al-Zuhrī's encounter with the caliph:

> Qabīṣa went in to see ʿAbd al-Malik b. Marwān, but I sat at the doorway for about an hour until the sun rose. Later he came out and said, "Where's that Qurashī from Medina?" "Right here!" I said. I stood up. I entered the presence of the Commander of the Faithful at [Qabīṣa's] side. I saw before him a copy of the Qurʾān that he had just closed and commanded to be taken away. No one else besides Qabīṣa sat in his presence. I offered him the salutations owed the caliph, and he said, "Who are you?" I said, "I am Muḥammad b. Muslim b. ʿUbaydallāh b. ʿAbdallāh b. Shihāb b. ʿAbdallāh b. al-Ḥārith b. Zuhra."[28]

After introducing himself to ʿAbd al-Malik by naming not only his forefathers but also the scholarly circles he attended in Medina, al-Zuhrī repeats the tradition he heard from the renowned Medinan scholar Saʿīd b. al-Musayyab (d. 94/712) on the question of the inheritance of slave women who bear their master children (*ummahāt al-awlād*), which he had been asked earlier by Qabīṣa.[29] The caliph is equally pleased with al-Zuhrī's answer. Encouraged by the caliph's sympathy, al-Zuhrī makes an appeal for restoring the stipends of his family. Although both Qabīṣa and ʿAbd al-Malik are slightly perplexed by the young man's boldness, al-Zuhrī manages to secure for himself first an advance payment of 100 dinars with some extras, and later the restoration of the stipends due to his family. Additionally, and more importantly, the caliph offers him the right to join his entourage with a commensurate salary (*rizq al-ṣaḥāba*).

As with Qabīṣa, the precise date of al-Zuhrī's visit to Damascus is unclear. However, al-Zuhrī's autobiographical account offers certain hints. After learning about al-Zuhrī's genealogy, the caliph immediately remarks that al-Zuhrī's clan Banū Zuhra participated in the second *fitna* on the side of the Zubayrids against the Umayyads. This information finds corroboration in other accounts, stating that two members of the Banū Zuhra served ʿAbdallāh b. al-Zubayr as

28 Ibid.

29 Saʿīd b. al-Musayyab is a Medinan expert on legal matters, whom both Qabīṣa and ʿAbd al-Malik held in high esteem. Another report illustrates how Saʿīd b. al-Musayyab shared a letter the Medinans received from ʿAbd al-Malik only with al-Zuhrī, who quickly memorized it, see Ṭaqī al-Dīn Aḥmad b. ʿAlī al-Maqrīzī, *Kitāb al-muqaffā al-kabīr*, ed. Muḥammad al-Yaʿlāwī (Beirut: Dār al-Gharb al-Islāmī, 1991), 7:136.

governors of Medina from 68/687 onwards, until the capture of the town by ʿAbd al-Malik's forces in 73/692.[30] The beginning of al-Zuhrī's account also makes it clear that the primary reason for al-Zuhrī's financial hardship was the Umayyad's suspension of the stipends for Banū Zuhra.[31] Evidently, this is due to the Banū Zuhra's involvement in the Zubayrid uprising. Given these indications, al-Zuhrī's visit to Damascus can only be dated to the period when the unrest of the civil war had subsided, i.e. after 72/692. Furthermore, we learn from two parallel accounts that the tradition al-Zuhrī reported to the caliph in order to help solve the inheritance question of *ummahāt al-awlād* was no neutral matter: it involved the inheritance rights of the family of Ibn al-Zubayr or, more precisely, the rights of a slave woman who bore Muṣʿab (the brother of ʿAbdallāh b. al-Zubayr) a son. After her son's death, Muṣʿab's wife asked for her share in the inheritance, which she was denied by the Zubayrid family. These accounts elucidate that ʿAbd al-Malik was informed about the matter when his governor in Medina wrote to him, asking for legal advice.[32] From this piece of information we can determine that the *fitna* was over and ʿAbd al-Malik in full control of the city, as he had his own appointed governor there. The governor is identified as Hishām b. Ismāʿīl, who was in charge of the city between 82/701–87/706.[33] This date conforms with other reports that date al-Zuhrī's arrival to the year of Ibn al-Ashʿath's revolt in 82/701.[34] The accounts also clearly

30 M. Lecker, "Biographical Notes," 47–48.

31 The biographical sources inform us that ʿAbd al-Malik, before being forced to leave Medina, was in charge of the *dīwān* that regulated the stipends distributed to Medinan families under the governorship of his father Marwān (I) and thus must have had first-hand knowledge of the genealogies of Medinan families and their payments. Al-Ṭabarī, *Tārīkh al-rusūl wa al-mulūk*, ed. M.J. de Goeje *et al.* (Leiden: E.J. Brill, 1879–1901), II, 837; Ibn Qutayba, *K. al-maʿārif*, ed. Shawkat ʿUkāsha (Cairo: Dār al-Maʿārif, 1971), 355.

32 Ibn ʿAsākir, TMD, 55:298–302.

33 Ibid. On Hishām b. Ismāʿīl's governorship, see al-Ṭabarī, *Tārīkh*, II, 1182. He is ʿAbd al-Malik's father-in-law, and the grandfather of his namesake, the caliph Hishām. Another report in al-Bukhārī's *al-Tārīkh al-saghīr* relates that after their first encounter ʿAbd al-Malik sent a letter through Hishām b. Ismāʿīl as intermediary to Saʿīd b. al-Musayyab inquiring about al-Zuhrī; see idem, ed. Yūsuf al-Marʿashlī (Beirut: Dār al-Maʿrifa, 1986), 1:217.

34 Ibid.; Abū Zurʿa's *Tārīkh* offers an abridged version of al-Zuhrī's encounter with Qabīṣa and ʿAbd al-Malik during his travel to Damascus and dates this visit to the time of Ibn al-Ashʿath's revolt: "*qadimtu Dimashqa zamāna taḥarruk Ibn al-Ashʿath wa ʿAbd al-Malik mashghūl yawmaʾidhin bi-shaʾnihi.*" Abū Zurʿa's *al-Tārīkh*, ed. Shukrullāh Niʿmatullāh al-Qūjānī (Damascus: Majmaʿ al-Lugha al-ʿArabiyya, 1980), 1:408–9, no. 946. Cf. Ibn ʿAsākir, TMD, 55:305. On Ibn al-Ashʿath's revolt, see al-Ṭabarī, *Tārīkh*, II, 1052. Cf. al-Dhahabī, *Siyar aʿlām al-nubalāʾ*, ed. Shuʿayb al-Arnāʾūṭ and Ḥusayn al-Amad (Beirut: Muʾassasat al-Riāla, 1996), 5:328: "*qadima Ibn Shihāb ʿalā ʿAbd al-Malik sanata ithnatayn wa thamānīn* (= 82/701)."

articulate that the people of Medina were living in a general state of destitution following the end of the civil strife, and that this prompted al-Zuhrī to undertake his journey to the Umayyad capital.[35] Thus, al-Zuhrī likely entered the service of the Umayyad government in the final years of ʿAbd al-Malik's reign, when he was somewhere between 23 and 31 years of age.[36]

---

35 Ibn ʿAsākir, *TMD*, 55:298–302.

36 My dating of al-Zuhrī's enterance to the Damascene court accords with the abovementioned abridged account preserved in Abū Zurʿa's *Tārīkh* (1:408–9, no. 946.). Cf. Abbott (*Studies in Arabic Literary Papyri II*, 21–22). An alternative date has been proposed by M. Lecker ("Biographical Notes," 47–48), who prefers to depend on a variant reading of the same report, found also in Abū Zurʿa's *al-Tārīkh* (1:583–584, no. 1643). This second report replaces Ibn al-Ashʿath's revolt in Iraq with Muṣʿab b. al-Zubayr's: "*wa kāna maqdam Ibn Shihāb Dimashqa zamāna Muṣʿab wa ʿAbd al-Malik mashghūl yawmaʾidhin bi-shaʾnihi.*" Therefore, M. Lecker dates al-Zuhrī's arrival in Damascus to the year 72/691. This reading is, however, unlikely for several reasons. Firstly, al-Zuhrī's father is reported to be a member of Muṣʿab b. al-Zubayr's troops in Iraq and it is unrealistic that ʿAbd al-Malik would have restored al-Zuhrī's and his family's stipends before the fight against Muṣʿab b. al-Zubayr was won, see Ibn Khallikān, *Wafayāt al-aʿyān wa anbāʾ abnāʾ al-zamān*, ed. Iḥsān ʿAbbās (Beirut: Dār Ṣādir, 1968–72), 4:178, and cf. Ibn Qutayba, *K. al-maʿārif*, 472. M. Lecker accepts Abū Zurʿa's second account in accordance with a reference found in al-Yaʿqūbī's *Tārīkh* (ed. M.T. Houtsma [Leiden, 1883], 22:311), which informs us that ʿAbd al-Malik quoted a Prophetic tradition during the conflict with the Zubayrids, transmitted by al-Zuhrī, that allowed pilgrimage to Jerusalem instead of Mecca; see M. Lecker, "Biographical Notes," 42–43. This isolated piece of information presented by al-Yaʿqūbī was first studied by I. Goldziher (*Muslim Studies*, 2:44–45) and has been extensively discussed in earlier scholarship: J. Horovitz, ʿA.ʿA. al-Dūrī, N. Abbott, and M.M. Aʿẓamī approached it with great skepticism and rejected it on the grounds that al-Zuhrī would have been too young a scholar to be considered an authority permitted to advise the caliph on a weighty subject like changing the pilgrimage ritual; see J. Horovitz, "The Earliest Biographies II," 35–36; ʿA. ʿA. al-Dūrī, "Al-Zuhrī," 11; N. Abbott, *Studies in Arabic Literary Papyri II*, 21; Muḥammad Muṣṭafā Aʿẓamī, *Studies in Early Hadith Literature* (Indianapolis: American Trust, 1978), 288–291. For various dates of al-Zuhrī's birth year (50/670, 51/671, 56/676 or 58/678), see M. Lecker, "Biographical Notes,"44, fn. 92. Another account, again found in Abū Zurʿa's *al-Tārīkh* (1:409), which reports that al-Zuhrī heard ʿAbd al-Malik preaching in Jerusalem before the outbreak of a plague, cannot be taken as a definite *terminus ante quem*, since it suggests no personal encounter between al-Zuhrī and ʿAbd al-Malik. Additionally, the plague that hit Syria during ʿAbd al-Malik's reign came in several waves. The last occurred in 86/705, coinciding with ʿAbd al-Malik's death. Moreover, in other versions of the report, the sermon which al-Zuhrī heard is either attributed to other figures or reported to have taken place in an unspecified place; see S.W. Anthony, *Muhammad and the Empires of Faith*, 136, fn. 21. Finally, an account which suggests that al-Zuhrī visited Syria as a young adolescent during the caliphate of Marwān I (r. 64–65/683–684) ("*wafadtu ʿalā Marwān wa anā muḥtalim*") is dubious and was rejected by Yaḥyā b. Bukayr (d. 231/845), an early transmitter of al-Zuhrī's material, who also questioned al-Zuhrī's age and commented that he must have been too young at the time to undertake such a journey; see Ibn ʿAsākir, *TMD*, 55:305 and al-Dhahabī, *Siyar*, 5:326. Yaḥyā is the transmitter of al-Zuhrī's

Al-Zuhrī's narration of his journey to Damascus and his admittance to the caliphal retinue reveal many details about al-Zuhrī's aspirations as a young Medinan scholar eager to pursue a career at the center of political power. At the same time, his admittance to the court attests to the caliph's interest in people of his profile. Apart from al-Zuhrī's successful performance during his initial encounters with Qabīṣa and ʿAbd al-Malik, there was another factor that facilitated al-Zuhrī's admittance to the Umayyad court: he had been a member of the Medinan scholarly network to which both ʿAbd al-Malik and Qabīṣa had had close affinities in their time. This may explain why al-Zuhrī's knowledge of traditions on the decisions of earlier Medinan caliphs, transmitted via revered scholars like Saʿīd b. al-Musayyab, was met with so much favor.[37] After his admittance to the court, al-Zuhrī remained in the service of the Umayyads until the end of his life, serving not only ʿAbd al-Malik but also four of his sons in various positions. He was at the peak of his influence during the caliphate of Hishām b. ʿAbd al-Malik (r. 105–125/724–743).

3 Service to the Caliphate

Although both Medinan scholars made their careers by joining ʿAbd al-Malik's court in Damascus, the details of their rise in the ranks differ. As noted above, Qabīṣa was a close confidant of the caliph and an influential advisor, who carried ʿAbd al-Malik's signet, was allowed to open his letters, and could enter his presence without prior announcement.[38] Moreover, he was in charge of the mint (*sikka*) and the caliphal information service or royal post (*barīd*).[39] According to a report in Khalīfa b. Khayyāt's *Tārīkh*, Qabīṣa was also responsible for the state treasury (*buyūt al-amwāl*) and storehouses (*khazāʾin*).[40] Thus he was clearly the most powerful figure after the caliph, and it can be argued that his rank was almost equal to that of a vizier, a post that was instituted by the Abbasids less than a century later.

material preserved on a papyrus fragment, which is called *Kitāb ʿuqayl*, see S.W. Anthony, *Muhammad and the Empires of Faith*, 143–144.

37 A report in al-Ṭabarī's *Tārīkh* (1:1313) suggests that Saʿīd b. al-Musayyab had close connections to ʿAbd al-Malik's father Marwān (I) at the time when the latter was the governor of Medina.

38 Ibn Saʿd, *Ṭabaqāt*, 7:174–175.

39 Ibid.

40 Khalīfa b. Khayyāt, *Tārīkh*, ed. Akram Ḍiyāʾ al-ʿUmarī (Riyadh: Dār Ṭayba, 1985), 299; Ibn ʿAsākir, *TMD*, 45:454.

Al-Zuhrī's narration offers glimpses into some of the roles Qabīṣa assumed at ʿAbd al-Malik's court. For example, Qabīṣa brings al-Zuhrī into the caliph's presence without asking for permission from any other courtier, he issues a special advance payment of 100 dinars to be paid to al-Zuhrī directly from the state's treasury on a document (*ruqʿa*) in his own handwriting without requiring any further authorization, and he advises ʿAbd al-Malik on various matters.[41] The classical sources offer a myriad of cases in which Qabīṣa directs the caliph's decisions, particularly in legal issues. For example, in a report in ʿAbd al-Razzāq's *al-Muṣannaf*, ʿAbd al-Malik shows Qabīṣa a private petition regarding the slander of a free person by a freed slave, and Qabīṣa pronounces the final ruling of eighty lashes.[42] In another report, Qabīṣa joins ʿAbd al-Malik during his pilgrimage in 75/695 and advises the caliph on a number of issues concerning the conduct of *ḥajj*.[43] The influential role he enjoyed is exceptional for someone with an exclusively Medinan scholarly background.

Al-Zuhrī's narration indicates that Qabīṣa pursued his profession as a distinguished scholar in Syria and held regular teaching circles at the Umayyad mosque, where he lectured his students in the mornings after the prayer. His expertise in the teachings and rulings of the Prophet as well as in legal matters is also mentioned in other accounts.[44] Mālik b. Anas' (d. 179/795) *al-Muwaṭṭaʾ*, for example, preserves a tradition from al-Zuhrī, transmitted on the authority of Qabīṣa, which settles another inheritance question (that of a grandmother).[45] Additionally, Qabīṣa is recorded in the biographical accounts as a teacher of secretaries or scribes (*muʿallim al-kuttāb*),[46] a task usually

41 There is a similar papyrus document from the late Umayyad period that institutes a payment to a *qāḍī* on top of his regular salary, addressed to the treasury's office and written by the head of the treasury in Egypt; see Wadād al-Qāḍī, "An Umayyad Papyrus in al-Kindī's Kitāb al-Quḍāt?," *Der Islam* 84, no. 2 (2007): 200–245.

42 ʿAbd al-Razzāq, *al-Muṣannaf*, ed. Ḥabīb al-Raḥmān al-Aʿẓamī (Beirut: al-Maktab al-Islāmī, 1970–1972), 7:437, no. 13787, cf. P. Crone and M. Hinds, *God's Caliph*, 47.

43 Ibn Saʿd, *Ṭabaqāt*, 7:228–229, 230. See also Qabīṣa's intervention in facilitating Ibn al-Ḥanafiyya's apology sent to ʿAbd al-Malik; ibid. 7:708–110.

44 He was known to be an expert on Zayd b. Thābit's rulings; see al-Bukhārī, *Tārīkh al-kabīr*, ed. Muḥammad ʿAbd al-Muʿīd Khān (Hyderabad: Maṭbaʿat Jamʿiyyat Dāʾirat al-Maʿārif al-ʿUthmāniyya, 1941–1958), 7:174–175; Ibn Ḥajar, *al-Iṣāba fī tamyīz al-ṣaḥāba* eds. ʿĀdil Aḥmad ʿAbd al-Mawjūd, ʿAlī Muḥammad Muʿawwaḍ (Beirut, Dār al-Kutub al-ʿIlmiyya, 1995), 5:391; al-Dhahabī, *Siyar*, 4:283.

45 Mālik b. Anas, *al-Muwaṭṭaʾ*, ed. Muḥammad Fuʾād ʿAbd al-Bāqī (Beirut: Iḥyā Turāth al-ʿArabī, 1985), 2:513 (book 27, section 8).

46 Ibn Ḥajar, *al-Iṣāba* 5:391; Ibn ʿAsākir, TMD, 49:255,257–8; Ibn Kathīr, *al-Bidāya wa al-nihāya* (Beirut: Maktabat al-Maʿārif, 1992), 8:313.

assumed by established secretaries of the chancery.[47] Although he is often mentioned as ʿAbd al-Malik's chief secretary (*kātib ʿAbd al-Malik*), Qabīṣa did not have the formal training of a secretary (*kātib*) working in the administrative offices of the state. In that regard it is indicative that Qabīṣa was not the head of the chancery (*kātib al-rasāʾil*), as the caliph's chief secretaries usually were. This post was occupied by Abū Zaʿzaʿa, the caliph's *mawlā*,[48] suggesting that Qabīṣa's title *kātib* somehow described his extraordinary, more complex role.

There is also no evidence that Qabīṣa educated scribes. Among those transmitting Prophetic traditions from Qabīṣa, we find only two who became influential officials of the Umayyad state in the subsequent period.[49] The first is his son Isḥāq (died after 120/738), who later became a government official in the *al-Urdunn* province, initially in charge of the office that looked after the invalids (*dīwān al-zamnā*) under Walīd b. ʿAbd al-Malik (r. 86–96/705–715), then in charge of the alms taxes (*dīwān al-ṣadaqāt*) under Hishām b. ʿAbd al-Malik.[50] Rajāʾ b. Ḥaywa (112/730), another transmitter of Qabīṣa's traditions, became an advisor to the caliph Sulaymān b. ʿAbd al-Malik (r. 96–99/715–717) and, according to some sources, rose to the rank of head of Sulaymān's *dīwān al-khatam* or chancery.[51] The remit of Qabīṣa's teaching activity hence apparently did not extend to the training of scribes. The sources suggest that he was also not responsible for the education of the children of the ruling elite, including the

---

47 The prime examples are Sālim Abū al-ʿĀlāʾ and his student and son-in-law ʿAbd al-Ḥamīd al-Kātib (d. 132/750), who both served as the head of the imperial chancery in successive periods, see Wadād al-Qāḍī "Identity Formation of the Bureaucracy of the Early Islamic State: ʿAbd al-Ḥamīd's 'Letter to the Secretaries'," in *Mediterranean Identities in the Premodern Era Entrepôts, Islands, Empires*, eds. John Watkins, Kathryn L. Reyerson (London: Routledge, 2016), 141–154. On Sālim, see Ibn ʿAsākir, *TMD*, 20:79–81. For refences about how, under the caliph ʿAbd al-Malik, the state chancery became a complex institution training professional scribes, see idem, "Early Islamic State Letters," in eds. Averil Cameron, Lawrence I. Conrad, *Byzantine and Early Islamic Near East, vol I: Problems in the Literary Source Material* (Princeton: Darwin Press, 1992), 215–222.

48 Khalīfa b. Khayyāṭ, *Tārīkh*, 299. His name is occasionally vocalized as Zuʿayziʿa.

49 Ibn Ḥajar, *Tahdhīb al-tahdhīb*, eds. Ibrāhīm al-Zaybaq, ʿĀdil Murshid (Beirut: Muʾassasat al-Risāla, 1995), 3:425–426. Those who transmitted from Qabīṣa are his son Isḥāq, al-Zuhrī, Rajāʾ b. Ḥaywa, ʿUthmān b. Isḥāq b. Kharasha, ʿAbdallāh b. Mawhab, ʿAbdallāh b. Abī Maryam, Makḥūl, and Abū Qilāba al-Jarmī.

50 There are two mosaic boards near the Umayyad market of Beisan with inscriptions that bear Isḥāq's name as the official in charge of the construction. More information on this inscription and on Isḥāq's biography can be found in M. Sharon, *CIAP*, 207–212.

51 *EI*² s.v. "Radjāʾ b. Ḥaywa," (Clifford E. Bosworth). On him, see N. Abbott, *Studies in Arabic Literary Papyri II*, 205; Clifford E. Bosworth, "Rajāʾ b. Ḥaywa al-Kindī and the Umayyad Caliphs" *Islamic Quarterly* 16, no. 1 (1972): 36–81.

princes. Rather, his scholarly reputation was based on his knowledge of the Prophetic tradition and his expertise in Medinan legal practice, which contributed to the formation of a new generation of Syrian scholars and reinforced the Umayyad state's interest in Medinan scholarship, particularly in the pursuit of legal knowledge.

Unlike Qabīṣa, who may have profited from his being acquainted with ʿAbd al-Malik since their Medinan times, al-Zuhrī was a newcomer at the Umayyad court, and the progression of his career was much slower. In his junior years, al-Zuhrī undertook various official positions with a rather modest authority. Reports suggest that he kept his residence in Medina and continued to pursue his scholarly life there.[52] Although al-Zuhrī entered into the service of the Umayyad state under ʿAbd al-Malik, there is no clear information about his official appointment during this caliph's rule. One report suggests that after having resided in Medina, al-Zuhrī was sent by ʿAbd al-Malik to his brother ʿAbd al-ʿAzīz b. Marwān (d. 86/705) in Egypt.[53] In another account, al-Zuhrī is mentioned as a member of Walīd I's court (*wa-huwa fī ʿaskarihi*), advising the caliph on legal conditions of marrying one sister and divorcing another.[54]

According to the biographical sources, al-Zuhrī's first official appointment was as a tax collector.[55] Although the task might appear unrelated to his scholarly qualifications at first sight, undertaking the job required a thorough knowledge of collecting alms (*ṣadaqāt*)[56] and provisions about payment of bloodwit

---

52 J. Horovitz, "The Earliest Biographies II," 43; ʿA.ʿA. al-Dūrī, *The Rise of Historical Writing*, 118.

53 Al-Maqrīzī, *al-Muqaffā*, 7:137. The account provides no details about al-Zuhrī's mission in Egypt, except for the information that al-Zuhrī met another Medinan scholar from his clan Banū Zuhra, named Ibrāhīm b. Qāriẓ (on him, see Ibn Ḥajar, *Tahdhīb*, 1:72) Accordingly, Ibrāhīm heard about al-Zuhrī's studies with Saʿīd b. al-Musayyab in Medina and advised him to go and study with the other Medinan companion, ʿUrwa b. al-Zubayr (94/712). The report, however, contains several peculiarities. It informs us that al-Zuhrī traveled to Egypt after having resided in Medina for eight years and after Ibn al-Musayyab's death. However, Ibn al-Musayyab died in the same year as ʿUrwa, and that is approximately seven years after the deaths of both ʿAbd al-Malik and his brother ʿAbd al-ʿAzīz.

54 Ibn ʿAsākir, *TMD*, 58:23.

55 M. Lecker, "Biographical Notes," 38.

56 Al-Maqrīzī, *al-Muqaffā*, 7:135; see M. Lecker, "Biographical Notes," 39. Al-Zuhrī memorized a text on alms (*kitāb al-ṣadaqa*) from Sālim b. ʿAbdallāh b. ʿUmar b. al-Khaṭṭāb (d. 106/724), which was a document preserved by the family of ʿUmar b. al-Khaṭṭāb. See, e.g., Ibn Zanjawayh, *Kitāb al-amwāl*, ed. Shākir Dhīb Fayyāḍ (Riyadh: King Faisal Center for Research and Islamic Studies, 1986), 2:853–855. It is reported that ʿUmar II also copied this document from Sālim and his brother ʿAbdallāh during his governorship in Medina (87–93/706–712) and used it as a template during his caliphal term, when he sent an edict to his governors defining the terms of collecting alms taxes. See M.J. Kister, "*Lā taqraʾū l-qurʾāna ʿalā l-muṣḥafiyyīn wa-lā taḥmilū l-ʿilma ʿani l-ṣaḥafiyyīn* …: Some Notes on the

(*ʿuqūl*),[57] which al-Zuhrī learned from two Medinan scholars. Additionally, a firm knowledge of tribal genealogies was mandatory for this task, which al-Zuhrī had studied already in his youth, whence he was considered an expert on *nasab*.[58] A jurist by training, al-Zuhrī's next post in service to the Umayyad state was that of a judge. The Egyptian jurist Layth b. Saʿd (b. 94/713–d. 175/791) names al-Zuhrī as the judge under ʿUmar II (r. 99–101/717–720), who settled

Transmission of Ḥadīth," in *The Ḥadīth: Critical Concepts in Islamic Studies*, ed. Mustafa Shah (London: Routledge, 2010), 1:270; cf. Ibn Zanjawayh, *Kitāb al-amwāl*, 2:800–803. For an epistle sent by ʿUmar II to the provinces, which includes provisions on levying alms, see Sean W. Anthony, "A 'Rediscovered' Letter of the Umayyad Caliph ʿUmar ibn ʿAbd al-ʿAzīz (r. 717–720 CE): Caliphal Authorship and Legal Authority in al-Risālah fī l-Fayʾ," in *Rulers as Authors in the Islamic World*, eds. Sonja Brentjes, Maribel Fierro, and Tilman Seidensticker (Brill, forthcoming).

57 Al-Zuhrī memorized a document on bloodwit (*kitāb al-ʿuqūl*) from Abū Bakr b. Muḥammad b. ʿAmr b. Ḥazm, who was the *qāḍī* of Medina until he was appointed as governor there. On him, see M. Lecker, "ʿAmr ibn Ḥazm al-Anṣārī and Qurʾān 2,256: 'No Compulsion Is There in Religion'," in *Oriens* 35 (1996): 1–9; S.C. Judd, *Religious Scholars and the Umayyads*, 153–154. Al-Nasāʾī's *Sunan* preserves various versions of a document sent by the Prophet to the people of Yemen with clauses on bloodwit (*ʿuqūl*), which al-Zuhrī transmitted from Abū Bakr b. Muḥammad, see idem, ed. Ḥasan ʿAbd al-Munʿim al-Shalbī (Beirut: Muʾassasat al-Risāla, 2001), 6:373–377 (*Kitāb al-qasāma: Bāb dhikr ḥadīth ʿAmr ibn Ḥazm fī al-ʿuqūl*). Al-Zuhrī reports that the document was in the possession of the Ḥazm family, cf. M.J. Kister, "*Lā taqraʾū l-qurʾāna ʿalā l-muṣḥafiyyīn*," 1:270.

58 According to Ibn Saʿd (*Ṭabaqāt*, 2:328–329), al-Zuhrī studied genealogy with the Medinan genealogist ʿAbdallāh b. Thaʿlaba (d. 89/708), who was an ally (*ḥalīf*) of Banū Zuhra, even before he commenced his studies on *fiqh* with Saʿīd b. al-Musayyab. Cf. Ibn ʿAsākir, TMD, 55:322; al-Dhahabī, *Siyar*, 3:503, 5:330. According to a statement attributed to Qurra b. ʿAbd al-Raḥmān Ḥaywaʾil/Ḥaywīl (d. 147/764), al-Zuhrī had a book on the genealogy of his own tribe. See al-Fasawī, *K. al-maʿrifa wa al-tārīkh*, ed. Akram Ḍiyāʾ al-ʿUmarī (Medina: Maktabat al-Dār, 1990), 1:641; al-Dhahabī, *Siyar*, 5:333; cf. Abū Zurʿa, *Tārīkh*, 1:641. In the *Kitāb al-aghānī* (19:57), there is a report that the Umayyad governor of Iraq, Khālid al-Qasrī (d. 126/743), commissioned Zuhrī to write a book on genealogy for him. Al-Zuhrī started out with the genealogy of the Muḍarites, but that work was left unfinished because of Khālid's hatred towards that tribe. G.R. Hawting suggests that Khālid was appointed as a governor of Iraq to end the intensifying inter-tribal feuds in the region, which primarily involved the Muḍarites, see *EI*[2] s.v. "ʿAbd Allāh al-Ḳasrī," (G.R. Hawting). For the indispensability of knowledge of *nasab* for the administration in the *dīwān* of the early period, especially for the settlement of troops and the payment of stipends (*ʿaṭāʾ*), see M.J. Kister and M. Plessner, "Notes on Caskel's *Ǧamharat an-nasab*," *Oriens* 25/26 (1976): 50–51. As W. al-Qāḍī pointed out, knowledge about newborns and deceased in each clan was essential for the payment of stipends; see idem, "A Documentary Report on Umayyad Stipends Registers: *Dīwān al-ʿAṭāʾ* in Abū Zurʿa's *Tārīkh*," *Quaderni di Studi Arabi Nuova Serie*, 4 (2009): 33–42. Moreover, the genealogical information about Arab tribes must have been essential to tax collection when no census declarations were available.

a property dispute in Fusṭāṭ, which he remembered from his childhood.[59] Several accounts, however, date al-Zuhrī's appointment as a judge to the reign of Yazīd (II) b. ʿAbd al-Malik (r. 101–105/720–724), which he held jointly with Sulaymān b. Ḥabīb al-Muḥārabī (d. 126/744).[60] A report in Wakīʿ's *Akhbār al-quḍāt* suggests that the location of this post was in the Ḥimṣ province of Syria, as he and Sulaymān adjudicated a dispute that arose among a number of treasure hunters who excavated some antiquities in the old town of Lattakia.[61] It must be during this post that al-Zuhrī finally took up a permanent residence in Syria, which lasted for about two decades, until he moved to the estates he owned in southern Palestine, near Ayla, towards the end of his life.[62]

In connection to these posts, al-Zuhrī is also mentioned to have served the Umayyad state as a *shurṭī*, i.e. as someone in charge of a special urban armed unit, typically attached to a governor or the caliph. Among a number of responsibilities, the *shurṭa* in the Umayyad period had the important function of imposing judicial decisions.[63] In many provinces the chief of the *shurṭa* often worked in close collaboration with the *qāḍīs*.[64] Several examples from Egypt show that some of the chief *qāḍīs* even held the office of *ṣāḥib al-shurṭa*

59 Ibn ʿAbd al-Ḥakam, *Futūḥ miṣr wa al-maghrib*, ed. Muḥammad ʿAlī ʿUmar (Cairo: Maktabat al-Thaqafiyya al-Dīniyya, 2004), 129–130. The account identifies the judge as Ibn Shihāb. Since no other Ibn Shihāb is mentioned, M. Lecker postulates that this must be al-Zuhrī. There are, however, some peculiarities about this report. First of all, we find information that ʿUmar II did not favor al-Zuhrī because of his earlier misdeeds as a tax-collector, and hence revoked his decision to appoint al-Zuhrī as his tax-collector or governor in Kufa. See S.W. Anthony, *Muhammad and the Empires of Faith*, 136, fn. 26. Secondly, al-Zuhrī is not listed as a judge in Egypt. The judges in Egypt under ʿUmar II were ʿAbdallāh b. ʿAbd al-Raḥmān b. Hujayra and ʿIyāḍ b. ʿAbdallāh al-Azdī (in office twice, 99–101/717–19). See, for example, the correspondence between ʿUmar II and ʿIyāḍ; W. al-Qāḍī, "An Umayyad Papyrus," 225, 243. If Layth b. Saʿd's testimony should be taken as valid, then al-Zuhrī's ruling over the dispute in Egypt should date to the end of ʿUmar II's reign, since Layth is born in 94/713. For further discussions on his appointment under ʿUmar II, see M. Lecker, "Biographical Notes," 37–38. An isolated report in Ibn ʿAsākir's *TMD* (55:387), stating that al-Zuhrī served ʿAbd al-Malik as a judge, seems to be mistaken.

60 Ibn Qutayba, *K. al-maʿārif*, 472; Ibn ʿAsākir, *TMD*, 55:325; al-Dhahabī, *Siyar*, 5:331. On Sulaymān b. Ḥabīb, see W. al-Qāḍī, "A Documentary Report on Umayyad Stipends Registers," 33–36.

61 Wakīʿ, *Akhbār al-quḍāt* (Beirut: ʿĀlam al-Kutub, n.d.), 3:211.

62 M. Lecker, "Biographical Notes," 48–56.

63 For a more detailed discussion of various functions of the *shurṭa* in the Umayyad period, especially of the units attached to the caliph, see F.M. Donner, "The Shurta in Early Umayyad Syria," in *Proceedings of the Third Symposium on the History of Bilâd al-Shâm during the Umayyad Period*, ed. M. Adnan Bakhit and Robert Schick (Amman, 1989), 2: 247–262.

64 *EI*[2] s.v. "Shurṭa," (J.S. Nielsen).

simultaneously.[65] As part of their duties, the *shurṭa* also actively helped to enforce the levying of taxes, which accounted for their image as merciless agents of the state.[66] Indeed, al-Zuhrī is also remembered for his ruthless punishment of a man who refused to pay his taxes by flogging him to death.[67] However, the details of al-Zuhrī's function as a *shurtī* remain otherwise unknown. He is possibly described as a *shurṭī* not because of a self-standing post that he held, but rather because he fulfilled that function in combination with the duties of a tax-collector or a *qāḍī*.[68] Overall it is evident that the traditional education al-Zuhrī had obtained in Medina, especially his expertise in jurisprudence, his knowledge of genealogy, as well as his easy access to first-hand knowledge on collecting alms and bloodwit, opened the doors to a rewarding career in the Umayyad state administration.

Al-Zuhrī's heyday as a senior scholar was during Hishām b. ʿAbd al-Malik's caliphate. Under Hishām, al-Zuhrī pursued his scholarly activities at the caliph's palace in Ruṣāfa in northeast Syria, where he began tutoring the caliph's children Saʿīd, Sulaymān, Maslama, and Yazīd.[69] In detailing al-Zuhrī's teaching activity, the sources emphasize how, at the caliph's behest, al-Zuhrī departed from the conventional methods of instruction and began dictating his knowledge to the princes.[70] One account, for example, describes a scene in which the prince Ibrāhīm b. Walīd appears before al-Zuhrī and asks for his teacher's

65 Yūnus b. ʿAṭiyya al-Ḥadramī (in office 83–85/702–705), ʿAbd al-Raḥmān b. Muʿāwīya b. Ḥudayj (85/705), and ʿImrān b. ʿAbd al-Raḥmān al-Ḥasanī (85–?/705–?) were appointed to the post that combined *qāḍī*ship and *ṣāḥib al-shurṭa* in Egypt. See S.C. Judd, *Religious Scholars and the Umayyads*, 163–164.

66 *EI*[2] s.v. "Shurṭa," (J.S. Nielsen).

67 M. Lecker, "Biographical Notes,", 38–39, Ibn Sayyid al-Nās, *al-Nafḥ al-shadhī fi sharḥ jāmiʿ al-tirmidhī*, ed. Aḥmad Maʿbad ʿAbd al-Karīm (Riyadh: Dār al-ʿĀṣima, 1409/1988), 544.

68 For the variety of the security positions under the Umayyads and an assessment of the gap in our knowledge about them, see W. al-Qāḍī, "Security Positions under the Umayyads: The Story of 'Maʿbad al-Ṭuruq'," in *Differenz und Dynamik im Islam: Festschrift für Heinz Halm zum 70. Geburtstag / Difference and Dynamism in Islam: Festschrift for Heinz Halm on his 70th Birthday*, eds. Hinrich Biesterfeldt, Verena Klemm (Würzburg: Ergon Verlag, 2012), 279–283. Another Medinan scholar from al-Zuhrī's clan, Saʿd b. Ibrāhīm (d. ca. 127/745), the father of the traditionist Ibrāhīm b. Saʿd (d. 185/801), is also known to have served as the chief *shurṭa* of Medina and officiated as the *qāḍī* of the town several times. In his capacity as a judge, he is reported to have administered several cases of beating to those who resisted his rulings. Like al-Zuhrī, he was also employed as a tax collector. See S.C. Judd, *Religious Scholars and the Umayyads*, 154–155. Cf. Ibn ʿAsākir, *TMD*, 20:206, 210; al-Dhahabī, *Siyar*, 4:29; al-Mizzī, *Tahdhīb al-kamāl*, 10:241, 23:427–436.

69 S.C. Judd, *Religious Scholars and the Umayyads*, 54–55.

70 Al-Fasawī, *Maʿrifa*, 1: 632; Ibn ʿAsākir, *TMD*, 20:80; 55:333; cf. S.W. Anthony, *Muhammad and the Empires of Faith*, 138–139.

permission to transmit the knowledge he wrote down in a notebook.[71] Such reports illustrate how al-Zuhrī allowed the caliph's children to write down the traditions he told them, but give no information about the content of his instruction. In addition to tutoring the caliph's children, al-Zuhrī established a teaching circle in Ruṣāfa[72] and allowed his transmissions to be written down by his other students as well, which significantly changed the nature of the transmission and the recording of knowledge, for which al-Zuhrī was severely criticized by other scholars.[73] The writings of al-Zuhrī's students preserved in later sources offer insight into what the content of al-Zuhrī's corpus would have looked like.[74] However, how much of that teaching activity extended to the education of the princes, remains unknown.

In his article *Lā taqra'ū l-qur'āna 'alā l-muṣḥafiyyīn*, M.J. Kister suggested that the traditions al-Zuhrī dictated to the princes must have been special topics, which would either have gotten lost lest they were written down, or were perplexing for the general Muslim public, which made their written preservation and wider dissemination permissible.[75] These were either subjects of official concern but largely unknown outside of Medinan circles, such as taxation and the treatment of non-Muslim populations and the so-called hypocrites, or topics of historical significance that vexed al-Zuhrī's contemporaries, such as the late conversions of some notable Qurashīs who used to be archenemies of the Prophet.[76] M.J. Kister's assessment of these topics, though plausible, did not take the curriculum of the princes as its starting point, but aimed to explain why al-Zuhrī allowed writing in his instruction of the princes. There hence remains a gap in our understanding of the *content* of the education pursued by the young members of the ruling house, in which al-Zuhrī played an active role.

We can obtain a fairly good idea of how such an education would have likely taken place by comparing it with the training the Umayyad scribes received. In his letter to the scribes, 'Abd al-Ḥamīd al-Kātib (d. 132/150), the head of

71 Al-Khaṭīb al-Baghdādī, *al-Kifāya fī 'ilm al-riwāya* (Hyderabad: Dā'irat al-Ma'ārif al-'Uthmāniyya, 1938), 266. For a detailed discussion of this account, see M. Lecker, "Biographical Notes," 22–23, 28–33.

72 For a detailed discussion of his residence in Ruṣāfa and his teaching activities, see S.W. Anthony, *Muhammad and the Empires of Faith*, 140–150.

73 Ibid., 136–137.

74 For al-Zuhrī's corpus, see ibid., 140–150, and 'Abd al-'Azīz al-Dūrī, "Al-Zuhrī," 1–12.

75 M.J. Kister, "*Lā taqra'ū l-qur'āna 'alā l-muṣḥafiyyīn*," 269–70.

76 M.J. Kister suggests that the traditions that were part of al-Zuhrī's instruction to the princes are preserved in Mālik's *Muwaṭṭa'*. For al-Zuhrī's entire corpus in this work (al-Zuhrī > Mālik), see Abū 'Umar Yūsuf Ibn 'Abd al-Barr, *Tajrīd al-tamhīd limā fī al-muwaṭṭa' min al-ma'ānī wa al-asānīd* (Cairo: Maktabat al-Qudsī, 1931), 116–154.

the chancery during Marwān II's (r. 127–132/744–750) caliphate, gives a long list of subjects: He states that scribes must acquire a general knowledge of all branches of learning, which includes "a thorough knowledge of the Qur'ān, religious duties, Arabic language, penmanship, poetry, the history of pre-Islamic Arabs and of the non-Arabs, and accounting."[77] Just as scribes were expected to be proficient in these above-mentioned subjects, the princes as future rulers or high ranking authorities in the state administration were expected to receive a similar education. This curriculum differs to some extent from the teaching that took place in the traditional circles, where a focus was placed on legal traditions, Prophetic sayings and the Prophet's expeditions – fields for which al-Zuhrī was considered a leading authority.

In a letter ʿAbd al-Malik sent to his governor in Iraq, al-Ḥajjāj (in office 74–95/694–714), he outlines the qualifications of a scholar fit to tutor his children as "someone who combines all kinds of knowledge and understanding (*rajul jāmiʿ li-l-ʿilm wa al-fiqh*), is intelligent (*ʿāqil*), sensible (*labīb*) and has outstanding manners and an audacious spirit (*fāḍil fī akhlāqihi wa muruwwatihi*)."[78] Al-Ḥajjāj thereupon suggested the Kufan scholar al-Shaʿbī (d. 103–109/721–727), who was known not only for his expertise in legal traditions, but also someone well versed in accounting (*ḥisāb*),[79] a master of the Arabic language, and a skillful poet.[80] Similar to al-Shaʿbī's versatility, al-Zuhrī is known to have possessed a wide array of knowledge and skills. Next to his expertise in tribal genealogies and knowledge on legal and religious traditions, he was a connoisseur of poetry, and had a masterful command of the Arabic language. According to one anecdote, the caliph Yazīd II summoned al-Zuhrī one night to his chamber in the palace, inquiring about the name of a poet whose verses mesmerized him, and al-Zuhrī immediately identified him as al-Aḥwaṣ b. Muḥammad (d. 105/723).[81] Al-Zuhrī's student Yūnus b. Yazīd reports that when he demanded al-Zuhrī to show him his own writings, he had nothing but poetry in them.[82] Moreover, al-Marzūbānī's *Muʿjam al-shuʿarāʾ* records some of the verses of a praise poem al-Zuhrī wrote for the

77 W. al-Qāḍī "Identity Formation," 147.

78 Ibn ʿAsākir, *TMD*, 25:384–385.

79 He learned *ḥisāb* from al-Ḥārith al-Aʿwar (d. ca. 60s/680s), a Kufan expert on the topic, who was one of the followers of ʿAlī b. Abī Ṭālib, see Ibn Ḥajar, *Tahdhīb*, 1:331.

80 For an account of the poetic competition he engaged in with the Umayyad poet al-Akhṭal in ʿAbd al-Malik's presence, see al-Iṣbahānī, *Kitāb al-aghānī*, 9:162.

81 *Kitāb al-aghānī*, 4:49; cf. J. Horovitz, "The Earliest Biographies II," 39.

82 Ibn ʿAbd al-Barr, *Jāmiʿ bayān al-ʿilm wa faḍlihi*, ed. Abū al-Ashbāl al-Zuhayrī (Riyadh: Dār Ibn al-Jawzī, 1994), 334, no. 445.

Umayyad prince ʿAbdallāh b. ʿAbd al-Malik.[83] Finally, Ḥammād b. Zayd relates how al-Zuhrī enthusiastically encouraged his students to recite poems and tell stories once his teaching was over.[84] As for al-Zuhrī's profound interest in the Arabic language, he is credited with the statement that "the people have not initiated a practice more pleasing to me than learning grammar and eloquent speech (*naḥw wa al-faṣāḥa*)."[85]

The diversity of al-Zuhrī's knowledge and scholarship, however, is not surprising given the profile of scholars during his era. Learned men like ʿUbaydallāh b. ʿAbdallāh b. ʿUtba and al-Shaʿbī, for instance, pursued an ideal of knowledge that encompassed a broad range of subjects, which defied the divisions of what we would today call religious and profane, or pious and impious.[86] The following statement attributed to Layth b. Saʿd about al-Zuhrī's command of various branches of learning exemplifies the qualifications required for serving as tutor of the caliph's children:

> I have never seen any scholar who is more versatile (*mā raʾaytu ʿāliman ajmaʿ*) and possesses more knowledge than Ibn Shihāb. If you were to hear him speak, exhorting men to goodness (*al-targhīb*), you would say, this man is an expert on this topic; if you were to hear him speak about the past prophets and the people of the book (*al-anbiyāʾ wa ahl al-kitāb*), you would say, this man is an expert on this topic; if you were to hear him speak about Arabs and their genealogy (*al-ʿarab wa al-ansāb*), you would say, this man is an expert on this topic; and when he speaks of the Qurʾān and the *sunna*, then his speech would become comprehensive (*nawʿan jāmiʿan*).[87]

83 Al-Marzūbānī, *Muʿjam al-shuʿarāʾ*, ed. Fārūq Aslīm (Beirut: Dār Ṣādir, 2005) 405, no. 766.

84 Ibn Qutayba, *Gharīb al-hadīth*, ed. ʿAbdallāh al-Jabūrī (Baghdad: Maṭbaʿat al-Ānī, 1977), 2:366; cf. J. Horovitz, "The Earliest Biographies II," 50.

85 Nabia Abbott, *Studies in Arabic Literary Papyri III: Language and Literature* (Chicago: University of Chicago Oriental Institute Publications, 1972), 31–32.

86 For a longer list of scholars from the Umayyad and early Abbasid period who pursued a variety of interests and gained expertise in multiple subjects, such as Prophetic traditions (*ḥadīth*), Qurʾānic recitation (*qirāʾa*), exegesis (*tafsīr*), jurisprudence (*fiqh*), Arabic language (*ʿarabiyya*), grammar (*naḥw*), lexicography (*lugha*), poetry (*shiʿr*), humorous anecdotes (*nawādir*), pre-Islamic battles (*ayyām*), genealogy (*nasab*), historical reports (*akhbār*), and belles-lettres (*adab*), see Monique Bernards, "Ibn Abī Isḥāq (d. ca. 125/743) and His Scholarly Network," in *Islam at 250: Studies in Memory of G.H.A. Juynboll*, eds. Petra M. Sijpesteijn and Camilla Adang (Leiden: Brill, 2020), 21–23.

87 Abū Nuʿaym, *Ḥilyat al-awliyāʾ wa ṭabaqāt al-aṣfiyāʾ* (Beirut: Dār al-Kutub al-ʿIlmiyya, 1988), 3:361; Ibn Ḥajar, *Tahdhīb*, 3:698; cf. J. Horovitz, "The Earliest Biographies II," 45.

4 Conclusion

The examples of the two Medinan scholars who made their way to the Damascene court are indicative of consecutive stages in the chronology of the Umayyad caliphate and its interactions with scholars. In Qabīṣa's case it is unclear how exactly he entered the Umayyad court (by invitation of ʿAbd al-Malik or out of his own initiative?), while al-Zuhrī initially seems to have travelled to Damascus to alleviate his financial constraints. Qabīṣa, perhaps by virtue of having known ʿAbd al-Malik since their Medinan times, enjoyed a power and influence that no later scholar of his training would ever acquire, making him almost equivalent to what would later be known as a vizier. By comparison, al-Zuhrī received recognition for his genealogical and legal expertise as well as his knowledge of the Arabic language and poetry, but never had long-lasting appointments until Hishām's reign, when he was invited to tutor the caliph's sons. It should be emphasized, however, that even under Hishām, al-Zuhrī's activity and influence remained confined to the intellectual sphere. He did not serve the caliph as a statesman with administrative functions. The differences in the two men's careers can be read against the changing circumstances after the establishment of a fully-fledged bureaucracy. While the extent of the power and influence of individual scholars such as Qabīṣa's may have been reduced in successive periods, the case of al-Zuhrī demonstrates how his Medinan scholarly education helped him fulfil a variety of official tasks. At the same time, the Umayyad state's interest in hiring experts with the kind of traditional education that al-Zuhrī had received in Medina shows how his qualifications were of value to the Umayyad state.

Acknowledgment

I would like to dedicate this article to Prof. Wadād al-Qāḍī on the occasion of her 78th birthday, in recognition of her path-breaking research on Umayyad bureaucratic history.

Bibliography

Abbott, Nabia. *Studies in Arabic Literary Papyri II: Qurʾānic Commentary and Tradition*. Chicago: University of Chicago Oriental Institute Publications, 1967.

Abbott, Nabia. *Studies in Arabic Literary Papyri III: Language and Literature*. Chicago: University of Chicago Oriental Institute Publications, 1972.

ʿAbd al-Razzāq al-Ṣanʿānī. *Al-Muṣannaf*. Edited by Ḥabīb al-Raḥmān al-Aʿẓamī. Beirut: al-Maktab al-Islāmī, 1970–1972.

Abū al-Faraj al-Iṣbahānī. *Kitāb al-aghānī*. Edited by Aḥmad al-Shinqiṭī. Cairo: Maṭbaʿat al-Taqaddum, 1323/1905.

Abū Nuʿaym al-Iṣbahānī. *Ḥilyat al-awliyāʾ wa ṭabaqāt al-aṣfiyāʾ*. Beirut: Dār al-Kutub al-ʿIlmiyya, 1988.

Abū Zurʿah al-Dimashqī. *Al-Tārīkh*. Edited by Shukrullāh Niʿmatullāh al-Qūjānī. Damascus: Majmaʿ al-Lughah al-ʿArabiyyah, 1980.

Anthony, Sean W. *Muhammad and the Empires of Faith: The Making of the Prophet of Islam*. Oakland: University of California Press, 2020.

Anthony, Sean W. "A 'Rediscovered' Letter of the Umayyad Caliph ʿUmar ibn ʿAbd al-ʿAzīz (r. 717–720 CE): Caliphal Authorship and Legal Authority in al-Risālah fī l-Fayʾ." In *Rulers as Authors in the Islamic World*, edited by Sonja Brentjes, Maribel Fierro, and Tilman Seidensticker. Leiden: Brill, forthcoming.

Aʿẓamī, Muḥammad Muṣṭafā. *Studies in Early Hadith Literature*. Indianapolis: American Trust, 1978.

Al-Balādhurī, Aḥmad b. Yaḥyā. *Ansāb al-ashrāf*. Edited by ʿAbd al-ʿAzīz al-Durī, ʿIṣām ʿUqla. Beirut, Berlin: Das Arabische Buch, 2001.

Bernards, Monique. "Ibn Abī Isḥāq (d. ca. 125/743) and His Scholarly Network." In *Islam at 250: Studies in Memory of G.H.A. Juynboll*, edited by Petra M. Sijpesteijn and Camilla Adang, 9–31. Leiden: Brill, 2020.

Bosworth, Clifford Edmund. "Rajāʾ b. Ḥaywa al-Kindī and the Umayyad Caliphs." *Islamic Quarterly* 16, no. 1 (1972): 36–81.

Al-Bukhārī. *Tārīkh al-kabīr*. Edited by Muḥammad ʿAbd al-Muʿīd Khān. Hyderabad: Maṭbaʿat Jamʿiyyat Dāʾirat al-Maʿārif al-ʿUthmāniyya, 1941–1958.

Al-Bukhārī. *Al-Tārīkh al-saghīr*. Edited by Yūsuf al-Marʿashlī. Beirut: Dār al-Maʿrifa, 1986.

Crone, Patricia, and Martin Hinds. *God's Caliph: Religious Authority in the First Centuries of Islam*. Cambridge: Cambridge University Press, 1986.

Al-Dhahabī, Muḥammad b. Aḥmad. *Siyar aʿlām al-nubalāʾ*. Edited by Shuʿayb al-Arnāʾūṭ and Ḥusayn al-Amad. Beirut: Muʾassasat al-Riṣāla, 1996.

Ḍirār b. ʿAmr al-Ghaṭafānī. *Kitāb al-taḥrīsh*. Edited by Hüseyin Hansu. Istanbul: Sharikat Dār al-Irshād, 2014.

Donner, Fred M. "The Formation of the Islamic State." *Journal of the American Oriental Society* 106 (1986): 283–96.

Donner, Fred M. "The Shurta in Early Umayyad Syria." In *Proceedings of the Third Symposium on the History of Bilâd al-Shâm during the Umayyad Period*, edited by M. Adnan Bakhit and Robert Schick, 2: 247–62. Amman: 1989.

Al-Dūrī, ʿAbd al-ʿAzīz. "Al-Zuhrī: A Study on the Beginnings of History Writing in Islam." *Bulletin of the School of Oriental and African Studies, University of London* 19, no. 1 (1957): 1–12.

Al-Dūrī, ʿAbd al-ʿAzīz. *The Rise of Historical Writing Among the Arabs*. Edited by Lawrence I. Conrad and Fred M. Donner, translated by Lawrence I. Conrad. Princeton: Princeton University Press, 1984.

EI^2 s.v. "ʿAbd Allāh al-Ḳasrī," (G.R. Hawting).

EI^2 s.v. "ʿAbd al-Malik," (H.A.R. Gibb).

EI^2 s.v. "Radjāʾ b. Ḥaywa," (C.E. Bosworth).

EI^2 s.v. "Al-Zuhrī," (Michael Lecker).

Al-Fasawī, Abū Yūsuf Yaʿqūb b. Sufyān. *K. al-maʿrifa wa al-tārīkh*. Edited by Akram Ḍiyāʾ al-ʿUmarī. Medina: Maktabat al-Dār, 1990.

Goldziher, Ignaz. *Muslim Studies*. Edited by S.M. Stern. Translated by C.R. Barber and S.M. Stern. London: Allen and Unwin, 1967–1971.

Horovitz, Josef. "The Earliest Biographies of the Prophet and Their Authors", translated by M. Pickthall. *Islamic Culture* 1 (1927): 535–559; 2 (1928): 22–50, 164–182, 495–523.

Ibn ʿAbd al-Barr, Abū ʿUmar Yūsuf. *Tajrīd al-tamhīd limā fī al-muwaṭṭaʾ min al-maʿānī wa al-asānīd*. Cairo: Maktabat al-Qudsī, 1931.

Ibn ʿAbd al-Barr, Abū ʿUmar Yūsuf. *Jāmiʿ bayān al-ʿilm wa faḍlihi*. Edited by Abū al-Ashbāl al-Zuhayrī. Riyadh: Dār Ibn al-Jawzī, 1994.

Ibn ʿAbd al-Ḥakam. *Futūḥ miṣr wa al-maghrib*. Edited by Muḥammad ʿAlī ʿUmar. Cairo: Maktabat al-Thaqafiyya al-Diniyya, 2004.

Ibn ʿAsākir, ʿAlī b. al-Ḥasan. *Tārīkh madīnat dimashq*. Edited by Muḥibb al-Dīn ʿUmar b. Gharāma al-ʿAmrawī. Beirut: Dār al-Fikr, 1995–2000.

Ibn Ḥajar al-ʿAsqalānī, Aḥmad b. ʿAlī. *Al-Iṣāba fī tamyīz al-ṣaḥāba*. Beirut: Dār al-Kutub al-ʿIlmiyya, 1995.

Ibn Ḥajar al-ʿAsqalānī, Aḥmad b. ʿAlī. *Tahdhīb al-tahdhīb*. Edited by Ibrāhīm al-Zaybaq and ʿĀdil Murshid. Beirut: Muʾassasat al-Risāla, 1995.

Ibn Kathīr, Ismāʿīl b. ʿUmar. *Al-Bidāya wa al-nihāya*. Beirut: Maktabat al-Maʿārif, 1992.

Ibn Khallikān, *Wafayāt al-aʿyān wa anbāʾ abnāʾ al-zamān*. Edited by Iḥsān ʿAbbās. Beirut: Dār Ṣādir, 1968–72.

Ibn Qutayba, ʿAbdallāh b. Muslim. *Gharīb al-hadīth*. Edited by ʿAbdallāh al-Jabūrī. Baghdad: Maṭbaʿat al-Ānī, 1977.

Ibn Saʿd, Muḥammad. *Kitāb al-ṭabaqāt al-kabīr*. Edited by ʿAlī Muḥammad ʿUmar. Cairo: Maktabat al-Khānjī, 2001.

Ibn Saʿd, Muḥammad. *The Men of Medina: The Volume II*. Translated by Aisha Bewley. London: Ta-Ha Publishers Ltd., 1997.

Ibn Sayyid al-Nās. *Al-Nafḥ al-shadhī fi sharḥ jāmiʿ al-tirmidhī*. Edited by Aḥmad Maʿbad ʿAbd al-Karīm. Riyadh: Dār al-ʿĀṣima, 1409/1988.

Ibn Zanjawayh. *Kitāb al-amwāl*. Edited by Shākir Dhīb Fayyāḍ. Riyadh: King Faisal Center for Research and Islamic Studies, 1986.

Judd, Steven C. *Religious Scholars and the Umayyads: Piety-Minded Supporters of the Marwānid Caliphate*. London, New York: Routledge, 2014.

Al-Khaṭīb al-Baghdādī. *Al-Kifāya fī ʿilm al-riwāya*. Hyderabad: Dāʾirat al-Maʿārif al-ʿUthmāniyya, 1938.

Kister, M.J. and M. Plessner. "Notes on Caskel's *Ǧamharat an-nasab*." *Oriens* 25/26 (1976): 50–51.

Kister, M.J. "*Lā taqraʾū l-qurʾāna ʿalā l-muṣḥafiyyīn wa-lā taḥmilū l-ʿilma ʿani l-ṣaḥafiyyīn* ...: Some Notes on the Transmission of Ḥadīth." In *The Ḥadīth: Critical Concepts in Islamic Studies*, edited by Mustafa Shah, 1:252–287. London: Routledge, 2010.

Lecker, Michael. "Biographical Notes on Ibn Shihāb al-Zuhrī." *Journal of Semitic Studies* 41 no. 1 (1996): 21–63.

Lecker, Michael. "ʿAmr ibn Ḥazm al-Anṣārī and Qurʾān 2,256: 'No Compulsion Is There in Religion'." *Oriens* 35 (1996): 1–9.

Mālik b. Anas. *Al-Muwaṭṭaʾ*. Edited by Muḥammad Fuʾād ʿAbd al-Bāqī. Beirut: Dār Iḥyā Turāth al-ʿArabī, 1985.

Al-Maqrīzī, Ṭaqī al-Dīn Aḥmad b. ʿAlī. *Kitāb al-muqaffā al-kabīr*. Edited by Muḥammad al-al-Yaʿlāwī. Beirut: Dār al-Gharb al-Islāmī, 1991.

Al-Mizzī, Yūsuf b. ʿAbd al-Raḥmān. *Tahdhīb al-kamāl fī asmāʾ al-rijāl*. Edited by Bashshār ʿAwwād Maʿrūf. Beirut: al-Muʾassasat al-Risāla, 1992.

Al-Nasāʾī. *Sunan*. Edited by Ḥasan ʿAbd al-Munʿim al-Shalbī. Beirut: Muʾassasat al-Risāla, 2001.

Al-Qāḍī, Wadād. "An Umayyad Papyrus in al-Kindī's Kitāb al-Quḍāt?" *Der Islam* 84, no. 2 (2007): 200–245.

Al-Qāḍī, Wadād. "Identity Formation of the Bureaucracy of the Early Islamic State: ʿAbd al-Ḥamīd's 'Letter to the Secretaries'." In *Mediterranean Identities in the Premodern Era. Entrepôts, Islands, Empires*, edited by John Watkins and Kathryn L. Reyerson, 141–154. London: Routledge, 2016.

Al-Qāḍī, Wadād. "Early Islamic State Letters." In *Byzantine and Early Islamic Near East, vol I: Problems in the Literary Source Material*, edited by Averil Cameron and Lawrence I. Conrad, 215–278. Princeton: Darwin Press, 1992.

Al-Qāḍī, Wadād. "A Documentary Report on Umayyad Stipends Registers: *Dīwān al-ʿAṭāʾ* in Abū Zurʿa's *Tārīkh*." *Quaderni di Studi Arabi Nuova Serie* 4 (2009): 7–44.

Al-Qāḍī, Wadād. "Security Positions under the Umayyads: The Story of 'Maʿbad al-Ṭuruq'." In *Differenz und Dynamik im Islam: Festschrift für Heinz Halm zum 70. Geburtstag / Difference and Dynamism in Islam: Festschrift for Heinz Halm on his 70th Birthday*, edited by Hinrich Biesterfeldt and Verena Klemm, 253–283. Würzburg: Ergon Verlag, 2012.

Robinson, Chase F. *ʿAbd al-Malik*. Oxford: Oneworld Publications, 2005.

Schacht, Joseph. *The Origins of Muhammadan Jurisprudence*. Oxford: Clarendon Press, 1950.

Sharon, Moshe. *Corpus Inscriptionum Arabicarum Palaestinae*. Vol. 2. Leiden: Brill, 1999.

Al-Ṭabarī, Abū Jaʿfar Muḥammad b. Jarīr. *Tārīkh al-rusul wa-al-mulūk*. Edited by M.J. de Goeje *et al.* Leiden: E.J. Brill, 1879–1901.

Al-Yaʿqūbī. *Tārīkh*. Edited by M.T. Houtsma. Leiden: Brill, 1883.

Zaman, Muhammad Qasim. *Religion and Politics Under the Early ʿAbbasids: The Emergence of the Proto-Sunni Elite*. Leiden: Brill, 1997.

Zaman, Muhammad Qasim. "The Caliphs, the ʿUlamāʾ, and the Law: Defining the Role and Function of the Caliph in the Early ʿAbbāsid Period." *Islamic Law and Society Islamic Law and Society* 4, no. 1 (1997): 1–36.

CHAPTER 2

Professional Mobility and Social Capital: A Note on the *muḥaddithāt* in *Kitāb Tārīkh Baghdād*

Nadia Maria El Cheikh

In the words of Michael Cooperson, "Biography is the archive of the Muslims." Biographical dictionaries have consequently been mined by historians for "information about kinship, marriage, political alliances, labor, social status, and the transmission of knowledge in pre-modern Muslim communities."[1] Biographies reveal the functions and backgrounds of individuals and glimpses on their lives; they offer perspective and insight as to their authors' motives and responsibilities. This genre of historical writing was rooted in "the desire of the urban notables to show that their native cities were major centers of Islamic piety and learning."[2]

One such work is *Kitāb Tārīkh Baghdād* by al-Khaṭīb al-Baghdādī (d. 463/1071), which contains biographies of thousands of *ḥadīth* scholars associated with Baghdad.[3] This biographical dictionary, containing some 7,800 entries, focused on the noted men and women who resided in the Abbasid capital, the city of Baghdad. *Ḥadīth* was al-Baghdādī's primary interest. He hoped to produce a reference work for traditionists through which chains of transmitters, relations between teachers and students, and questions on the reliability of *ḥadīth* scholars could be checked and tackled.[4]

The last part of this fourteen-volume biographical dictionary includes a record of thirty-two female scholars (*muḥaddithāt*) who lived between the second/eighth century and al-Baghdādī's own days in the fifth/eleventh century. Listed with no regard to either chronology or alphabetical order, the entries on women start with Khayzurān, wife of the Abbasid caliph al-Mahdī (r. 159/775–169/785), and end with Khadīja l-Shāhjāniyya (d. 460/1067), all having lived in Baghdad. What these women had in common was their relationship to the

1 Michael Cooperson, *Classical Arabic Biography: The Heirs of the Prophets in the Age of al-Ma'mūn* (Cambridge: Cambridge University Press, 2000), preface.

2 R. Stephen Humphreys, *Islamic History: A Framework for Enquiry* (Princeton, NJ: Princeton University Press, 1991), 132.

3 *Ḥadīth*, or tradition, is "an account of what the Prophet said or did, or of his tacit approval of something said or done in his presence." In "Ḥadīth," *Encyclopedia of Islam*, 2nd ed.

4 "Al-K͟haṭīb al-Bag͟hdādī," *Encyclopedia of Islam*, 2nd ed.

 | DOI:10.1163/9789004467637_004

transmission of *ḥadīth* that they acquired mostly from their male relatives, who belonged to the *ʿulamāʾ* religious scholars network. This article explores the professional, social, and geographical mobility of these women by answering the following questions: What can we learn from al-Khaṭīb's final, slim volume about women's education in the fourth/tenth and fifth/eleventh centuries? What kind of knowledge did these women acquire and who were the people involved in mediating this knowledge? Did their education involve professional mobility, upward mobility, or geographical mobility? How did their status as *muḥaddithāt* (traditionists) increase their professional or social mobility or add to the social capital of their families?

1 Women's Education

The most widespread institution for elementary education of the era was the *kuttāb*, where the curriculum was limited to committing the Qurʾan to memory, some writing and some arithmetic, and penmanship.[5] The *ḥisba* literature supplies information concerning special *kuttāb* for girls staffed by female teachers. These, however, were limited in number.[6] Girls could attend the boys' *kuttāb* but with difficulty, and only at the risk of undergoing substantial social pressure. Authors of the *ḥisba* manuals demanded that girls be educated at home and taught there how to pray, cook, and weave. Even those emphasizing the importance of religious education for girls informed their readers of the possible dangers for the social order that would follow when women were taught such inappropriate skills as writing.[7]

The major site of religious learning was the *ḥalqa* or *majlis*, which took place in the mosque. The second important educational structure in the mosque was that of the *zāwiya*, differentiated from the *ḥalqa* by its institutional character. Education in the mosque concentrated on the study of the *Qurʾān*, *ḥadīth*, and *fiqh* (jurisprudence). After several centuries of self-sustained growth, Islamic

5 Hisham Nashabe, *Muslim Educational Institutions: A General Survey Followed by a Monographic Study of al-Madrasah al-Mustanṣirīyah in Baghdād* (Beirut: Makassed Philanthropic Islamic Association, 1989), 18 and 30.

6 *Ḥisba* can mean "the duty of every Muslim to 'promote good and forbid evil'" or "the function of the person who is effectively entrusted in a town with the application of this rule in the supervision of moral behavior and more particularly of the markets." In "Ḥisba," *Encyclopedia of Islam*, 2nd ed.

7 Avner Giladi, "Gender Differences in Child Rearing and Education: Some Preliminary Observations with Reference to Medieval Muslim Thought," *Al-Qantara* 16, no. 2 (January 1995): 291–308.

education received direct attention from Islamic governments, ministers, and kings. Making its definitive appearance in the late fifth/eleventh century, the *madrasa* came to dominate learning in the Islamic East, and the most important subject taught in the *madrasa* was the science of jurisprudence.[8]

In the period preceding the establishment of the *madrasa*, the most frequently mentioned site of teaching after the mosque, was the teacher's own home.[9] Women's education, both elementary and advanced, took place within the latter. The evidence gathered from the biographical dictionaries confirms that a girl's primary education was inculcated at home by close family members. The spread of institutions devoted to religious education did not benefit women who played neither role as teachers or students. Women were excluded from formal enrollment in mosques, Sufi convents, and *madrasas*.[10] Higher institutions of learning for girls' education were not thought of as a viable alternative. The confinement of this particular class of women, the *ʿulamāʾ* class, mostly to their homes, and their inaccessibility to higher institutions of learning, reveals a great deal about the type and the aim of education deemed proper for women. Whatever education was dispensed was not systematic, organized, or continuous, nothing similar to the *madrasa*, or the mosque, available to men.[11]

Ḥadīth was the most important subject studied by the women of our compilations. In fact they modeled their learning after the pious women of early Islam. In addition to ʿĀʾisha, the Prophet's wife, many women of the first generation (the generation of the Prophet) were recognized as important sources of *ḥadīth*. Once established "as legitimate, and even essential, sources of *hadith*, the norm was set that legitimized women traditionists."[12] While the education of the *muḥaddithāt* was by and large limited to the confines of the family and their mobility was consequently constrained, this did not prevent a few of them from becoming distinguished scholars of *ḥadīth*.

---

8 This brief discussion is based on Roy Mottahedeh's *The Mantle of the Prophet: Religion and Politics in Iran* (New York: Pantheon, 1985), 89–90.

9 Christopher Melchert, "The Etiquette of Learning in the Early Islamic Study Circle," in *Law and Education in Medieval Islam: Studies in Memory of Professor George Makdisi*, eds. Joseph Lowry, Devin Stewart, and Shawkat Toorawa (Cambridge: E.G.W. Gibb Memorial Trust, 2004), 33–44.

10 Jonathan Porter Berkey, *The Transmission of Knowledge in Medieval Cairo: A Social History of Islamic Education* (Princeton, NJ: Princeton University Press, 1992), 167.

11 For these institutions, see George Makdisi, "Muslim Institutions of Learning in Eleventh-Century Baghdad," *Bulletin of the School of Oriental and African Studies* 24, no. 1 (February 1961): 1–56.

12 Ruth Roded, *Women in Islamic Biographical Collections: From Ibn Saʿd to Who's Who* (Boulder, CO: L. Rienner, 1994), 29.

2 Women, Baghdad, and *Ḥadīth*

Al-Khaṭīb al-Baghdādī asserts that the participation of women in *ḥadīth* transmission is acceptable. He upholds that gender is not a consideration, and that the narrations of women are to be accepted on a par with those of men.[13] Women and men are deemed equal with respect to the legal conditions for receiving and transmitting *ḥadīth*, the qualifications for both being personal qualities including "truthfulness and integrity, a competent and accurate memory, and being free of prejudice or compulsion of any sort that might be presumed to distort the reporting."[14]

In the third/ninth century, Baghdad emerged as a center for women's *ḥadīth* scholarship. This is clear, for instance, from the biography of Umm ʿUmar bint Abī l-Ghuṣn Ḥassān al-Thaqafiyya, in *Tārīkh Baghdād*: "She narrated from her father and from her husband. In turn, Abū Ibrāhīm al-Turjumānī, Aḥmad b. Ḥanbal, Muḥammad b. al-Ṣabbāḥ al-Jarajarāʾī … ʿAlī b. Muslim al-Ṭūsī narrated from her."[15] Developments in the fourth/tenth century brought *ḥadīth* sciences to the fore, a factor that allowed for increased women's participation in *ḥadīth* transmission. *Ḥadīth* came to occupy a predominant place in the culture of classical Sunni Islam, and women's participation was enhanced by the increasing reliance on written transmission of *ḥadīth* in parallel with its oral transmission. Written transmission gave women access to a corpus without having to learn directly from *ḥadīth* scholars, which often required traveling. Finally, this century witnessed the increasing fragmentation of Abbasid authority, leading to the strengthening and proliferation of *ʿulamāʾ* kinship networks. Women's participation in the transfer *of ḥadīth* "became part of the cultural and social capital that enabled the survival and flourishing of the scholarly elite."[16] Women's role in *ḥadīth* transmission within these kinship networks gained priority, a matter that allowed flexibility in their personal contact with the *ḥadīth* scholars within their network.

The information provided in al-Baghdādī's biographical dictionary reveals that a significant number of these women received their religious education, especially in *ḥadīth*, from their closest male relatives, in particular, their fathers.

---

13 Al-Khaṭīb al-Baghdādī, *Al-Kifāya fī ʿilm al-riwāya* (Beirut: Dār al-Kutub al-ʿIlmiyya, 1988), 94–95.

14 Mohammad Akram Nadwi, *Al-Muḥaddithāt: The Women Scholars in Islam* (London: Interface, 2007), 17.

15 Al-Khaṭīb al-Baghdādī, *Tārīkh Baghdād*, vol. 14 (Beirut: Dār al-Kutub al-ʿIlmiyya, 1997), 432; Nadwi, *Al-Muḥaddithāt*, 253.

16 Asma Sayeed, *Women and the Transmission of Religious Knowledge* (Cambridge: Cambridge University Press, 2013), 113.

Zaynab bint Sulaymān, Umm ʿUmar bint Ḥassān al-Thaqafiyya, ʿAbda bint ʿAbd al-Raḥmān, Samāna bint Ḥamdān, and Ṭāhira bint Aḥmad al-Tanūkhiyya all transmitted tradition on the authority of their respective fathers.[17] According to *Tārīkh Baghdād*, ʿAbda bint ʿAbd al-Raḥmān al-Anṣāriyya transmitted traditions on the authority of her father. But, later, she became an authority herself:

> Muḥammad b. Makhlad al-Dūrī and Sulaymān b. Aḥmad al-Ṭabarānī transmitted on her authority.... Al-Ṭabarānī said: We heard a tradition by ʿAbda bint ʿAbd al-Raḥmān ... in Baghdad in her house ... she said: I heard from ʿAbd al-Raḥmān who heard from his father Muṣʿab, who heard from his father Thābit, who heard from his father ʿAbdallāh b. Abī Qatāda, who heard from his father Abū Qatāda l-Ḥārith b. Rabʿī. The Prophet said: the best of our knights is Abū Qatāda; the best of our foot-soldiers Salma b. al-Akwaʿ ... Al-Ṭabarānī said: no one mentioned these traditions of Abū Qatāda except his children and we only heard it from ʿAbda who was a wise, eloquent and pious woman.[18]

As al-Ṭabarānī confirms, he heard traditions in ʿAbda bint ʿAbd al-Raḥmān's house in Baghdad. Learned women traditionists provided *ḥadīth* instructions from their homes, which became learning centers. They practiced their work in the informal arena of homes and "were not officially appointed to any formal state position or educational institutions such as the *madrasa* or *dār al-ḥadīth*."[19]

Women also transmitted traditions from their grandfathers, husbands, and brothers. Al-Baghdādī reports that Umm ʿUmar bint Ḥassān al-Thaqafiyya transmitted traditions on the authority of her husband Saʿīd b. Yaḥyā b. Qays; Zaynab bint Sulaymān and Samāna bint Ḥamdān transmitted tradition on the authority of their fathers and grandfathers; al-Ḥawwāriyya transmitted traditions on the authority of her brother Abū Saʿīd Aḥmad al-Kharrāz.[20]

Thus, these women, who belonged mostly to the scholarly classes, seem to have been informally trained through their close male relatives. Jawhar, wife of al-Barāthī, and al-ʿAbbāssa, wife of Aḥmad b. Ḥanbal, along with others, had studied with close relatives who were important scholars. Indeed, women of learning often came from households in which a close relative was already

17 Al-Baghdādī, *Tārīkh Baghdād*, vol. 14, 432, 434–35, and 439–40.
18 Al-Baghdādī, *Tārīkh Baghdād*, vol. 14, 439–40.
19 Omaima Abou-Bakr, "Teaching the Words of the Prophet: Women Instructors of the Hadith (Fourteenth and Fifteenth Centuries)," *Hawwa* 1, no. 3 (January 2003): 306–28.
20 Al-Baghdādī, *Tārīkh Baghdād*, vol. 14, 432, 434, and 439–40.

learned and took an active role in teaching Qur'anic recitation, *ḥadīth*, and the study of other religious texts.

The women traditionists mentioned in the last section of *Tārīkh Baghdād* had contact with the scholarly world. No less than eighteen women had studied with the leading scholars of the day, mostly their male relatives, but later, as they progressed in age, they learned with great scholars who were not related to them, scholars of the caliber of Aḥmad b. Ḥanbal and al-Tanūkhī:

> Ṭāhira bint Aḥmad b. Yūsuf al-Azraq [d. 436/1044] ... al-Tanūkhiyya transmitted traditions on the authority of her father. We studied with her in the house of the judge Abū l-Qāsim al-Tanūkhī. She studied his book with him ... Ṭāhira told us: 'I was born at the beginning of Shaʿbān in the year 359 [AD 969]. I studied with Abū Muḥammad b. Māsī, and Makhlad b. Jaʿfar al-Bāqarḥī, and Abū l-Ḥasan b. Lu'lu', and Abū Bakr b. Ismāʿīl al-Warrāq, and Abū l-Ḥusayn b. al-Bawwāb and others, but all my works are gone.'[21]

The women included in al-Baghdādī's text were mostly traditionists specializing in *ḥadīth* as a distinct subject of study. Their education allowed them to play a critical role in the transmission of the fundamental field of traditional Islamic learning. Indeed, the level of knowledge of *ḥadīth* that some of these women attained rendered them authorities. The *muḥaddithāt* "were trustworthy links in *isnāds* [chains of transmissions] which served as vehicles for authenticating not just individual traditions but books in their entirety.... These practices promoted Sunni culture as it was coalescing."[22] As is already clear from this compilation, once they acquired knowledge, some women became transmitters in their own right. At least twelve women out of the thirty-two are listed as having taught other scholars. Not only did their brothers transmit traditions on the authority of their sisters,[23] but al-Khaṭīb himself studied with four of these: Ṭāhira al-Tanūkhiyya, Fāṭima l-Kurjiyya, Khadīja bint al-Baqqāl, and Sutayta bint al-Qāḍī b. Abī ʿAmr. These female teachers had a high reputation among the scholars of their times.[24]

---

21 Al-Baghdādī, *Tārīkh Baghdād*, vol. 14, 445. According to Maleeha Rahmatallah, the statement concerning Ṭāhira's lost works may imply that these may have been banned or destroyed, considering her family's Muʿtazilī background. In *The Women of Baghdad in the Ninth and Tenth Centuries, as Revealed in the History of Baghdad of al-Hatib* (Baghdad: Times Press, 1952), 68.

22 Sayeed, *Women and the Transmission of Religious Knowledge*, 110.

23 Al-Baghdādī, *Tārīkh Baghdād*, vol. 14, 441.

24 Rahmatallah, *Women of Baghdad*, 59.

A number of important male traditionists transmitted *ḥadīth* on the authority of women. Abū Ibrāhīm al-Turjumānī, Aḥmad ibn Ḥanbal, al-Jarajarāʾī, Ibrāhīm b. ʿAbdallāh al-Harawī, and ʿAlī b. Muslim al-Ṭūsī transmitted tradition on the authority of Umm ʿUmar al-Thaqafiyya.[25] ʿAlī l-Wāsiṭī and others transmitted *ḥadīth* on the authority of Zaynab bint Sulaymān, while transmitters on the authority of ʿAbda bint ʿAbd al-Raḥmān included Muḥammad b. Makhlad al-Dūrī and Sulaymān ibn Aḥmad al-Ṭabarānī.[26] The scholar Abū Ḥafṣ b. Salm heard Khadīja bint Mūsā b. al-Baqqāl, the preacher, and copied traditions from her because he considered her highly reliable and a woman of high moral character.[27] The serious study of *ḥadīth* constituted a cardinal element in a scholar's and jurist's education; and it was *ḥadīth* that provided entry into the world of learning for women.

Women who received a more extensive education in the religious sciences participated in the transmission of texts that embodied Muslim learning. Some women received *ijāza*s, a teacher's certification that a student was qualified to teach a particular subject or transmit a specific book or collection of traditions. Al-Baghdādī mentions that Khadīja bint Abī Bakr transmitted from her father *Kitāb al-Jumal* by Ziyād b. ʿAbdallāh;[28] and that Ṭāhira bint Aḥmad al-Tanūkhiyya studied judge Abū l-Qāsim al-Tanūkhī's book with him.[29]

Women's achievements in *ḥadīth* transmission translated into social capital, and their roles and contributions came to be incorporated in Abbasid biographical literature.[30] Asma Sayeed has traced this development to the new political environment "characterized by the heightened use of state power to control the *ʿulamāʾ* and by increased military and political instability." The *ʿulamāʾ* hence elaborated on "strategies of personal and group survival," notably that of drawing in increasing numbers of their family members into the circle of religious learning. Women's entry into *ḥadīth* learning, starting the late third/ninth century, is thus intimately connected with these changes. Women became central to this survival, by creating dynasties of *ʿulamāʾ* through marriages. But since they were also shielded from political and factional pressures because of their gender, they managed to preserve the tradition of *ḥadīth* transmission, an epicenter of the culture of religious learning and piety of the *ʿulamāʾ* class.[31]

25 Al-Baghdādī, *Tārīkh Baghdād*, vol. 14, 432.
26 Al-Baghdādī, *Tārīkh Baghdād*, vol. 14, 443 and 439.
27 Al-Baghdādī, *Tārīkh Baghdād*, vol. 14, 446.
28 Al-Baghdādī, *Tārīkh Baghdād*, vol. 14, 443.
29 Al-Baghdādī, *Tārīkh Baghdād*, vol. 14, 445.
30 Sayeed, *Women and the Transmission of Religious Knowledge*, 114.
31 Sayeed, *Women and the Transmission of Religious Knowledge*, 141.

3 Learning, *Ḥadīth*, and Mobility

George Makdisi stated that Muslim education "shifted early on from a cumulative phase to one of critical understanding and creative inquiry," abandoning the *ḥadīth* phase based on transmission (*riwāya*), to pass on through understanding (*dirāya*), to the *fiqh* phase. What is important about the *fiqh* phase is that it is a system "based on the confrontation of legal opinions and disputation." This legal methodology prepared the ability to analyze and synthesize.[32] *Muḥaddithāt* and women, in general, rarely received any education in jurisprudence. Concomitant with this lack in legal training is the absence of *munāẓara*, the disciplined disputation of fine points of the law and the resolution of controversial questions.[33] This absence concerns not only a field of knowledge but the absence of a fundamental intellectual training: specifically, developed critical and analytical skills.[34] In the words of Brinkley Messick, "The shift from the Quranic school to *darasa* instruction also recapitulates the general movement from the Quran (and the Sunna) to the jurisprudence of the *shariʿa*, a movement from basic text to expansive commentary, from sacred to humanly constituted discourse."[35] Women were, on the whole, confined to the sacred discourse of *ḥadīth*, managing only rarely, if at all, to move in the direction of the humanly constituted discourse of jurisprudence.

A close reading of this major Abbasid source reveals that women's education in the third/ninth and fourth/tenth centuries did not seem to have gone beyond the *ḥadīth* phase. The much later ninth/fifteenth century biographical dictionary by al-Sakhāwī, *al-Dawʾ al-lāmiʿ li-ahl al-qarn al-tāsiʿ*, confirms this conclusion. Granted, these were compilations that focused on women who were trained in *ḥadīth*. However, other texts, focusing of early Sufi women for instance, similarly uphold this conclusion. Abū ʿAbd al-Rahmān al-Sulamī's compilation on early Sufi women indicates that they did not receive a formal education but that these women's "knowledge" was in large part in the ways of asceticism (*zuhd*), reclusiveness, scrupulousness, self-denial, spiritual states, and gnosis.[36]

---

32 George Makdisi, *The Rise of Colleges: Institutions of Learning in Islam and the West* (Edinburgh: Edinburgh University Press, 1981), 284.

33 Berkey, *Transmission of Knowledge*, 180.

34 Makdisi, *Rise of Colleges*, 284.

35 Brinkley Messick, *The Calligraphic State: Textual Domination and History in a Muslim Society* (Berkeley: University of California Press, 1992), 85.

36 Abū ʿAbd al-Rahmān al-Sulamī', *Early Sufi Women*, Arabic with facing English translation by Rkia E. Cornell (Fons Vitae: Louisville KY, 1999), 86–87; 122–125, 130–31, 218–19. Sufi women started receiving a more formal education around the sixth/twelfth century.

Tārīkh Baghdād includes, nevertheless, biographies of a few women who seemed to have, exceptionally, moved beyond *ḥadīth*. The entry on Amat al-Wāḥid (d. 377/987) reflects the inherent potential:

> Amat al-Wāḥid, daughter of the Qāḍī Abū ʿAbdallāh al-Ḥusayn … al-Maḥāmilī. She transmitted traditions on the authority of her father and others.… She was virtuous and learned, one of the most prominent individuals to have committed to memory Shāfiʿī jurisprudence.… Abū Bakr al-Barqānī said: The daughter of al-Maḥāmilī used to deliver legal opinions along with Abū ʿAlī b. Abī Hurayra.… Abū l-Ḥasan al-Dāraquṭnī said: she studied with her father, with Ismāʿīl b. al-ʿAbbās al-Warrāq, with ʿAbd al-Ghāfir b. Salāma al-Ḥumṣī, with Abū l-Ḥasan al-Miṣrī, with Ḥamza l-Hāshimī, and others. She committed to memory the Qurʾan and Shāfiʿī jurisprudence, the rules of inheritance, and the calculation of heir's portions, grammar and other religious sciences.[37]

For Amat al-Wāḥid to give legal decisions she must have had an exhaustive education in the science of *fiqh*. Al-Baghdādī gives evidence of one other woman, Umm ʿĪsā, giving decisions in jurisprudence. While these women were exceptional in their training in jurisprudence, it is evidence, nonetheless, of the window, albeit narrow, of possibilities.

The information in *Tārīkh Baghdād*'s last volume clearly reveals a development in the role of women *muḥaddithāt* "from the stage of memorizing, preserving and transmitting … to another advanced stage of interactive instruction and teaching the material to students."[38] At times, as mentioned earlier, they specialized in teaching particular collections.

Given the informal network to which such privileged women had access, male scholars encouraged female students to seek female scholars whenever possible. The biographies of women traditionists in *Tārīkh Baghdād*, however, lists only Fāṭima bint Aḥmad al-Sāmarriyya as having transmitted traditions on the authority of a woman, namely, al-Ḥawwāriyya, sister of Abū Saʿīd.[39]

In any event, the small number of existing female scholars meant that such women had to pursue their higher education with male scholars within a socially restricted context. This limited relationship between women and their male teachers has to be contrasted with the intimate relationship that male students could potentially acquire with their masters. Al-Ghazālī, in the passages

37 Al-Baghdādī, *Tārīkh Baghdād*, vol. 14, 442–43.
38 Abou-Bakr, "Teaching the Words of the Prophet," 306–28.
39 Al-Baghdādī, *Tārīkh Baghdād*, vol. 14, 439 and 444.

he devotes to the relationship between master and student, stresses that a master is not only the one who teaches but at the same time the "Murshid," the spiritual guide.[40] Such ties had "much in common with those that bound Sufis to their disciples."[41] This master-student relationship, indicated by the word *ṣuḥba*, implied an extremely close personal and intellectual relationship. The teacher was more than an expert in a body of knowledge. The companionship it entailed was infused with the quest by the student to model himself after the sheikh in his morals and manners.[42] If the master-student relationship was crucial for the correct completion of education, how could a woman attain the same level and depth of knowledge? Women's education, circumscribed by the social restrictions, including travel in the quest of learning, affected women's acquisition of knowledge and limited their professional mobility.

4 Conclusion

Through an analysis of al-Baghdādī's short section on women in his *Tārīkh Baghdād*, one is able to spot several issues pertaining to women's education within the Abbasid context. I have pointed to the absence of formal institutions of learning for women, to the crucial initiative and encouragement given by their family members, and to the limited intellectual training accessible to women. While we have a record of a small number of women who integrated into the system of transmission of higher knowledge, it appears that these women partook fully in only one of the major religious sciences, namely *ḥadīth*. Some of them succeeded, through the encouragement of their relatives, to become important *ḥadīth* scholars and had mostly informal access to teachers and students. Most of these women, however, were constrained in their education by a number of factors that limited their access, possibilities, expectations, and mobility. These women were seldom allowed to travel to different cities in order to learn *ḥadīth* from major traditionists, and the lack of facility to undertake such journeys affected their acquisition of knowledge. Moreover, the actual form in which tuition was received and, in particular, the absence of strong bonds between the female students and their male teachers

40 Louis Gardet, "Notions et principes de l'éducation dans la pensée arabo-musulmanne," in *L'enseignement en Islam et en Occident au Moyen Age*, eds. George Makdisi, Dominique Sourdel, and Janine Sourdel-Thomine (Paris: Colloques internationaux de la Napoule, 1977), 1–13.

41 Michael Chamberlain, *Knowledge and Social Practice in Medieval Damascus, 1190–1350* (Cambridge: Cambridge University Press, 1994), 108.

42 Chamberlain, *Knowledge and Social Practice*, 109.

was surely a factor that constrained their learning. Their geographical and spatial immobility constituted a major factor in preventing their upward professional mobility: notably, in the absence of career choices.

While men went ahead to become paid teachers or judges, or use their knowledge in some practical capacity, women were limited to only a training of the mind, or learning for its own sake. Nevertheless, the *muḥaddithāt* played a major role during this period of Sunni consolidation. By becoming a *muḥadditha*, the learned woman served her family, hence increasing its social capital. This strategy, followed by *ʿulamāʾ* families starting the late third/ninth century, boosted "the status and competitive capacity of the family as a whole."[43] The increasing number of *muḥaddithāt* starting in the third/ninth century continued to increase into Mamluk times, culminating in the ninth/fifteenth-century al-Sakhāwī's *al-Ḍawʾ al-lāmiʿ li-ahl al-qarn al-tāsiʿ*, a unique compilation, as it is the only biographical dictionary where we "find such a constellation of women who study *ḥadīth*."[44] Women's participation in the transfer of *ḥadīth* became part of the cultural and social capital that enabled the survival and flourishing of the scholarly elite, the *ʿulamāʾ*. However, that few of these women attained the status of important *ḥadīth* scholars does not diminish the general dearth and condition of women's education during this period and the consequent restrictions on their mobility in its multiple dimensions.

Bibliography

Abou-Bakr, Omaima. "Teaching the Words of the Prophet: Women Instructors of the Hadith (Fourteenth and Fifteenth Centuries)." *Hawwa* 1, no. 3 (January 2003): 306–28.

Berkey, Jonathan Porter. *The Transmission of Knowledge in Medieval Cairo: A Social History of Islamic Education*. Princeton, NJ: Princeton University Press, 1992.

Chamberlain, Michael. *Knowledge and Social Practice in Medieval Damascus, 1190–1350*. Cambridge: Cambridge University Press, 1994.

Cooperson, Michael. *Classical Arabic Biography: The Heirs of the Prophets in the Age of al-Maʾmūn*. Cambridge: Cambridge University Press, 2000.

43 Sayeed, *Women and the Transmission of Religious Knowledge*, 140.

44 Basim Musallam, "The Ordering of Muslim Societies," in *The Cambridge Illustrated History of the Islamic World*, ed. Francis Robinson (Cambridge: Cambridge University Press, 1996), 164–207.

Gardet, Louis. "Notions et principes de l'éducation dans la pensée arabo-musulmanne." In *L'enseignement en Islam et en Occident au Moyen Age*, edited by George Makdisi, Dominique Sourdel, and Janine Sourdel-Thomine, 1–13. Paris: Colloques internationaux de la Napoule, 1977.

Giladi, Avner. "Gender Differences in Child Rearing and Education: Some Preliminary Observations with Reference to Medieval Muslim Thought." *Al-Qantara* 16, no. 2 (January 1995): 291–308.

Humphreys, R. Stephen. *Islamic History: A Framework for Enquiry*. Princeton, NJ: Princeton University Press, 1991.

al-Khaṭīb al-Baghdādī. *Al-Kifāya fī ʿilm al-riwāya*. Beirut: Dār al-Kutub al-ʿIlmiyya, 1988.

al-Khaṭīb al-Baghdādī. *Tārīkh Baghdād*. Vol. 14. Beirut: Dār al-Kutub al-ʿIlmiyya, 1997.

Makdisi, George. "Muslim Institutions of Learning in Eleventh-Century Baghdad." *Bulletin of the School of Oriental and African Studies* 24, no. 1 (February 1961): 1–56.

Makdisi, George. *The Rise of Colleges: Institutions of Learning in Islam and the West*. Edinburgh: Edinburgh University Press, 1981.

Melchert, Christopher. "The Etiquette of Learning in the Early Islamic Study Circle." In *Law and Education in Medieval Islam: Studies in Memory of Professor George Makdisi*, edited by Joseph Lowry, Devin Stewart and Shawkat Toorawa. Cambridge: E.G.W. Gibb Memorial Trust, 2004.

Messick, Brinkley. *The Calligraphic State: Textual Domination and History in a Muslim Society*. Berkeley: University of California Press, 1992.

Mottahedeh, Roy. *The Mantle of the Prophet: Religion and Politics in Iran*. New York: Pantheon, 1985.

Musallam, Basim. "The Ordering of Muslim Societies." In *The Cambridge Illustrated History of the Islamic World*, edited by Francis Robinson, 164–207. Cambridge: Cambridge University Press, 1996.

Nadwi, Mohammad Akram. *Al-Muḥaddithāt: The Women Scholars in Islam*. London: Interface, 2007.

Nashabe, Hisham. *Muslim Educational Institutions: A General Survey Followed by a Monographic Study of al-Madrasah al-Mustanṣirīyah in Baghdād*. Beirut: Makassed Philanthropic Islamic Association, 1989.

Rahmatallah, Maleeha. *The Women of Baghdad in the Ninth and Tenth Centuries, as Revealed in the History of Baghdad of al-Hatib*. Baghdad: Times Press, 1952.

Roded, Ruth. *Women in Islamic Biographical Collections: From Ibn Saʿd to Who's Who*. Boulder, CO: L. Rienner, 1994.

Sayeed, Asma. *Women and the Transmission of Religious Knowledge*. Cambridge: Cambridge University Press, 2013.

CHAPTER 3

The Aqīt Household: Professional Mobility of a Berber Learned Elite in Premodern West Africa

Marta G. Novo

1 Introduction

The social advancement of the Aqīts, the most powerful scholarly household of 10th/16th century Timbuktu, has traditionally been considered as meteoric, and although their prior socioeconomic condition has not received sufficient attention, it is a good example of how specialized scholarship aided powerful households to reach and consolidate social and political leadership. Just a few decades after their arrival in the city, and without previous dedication to scholarship, the Aqīt household reached the top of its learned elites in what has been known as Timbuktu's golden age. Their story, which was told by the last of the members of the prestigious lineage, Aḥmad Bābā al-Tinbuktī (963/1556–1036/1627), as well as by other contemporary sources, exemplifies the careers of the elite of the *ʿulamāʾ* in premodern West Africa.[1] In fact, the history of the Aqīts is one of the very rare accounts of learned households which can be drawn from West African sources before the 11th/17th century, an account for which the information available is relatively sufficient enough in order to be considered as representative of the intellectual life of the premodern *bilād al-sūdān* before the Moroccan invasion of the Songhay Empire in the year 999/1591, in spite of the evident tendentiousness of the sources.[2]

1 About Aḥmad Bābā al-Tinbuktī, see Zouber, M., *Aḥmad Bābā de Tombouctou (1556/1627): sa vie et son œuvre*, Paris: Maisonneuve et Larose, 1977; Hunwick, J.O., "A new source for the biography of Aḥmad Bābā al-Tinbuktī (1556–1627)", *Bulletin of the School of Oriental and African Studies*, 27, 3 (1964), 568; by the same author "Further light on Aḥmad Bābā al-Tinbuktī", *Research Bulletin, Centre of Arabic Documentation*, 1, 2 (1966), 19–31. See also Hunwick, J.O. (ed.), *Arabic Literature of Africa IV*, Leiden: Brill, 2003, 17–31; Sadki, Ḥ., *Makhṭūṭāt Aḥmad Bābā al-Tinbuktī fī-l-khazāʾin al-maghribiyya*, Rabat: Institut des Études Africaines, 1996.

2 Hunwick, J.O., "Aḥmad Bābā and the Moroccan invasion of the Sudan (1591)", *Journal of the Historical Society of Nigeria*, 2/3 (1962), 311–328; Castries, H. de, "La conquête du Soudan par Moulaye Ahmed el-Mansôur", *Hespéris*, III (1923), 438–88; Pianel, G., "Les préliminaires de la conquête du Soudan par Moulaye Ahmed el-Mansôur, d'après trois documents inédits", *Hespéris*, XL (1953), 185–97; García-Arenal, M., *Aḥmad al-Manṣūr. The Beginnings of Modern Morocco*, London: Oneworld, 2009, 91. About the bias in the sources, see Novo, M.G., "Writing

 | DOI:10.1163/9789004467637_005

Members of this household occupied the judgeship (*qaḍāʾ*) of Timbuktu for almost a century, which coincided with the period in which the Askya dynasty ruled over the Songhay Empire. This was also the period of the city's intellectual splendor, as Timbuktu became the main hub of West African Islamic scholarship. Rulings by the Aqīt *quḍāt* can be found in *fatwa* compilations from the 11th/17th century onwards, all over the *bilād al-sūdān*. They constitute a significant part of West Africa's earliest pieces of Islamic jurisprudence, and this is one of the reasons that make historians consider them as fundamental parts in the development of the Islamic legal system beyond the southern shore of the Sahara.

This chapter addresses the issue of the spatial and social mobility of the *ʿulamāʾ* in premodern West Africa through the careers of the Aqīt household, focusing on how their scholarly network was set up and how it promoted their social advancement, to the point of becoming relevant sociopolitical actors in the Niger Bend area during the apogee of the Songhay Empire. It will also analyze how spatial mobility might have reinforced the network, as well as the symbolic capital derived from it. In order to achieve this, it will focus on the information on Islamic scholarship in premodern West Africa through its main sources, Aḥmad Bābā's biographical works and the so-called *Timbuktu Chronicles*.[3] While the *Timbuktu Chronicles* provide a more general overview about the professionalization of the *ʿulamāʾ* in Imperial Songhay, Aḥmad Bābā's

---

the history of Islamic law in West Africa: scholars from the *bilād al-sūdān* in Aḥmad Bābā al-Tinbuktī's biographical works", *Die Welt des Islams* (forthcoming). Also, Stewart, C., "Calibrating the scholarship of Timbuktu", and Hall, B., "Rethinking the place of Timbuktu in the Intellectual History of Muslim West Africa", in Green, T., and Rossi, B. (eds.), *Landscapes, Sources and Intellectual Projects of the West African Past*, Leiden: Brill, 2018, 220–238 and 239–258.

3 These are the *Taʾrīkh al-sūdān* and the writings of Ibn al-Mukhtār. See ʿAbd al-Raḥmān b. ʿAbd Allāh al-Saʿdī, *Taʾrīkh al-sūdān*. Arabic text and French translation by O. Houdas (Paris: Ernest Leroux, 1900). English translation in Hunwick, J.O., *Timbuktu and the Songhay Empire. Al-Saʿdī's* Taʾrīkh al-sūdān *down to 1613 and Other Contemporary Documents*, Leiden: Brill, 1999. Also Maḥmūd Kaʿtī Ibn al-Ḥājj al-Mutawakkil, *Taʾrīkh al-fattāsh fī akhbār al-buldān*, Arabic text and French translation by Houdas, O., and Delafosse, M., Paris: Ernest Leroux, 1913. See also Hunwick, J.O., "Studies in the *Tārīkh al-fattāsh* I: Its Authors and Textual History," *Research Bulletin – Centre of Arabic Documentation*, 5 (1969), 57–65; Levtzion, N., "A Seventeenth-Century Chronicle by Ibn al-Mukhtār: A Critical Study of *Taʾrīkh al-fattāsh*," *Bulletin of the School of Oriental and African Studies*, 34, 3 (1971), 571–593; and Hunwick, J.O., "Studies in the *Taʾrīkh al-fattāsh* II: An Alleged Charter of Privilege Issued by Askiya *al-Ḥājj* Muḥammad to the Descendants of Mori Hawgāro," *Sudanic Africa*, 3 (1992), 133–148. Also Nobili, M., *Sultan, Caliph, and the Renewer of the Faith: Ahmad Lobbo, the Tārīkh Al-Fattāsh and the Making of an Islamic State in West Africa*, Cambridge: Cambridge University Press, 2020.

biographies of West African scholars are richer in very important details, such as transmission chains and the geographical origin of their knowledge, or their main subjects of interest, as well as significant references to their role as socio-political actors.

Aḥmad Bābā al-Tinbuktī is a paramount figure of premodern West African Islamic scholarship. He acquired great renown in his time and after it as the author of two Mālikī biographical dictionaries, the famous *Nayl al-ibtihāj bi-taṭrīz al-Dībāj* (written ca. 1012/1603) and its abridged version, called *Kifāyat al-muḥtāj li-maʿrifat man laysa fī-l-Dībāj* (written ca. 1015/1606).[4] His legal opinions, many of which have been preserved in a number of North and West African public and private libraries, and also reproduced in later compendia, contributed to extend his fame as a jurist and *muftī*. His rulings on slavery transcended his times and brought his renown up to the present, in recognition of his clear stance against racial prejudices in this domain.[5] The great variety of his works and the deepness of his thought clearly show him as one of the greatest authors of his time, as pointed out already in contemporary sources. Although he was a member of the powerful Aqīt clan, Aḥmad Bābā himself was never appointed to any post of relevance in local or Imperial Songhay administration, nor did his father or his grandfather, who both were brothers of the great *qāḍī*s of their time, Maḥmūd b. ʿUmar Aqīt and his son, al-ʿĀqib. Being apart from the "great affairs", as he put it, allowed him to focus on learning, and after completing the finest education, Aḥmad Bābā started writing his own works. Part of them were dedicated to Arabic grammar and to logic, together with commentaries to the most cultivated subject by the West African *ʿulamāʾ* of the moment as well as of later periods, the *Mukhtaṣar* of Khalīl b. Isḥāq.[6] At this point he also started reflecting on the role of Islamic scholars and scholarship in society. It was a moment of great social and political

4 Aḥmad Bābā al-Tinbuktī, *Nayl al-ibtihāj bi-taṭrīz al-Dībāj*, ed. ʿAmar, M., Cairo: Maktabat al-thaqāfa al-dīniyya, 2004, 2 vols.; ed. al-Harrāma, ʿA.H., Tripoli (Libya): Kulliyyat al-daʿwa al-islāmiyya, 2000; ed. on the margins of Ibn Farḥūn's *al-Dībāj al-mudhhab*, Cairo: Maṭbaʿat al-Maʿāhid, 1932. By the same author, *Kifāyat al-muḥtāj li-maʿrifat man laysa fī l-Dībāj*, intr. and ed. Mutīʿ, M., Rabat: Wizārat al-awqāf wa-l-shuʾūn al-islāmiyya, 2000.

5 For Aḥmad Bābā's legal opinions on slavery, see J.O. Hunwick's and F. Ḥarrāq's edition and English translation in Aḥmad Bābā al-Tinbuktī, *Miʿrāj al-ṣuʿūd. Aḥmad Bābā's Replies on slavery*, Rabat: Institut des Études Africaines, 2000. See also García Novo, M., "Islamic law and slavery in premodern West Africa", *Entremóns. UPF Journal of World History*, 2 (2011), 1–20.

6 Khalīl Ibn Isḥāq b. Mūsā b. *S̲h̲uʿayb*, Abū l-Mawadda Ḍiyāʾ al-Dīn, Ibn al-Jundī (d. ca. 776/1374), Egyptian jurist, one of the main figures of the Mālikī *madhhab*. See Ben Cheneb, M., "K̲h̲alīl b. Isḥāḳ", in: *Encyclopaedia of Islam*, Second Edition, edited by: P. Bearman, Th. Bianquis, C.E. Bosworth, E. van Donzel, W.P. Heinrichs. Consulted online on 6 April 2020 <http://dx.doi.org/10.1163/1573-3912_islam_SIM_4162>. About his most famous work, the

upheaval due to the constant fight for power between the descendants of Askya *al-Ḥājj* Muḥammad since he was removed from power in his later years. The political decline of the Songhay Empire inspired one of the works of what historians have come to name as Aḥmad Bābā's "first Timbuktu period", called *Jalb al-niʿma wa-ḍafʿ al-niqma bi-mujānabat al-wulāt al-ẓalama*. As M. Zouber described it in his work on the life and works of the renowned Timbuktu scholar, it is an essay against frequenting wrongful rulers (*al-wulāt al-ẓalama*), where the author explains that this may imply moral corruption or end in an ill fate, drawing examples from early Islamic history.[7]

He continued to write about the *ʿulamāʾ* after the fall of the Songhay Empire and the establishment of Moroccan rule over part of its territories, including Timbuktu, and also during the period of his deportation to the Saʿdid capital, Marrakech, where he was forced to reside along with a great part of the members of his powerful clan. Between the years 1002/1593–1016/1607, Aḥmad Bābā accomplished his famous *ṭabaqāt* works *Nayl al-ibtihāj* and *Kifāyat al-muḥtāj*, the first of which he may have already started before the Saʿdid expedition to the *bilād al-sūdān*. From his "Moroccan period" dates another essay, called *Tuḥfat al-fuḍalāʾ bi-baʿḍ faḍāʾil al-ʿulamāʾ*, which is a treaty on the virtues of scholars and their role as models and guides for the community, and on the primacy of scholars over saints (*awliyāʾ*), and that of religious knowledge (*ʿilm*) over cult practices (*ʿibādāt*).[8] The role of scholarship in society and the piety and devotion of scholars were a main theme in Aḥmad Bābā's thought, to which he dedicated the greatest part of his writings also in the period of his greatest literary and intellectual standing. As we may see later on, this was so also in a self-biographical manner, as a reflection on his own *métier*.

2 Building a Network

As we can read in the first passages of the autobiography of Aḥmad Bābā al-Tinbuktī, where the author explained how he came to be an *ʿālim*, when the first scholar in the Aqīt lineage started his career in Islamic jurisprudence, he was already very close to the highest levels. The text, which can be found at the end of the *Kifāyat al-muḥtāj*, goes as follows:

Mukhtaṣar fī l-furūʿ, see Brockelmann, C., *Geschichte der arabischen Litteratur*, Leiden: Brill, 1937–1942, S II, 83, 86.

7 Zouber, M. *Aḥmad Bābā de Tombouctou*, 156–162.

8 Aḥmad Bābā al-Tinbuktī, *Tuḥfat al-fuḍalāʾ bi-baʿḍ faḍāʾil al-ʿulamāʾ*, ed. Sāmī, S., Rabat: Institut des Études Africaines, 1992.

> The first of my ancestors who dedicated himself to scholarship (*ʿilm*) was the faqīh Maḥmūd And-Ag-Muḥammad, grandfather of my maternal grandfather. He was the qāḍī of Timbuktu in the middle of the 9th(–14th) century. After him, ʿUmar, father of my grand-father, was a pious jurist who studied under the pious judge, the muʾaddib Muḥammad al-Kābarī. Then his sons, my grandfather Aḥmad and his two brothers, Maḥmūd and ʿAbd Allāh. Knowledge (*ʿilm*) spread in their lineage together with leadership (*riyāsa*). The judgeship was conferred to some of them with abundant wealth (*mutamawwal^an^*).[9]

Although slightly enigmatic, with some determinant factors omitted, these few lines in al-Tinbuktīs *tarjama* reveal the constituent elements in the birth of his scholarly lineage. Thus, even if the text does not specify how ʿUmar b. Muḥammad Aqīt came to marry Sitta, *qāḍī* And-Ag-Muḥammad's daughter, and how he became the student of one of the most relevant figures in the transmission of Islamic jurisprudence in the Niger Bend, Modibbo Muḥammad al-Kābarī, we may assume that some conditions were necessary for it.[10]

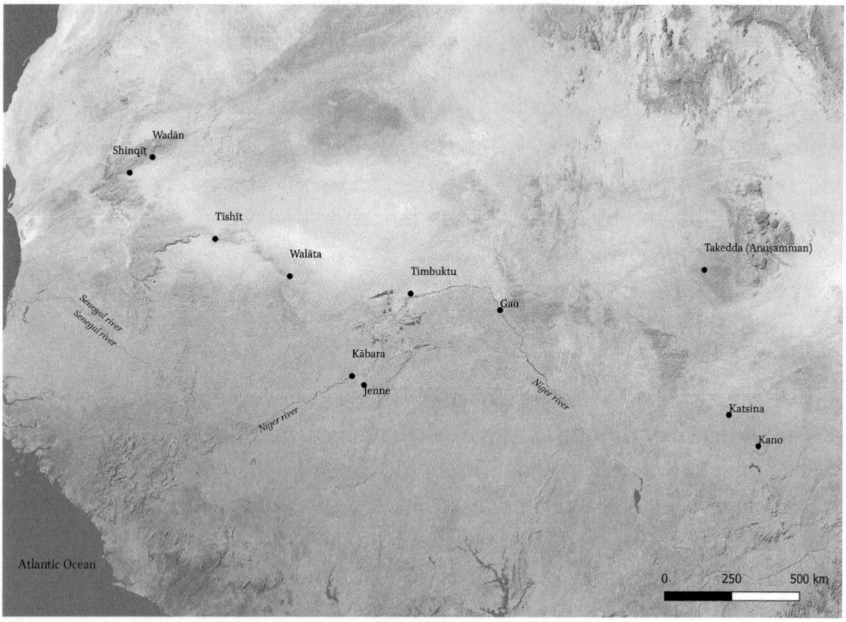

MAP 3.1 Locations for Islamic learning in West Africa ca. 1100–1600

9 Aḥmad Bābā al-Tinbuktī, *Kifāyat al-muḥtāj*, vol. 2, 281.
10 For his biography see Hunwick, J.O. (ed.), *Arabic Literature of Africa IV*, 12.

The first of them probably was wealth, obtained through the participation in trans-Saharan commercial networks, combined with some social relevance due to a noble descent. We can deduce that, in absence of other significant factors, such as kinship, renowned scholarship or sainthood (*wilāya*), it is very likely that the Aqīts' very propitious starting position in the intellectual milieu of Timbuktu was made possible through their economic means. Their origin in Masina, the region between Timbuktu and Jenne, would explain how the Aqīts may have become partners of other Ṣanhāja trading households northwards in the trans-Saharan trade routes, such as the Timbuktu And-Ag-Muḥammads, and develop alliances with them. H.T. Norris's investigation of the Aqīt *nisbas* showed that when Muḥammad Aqīt arrived in this town he was probably no ordinary man, but the leader of the Massūfa clan of the Uqītūn.[11] Muḥammad Aqīt's unsettled quarrel with Akil, the Tuareg sultan of the Timbuktu, may be considered as another sign of his position, as it could hardly be expected from someone of a low social condition to be able to confront one of the chiefs of the city.[12] It was also hardly expectable from an ordinary man to establish a marriage with the city's leading scholarly household, but not as much so from a powerful, noble and wealthy stranger. Once again, wealth and social relevance are the most likely explanations of how Muḥammad Aqīt could marry his son to the daughter of one of the city's most relevant figures, *qāḍī* And-Ag-Muḥammad. The marriage alliance between the Aqīt and the And-Ag-Muḥammad households shows that this kind of strategies were used to promote the social mobility of scholars in premodern West Africa.

The marriage of ʿUmar b. Muḥammad Aqīt and Sitta bt. And-Ag-Muḥammad allowed the Aqīts to rapidly reach the highest level in Timbuktu's learned circles, the judgeship (*al-qaḍāʾ*), which they held for over a century. But we can guess that ʿUmar must have had some relevance or some potential as an *ʿālim* in order to be able to found a scholarly branch in the Aqīt family, or otherwise some other kind of marriage alliance, one that remained within the trading families of the Aqīt and And-Ag-Muḥammad clans, was more likely to have taken place. The basically economic character of the Aqīts before their establishment in Timbuktu, and the specialized scholarly character of the And-Ag-Muḥammads suggest that this scholarly household was the religious branch of a trading clan, especially since it appears that being involved in commercial activities was considered as putting at risk the *wilāya* of some

11 Norris, H.T., "Ṣanhājah Scholars of Timbuctoo", *Bulletin of the School of Oriental and African Studies*, 30, 3 (1967), 634–640.

12 Al-Saʿdī, *Taʾrīkh al-sūdān*, ed. Houdas, 36; English translation by Hunwick, J.O., *Timbuktu and the Songhay Empire*, 50.

of the great *ʿulamāʾ*, which, perhaps significantly, were not those who were in charge of worldly affairs, such as the *quḍāt*, but eminent scholars who focused on piety and devotion. For instance, The *Taʾrīkh al-sūdān* recalls the anecdote of how Sīdī Yaḥyà, the revered 9th/15th century North African scholar who settled in Timbuktu, whose name bears one of the mosques and is considered as one of the greatest saints of the city, lost his *wilāya* by getting involved in trade, which he did because he did not want to depend on others.[13] As will be discussed hereunder, and as shown by the opening paragraphs of al-Tinbuktī's biography, the Aqīt *quḍāt* were extraordinarily wealthy and had an important role in the political affairs of Imperial Songhay, and it may be assumed that such prominent positions entailed a complex social and economic human structure. As happened elsewhere in the lands of Islam, the accumulation of wealth, that liberated the most talented in the family from work and allowed them to become scholars, made the birth of the scholarly network possible, and reinforced it, causing the social advancement of the group, which was more pronounced in the case of the most influential of its members, the elite of the *ʿulamāʾ*. It should also be noted that a context of lack of a strong authoritative power, as was the case of the decline of Imperial Songhay, favored that members of the scholarly elites, such as the Aqīts in the *bilād al-sūdān*, contested weak political powers and tried to replace them, as will be discussed later in this chapter.

Though scholarship was not completely absent from the ensemble of elements that made the alliance with Aqīts interesting for the And-Ag-Muḥammads, a solid tradition of learning on behalf of the Aqīts was probably not necessary for the alliance to work. However, once the alliance was set up, the Aqīts, and more specifically ʿUmar b. Muḥammad Aqīt, the only figure in his generation in the Aqīt household for which we may find some references, had access to all the learning resources, that is, teachers and libraries, of the And-Ag-Muḥammads'. As his great-grandson declares, he studied under one of the greatest scholars of his time, Muḥammad al-Kābarī, as well as under his father-in-law, *qāḍī* And-Ag-Muḥammad. We can guess that he and his offspring made the most of the network of their maternal relatives, as their success in becoming great *ʿulamāʾ* was the key differential factor for their social advancement, for a second and greater time in the patriline if we consider that ʿUmar b. Muḥammad Aqīt must have had some talent as a scholar that he could exploit in order to become related to a scholarly lineage.

13 Hunwick, J.O. (ed.), *Arabic Literature of Africa IV*, 12–13, for Sīdī Yaḥyà's biography. Al-Saʿdī, *Taʾrīkh al-sūdān*, ed. Houdas, 50–51; English translation by Hunwick, J.O., *Timbuktu and the Songhay Empire*, 72–73.

ʿUmar's son, Maḥmūd (d. 955/1548), succeeded his maternal grandfather in the judgeship of Timbuktu, and became even greater than him as a *qāḍī*. And the same occurred with Maḥmūd's sons, Muḥammad (d. 973/1565) and al-ʿĀqib b. Maḥmūd b. ʿUmar (d. 991/1583).[14] What made them overtake their relatives in the And-Ag-Muḥammad lineage, as well as other scholarly lineages in Timbuktu or elsewhere in the *bilād al-sūdān* is not clear in the textual evidence available, since there are almost no detailed references to the careers of scholars outside the Aqīt household in the sources. A closer look at the different levels of religious learning and professionalization of scholars may be useful in order to evaluate it.

3 Professionalization and Vertical Mobility

The alliance between the Aqīts and the And-Ag-Muḥammads illustrates how new kinship ties potentiated intellectual and commercial profit. The knowledge transfer for social capital, which was so palpable in the Aqīt lineage, had different outcomes that were probably directly related to the student's socioeconomic background in the premodern *bilād al-sūdān*. As could be expected, the sources pay very little attention to ordinary scholars, although we may still glimpse that a rudimentary Islamic education opened the way for administrative positions in Imperial Songhay. The only post related to scholarship in the political structure of the Empire that has been referred to in the *Timbuktu Chronicles* is that of *kātib*, but with no detail to the number of secretaries at the court, their possible hierarchy, or other aspects that may be relevant for the study of the professionalization of *sūdānī* scholars. There is a considerable gap in the information available between the period of the first Muslim communities that established themselves in the *bilād al-sūdān*, and the period in

14 About Maḥmūd b. ʿUmar b. Muḥammad Aqīt, see Aḥmad Bābā al-Tinbuktī, *Nayl al-ibtihāj*, ed. al-Harrāma, #746, 607–608; *Kifāyat al-muḥtāj*, ed. Muṭīʿ, II, #655, 245–246. Also, Makhlūf, M., *Shajarat al-nūr al-zakiyya fī ṭabaqāt al-mālikiyya*, Cairo: 1930, 1043; Hunwick, J.O. (ed.), *Arabic Literature of Africa IV*, 13–14; Kaḥḥāla, ʿU.R., *Muʿjam al-muʾallifīn. Tarājim muṣannifī al-kutub al-ʿarabiyya*, Damascus: al-Maktaba al-ʿarabiyya, 1957–1961, XII, 85; Cherbonneau, M., *Essai sur la littérature arabe au Soudan d'après le Takmilet-ed-dibadje d'Ahmed Baba, le Tombouctien*, Constantine-Paris: Abadie, A. Leleux, 1861, 14–16. For the biography of Muḥammad b. Maḥmūd b. ʿUmar b. Muḥammad Aqīt, see Aḥmad Bābā al-Tinbuktī, *Nayl al-ibtihāj*, ed. al-Harrāma, #730, 597–8; *Kifāyat al-muḥtāj*, ed. Muṭīʿ, II, #641, 234; Cherbonneau, M., *Essai*, 19–20; "Muḥammad b. Maḥmūd b. ʿUmar b. Muḥammad Aqīt", in Hunwick, J.O. (ed.), *Arabic Literature of Africa IV*, 14–15. About al-ʿĀqib b. Maḥmūd b. ʿUmar b. Muḥammad Aqīt, see Aḥmad Bābā al-Tinbuktī, *Nayl al-ibtihāj*, ed. al-Harrāma, #459, 353–4; *Kifāyat al-muḥtāj*, ed. Muṭīʿ, I, #393, 377–8.

which the Mālīan State became mostly Islamized, and therefore the origins of this professionalization remain uncertain due to the lack of textual evidence. Earlier sources, such as Ibn Baṭṭūṭa, mention that in the Empire of Mālī, Muslim foreign traders were designated as mediators and charged of taking care of the affairs of their community, probably with only a basic knowledge of Islamic jurisprudence.[15] It is also likely that Muslim foreigners may have occupied positions in the administration, as well as served as teachers for *sūdānī* scholars-to-be, as this could be expected from the project of state-islamization carried out by Mālian Emperors, which included the establishment of diplomatic relations with North-African rulers, that were also used for travel *fī ṭalab al-ʿilm* to several North African locations.[16]

It may be inferred from Aḥmad Bābā's biographical works that the ordinary curriculum followed by students of religious sciences was adapted to the circumstances of recent Islamization and Arabization, as denoted by the strong presence of the subjects of grammar and rhetoric among the works that were learned by the *sūdānī* scholars of the 10th/16th century, and many of the works composed by West African scholars are commentaries to works related to the Arabic language.[17] A great interest was put in the domain of logic, probably under influence of al-Sanūsī's works, but it is likely that this subject was not dealt with in the most elementary levels of learning, from which there is no specific information at all.[18] It is hard to ascertain from the biographies of the intellectual elite what would the essential learning of West African scholars be like, but it would be reasonable to guess that the more known curricula followed by non-Berber groups such as the Dyula could not be so different from the basics in 10th/16th century *bilād al-sūdān*, that is, some of the key works in the domain of *ḥadīth*, the works of Muslim or Bukhārī, as well as the

---

15 Ibn Baṭṭūṭa, *Tuḥfat al-nuẓẓār fī gharāʾib al-amṣār wa-ʿajāʾib al-asfār*, ed. Defrémery, C., and Sanguinetti, B.R., Paris: Anthropos, 1968, IV, 394–5 and 397–8.

16 The beginnings of islamization of West Africa have been analyzed, among others, by Cuoq, J., *Histoire de l'islamisation de l'Afrique de l'Ouest*, Paris: Geuthner, 1984, and Levtzion, N. and Pouwells, R., *The History of Islam in Africa*, Athens, OH: Ohio University Press, 2000. See also Gomez, M.A., *African Dominion: A New History of Empire in Early and Medieval West Africa*, Princeton, New Jersey: Princeton University Press, 2019.

17 The complete reference to all the learnt, transmitted and composed works by *sūdānī* scholars in Aḥmad Bābā's biographical works can be consulted in Novo, M.G., "Writing the history of Islamic law in West Africa", *op. cit.* A wider study, chronologically and geographically, is that of, C. Stewart and Hall, B., "The historic 'core curriculum' and the book market in Islamic West Africa", in Krätli, G., and Lydon, G., eds., *The Trans-Saharan Book Trade*, Leiden: Brill, 2011, 109–174.

18 See Van Dalen, D., *Doubt, Scholarship and Society in 17th-Century Central Sudanic Africa*, Leiden: Brill, 2016, 90, 109–119.

most popular *fiqh* work in the region, the *Mukhtaṣar* of Khalīl b. Isḥāq, or the *Muwaṭṭa'* of Mālik b. Anas.[19] In any case, the available textual evidence does not permeate anything in what regards the process of specialization within the learning careers, as so far no specific texts mention the process. We can read in Aḥmad Bābā's biographic works that, in 10th/16th century Timbuktu, teachers taught in their homes, as well as in places of worship, as can be observed in the biography of al-Tinbuktī's *shaykh*, Muḥammad b. Maḥmūd b. Abī Bakr Baghayogho al-Wangarī (d. 1002/1594).[20] The verb used for learning a work is *qara'a*, and there is no trace of the terminology used in other *tabaqāt* works in other contexts of the Islamic world, such as *ḥaddatha* or *akhbara*. We may assume that a certain degree of oral transmission took place, but it is not possible to know specifically which works were taught orally and learnt from different teachers, as could be the case of the *ummahāt* of the Mālikī law school, and which ones were just consulted individually through the copies obtained from the Maghrib or from the central lands of Islam.

References to other positions more directly related to religious learning and practice are more common in West African sources, though still scarce, as only *khaṭībs*, *imāms* and *qāḍīs* appear, quite often without any further detail. These positions are linked only to the most prominent locations in the area, Gao, Jenne and Timbuktu, though we may assume that there must have been at least *imāms* in minor towns, and perhaps *khaṭībs*. There are a very few mentions to the *khaṭīb* of Gao and Jenne in the *Ta'rīkh al-sūdān*, and some mentions to *khaṭībs* in Timbuktu, but if this position was part of the political administration is not specified. There are no specifications of the tasks, nor if the *khaṭīb* of the capital ranked higher than others in dependent territories. In a very interesting passage of al-Sa'dī's work, we read that the people of Jenne

19 Wilks, I., "The transmission of Islamic learning in the Western Sudan", in Goody, J. (ed.), *Literacy in Traditional Societies*, Cambridge: Cambridge University Press, 1968, 162–197.

20 Aḥmad Bābā al-Tinbuktī, *Nayl al-ibtihāj*, ed. al-Harrāma, #736, 600–3; *Kifāyat al-muḥtāj*, ed. Muṭī', II, #646, 237–40. For Muḥammad Baghayogho's biography and works, see Hunwick (ed.), J.O., *Arabic Literature of Africa IV*, 31–32. Also al-Qādirī, *Nashr al-mathānī*, ed. Ḥajjī, M. and Tawfīq, A., Rabat: al-Jama'iyya al-maghribiyya li-l-ta'līf, 1986, IV, 40; al-Muḥibbī, *Khulāṣat al-athar fī a'yān al-qarn al-ḥādī 'ashar*, Beirut: Dār Ṣāḍir, 1966, IV, 211–2; al-Bagdādī, *Hādiyat al-'ārifīn, asmā' al-mu'allifīn wa-āthār al-muṣannifīn*, ed. Bilge, R. and Inal, M.K., Istanbul: Wikālat al-ma'ārif, 1951–1955, II, 260; al-Baghdādī, *Īḍāḥ al-maknūn fī l-dhayl 'alà kashf al-ẓunūn 'an asāmī l-kutub wa-l-funūn*, ed. Yaltakaya, S., Beirut: Dār al-kutub al-'ilmiyya, 1992, II, 697; Kaḥḥāla, *Mu'jam al-mu'allifīn*, XI, 315. Cherbonneau, M., *Essai*, 25–31; see also Hunwick, J.O., "Further light on Aḥmad Bābā al-Tinbuktī", 22–5; and Hunwick, J.O., "A contribution to the study of Islamic teaching traditions in West Africa: the career of Muḥammad Baghayogho, 930/1523–4", *Islam et Sociétés au Sud du Sahara* (1990), 149–62.

used to settle their affairs by the *khaṭīb*, "as is the custom of the *sūdān*" and that only in the 10th/16th century did they start to judge them according to the *sharīʿa*, litigating before *qāḍīs* like the *bīḍān*.[21] The ethnic distinction of justice authorities among the Berber and non-Berber West Africans made by al-Saʿdī's text raises many questions about how the practice of Islamic jurisprudence took place south of the Sahara, which unfortunately cannot yet be answered with the scarce textual evidence available. Although the fragment clearly tries to differentiate and hierarchize the Berber and non-Berber traditions of learning, what we can hardly glimpse from the description of the intellectual life of the *bilād al-sūdān* more likely suggests that *bīḍān* and *sūdān* alike shared the same scholarly background, as will be discussed later in this chapter. It is probable, as will be shown, that the divide presented by al-Saʿdī may have intended to emphasize the difference as part of a self-conscious attitude of superiority by the Ṣanhāja elites, which were at the time involved in the process of building their sociopolitical dominion in the Niger Bend area.

The *Timbuktu Chronicles* dedicate more attention to the position of *imām*, which is referred to in Gao and Jenne only briefly, and in a more detailed manner in the case of Timbuktu. The chronicles refer to the post of *imām* of the different mosques in the city, Jingereber, Sidi Yaḥyà and Sankore, and these positions were appointed by the *qāḍī* of Timbuktu. It is perhaps significant that the *imāms* were more varied from the point of view of ethnicity than the judges: while *imāms* had many different ethnic backgrounds such as Fulbe, Soninke or from different North African backgrounds, Arab or Berber, those who were appointed as *qāḍīs* came only from the Ṣanhāja, which shows the predominance of this Berber clan over other ethnic groups involved in the intellectual and religious life of the city. The *Timbuktu Chronicles* also refer to the appointment of *khaṭībs* for the abovementioned mosques, which was as well made by the *qāḍī*. No reference is made in the sources as to how were *khaṭībs* paid, while the *Taʾrīkh al-sūdān* specifies that *imāms* were paid on an annual basis "by notable families", with equal participation of every one of them.[22] This may lead to think that, even though only the Askyas, the highest political authorities, appointed the *qāḍīs*, in Jenne and Timbuktu, there may have been some sort of collegiate designation before this appointment, except of course in the case of the *qāḍī* appointed by Sonni ʿAlī. It is also probable that

21 Al-Saʿdī, *Taʾrīkh al-sūdān*, ed. Houdas, 18; English translation by Hunwick, J.O., *Timbuktu and the Songhay Empire*, 26. Hunwick suggests that in Gao the *khaṭīb* was also the *qāḍī*, see *Timbuktu and the Songhay Empire*, 366.

22 Al-Saʿdī, *Taʾrīkh al-sūdān*, ed. Houdas, 60–61; English translation by Hunwick, J.O., *Timbuktu and the Songhay Empire*, 86.

the Askyas appointed someone that was already a leading member of the community of scholars, the *jamāʿa*. The regular payments of the notables suggest that they considered themselves as part of the *khāṣṣa*.

The sources do not specify other possible sources of income of the scholars that appear in them, whether they were private or whether they came from higher authorities. It is difficult to know to what extent the dedication to learning was affordable for ordinary families, as determining the cost of living in 10th/16th premodern *bilād al-sūdān* with the present textual evidence may only be an approximative guess. West African sources do not feature any references to any institution of learning other than the relationship between student and teacher, so we may assume that this sort of professionalization was sustained by the student's own wealth; that is, the wealth of a household. The sources are particularly silent about how the *ʿulamāʾ* met their day-to-day needs. On the one hand, there are just a couple of mentions of economic activities related to scholars, which are trade and the exploitation of slave labor, as could be expected, and only one of the West African *ʿulamāʾ* that appears in Aḥmad Bābā's biographical works was not a full-time student in the beginning of his career.[23] On the other hand, some scholars are described as being extremely wealthy, and we may assume that this wealth came, at least partially, from trade, probably not carried out by themselves, but by associated relatives, and also from the donations received from rulers, or, as we have seen in the case of the *imāms* of Timbuktu, from the *jamāʿa*. We also do not know if teachers admitted every student at their lectures, regardless of origin or intellectual qualities, or if the access to the most prestigious teaching networks in the city was only open for students with great achievements or social connections.[24] We may assume that collaboration between learning households included the introduction of students in these networks, as permeates from the *Taʾrīkh*

23 This is the case of Makhlūf b. ʿAlī b. Ṣāliḥ al-Balbālī (d. 940/1533), a Walātī scholar whose *fatwas* had a considerable impact in the *bilād al-sūdān*, see Aḥmad Bābā al-Tinbuktī, *Nayl al-ibtihāj*, ed. al-Harrāma, #747, 608; *Kifāyat al-muḥtāj*, ed. Muṭīʿ, II, #656, 24. Also "Makhlūf b. ʿAlī b. Ṣāliḥ al-Balbālī", in: *Arabic Literature of Africa Online*, General Editors J.O. Hunwick, R.S. O'Fahey. Consulted online on 10 April 2020 <http://dx.doi.org/10.1163/2405-4453_alao_COM_ALA_20001_1_4>; Cherbonneau, *Essai*, 7; Bivar, H.D., and Hiskett, M., "The Arabic Literature of Nigeria to 1804: a provisional account", *Bulletin of the School of Oriental and African Studies*, 25, 3 (1962), 110–1.

24 The teaching networks of the city were thoroughly described by Saad, E.N., *Social History of Timbuktu. The role of Muslim Scholars and Notables, 1400–1900*, Cambridge: Cambridge University Press, 1983.

al-sūdān, but we ignore if the rivalries that certainly existed between prominent households caused the exclusion of rivals from them.[25]

In the case of the only post that was appointed by the Askya, which was the *qāḍī*, there is no mention of regular payments, but of diverse "gifts", that were also made to other persons of relevance, such as *imāms* or even secretaries. There are also no references to *qāḍī-l-quḍāt* or *qāḍī-l-jamāʿa* in the sources. Leo Africanus briefly mentions that "in Timbuktu there are numerous judges, scholars and priests, all well paid by the King".[26] The generosity of the Askya as portrayed in the *Timbuktu Chronicles* does not match the great expenses that are referred to from some members of the Timbuktu *jamāʿa*, especially of *qāḍī* al-ʿĀqib, who seems to embody this generosity to its highest degree, in one of the signs of the sources' self-centered character. Once again, there are no mentions to the origins of al-ʿĀqib's wealth, so we can just guess that part of his fortune came from the Askya's gifts. It is also probable to argue that being a *qāḍī* was profitable in the economic sense of the term, since this position allowed not only to intervene in the social and economic life in a way that could favor the social group of origin, but also to obtain a significant symbolic capital in the form of prestige, and to configure the social reality through the interpretation of divine norms. The textual evidence available does not allow to infer that judges took advantage of their position, as none of the *qāḍīs* that appear in the sources were accused of corruption, but this must also be taken cautiously, given their palpable self-centered character. It could be argued that no such accusations would make their way into the *Timbuktu Chronicles* or into Aḥmad Bābā's *tarājim* of his fellowmen, written with a more than evident intention of self-praise.

4 Spatial Mobility

The mobility of scholars to and from the *bilād al-sūdān* and within it appears early in Arabic geographical sources, from which we learn that Islam was introduced in the area through the contact of Muslim traders with local ones. Unfortunately, the information about this is vague. Mentions of African scholars travelling to Fez in expeditions sent by the rulers of the first great West African political entities, especially Mālī, do not come into detail, and so the names of these scholars and their teachers, and of the works they learnt, remain

25 Al-Saʿdī, *Taʾrīkh al-sūdān*, ed. Houdas, 76–77; English translation by Hunwick, J.O., *Timbuktu and the Songhay Empire*, 110–111.

26 Translated by Hunwick, J.O., *Timbuktu and the Songhay Empire*, 281.

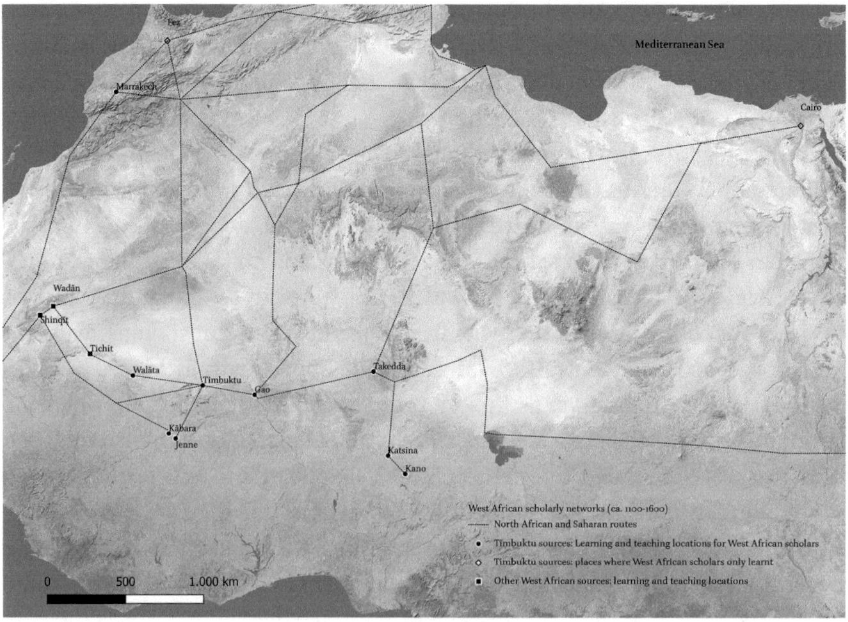

MAP 3.2 West African scholarly networks ca. 1100–1600

obscure. We may just assume that, before the 9th/15th century, there may have been a certain mobility of West African scholars towards the Maghrib, and from North African scholars into the *bilād al-sūdān*, following the trans-Saharan trade routes. However, in the 10th/16th-century the impact that the Orient had in the diffusion of Islamic learning in West Africa was probably bigger, although its reach probably was reduced to the elite of the *ʿulamāʾ*.

Aḥmad Bābā's biographical works include what may be considered, up to our present knowledge, as the first West African detailed account on the intellectual activities of scholars from the *bilād al-sūdān*. His works *Nayl al-ibtihāj* and *Kifāyat al-muḥtāj* include the biographies of fifteen *ʿulamāʾ*, including himself, among hundreds of other jurists of the Mālikī *madhhab*. In these works, as well as in the so-called *Timbuktu Chronicles*, there are barely any references of scholars traveling to the Maghrib *fī ṭalab al-ʿilm* in the 10th/16th century and beyond. Only one of the *sūdānī* scholars that appear in Aḥmad Bābā's *ṭabaqāt* works, Makhlūf al-Balbālī,[27] traveled to study at Fez and other locations in the Maghrib. This is striking, since mentions to North African scholarly communities and networks (Tuwātīs, Ghadāmisīs) in the *Timbuktu Chronicles* suggest that intellectual ties with North Africa, and especially the Central Maghrib,

27 *V. supra*, footnote 23.

were strong at this moment. However, it does seem that the mobility of scholars between the Maghrib and West Africa took place mainly southwards, where Timbuktu as well as other cities, such as Jenne, Gao, Kano or Katsina, attracted scholars who settled there to teach.[28]

Mobility within the *bilād al-sudān* followed the routes of the expansion of Islam, with the earliest Muslim communities, and also most important trade hubs, Jenne being probably one of these first nuclei, acting as poles for the diffusion of scholars who settled in newer locations and spread their knowledge. In later periods, from the 9th/15th century onwards, scholars also moved to other locations in order to learn from specific, more prestigious teachers, and this caused concentrations of scholarly households in places such as Timbuktu, and others such as Kābara probably before it, which later became the main hubs in West Africa. From this city, the teaching networks in the *bilād al-sūdān* were extended to other locations, such as Kano or Katsina, following the direction of the consolidation of Islam in other West African territories. This was the case of some of the members of the Aqīt household, who became *qāḍī*s in Kano or Katsina.[29] Some places of learning were abandoned by the *ʿulamāʾ* when their commercial importance declined: this was the case of Walāta, which flourished during the 9th/15th century, and lent its place to Timbuktu in the period that followed.[30] Political upheaval was another cause of migration for West African scholars, as shows the episode of the escape of some of the Timbuktu scholarly households (we may assume that they were accompanied by relatives engaged in commercial activities) due to their persecution by the Songhay ruler Sonni ʿAlī Ber in the early 10th/16th century. The notables moved back to Walāta for some time running away from his reprisals,

28 The mentions are especially abundant in the case of scholars from Tuwāt. See Voguet, É., "Tlemcen-Touat-Tombouctou: un réseau transsaharien de difussion du Mālikisme (fin VIII/XIVème–XI/XVIIème siècles)", *Revue des Mondes Musulmans et de la Méditerranée*, 141 (2017), 259–279. About the influence of North Africa, see Cuoq, J., *Histoire de l'islamisation de l'Afrique de l'Ouest*, 108–110; Levtzion, N., *Ancient Ghana and Mali*, London: Methuen, 1973, 201–202. Also, Konate, D., "Les relations culturelles entre Fès et le Mali entre le XIVème et le XVIème siècles", in *Fès et l'Afrique. Relations économiques, culturelles et spirituelles*, Rabat: Publications de l'Institut des Études Africaines, 1995, 48–49.

29 About the diffussion of Islamic learning in the area of the Central Sahel, see Hamani, D., *L'islam au Soudan central*, Paris: L'Harmattan, 2007.

30 About this Saharan town in the Southwest of present-day Mauritania, see Cleaveland, T., "Timbuktu and Walāta: lineages and higher education", in Bachir Diagne, S., and Jeppie, S., *The Meanings of Timbuktu*, Cape Town: HSRC, 2008, 77–93. And from the same author, *Becoming Walāta. A History of Saharan Formation and Transformation*, Portsmouth (NH): Heinemann, 2002. Also Osswald, R., *Schichtengesellschaft und islamisches Recht. Die* zawāyā *und Krieger der Westsahara im Spiegel von Rechtsgutachten des 16.–19. Jahrhunderts*, Wiesbaden: Harrassowitz, 1993.

then returned to Timbuktu. Quite surprisingly, the biographies featured in Aḥmad Bābā's *ṭabaqāt* works do not mention the intellectual activities that these scholars engaged in in Walāta, nor anything related to the relevance of the tradition of learning of that town.

Timbuktu was also one of the main centers of the book trade of the *bilād al-sūdān* and of the book copying industry that "distributed" knowledge into the area. The mobility of manuscripts was also propitiated by trans-Saharan trade, as has been shown in studies of this domain.[31] From what we can infer from the manuscript copies that have been preserved in public and private libraries south of the Sahara, works from every part of the Islamic world, early or late, were known and discussed by the elite of the *ʿulamāʾ* in the *bilād al-sūdān*. A great amount of these works, especially in the domains of law and jurisprudence, came from the Maghrib. What has been described as the "core curriculum" of West African *ʿulamāʾ* included the fundamental works of the Mālikī school of law, mainly from North African authors. However, this predominance was accompanied by the central role of certain Eastern figures of this *madhhab*, such as Khalīl b. Isḥāq and his *Mukhtaṣar*, which became the most popular legal work in the region. The *Mukhtaṣar*'s foremost place in *sūdānī* legal literature did not have any parallel in other genres, but many other Egyptian works made their way beyond the Sahara, their arrival being however hard to date.

From the 10th/16th century onwards, which is the first period to be dealt with in West African sources, the knowledge transfer from Eastern teachers takes place directly during the stay in Cairo of some of the West African *ʿulamāʾ* on the occasion of the pilgrimage to Mecca. While the *Timbuktu Chronicles* mention that "a large number of scholars" accompanied Mansā Mūsà, ruler of the Mālian Empire, when he performed the *ḥajj*, this account does not specify the names, households or ethnic affiliation of these *ʿulamāʾ*, nor if they learnt from Egyptian scholars, though we may suppose that they did.[32] Later travels, always related to pilgrimage to Mecca, are related by 11th/17th century West African sources in a much more detailed way, especially in Aḥmad Bābā's biographical works, but not with a broad scope from which we could infer how this phenomenon affected the *bilād al-sūdān* as a whole.[33] These works focus

31 Brigaglia, A., and Nobili, M., eds., *The Arts and Crafts of Literacy*, Berlin, Boston: De Gruyter, 2017. Also Krätli, G., and Lydon, G., eds., *The Trans-Saharan Book Trade*, *op. cit.*

32 Al-Saʿdī, *Taʾrīkh al-sūdān*, ed. Houdas, 7–8; English translation by Hunwick, J.O., *Timbuktu and the Songhay Empire*, 9–11.

33 Eight out of the fifteen *sūdānī* scholars included in al-Tinbuktī's *ṭabaqāt* spent some time learning in Cairo on the occasion of their pilgrimage to Mecca. See Novo, M.G., "Writing the History of Islamic Law in Africa", *op. cit.*

on scholars from Timbuktu or with a strong relationship to this city. In the case of Aḥmad Bābā's *ṭabaqāt* works, from which later West African historical and biographical works draw, they only refer to the intellectual development achieved during the stay in Cairo of members of the Aqīt household, or scholars that were very close to it, such as Muḥammad Baghayogho.[34] His account omits scholars from other prominent households of the city, and from other relevant places of learning, such as Walāta or Jenne, just to name two very important traditions of Islamic scholarship in the *bilād al-sūdān*, and makes it difficult to discern if the mobility of West African scholars towards Egypt was somehow encouraged or supported by political rulers. The mentions to royal expeditions in Imperial Mālī and Songhay with the participation of notable scholars in them may point at some degree of collaboration or economic support of travel *fī ṭalab al-ʿilm*, but this issue remains quite unclear.

It is more evident that spending some time in Cairo could not have been a generalized practice in premodern *bilād al-sūdān* because of the economic resources that it implied, and still, shows to what extent the scholarly elites of premodern West Africa may have been wealthy. Although it is very possible that more scholars than those that appear in the sources did travel to Egypt, the effect of those who effectively stayed in Cairo was potentiated as their knowledge spread through the West African scholarly networks when they returned home. The knowledge that they obtained in the central lands of Islam, once again, was transferred for social capital, as these *ʿulamāʾ* became the most prestigious and revered teachers of the region, being sought after by scholars from their cities and other places in West Africa. In the case of the Aqīts, what we could define as their "Egyptian capital" coincides with their intellectual and sociopolitical century of grandeur, in which they monopolized the judgeship of Timbuktu. It is difficult to try to find out what came before, if their power or their knowledge, but it seems difficult that they would occupy the most prominent place in an environment that busted with scholars if they wouldn't have overshadowed their neighbors, their rivals, with the distinction brought about by what they had learnt in the Orient. The scope of the Egyptian influence over West African *ʿulamāʾ* is also witnessed by the abundance of summaries,

34 The *Timbuktu Chronicles* draw on Aḥmad Bābā's *Kifāya* for their *tarājim* of some ʿulamāʾ, but so do later works such as the biographical dictionary of al-Bartaylī (Muḥammad b. Abī Bakr b. Ṣiddīq al-Walātī, d. 1805), *Fatḥ al-shakūr li-maʿrifat aʿyān ʿulamāʾ al-Takrūr*, ed. al-Kattānī, M.I., and Ḥajjī, M., Beirut, Dār al-gharb al-islāmī, 1981; French translation in El Hamel, C., *La vie intellectuelle islamique dans le Sahel Ouest-Africain*, Paris: L'Harmattan, 2002; and is also the case of Muḥammad Bello's (d. 1837), *Infāq al-maysūr fī taʾrīkh bilād Takrūr*, Rabat: Institut des Études Africaines, 1996.

commentaries and works inspired by Egyptian authors that were produced in the *bilād al-sūdān*, as has already been brought up by several authors.[35]

There is another relevant aspect in what refers to geographic mobility in Aḥmad Bābā's *ṭabaqāt*, which should be taken into consideration: the deportation of the author himself, and its consequences in his writings. Although the work *Nayl al-ibtihāj* was probably started before the Saʿdian invasion of the *bilād al-sūdān*, a great part of it, and probably some of the biographies of members of the Aqīt Household that were featured in it, were composed during the period of forced exile that he suffered in Marrakech, where he was taken along with other prominent members of his clan as a punishment for their opposition to Moroccan rule over the Songhay territories. In such a context, the *tarājim* of the Aqīts can be understood as his credentials to the learned elites of the Saʿdid capital, who revered his vast knowledge, but really could not "contextualize" his social position. His omission of scholars other than those from his own household, which clearly obscures the trajectories of many other West African scholars, from Timbuktu and from other relevant locations, may have intended to emphasize his role as a reference on *sūdānī* matters for North African scholars. Some of the legal opinions that he issued for the Maghribian audience are related to trade affairs between North Africa and the *bilād al-sūdān*, of which his legal responses (*Ajwiba*) on slavery, forerunning his renowned *fatwa*, the work *Miʿrāj al-ṣuʿūd*, are a paramount example.[36] The beginnings of the 11th/17th century witnessed a sharp increase of trade between the *bilād al-sūdān* and North Africa, which may also explain the author's popularity as an informed but unofficial *muftī*, who could authoritatively deliver legitimate opinions about a region that most North Africans very much ignored.

The context in which the works *Nayl al-ibtihāj* and *Kifāyat al-muḥtāj* were composed, that of Aḥmad Bābā's forced exile in Marrakech, as mentioned before, could explain his silence on the intellectual ties of the *bilād al-sūdān* and the Maghrib, in the sense that he may have intended to differentiate himself from the *ʿulamā* of Marrakech by highlighting the Egyptian background of his knowledge, while obscuring the one with a clear North African origin. However, it is also possible that his emphasis on his Oriental learning, although an effective way to distinguish himself from the *ʿulamāʾ* of Marrakech, may also

35 See Hall, B.S. and Stewart, C.S., "The historic 'core curriculum'", *op. cit.*

36 Aḥmad Bābā's *Ajwiba* on slavery were issued in the *zāwiya* of Tamgrout, in present-day Southern Morocco, where he stopped for un unknown period of time on his way back to Timbuktu, after being released from his forced exile in Marrakech in 1016/1607. The work *Miʿrāj al-ṣuʿūd* was finished in 1024/1616, almost ten years later.

reflect the change of trend in the geographical mobility of scholars in premodern West Africa. While traveling to the Maghrib, where Fez was the main scholarly destination, took place in the earlier stages of the spread of Islam in West Africa, it is possible that the high economic levels reached in the Empire of Mālī and after it allowed wealthy households to travel to Egypt instead, where intellectual life could be considered as more attractive. If the relevance of the references was not so little, perhaps it could be significant that a not so wealthy scholar, who used to work in order to make a living, Makhlūf al-Balbālī, was the only West African scholar in Aḥmad Bābā's biographical works who traveled to Fez instead of Egypt.[37] Unfortunately, the available textual evidence does not allow to make any substantial conclusion about the mobility of West African *ʿulamāʾ* up to the 11th/17th century.

5 Conclusions

Our knowledge of the intellectual life of West Africa before the turn of the 11th/17th century remains sketchy, although we may conclude that the processes of professionalization of Islamic knowledge were clearly those of a context of recent and ongoing Islamization, which were considerably less specialized in the periphery than in the central lands of Islam. It is tempting to identify the self-conscious attitude that emanates from Aḥmad Bābā's *tarājim* of West African scholars with the emergence of the Ṣanhāja and of the dominion of the *bīḍān* in the Sahel. The self-consciousness of the Timbuktu *ʿulamāʾ* is clearly distinguishable in the sources that have been reviewed in this chapter, and some details may point at an already existing divide among non-Berber *sūdān* and Berber *bīḍān*, such as the almost complete omission of non-Berbers among the West African scholars featured in Aḥmad Bābā's *ṭabaqat*.[38] This occurs, too, but is much vaguer in the *Timbuktu Chronicles*, as has been mentioned above in this chapter and it could mean that the self-consciousness of the elite of the *ʿulamāʾ* as a body may have been stronger at the time than the ethnic divisions among the *jamāʿa*.

In what refers to the process of learning of the Islamic sciences, the sources include too few transmission chains, but they allow us to argue that in the premodern *bilād al-sūdān* Berbers and non-Berbers alike shared the same scholarly background, in whose creation many ethnic groups had participated. It

37 *V. supra*, footnote 23.

38 See Hall, B., *A History of race in Muslim West Africa*, Cambridge: Cambridge University Press, 2011, 55–68.

is highly probable that the Timbuktu tradition on which Aḥmad Bābā prided himself before his Maghribian peers flourished from a prior non-Berber tradition, that must have had its origins in locations that he deliberately omitted from his account, such as Kābara, Jenne or Walāta. This tradition of learning had strong ties with the Maghrib, and Maghribian Mālikī jurisprudence remained at the core of the teaching of Islam in the premodern *bilād al-sūdān*. There are, again, too few references of the mobility of West African scholars towards the Maghrib, but it seems quite clear that the influence of the North African communities who settled in different locations south of the Sahara had a determining influence in the intellectual life of the *bilād al-sūdān*, to which, in later periods, a close contact with Cairene scholars would add specialized knowledge on logic and Sufism, among other subjects of study.

Early in his career, in the *opusculum* called *Jalb al-niʿma*, Aḥmad Bābā started reflecting on the social and political circumstances around him, which were those of the violent strife of the descendants of Askya Muḥammad, which lasted for decades.[39] The situation may explain his interest in the nature of political power and social leadership, *riyāsa*, a term that occurs a number of times in his biographies of members of his household. Al-Tinbuktu's interest in the sociopolitical role of the *ʿulamāʾ* may also have its origin in the very close relationships of Songhay rulers with the scholarly elites of Timbuktu, to which he belonged. We only know one side of this relationship, as what we can read in the *Timbuktu Chronicles* is certainly the view of the city's *ʿulamāʾ*. So it is difficult to try to evaluate the extent to which they participated in the successional conflict of the Songhay princes, though some mentions indicate that they did collaborate with some of the throne pretenders.[40] The Timbuktu notables had a history of getting involved in political conflicts, as was the case when Sonni ʿAlī, first ruler of the Songhay Empire, came to power at the end of the 9th/15th century, the *jamāʿa* of Sankoré had backed Akil, and therefore the Tuareg, in his conflict with the new power, probably by questioning the religious legitimacy of Sonni ʿAlī. This was clearly reflected in the animosity with which the *Timbuktu Chronicles* portray the new ruler, almost as a pagan.[41]

Despite the image of power and moral victory of the Timbuktu *jamāʿa* over Songhay rulers that can be observed in Aḥmad Bābā's biographical works as well as in the Timbuktu *Tawārīkh*, the symbiosis that existed between the

39 *V. supra*, footnote 7.

40 The Timbuktu *ʿulamāʾ* took the side of one of the pretenders of the Songhay throne, Muḥammad al-Ṣādiq, whose rebellion is described in al-Saʿdī, *Taʾrīkh al-sūdān*, 121–124; English translation in Hunwick, J.O., *Timbuktu and the Songhay Empire*, 168–171.

41 See Gomez, M.A., *African dominion*, 183–184.

Empire and its preeminent scholars allowed for some independence on their behalf, though surely less than what we can read in the sources.[42] It is highly doubtful that the elite of the *ʿulamāʾ*, as a representative of the interests of the major households of Timbuktu, could directly challenge the rule of Gao and its intricate administrative organization, which responded to tax collection and the keeping of order and safety, especially in the trade routes that were fundamental for the economic functioning of the Empire.[43] A body of *ʿulamāʾ*, from scholars in religious positions to secretaries, and from *imāms* to the great *quḍāt*, was a fundamental structure for the political authorities, although their power, the symbolic capital derived from religious legitimacy, may have at times been hard to handle, since, as we have seen through the history of the Aqīt household, a knowledge career in 10th/16th century *bilād al-sūdān* could promote social advancement, even to the highest levels of sociopolitical leadership.

Acknowledgments

This article is part of the results of the Research Group (GIF) MASYG (University of Alcalá, UAH) and the Research Sub-Project "Human Dynamics in North Africa: peoples and landscapes in historical perspective (DHUNA)" (HAR2017-82152-C2-2-P; P.I.: de Felipe, E., University of Alcalá), which, together with the Research Sub-Project "Cultural Geography of the Medieval and Modern Islamic Maghreb Online (GEOMAGRED)" (HAR2017-82152-C2-1-P; P.I.: Manzano, M.Á., IEMYRhd, University of Salamanca), is integrated in the Coordinated Research

42 In Aḥmad Bābā's biographical works, see the description of the author's father, Aḥmad b. Aḥmad b. ʿUmar b. Muḥammad Aqīt (d. 991/1583), in Aḥmad Bābā al-Tinbuktī, *Nayl al-ibtihāj*, ed. al-Harrāma, #144, 141–2; *Kifāyat al-muḥtāj*, ed. Muṭīʿ, I, #94, 137–9; Al-Bartaylī, *Fatḥ al-shakūr*, VI, 29–30; Kaḥḥāla, ʿU.R., *Muʿjam al-muʾallifīn*, II, 33; Cherbonneau, M., *Essai*, 21–4. Also see Hunwick, J.O. (ed.), *Arabic Literature of Africa IV*, 15–17. See also in the biographies of the *qāḍīs* Maḥmūd b. ʿUmar Aqīt and his son, al-ʿĀqib, *v. supra*, footnote 14. For the Timbuktu *Tawārīkh*, see Al-Saʿdī, *Taʾrīkh al-sūdān*, 110; English translation in Hunwick, J.O., *Timbuktu and the Songhay Empire*, 154. See also De Moraes Farias, P., "Intellectual innovation and reinvention of the Sahel: the seventeenth-century Timbuktu Chronicles", in Jeppie, S., and Bachir Diagne, S. (eds.), *The meanings of Timbuktu*, Cape Town: Human Sciences Research Council, 2008, 97. Also, *v. supra* the works of Stewart, C., and Hall, B., footnote 2.

43 The institutions and authorities of Songhay administration were brightly described by Hunwick in "Songhay: an interpretative essay", the introduction of his *Timbuktu and the Songhay Empire*.

Project "Cultural Geography of the Maghreb and Human Dynamics in North Africa (MAGNA)" (HAR2017-82152-C2-1-P) (Coord.: Manzano, M.Á.), funded by the Spanish Ministry of Science, Innovation and Universities and the FEDER Program of the European Union. The author wishes to thank Kaj Öhrnberg for his thorough revision and insightful comments, and Juan Javier García-Abad Alonso for his aid regarding Geographic Information Systems, as well as the two anonymous reviewers of the chapter.

Bibliography

Sources

ʿAbd al-Raḥmān b. ʿAbd Allāh al-Saʿdī. *Taʾrīkh al-sūdān*. Arabic text and French translation by O. Houdas (Paris: Ernest Leroux, 1900). English trans. and ed. Hunwick, J.O. *Timbuktu and the Songhay Empire. Al-Saʿdī's* Taʾrīkh al-sūdān *down to 1613 and Other Contemporary Documents*, Leiden: Brill, 1999.

Aḥmad Bābā al-Tinbuktī. *Kifāyat al-muḥtāj li-maʿrifat man laysa fī l-Dībāj*, intr. and ed. Mutīʿ, M., Rabat: Wizārat al-awqāf wa-l-shuʾūn al-islāmiyya, 2000, vol. 2, 281.

Aḥmad Bābā al-Tinbuktī. *Miʿrāj al-ṣuʿūd. Aḥmad Bābā's Replies on slavery*, ed. and trans. Hunwick, J.O., and Harrak, F., Rabat: Institut des Études Africaines, 2000.

Aḥmad Bābā al-Tinbuktī. *Nayl al-ibtihāj bi-taṭrīz al-Dībāj*, ed. ʿAmar, M., Cairo: Maktabat al-thaqāfa al-dīniyya, 2004, 2 vols.; ed. al-Harrāma, ʿA.H., Tripoli (Lybia): Kulliyyat al-daʿwa al-islāmiyya, 2000; ed. on the margins of Ibn Farḥūn's *al-Dībāj al-mudhhab*, Cairo: Maṭbaʿat al-Maʿāhid, 1932.

Aḥmad Bābā al-Tinbuktī. *Tuḥfat al-fuḍalāʾ bi-baʿḍ faḍāʾil al-ʿulamāʾ*, ed. Sāmī, S., Rabat: Institut des Études Africaines, 1992.

Al-Baghdādī. *Hādiyat al-ʿārifīn, asmāʾ al-muʾallifīn wa-āthār al-muṣannifīn*, ed. Bilge, R., and Inal, M.K., Istanbul: Wikālat al-maʿārif, 1951–1955.

Al-Baghdādī. *Īḍāḥ al-maknūn fī l-dhayl ʿalà kashf al-ẓunūn ʿan asāmī l-kutub wa-l-funūn*, ed. Yaltakaya, S., Beirut: Dār al-kutub al-ʿilmiyya, 1992.

Al-Bartaylī. *Fatḥ al-shakūr li-maʿrifat aʿyān ʿulamāʾ al-Takrūr*, ed. al-Kattānī, M.I., and Ḥajjī, M., Beirut, Dār al-gharb al-islāmī, 1981; French translation in El Hamel, C., *La vie intellectuelle islamique dans le Sahel Ouest-Africain*, Paris: L'Harmattan, 2002.

Al-Muḥibbī. *Khulāṣat al-athar fī aʿyān al-qarn al-ḥādī ʿashar*, Beirut: Dār Ṣāḍir, 1966.

Al-Qādirī. *Nashr al-mathānī*, ed. Ḥajjī, M., and Tawfīq, A., Rabat: al-Jamaʿiyya al-maghribiyya li-l-taʾlīf, 1986.

Bello, M. *Infāq al-maysūr fī taʾrīkh bilād Takrūr*, ed. and trans. Chadli, B., Rabat: Institut des Études Africaines, 1996.

Ibn Baṭṭūṭa. *Tuḥfat al-nuẓẓār fī gharā'ib al-amṣār wa-ʿajā'ib al-asfār*, ed. Defrémery, C., and Sanguinetti, B.R., Paris: Anthropos, 1968, IV, 394–5 and 397–8.

Maḥmūd Kaʿtī Ibn al-Ḥājj al-Mutawakkil. *Ta'rīkh al-fattāsh fī akhbār al-buldān*, Arabic text and French translation by Houdas, O., and Delafosse, M., Paris: Ernest Leroux, 1913.

Studies

Bivar, H.D., and Hiskett, M. "The Arabic Literature of Nigeria to 1804: a provisional account", *Bulletin of the School of Oriental and African Studies*, 25, 3 (1962), 110–1.

Brigaglia, A., and Nobili, M. eds., *The Arts and Crafts of Literacy*, Berlin, Boston: De Gruyter, 2017.

Brockelmann, C. *Geschichte der arabischen Litteratur*, Leiden: Brill, 1937–1942.

Castries, H. de. "La conquête du Soudan par Moulaye Ahmed el-Mansôur", *Hespéris*, III (1923), 438–88.

Cherbonneau, M. *Essai sur la littérature arabe au Soudan d'après le Takmilet-ed-dibadje d'Ahmed Baba, le Tombouctien*, Constantine-Paris: Abadie, A. Leleux, 1861.

Cleaveland, T. "Timbuktu and Walāta: lineages and higher education", in Bachir Diagne, S., and Jeppie, S. *The Meanings of Timbuktu*, Cape Town: HSRC, 2008.

Cleaveland, T. *Becoming Walāta. A History of Saharan Formation and Transformation*, Portsmouth (NH): Heinemann, 2002.

Cleaveland, T. "Timbuktu and Walāta: lineages and higher education", in Bachir Diagne, S., and Jeppie, S. (eds.), *The Meanings of Timbuktu*, Cape Town: HSRC, 2008, 77–94.

Cuoq, J. *Histoire de l'islamisation de l'Afrique de l'Ouest*, Paris: Geuthner, 1984.

De Moraes Farias, P. "Intellectual innovation and reinvention of the Sahel: the seventeenth-century Timbuktu Chronicles", in Bachir Diagne, S., and Jeppie, S. (eds.), *The Meanings of Timbuktu*, Cape Town: HSRC, 2008, 95–108.

García Novo, M. "Islamic law and slavery in premodern West Africa", *Entremóns. UPF Journal of World History*, 2 (2011), 1–20.

García Novo, M. "Writing the history of Islamic law in West Africa: scholars from the *bilād al-sūdān* in Aḥmad Bābā al-Tinbuktī's biographical works", *Die Welt des Islams* (forthcoming).

García-Arenal, M. *Aḥmad al-Manṣūr. The Beginnings of Modern Morocco*, London: Oneworld, 2009.

Gomez, M.A. *African Dominion: A New History of Empire in Early and Medieval West Africa*, Princeton, New Jersey: Princeton University Press, 2019.

Hall, B. *A History of race in Muslim West Africa*, Cambridge: Cambridge University Press, 2011.

Hall, B. "Rethinking the place of Timbuktu in the Intellectual History of Muslim West Africa", in Green, T., and Rossi, B. (eds.), *Landscapes, Sources and Intellectual Projects of the West African Past*, Leiden: Brill, 2018, 239–258.

Hamani, D. *L'islam au Soudan central*, Paris: L'Harmattan, 2007.

Hunwick, J.O. "Aḥmad Bābā and the Moroccan invasion of the Sudan (1591)", *Journal of the Historical Society of Nigeria*, 2/3 (1962), 311–328.

Hunwick, J.O. "A new source for the biography of Aḥmad Bābā al-Tinbuktī (1556–1627)", *Bulletin of the School of Oriental and African Studies*, 27, 3 (1964), 568.

Hunwick, J.O. "Further light on Aḥmad Bābā al-Tinbuktī", *Research Bulletin, Centre of Arabic Documentation*, 1, 2 (1966), 19–31.

Hunwick, J.O. "Studies in the *Tārīkh al-fattāsh* I: Its Authors and Textual History," *Research Bulletin – Centre of Arabic Documentation*, 5 (1969), 57–65.

Hunwick, J.O. "A contribution to the study of Islamic teaching traditions in West Africa: the career of Muḥammad Baghayogho, 930/1523–4", *Islam et Sociétés au Sud du Sahara* (1990), 149–62.

Hunwick, J.O. "Studies in the *Ta'rīkh al-fattāsh* II: An Alleged Charter of Privilege Issued by Askiya *al-Ḥājj* Muḥammad to the Descendants of Mori Hawgāro," *Sudanic Africa*, 3 (1992), 133–148.

Hunwick, J.O. (ed.) *Arabic Literature of Africa IV*, Leiden: Brill, 2003.

Kaḥḥāla, ʿU.R. *Muʿjam al-mu'allifīn. Tarājim muṣannifī al-kutub al-ʿarabiyya*, Damascus: al-Maktaba al-ʿarabiyya, 1957–1961.

Konate, D. "Les relations culturelles entre Fès et le Mali entre le XIVème et le XVIème siècles", in *Fès et l'Afrique. Relations économiques, culturelles et spirituelles*, Rabat: Publications de l'Institut des Études Africaines, 1995, 48–49.

Levtzion, N. "A Seventeenth-Century Chronicle by Ibn al-Mukhtār: A Critical Study of *Ta'rīkh al-fattāsh*," *Bulletin of the School of Oriental and African Studies*, 34, 3 (1971), 571–593.

Levtzion, N. *Ancient Ghana and Mali*, London: Methuen, 1973.

Levtzion, N., and Pouwells, R. *The History of Islam in Africa*, Athens: Ohio University Press, 2000.

Makhlūf, M. *Shajarat al-nūr al-zakiyya fī ṭabaqāt al-mālikiyya*, Cairo: 1930.

Nobili, M. *Sultan, Caliph, and the Renewer of the Faith: Ahmad Lobbo, the Tārīkh Al-Fattāsh and the Making of an Islamic State in West Africa*, Cambridge: Cambridge University Press, 2020.

Norris, H.T. "Ṣanhājah Scholars of Timbuctoo", *Bulletin of the School of Oriental and African Studies*, 30, 3 (1967), 634–640.

Osswald, R. *Schichtengesellschaft und islamisches Recht. Die* zawāyā *und Krieger der Westsahara im Spiegel von Rechtsgutachten des 16.–19. Jahrhunderts*, Wiesbaden: Harrassowitz, 1993.

Pianel, G. "Les préliminaires de la conquête du Soudan par Moulaye Ahmed el-Mansôur, d'après trois documents inédits", *Hespéris*, XL (1953), 185–97.

Saad, E.N. *Social History of Timbuktu. The role of Muslim Scholars and Notables, 1400–1900*, Cambridge: Cambridge University Press, 1983.

Sadki, Ḥ. *Makhṭūṭāt Aḥmad Bābā al-Tinbuktī fī-l-khazā'in al-maghribiyya*, Rabat: Institut des Études Africaines, 1996.

Stewart, C. "Calibrating the scholarship of Timbuktu", in Green, T., and Rossi, B. (eds.), *Landscapes, Sources and Intellectual Projects of the West African Past*, Leiden: Brill, 2018, 220–238.

Stewart, C., and Hall, B. "The historic 'core curriculum' and the book market in Islamic West Africa", in Krätli, G., and Lydon, G., eds., *The Trans-Saharan Book Trade*, Leiden: Brill, 2011, 109–174.

Van Dalen, D. *Doubt, Scholarship and Society in 17th-Century Central Sudanic Africa*, Leiden: Brill, 2016.

Voguet, É. "Tlemcen-Touat-Tombouctou: un réseau transsaharien de difussion du Mālikisme (fin VIII/XIVème–XI/XVIIème siècles)", *Revue des Mondes Musulmans et de la Méditerranée*, 141 (2017), 259–279.

Wilks, I. "The transmission of Islamic learning in the Western Sudan", in Goody, J. (ed.), *Literacy in Traditional Societies*, Cambridge: Cambridge University Press, 1968, 162–197.

Zouber, M. *Aḥmad Bābā de Tombouctou (1556/1627): sa vie et son œuvre*, Paris: Maisonneuve et Larose, 1977.

PART 2

Social Mobility and Professionalization

CHAPTER 4

The Professional Mobility of Qāḍī ʿAbd al-Jabbār between the Quest for Knowledge and the Confluence with Power

Amal Belkamel

1 The Main Mobility Stages in ʿAbd al-Jabbār's Quest for Knowledge

ʿAbd al-Jabbār, born around 325/930 in Asadābād around the city of Hamadhān, would become one of the most famous Sunnī-Muʿtazilī theologians.[1] His quest for knowledge led him through several cities and can be summarized in two main stages. The first stage, from 340/950–1 until 346/957–8, was when he studied the foundations of his religious education, including the Qurʾanic exegesis and ḥadīth in Hamadhān. Al-Khaṭīb al-Baghdādī reports that ʿAbd al-Jabbār studied ḥadīth and Shāfiʿī *fiqh* with Zubayr b. ʿAbd al-Wāḥid al-Asadābādī (d. 347/958–9) and Abū-l-Ḥasan ʿAlī b. Ibrahīm b. Salāma al-Qaṭṭān (d. 345/956–7), received teaching from ʿAlī b. Brāhīm b. Salama al-Qazwīnī (d. 345/956–7), ʿAbdallāh b. Jaʿfar al-Iṣbahānī (d. 346/958) and ʿAbd al-Raḥmān b. Ḥamdān al-Jallāb (d. 342/954).[2] Some sources claimed that at this time he also learned the Ashʿarī doctrine.[3] The second stage was characterised by his departure to

---

1 According to al-Subkī (d. 771/1370), his full name is Abu-l-Ḥasan ʿAbd al-Jabbār b. Aḥmad b. ʿAbd al-Jabbār b. Aḥmad b. al-Khalīl b. ʿAbdallāh al-Qāḍī al-Hamadhānī al-Asadābādī. See al-Subkī, *Tabaqāt al-Shāfiʿiyya al-Kubrā*, ed. Maḥmūd Muḥammad al-Ṭanāhi and Abd al-Fattāḥ Muḥammad al-Ḥilw (Cairo: Maṭbaʿat ʿĪsa al-Bābī, 1964–76), 5: 443. For the sources and monographies relating the life and works of ʿAbd al-Jabbār, see Johannes Reinier Peters, *God's created speech: A study in the Speculative Theology of the Muʿtazilî Qâḍî l-Quḍât Abū l-Ḥasan ʿAbd al-Jabbâr bn Aḥmad al-Hamaḏânî.* (Leiden: E.J Brill, 1976), 8 n. 23.
The combination of Sunnī-Muʿtazilī expression here refers to the fact that ʿAbd al-Jabbār embraces the Shāfiʿī doctrine in the branches of the law and Muʿtazilī principles in the foundations of the theology (*kāna yantaḥilu madhhab al-Shāfiʿī fi-l-furūʿ wa madhāhib al-Muʿtazila fi-l-uṣūl*). See al-Khaṭīb al-Baghdādī, *Tārīkh Baghdād*, ed. Bashshār ʿAwwād Maʿrūf, 17 vols. (Beirut: Dār al-Gharb al-Islāmī, 2001), 12:414.

2 Al-Baghdādī, *Tārīkh Baghdād*, 12:414–16. For more details, see Wilferd Madelung, "ʿAbd al-Jabbār B. Aḥmad," *Encyclopeadia Iranica*, 1/2, 116–17; Gabriel Said Reynolds, *A Muslim theologian in the sectarian milieu ʿAbd al-Jabbār and the critique of Christian origins* (Leiden, Boston: Brill, 2004), 45–6.

3 Peters mentioned the views of al-Jushamī and Ibn al-Murtaḍā and set this conversion during ʿAbd al-Jabbār's stay in Hamadhān and Iṣfahān. Peters, *God's created speech*, 9. Several

 | DOI:10.1163/9789004467637_006

Baṣra, in 346/957–8, where he was initiated into speculative theology (*kalām*) with the Baṣran theologian Abū Isḥāq b. ʿAyyāsh (d. 386/996) who was the pupil of Abū Hāshim al-Jubbāʾī, Abū ʿAbdallāh al-Baṣrī (d. 369/980) and Abū ʿAli b. Khallād.[4] Although he attended different circles (*ikhtalafa ilā majālis al-ʿulamāʾ*) when he began to study *kalām* in Baṣra, the sources unanimously report the name of Abū Isḥāq b. ʿAyyāsh in Baṣra and Abū Abdallah al-Baṣrī in Baghdād, both Muʿtazilī.[5]

ʿAbd al-Jabbār would have met Abū Isḥāq b. ʿAyyāsh in ʿAskar Mukram, known to shelter the fervor of Muʿtazilī theological discussions. At this very place ʿAbd al-Jabbār attended the assemblies of Sheikh Abū Aḥmad b. Salāma, who was among the circle of Baghdādī theologians. ʿAbd al-Jabbār said that he was among the rigorist ones toward his companions (*kāna mina al-mutaʿaṣṣibīn alā aṣḥābinā*).[6] The companions mentioned by ʿAbd al-Jabbār are none other than Abū Hāshim al-Jubbāʾī and his pupils, the masters of his mentors Abū Isḥāq b. ʿAyyāsh and Abū ʿAbdallāh al-Baṣrī.[7] The affirmation of ʿAbd al-Jabbār

---

sources support the formation of ʿAbd al-Jabbār following the Shāfiʿī *fiqh* but very few mention the change of his credo at the *uṣūl* level. Al-Ḥākim al-Jushamī, *Sharḥ al-ʿUyūn*, ed. Fuʾād Sayyid (Tunis: al-Dār al-Tūnusiyya li-l-Nashr, 1393/1974), 366. At this stage of my research, I have not found any evidence directly from the works of ʿAbd al-Jabbār where he affirms it himself. The fact that he had received the basis of the teachings of the Shāfiʿī *fiqh* before starting his study of *kalām* did not convert him, de facto, to Ashʿarism, whose main figures were Shāfiʿī.

4 Two different formulations are found in the sources: Abū Isḥāq b. ʿAbbās or Abū Isḥāq b. ʿAyyāsh. In Fuʾād Sayyid's edition of *Faḍl al-iʿtizāl wa ṭabaqāt al-Muʿtazila*, it is referred to as Abū Isḥāq b. ʿAbbās, see *Faḍl al-iʿtizāl wa ṭabaqāt al-Muʿtazila*, ed. Fuʾād Sayyid (Tunis: al-Dār al-Tūnusiyya li-l-Nashr,1974), 328. In his notice on ʿAbd al-Jabbār Madelung uses the name Abū Isḥāq b. ʿAyyāsh, see Wilferd Madelung, "ʿAbd al-Jabbār B. Aḥmad," *Encyclopeadia Iranica*, 1/2, 116–17. Reynolds does the same, see *A Muslim Theologian in the Sectarian Milieu*, 46, n. 129. I will follow the same formulation. For the mentors of ʿAbd al-Jabbār, see ʿAbd al-Jabbār al-Hamadhānī, *Faḍl al-iʿtizāl wa ṭabaqāt al-Muʿtazila*, 325.

5 Al-Jushamī, *Sharḥ al-ʿUyūn*, 366. During his stay in Baghdād he studied under Abū ʿAbdallāh al-Ḥusayn b. ʿAlī (d. 367/978). See George F. Hourani, *Islamic rationalism: The Ethics of ʿAbd al-Jabbār* (Oxford: Clarendon Press, 1971), 6. Al-Baghdādī reports that ʿAbd al-Jabbār entered Baghdād as a pilgrim (*ḥājjan*) and gave *hadīth* there. See al-Baghdādī, *Tārīkh Baghdād*, 12:414. The first pilgrimage might be dated in the year 339/950, the second in 379/989. See Reynolds who bases his sources on Abū l-Ḥusayn Hilāl b. al-Muḥassin al-Ṣābiʾ, *Tuḥfat al-umarāʾ fī tārīkh al-wuzarāʾ*, ed. Aḥmad Farrāj (Cairo: Dār Iḥyāʾ al-Kutub al-ʿArabiyya, 1958). Reynolds, *A Muslim theologian in the sectarian milieu*, 45 n. 127.

6 Abd al-Jabbār counts him among the circle of Abū ʿAbdallāh Muḥammad Ibn ʿUmar al-Ṣaymarī and the *mutakallimīn* of Baghdād. See ʿAbd al-Jabbār al-Hamadhānī, *Faḍl al-iʿtizāl wa ṭabaqāt al-Muʿtazila*, 308, 333. For more details about ʿAskar Mukram see C.E. Bosworth, "ʿAskar Mokram," *Encyclopædia Iranica* (December 1987) online at http://www.iranicaonline.org/articles/askar-mokram-lit (accessed March 10, 2019).

7 Al-Jushamī, *Sharḥ al-ʿUyūn*, 365.

indicated that during his stay in Baṣra, while he received a solid knowledge of Muʿtazilī teachings, he already had a clear inclination for the school of Abū Hāshim al-Jubbāʾī, whose principles he would rigorously defend until the end of his life.

Baṣra would be a turning point for ʿAbd al-Jabbār as he moved towards *iʿtizāl*.[8] One point is certain, *kalām* finds more resonance in him than *fiqh*. According to reports from al-Ḥākim al-Jushamī (d. 494/1101) ʿAbd al-Jabbār had reached new heights in the knowledge of *fiqh* but chose to focus on *kalām*. He did so by affirming that "the *fiqh* concerns those who seek worldly things while the science of *kalām* has no other purpose than God".[9] By preferring theology (*kalām*) to law (*fiqh*), he gives primacy to the dialectics of theologians rather than to the casuistry of the jurists. Although he was going to be a chief judge (*qāḍī al-quḍāt*) later on, the concern for rational argumentation on divine questions takes precedence over following legal methods of the jurists (*fuqahāʾ*) who deal with worldly questions. In his path to *iʿtizāl*, ʿAbd al-Jabbār moved to Baghdād (the political capital of the ʿAbbasid caliphate) where he studied with Abū ʿAbdallāh al-Baṣrī (d. 369/980) – a renowned theologian and former master of the Muʿtazilī school in Baṣra – and began the composition of his own works including *Mutashābih al-Qurʾan* (an exegesis of the ambiguous verses of the Qurʾan).[10] His devotion to his master was such that he considered

8 According to the account of the opponents of the Muʿtazila, this term originates from a dispute over the status of the Muslim sinner (*fāsiq*) between Ḥasan al-Baṣrī (d. 110/728) and Wāṣil b. ʿAṭāʾ (d. 131/748) (and ʿAmr b. ʿUbayd (d. 145/762)) where the latter separated (*iʿtazala*) from him. For Wāṣil the *fāsiq* was neither totally a believer nor totally infidel but was in an intermediate state (*al-manzila bayn al-manzilatayn*). This position will give rise to one of the five fundamental principles of the Muʿtazila in addition to Divine unicity (*tawḥīd*) and justice (*ʿadl*), Commanding right and forbidding wrong (*amr bi-l-maʿrūf wa-l-nahy ʿan al-munkar*) and, the Promise and the Threat (*waʿd wa-l-waʿīd*). The *iʿtizāl* founded one of the most important theological schools of Islam. See Daniel Gimaret, "Muʿtazila," *Encyclopaedia of Islam*, Second Edition, ed. P. Bearman, Th. Bianquis, C.E. Bosworth, E. van Donzel, W.P. Heinrichs (Leiden: Brill, 1960–2004). ʿAbd al-Jabbār reports that the Muʿtazila were the only sect that would not have refused the appellation (*laqab*) that has been attributed to them. The Muʿtazila are the people of the middle way (*muqtaṣida*) who moved away from excess and simplification (*iʿtazalat al-ifrāṭ wa-l-taqsīr*) and followed the indications (*salakat al-adilla*). ʿAbd al-Jabbār al-Hamadhānī, *Faḍl al-iʿtizāl wa ṭabaqāt al-Muʿtazila*, 165.

9 Al-Jushamī, *Sharḥ al-ʿUyūn*, 367.

10 Reynolds, *Muslim Theologian in the Sectarian Milieu*, 47. ʿAbd al-Jabbār refers to the introduction of *Mutashābih al-Qurʾan* and states that he was dictating this book during the composition of *al-Mughnī*. See ʿAbd al-Jabbār al-Hamadhānī, *Kitāb al-Mughnī fī abwāb al-tawḥīd wa-l-ʿadl*, 10 vols. (Beirut: Dār al-Kutub al-ʿIlmiyya, 2012), 20/2:243, 17:94. For the place of Baghdād during the fourth/tenth century see Marius Canard, "Baġdād au IVe siècle de l'Hégire (Xe siècle de l'ère chrétienne)," *Arabica* 9/3 (October 1962): 267–87.

switching from the Shāfiʿī to the Ḥanafī *madhhab*, the same as al-Baṣrī.[11] ʿAbd al-Jabbār describes his mentor as one who surpassed his own masters by forging the heights of *kalām* and *fiqh* through his effort and perseverance.[12] Abū ʿAbdallāh al-Baṣrī was an important figure of Muʿtazilism and was consulted by the Būyids governor of Baghdād ʿAḍud al-Dawla on issues relating to *ijtihād*. This fact shows the notoriety and the important rank that the master of ʿAbd al-Jabbār has reached in the eyes of the political system in Baghdād, a place where he established a solid foundation in Baṣran Muʿtazilism.[13]

In 360/970 when ʿAbd al-Jabbār went to Rāmhurmuz, he confirmed his willingness to follow the Jubbāʾī teachings by joining the circle of Abū Muḥammad ʿAbdallāh b. ʿAbbās al-Rāmhurmuzī, one of Abū ʿAlī al-Jubbāʾī's companions, who owned a mosque in Rāmhurmuz where ʿAbd al-Jabbār claimed to spend a certain amount of time.[14] In this very mosque he began to dictate his theological *summa*, *Kitāb al-Mughnī fī abwāb al-tawḥīd wa-l-ʿadl*.[15] Afterward, he went to Iṣfahān to join the Būyid vizier Ibn ʿAbbād al-Ṭalaqānī al-Iṣfahānī who appointed him *qāḍī al-quḍāt* of Rayy.[16] In what political and cultural context did ʿAbd al-Jabbār pursue his professional mobility? What were the circles of knowledge and power that enabled him to access the highest function of *qāḍī al-quḍāt*?

---

11 Ibn al-Murtaḍā reports that ʿAbd al-Jabbār wanted to study al-Baṣrī's Ḥanafī *fiqh* but the latter would tell him: "This [*fiqh*] is a science. Any *mujtahid* (person who tries to understand the precepts of the law in order to practice them) achieves its goal. I am Ḥanafī and you are Shāfiʿī". See Ibn al-Murtaḍā, *Ṭabaqāt al-Muʿtazila* (Beirut: Dār al-Muntaẓar, 1988), 112; al-Jushamī, *Sharḥ al-ʿUyūn*, 367. We don't know if ʿAbd al-Jabbār considered at this time being lately a chief judge. According to Aḥmad Taymūr, since the reign of Hārūn al-Rashīd (r. 170/786–193/809) the judges who were appointed in Iraq and Khurāsān followed the Ḥanafī *madhhab*. Also, he reports that the people in Jurjān and in some parts of Ṭabaristān in the Daylam region (where the Būyids were originally from) were Ḥanafī. See Aḥmad Taymūr, *Naẓra tārīkhiyya fī ḥudūth al-madhāhib al-arbaʿa* (Beirut: Dār al-Qādirī, 1411/1990), 51, 59.

12 ʿAbd al-Jabbār al-Hamadhānī, *Faḍl al-iʿtizāl wa ṭabaqāt al-Muʿtazila*, 325.

13 See Schwarb, Gregor M., "Abū ʿAbdallāh al-Baṣrī," *Encyclopaedia of Islam*, Third Edition, eds. Kate Fleet, Gudrun Krämer, Denis Matringe, John Nawas, Everett Rowson.

14 Al-Khaṭīb al-Baghdādī, *Tārīkh Baghdād*, 12:414–16. See also ʿAbd al-Jabbār al-Hamadhānī, *Faḍl al-iʿtizāl wa ṭabaqāt al-Muʿtazila*, 312; Wilferd Madelung, "ʿAbd al-Jabbār b. Aḥmad," *Encyclopeadia Iranica*, 1/2, 116–17; Reynolds, *A Muslim theologian in the sectarian milieu*, 47 n. 134.

15 ʿAbd al-Jabbār states that the dictation of *al-Mughnī* was between 360 and 380 AH. See *al-Mughnī fī abwāb al-tawḥīd wa-l-ʿadl*, 20/2:243. Al-Jushamī claimed that ʿAbd al-Jabbār sent a copy of *al-Mughnī* while he was *qāḍī al-quḍāt*. Al-Jushamī, *Sharḥ al-ʿUyūn*, 369–70.

16 ʿAbd al-Jabbār al-Hamadhānī, *Faḍl al-iʿtizāl wa ṭabaqāt al-Muʿtazila*, 315. Madelung reports that it occurs during the rule of Mu'ayyid al-Dawla (d. 373/984). Madelung, "ʿAbd al-Jabbār B. Aḥmad," *Encyclopeadia Iranica*, 1/2, 116–17.

2 The Decentralization of ʿAbbāsid Power and Its Relationship with the Būyids

The fourth/tenth century witnessed the dismantling of the ʿAbbāsid empire and consequently the proliferation of several independent states. Around the year 324/935, ten years before the Būyids entered Baghdād, the ʿAbbāsid empire disintegrated into small states. Iraq was for the first time under the operative control of Abū Bakr Muḥammad b. Rāʾiq (d. 330/942), the head of the armies promoted to *amīr al-ʾumarāʾ* in 324/936.[17] Caliphal power decreased; effective expression of the amīr's power is reflected in the fact that both political and administrative powers were both clustered at *Dār al-imāra* and no longer at *Dār al-khilāfa* as had been the case when the administration was the caliph's exclusive domain.[18] However, the division of the prerogatives of the caliph and the amīr did not concern the religious field; the caliph reigned, according to his religious prerogatives as God's representative on Earth, the amīr governed according to the effective powers conferred on him. Faced with the weakening of ʿAbbasid political power and the influence of new Būyid contenders, new cultural centres and religious trends flourished.[19] At that time, Baghdād and Baṣra were still the cultural centers of the ʿAbbasids, even as other cities began to emerge such as Cairo, Ḥalab, Rayy or Bukhāra, Iṣfahān, and Shīrāz which attracted the *udabāʾ* and the *falāsifa*.[20]

The Būyids, originally from Daylam – under Zaydī political hegemony around the year 900 – were Shīʿī.[21] Originally, al-Ḥasan b. Zayd, al-Dāʿī al-Kabīr (d. 270/884) spread the Shīʿī doctrine throughout the Daylam region before the defenders of the Ismāʿīlī branch took over at the beginning of the third/ninth

17 During the reign of al-Rāḍī (r. 322–29/934–40), the effective power switched from the caliph to the head of armies known as *amīr al-umarāʾ* untill the reign of Muʿizz al-Dawla in 334/946. See D. Waines, "The Pre-Buyid Amirate, Two views from the past," *International Journal of Middle East Studies*, vol. 8 no. 3 (July 1977): 339–49; Kraemer, *Humanism in the renaissance of Islam* (Leiden: E.J. Brill, 1986), 34–5.

18 Kraemer, *Humanism in the renaissance of Islam*, 38.

19 Nyberg reports that in the fourth century while the ʿAbbāsid power was receding the Shīʿa was flourishing. Nyberg, H.S., "al-Muʿtazila," *Encyclopaedia of Islam*, First Edition (1913–1936).

20 Maḥmūd Ghanāwī al-Zuhayrī, *al-Adab fī ẓill banī buwayh* (Cairo: Maṭbaʿat al-Amāna, 1368/1949), 120. Peters, *God's created speech*, 6.

21 Claude Cahen states: "The Buwayhids were Zaydis because Daylam had been the scene of the activity of the emissaries of these same Zaydis who had set up political hegemonies in Ṭabaristān and, on the very borders of Daylam itself, by those of their rival al-ʿUṭrūsh, around the year 900". Claude Cahen, "Buwayhids," *Encyclopaedia of Islam*, Second Edition, 1350–7.

century and spread their propaganda to the Daylamite leaders Shīrawayh (Asfār b. Shīrūya, d. 319/931) and Mardāwij (d. 323/935).[22] The Daylamites crossed the Persian West and successively established small dynasties until the first generation of the Būyids brothers entered the land. The three sons of Būwayh (or Būya), ʿAlī, Ḥasan and Aḥmad – who the caliph al-Mustakfī later named ʿImād al-Dawla (d. 338/944), Rukn al-Dawla (d. 366/977) and Muʿizz al-Dawla (d. 356/967) – divided the conquered lands. ʿAlī ruled the province of Fārs, Ḥasan ruled almost all of Jibāl, and Aḥmad ruled Kirmān and Khūzistān at the border of Baṣra near Baghdād.[23] In 334/945, after a major struggle, Aḥmad (Muʿizz al-Dawla) entered Baghdād – which had witnessed before the execution of al-Ḥallāj in 309/922 – and ensured mediation between the Sunnī and Shīʿī fractions. When in 351/962 the Shīʿīs desecrated the names of the Prophet's companions, he stopped their offensive.[24]

A new fraternal triad founded the second Būyid reign. Upon the death of the Būyid brothers, the sons of Rukn al-Dawla took power: ʿAḍud al-Dawla (d. 372/983) in Fārs-Kimān (Shirāz) and later in Baghdād, Muʾayyid al-Dawla (d. 373/984) in Jibāl (Rayy and Iṣfahān) and Fakhr al-Dawla (d. 387/997) in Hamadhān and Dīnawar (Kurdistan Jibāl).[25] It was between 366/977 and 403/1012, which began with the reign of ʿAḍud al-Dawla in Baghdād and his brothers Muʾayyid al-Dawla and Fakhr al-Dawla, that ʿAbd al-Jabbār assumed the supreme function of *qāḍī al-quḍāt* in Rayy and the surrounding provinces. The reign of ʿAḍud al-Dawla was considered as the most important since he embodied the role of governor and was decorated with the *malik al-muluk* (*Shāhanshāh*) title.[26] The solidarity of the Būyid brothers was transformed

22 Kraemer states: "Mardāwij b. Ziyār al-Jīlī, founder of the Ziyārid dynasty in Ṭabaristān and Jurjān (...) aspired to replace the regime of the Arabs (*dawlat al-ʿarab*) with the regime of the Persians (*dawlat al-ʿajam*)". Kraemer, *Humanism in the renaissance of Islam*, 33–4.

23 Abū-l-Faraj Ibn al-Jawzī, *Al-Muntaẓam fī tārīkh al-mulūk wa-l-umam* (Beirut: Dār al-Kutub al-ʿIlmiyya, 1412/1992), 13:366. According to Richard N. Frye "the name al-Jibal was applied primarily to the plateau area which the three main cities of Hamadhān, Iṣfahān and Rayy, all ancient centres". Richard N. Frye, *The Golden Age of Persia The Arabs in the East* (London: Weidenfeld and Nicolson, 1975), 112. For more details about the Būyids see Claude Cahen, "Buwayhids," *Encyclopaedia of Islam*, Second Edition, 1350–7.

24 The regime Muʿizz al-Dawla introduced would continue until the year 447/1055. See Cahen, "Buwayhids," *Encyclopaedia of Islam*, First Edition, 1350–7. For the religious interference between Sunnī and Shīʿī see Kraemer, *Humanism in the renaissance of Islam*, 40–3.

25 A struggle broke out between ʿAḍud al-Dawla and his cousin ʿIzz al-Dawla (Bakhtiyār), son of Muʿizz al-Dawla. Harold Bowen, "ʿAḍud al-Dawla," *Encyclopaedia of Islam*, Second Edition, 211–12.

26 Kraemer reports that the Būyids "initially assumed the title of emir but beginning with Rukn al-Dawla and his son ʿAḍud al-Dawla the main Buyid ruler was also called king

from the third generation onwards into a struggle that split the power of the Būyid dynasty before it was finally dissolved in 446/1055.[27] How did the "inner circle of knowledge" of ʿAbd al-Jabbār – made up of his master al-Baṣrī and his pupils – become so decisive that it took him to the highest levels?

3 The Inner Circle of Knowledge: Key Element of ʿAbd al-Jabbār's Professional Mobility

In terms of the intellectual background, the *miḥna* – bequeathed by the reign of al-Māmūn (d. 218/833), achieved under the reign of al-Mutawakkil (d. 247/861) – made it easier to impose Muʿtazilism as a state doctrine and, consequently, established a rational approach to creed relating to the creation of the Qurʾan and human freedom issues.[28] It also contributed to enhance their detractors who deployed the same rhetorical enthusiasm to counter the Muʿtazilī arguments. Sunnism restored by al-Mutawakkil put the Muʿtazila in crisis and encouraged other theological groups. Thus al-Ashʿarī (d. 324/935), one of the prominent theologians of what would later become Sunnī orthodoxy, turned away from the Muʿtazila, founded his own movement, and gained pupils – including al-Bāqilānī, ʿAḍud al-Dawla son's tutor –, the leading figure countering the Muʿtazila. However, *iʿtizāl*, thanks to the Būyids, would be reborn in the Iranian provinces and would flourish in Baṣra, the city where ʿAbd al-Jabbār studied the bases of this doctrine. The geographer and chronicler Ibn Ḥawqal attested, during his stay in Khūzistān and Fārs between 350/961 and 358/969 that in these locations the doctrines were mainly Muʿtazilī (*al-ghālib ʿalayhum al-ʾiʿtizāl*).[29] At that time, the schools of *kalām* were transferred from Baṣra to Baghdād with an active branch in Rayy. This mobility of ideas and people operated a syncretism of *madhāhib* composed of Ashʿarī theologians, mainly Sunnī, and Muʿtazilī theologians both Sunnī and Shīʿī (who were

(*malik*)". Kraemer, *Humanism in the renaissance of Islam*, 35. For more details about the *Shāhanshāh* title see Wilferd Madelung, "The Assumption of the Title Shāhānshāh by the Būyids and The Reign of the Daylam (Dawlat Al-Daylam)," *Journal of Near Eastern Studies*, 28, no. 3 (July, 1969): 168–183.

27 Cahen, "Buwayhids," *Encyclopaedia of Islam*, Second Edition, 1350–7.

28 For more details about the *miḥna* see John A. Nawas, "The Miḥna of 218 A.H./833 A.D. Revisited: An Empirical Study," *Journal of the American Oriental Society* 116, no. 4 (October–December 1996): 698–708; J.P. Turner, "The end of the Miḥna," *Oriens* 38 (2010): 89–106. For the history of the Muʿtazila and their close connexion to the ʿAbbāsids see Nyberg, H.S., "al-Muʿtazila," *Encyclopaedia of Islam*, First Edition (1913–1936).

29 Abū l-Qāsim Ibn Ḥawqal, *Ṣūrat al-ʾarḍ* (Beirut: Manshūrāt Dār Maktabat al-Ḥayāt, 1996), 230.

specifically supporters of Zaydism).[30] Once again, the return of Muʿtazilism emanated from the political power, in particular from the Būyid fraternal triad that seized the eastern regions of Iran and Baghdād. The political issue, coextensive with the religious question, combined the Sunnī obedience of the ʿAbbasid caliph with the incoming Shīʿī Būyid leaders. The Būyids, preferring politics to religion, had no claim to impose Shīʿism as the political doctrine of the state.[31] They welcomed the various doctrinal opinions indiscriminately and the religious mixture displayed all spheres. The Shīʿī doctrine of the Būyid rulers and the Sunnī majority of the Baghdādī population reflected the two religious tendencies represented even in the ranks of the army. In this context of political adversity and religious syncretism "the idea of *mamlakat al-islām*" allowed Muslims to move through many cities to seek knowledge and prosper.[32] The decentralization of ʿAbbasid power in the face of the Būyid's hegemony created a conducive climate to the mobility of people and the circulation of ideas and cultures. ʿAbd al-Jabbār travelled to perfect his knowledge, which led him to study under the authority of Abū ʿAbdallāh al-Baṣrī who was the master of al-Ṣāḥib Ismaʿīl b. ʿAbbād al-Ṭālaqānī (d. 385/995), vizier of Mu'ayyid al-Dawla and Fakhr al-Dawla. Ibn ʿAbbād known for his intellectual prosperity will be a fervent defender of the Muʿtazilī doctrine of the Bahshamite branch (supporters of Abū Hāshim al-Jubbā'ī).

The inner circle of knowledge of ʿAbd al-Jabbār – consolidated both by the teachings of the *fiqh* (Abū ʿAbdallāh al-Baṣrī and Ibn ʿAbbād were both Ḥanafī, ʿAbd al-Jabbār was Shāfiʿī) and by the Muʿtazilī doctrine (all three were supporters of the movement of the Baṣran school) – gave him the opportunity to take advantage of his formative years. Thus, he was recommended by his master, al-Baṣrī, to work with the vizier Ibn Abbād, his former pupil and at this time advisor of the Būyid ruler Mu'ayyid al-Dawla (d. 373/984).[33] In 367/977,

30 Louis Gardet, "ʿIlm al-Kalām," *Encyclopaedia of Islam*, Third Edition, 1141–50; Kraemer, *Humanism in the renaissance of Islam*, 72. For the Baghdādī theologians who belonged to the Zaydiyya see Nyberg, H.S., "al-Muʿtazila," *Encyclopaedia of Islam*, First Edition (1913–1936).

31 Cahen persistently asserts that politically the Būyids advocated the doctrine of the Twelver theology. Cahen, "Buwayhids," *Encyclopaedia of Islam*, Second Edition, 1350–7.

32 Kraemer, *Humanism in the renaissance of Islam*, 31.

33 In his youth, Ibn ʿAbbād studied ḥadīth in Iṣfahān with his father who was one of the supporters of Ḥanafī *madhhab*. See Maurice A. Pomerantz, "A political biography of al-Ṣāḥib Ismāʿīl b. ʿAbbād," *Journal of the American Oriental Society*, 134/1 (January–March 2014): 4–5. Al-Tawḥīdī portrays the connection between the vizier and the qāḍī by stating that the latter "was like the mouse in the hands of the feline" (*al-Hamadhānī mithl al-fāra bayna yaday al-sinnūr*). See also Abū Ḥayyān al-Tawḥīdī, *Akhlāq al-wazīrayn* (Beirut: Dār ṣādir, 1992), 97. Reynolds points out the "personal interest" of Ibn ʿAbbād in ʿAbd

the vizier appointed ʿAbd al-Jabbār *qāḍī al-quḍāt* of Rayy, the capital of the province of Jibāl. His judicial authority would later extend to other provinces. Many scholars see in the proximity at the level of the Muʿtazilī principles uniting al-Baṣrī, Ibn ʿAbbād and ʿAbd al-Jabbār the indication of a common obedience of the latter to Zaydism. While some Western scholars are content to point out the Shīʿī-Imamī inclination of the Būyids, others argue in favour of the supposed Shīʿī-Zaydī inclination of Abū ʿAbdallāh al-Baṣrī and Ibn ʿAbbād.[34] Finally, some remain cautious and see it more as a way to court the Zaydī power.[35]

The hint of a Zaydī inclination would hang over ʿAbd al-Jabbār because of the close connection he had with Ibn ʿAbbād, the content of his writings inclined in favour of *amīr al-muʾminīn*, and his Zaydī pupils.[36] Taking into account the Muʿtazilī theoretical standpoint which could be transposed both on Sunnī and Shīʿī branches and the religious practical aim of the Shīʿīs, it is the Muʿtazila which would have influenced the Zaydīs and not the other way around.[37] Nevertheless, beyond doctrinal considerations, the Muʿtazilī theological inclinations of some Sunnī jurists did not prevent them from being respected by the population, just as the Shīʿī inclinations of the Būyid leaders did not prevent them from courting Sunnī scholars. The mobility of ʿAbd al-Jabbār in the quest for knowledge had enabled him to meet influential people, to enter the sphere of the *ʿulamāʾ* of his time, and to be courted by the political elite.

---

al-Jabbār's Muʿtazilī success to promote this doctrine. Gabriel Said Reynolds, "The Rise and Fall of Qadi ʿAbd al-Jabbar," *International Journal of Middle East Studies*, vol. 37, no. 1 (February 2005), 6.

34 For the different points of views, see Cahen, "Ibn ʿAbbād," *Encyclopaedia of Islam*, Second Edition, 3:672; Peters, *God's created speech*, 7; Reynolds, *A Muslim theologian in the sectarian milieu*, 48 n. 140. Kraemer describes him as "Zaydī Shīʿī" noting that he was pro-ʿAlī b. Abī Ṭālib and mentionnes the book *Kitāb al-Tafḍīl*. Kraemer, *Humanism in the renaissance of Islam*, 178–9. See also Pomerantz, "*A political*," 4 n. 20.

35 Van Ess, "Abu Abdallah al-Baṣrī," *Encyclopaedia of Islam*, Second Edition.

36 Kraemer, *Humanism in the renaissance of Islam*, 73; Reynolds, *A Muslim theologian in the sectarian milieu*, 48 n. 143. In *Faḍl al-iʿtizāl*, ʿAbd al-Jabbār argues by citing traditions from *amīr al-muʾminīn* (ʿAlī b. Abī-Ṭālib). See ʿAbd al-Jabbār al-Hamadhānī, *Faḍl al-iʿtizāl*, 150. Although, as Madelung notes, ʿAbd al-Jabbār advocates in *al-Mughnī* the *imāma* of ʿAlids, he accused the majority of Imāmīs of following excessiveness (*ġuluww*). See ʿAbd al-Jabbār al-Hamadhānī, *al-Mughnī fī abwāb al-tawḥīd wa-l-ʿadl*, 20/1:41. See also Wilferd Madelung, "Imāma," *Encyclopaedia of Islam*, Second Edition, ed. P. Bearman, Th. Bianquis, C.E. Bosworth, E. van Donzel, W.P. Heinrichs, P.J. Bearman (volumes X, XI, XII).

37 Kraemer states that at the end of the fourth/tenth century "Muʿtazilī influence on Zaydī Shīʿism reached a high point". Kraemer, *Humanism in the renaissance of Islam*, 73. For the connection between Muʿtazilism and the Imāmī Shīʿism, see Martin J. McDermott, *The Theology of al-Shaikh al-Mufīd* (Beirut: Dār al-Mashreq, 1978), 4–5.

The mobility carried out to acquire religious, legal, and theological knowledge led him to a mobility tending to fulfil legal and later didactic functions. What was the nature and extent of ʿAbd al-Jabbār's judicial function in the context of his relationship with the political power?

4 ʿAbd al-Jabbār's Judicial Function: Spatial Mobility and the Relationship to Power

During the period preceding the advent of the Būyids, judicial authority was under the aegis of the caliph who held all the powers. The emergence of the function of *qāḍī al-quḍāt* under the reign of Hārūn al-Rashīd, with its dual involvement both in the social life of individuals and relating to legislative precepts, had enabled caliphs to keep this position for admired and respected scholars among the population, especially in Baghdād.[38] The Būyid amīrs of the region of Jibāl (which included Rayy and Iṣfahān) and Hamadhān do not derogate from this rule. When al-Ṣāḥib b. ʿAbbād, an educated and experienced advisor, becomes the vizier of Mu'ayyid al-Dawla and Faḫr al-Dawla, he sent a letter to his master al-Baṣrī asking to send him "a man who exhorts people with his spirit more than he exhorts them by his knowledge or action (*urīdu an tabʿatha lī rajulan yadʿū al-nās bi-ʿaqlihi akthar mimmā yadʿūhum bi ʿilmihi wa ʿamalihi*)".[39] Al-Baṣrī sent him ʿAbd al-Jabbār, who had previously been reluctant to go but later gave in to Ibn ʿAbbād's insistence and honoured his mentor's recommendation and went.

Towards the end of the fourth/tenth century, Iraq was the homeland of Shīʿism which extended to Khūzistān, Fārs and Qūm (on the Rayy border).[40] Failing to have a doctrine of *kalām* proper for them, the Būyid leaders focused

38 Ṣafia Saʿāda, *Min tārīkh Baghdād al-ijtimāʿī: Taṭayyur manṣib qāḍī al-quḍāt fī-l-fatratayn al-buwīhiyya wa al-saljūqiyya* (Beirut: Dār Amwāj, 1986), 9, 120–5; Emile Tyan, *Histoire de l'organisation judiciaire en pays d'Islam* (Leiden: E.J. Brill, 1960), 128. See also ʿAbd al-Razzāk ʿAlī al-Anbārī, *Manṣib qāḍī-l-quḍāt fī-l-dawla al-ʿAbbāsiyya: mundhu nash'atihi ḥattā nihayat al-ʿahd al-Saljūqī* (Beirut: al-Dār al-ʿArabiyya li-l-Mawsūʿāt, 1987), 140.

39 Under the vizierate of Ibn ʿAbbād – from 366/976 to his death in 385/995 – the Būyid amīrs won several military victories. See Pomerantz, "*A political*," 1. The letter is written following the dismissal by Ibn ʿAbbād of a first contender for the position of *qāḍī al-quḍāt*, a certain Abā Isḥāq al-Naṣībī, although scholarly and eloquent, would not have behaved well with Ibn ʿAbbād. Al-Ṣafadī, *al-Wāfī bi-l-wafayāt*, 18:21.

40 According to al-Khawārizmī's words: "*al-tashayyuʿ ʿirāqī*". See Abī Bakr al-Khawārizmī, *Rasā'il* (Constantinople: Maṭbaʿat al-Jawā'ib, 1297), 49.

on the Muʿtazilī doctrine which has a common foundation with Zaydism.[41] By appointing ʿAbd al-Jabbār to the highest judicial function, Mu'ayyid al-Dawla relied on a Muʿtazilī-Shāfiʿī authority, whose reputation had been established in several other cities. Through the mobility he undertook to acquire and consolidate his knowledge in *fiqh* and *kalām*, ʿAbd al-Jabbār became the authority figure of the Muʿtazila of his time and created consensus among his fellow scholars.[42] He begun composing his works in several cities and his scholarly reputation grew. When he was in Rayy he gave theological lessons to pupils who came from distant lands and went to Iṣfahān and ʿAskar Mukram to teach lessons from his theological *summa*.[43] Ibn ʿAbbād, in a laudatory statement, describes ʿAbd al-Jabbār as "the best" or "most learned of men among the people of the Earth" applying God's justice.[44] The one whom the vizier called the great glorious judge (*al-qāḍī al-quḍāt al-ajall*) was, in his eyes, a man whose path was devotion and the truth his guide.[45]

As soon as he took up his legal duties in Rayy in 367/977, a new phase of professional mobility began for the man who holds the title of *qāḍī al-quḍāt* among all the Muʿtazila.[46] According to what Ibn ʿAbbād reports in his *Rasā'il*, in close collaboration with the caliph *amīr al-mū'minīn* al-Ṭā'iʿ li-llāh, Mu'ayyid al-Dawla appointed ʿAbd al-Jabbār *qāḍī al-quḍāt* of Rayy, Qazwīn, Suhraward, Qumm and Sāwa.[47] The Būyid amīr found in ʿAbd al-Jabbār someone who

41 Adam Mitz, *al-Ḥaḍāra al-islāmiyya fī-l-qarn ar-rābiʿal-hijrī* (Beirut: Dār al-Kitāb al-ʿArabī, 1947), 121–4.

42 Al-Jushamī reports: "*ittafaqa lahu min al-aṣḥāb mā lam yattafiq li aḥad min ru'asā' al-kalām*". Al-Jushamī, *Sharḥ al-ʿUyūn*, 369.

43 Reynolds, *A Muslim Theologian in the Sectarian Milieu*, 50–1.

44 Al-Jushamī, *Sharḥ al-ʿUyūn*, 366.

45 Ibn ʿAbbād, *Rasā'il*, 139. According to Ibn ʿAbbād's words "*al-waraʿu markabuhu wa sabīluhu, al-ḥaqq maqsaduhu wa dalīluhu*". See Ibn ʿAbbād, *Rasā'il*, 34.

46 For the arrival and the nomination of *qāḍī al-quḍāt* we found two dates: both al-Jushāmī and Ibn al-Murtaḍā reports that Ibn ʿAbbād invited ʿAbd al-Jabbār in Rayy after the year 360/970. See al-Jushamī, *Sharḥ al-ʿUyūn*, 366; Ibn al-Murtaḍā, *Ṭabaqāt al-Muʿtazila*, 112. Al-Rāfiʿī reports the date of the act of nomination of ʿAbd al-Jabbār in the early of Muḥarram of the year 367/977. See al-Rāfiʿī, *al-Tadwīn fī akhbār Qazwīn*, 125. As Reynolds pointed it out the last date seems chronologically more accurate since Ibn ʿAbbād, which will supervise the appointment of ʿAbd al-Jabbār, only would have accessed his functions as vizier in 366/976. Reynolds, *A Muslim Theologian in the Sectarian Milieu*, 49 n. 145. Although there are no sources on the date of the appointment of Ibn ʿAbbād as vizier, Pomerantz leans on the year 356/966 since Mu'ayyid al-Dawla was crowned prince the same year. See Pomerantz, "A political," 13 n. 80. For the appellation of ʿAbd al-Jabbār as *qāḍī al-quḍāt* among the *Muʿtazila* see al-Subkī, *Ṭabaqāt al-shāfiʿiyya al-kubrā*, 5:443.

47 Ibn ʿAbbād, *Rasā'il*, 42. Al-Rāfiʿī adds Abhar and Zanjān. See al-Rāfiʿī, *al-Tadwīn fī akhbār Qazwīn*, 119.

could feed people with his devoutness and guide them with his knowledge and extended his judicial authority to Jurjān and Ṭabaristān.[48]

Unfortunately, sources are scarce to trace the geographical mobility and the modalities of the judicial authority of qāḍī ʿAbd al-Jabbār in Rayy because the works of the scholars consulted mainly concern the *qāḍī al-quḍāts* of Iraq or Egypt. It seems that the prerogatives of the qāḍī covered both legal and administrative functions and its authority extended geographically to the Jibāl region and beyond to Jurjān and Ṭabaristān.[49] In his book *Adab al-qāḍī*, al-Māwardī (d. 450/1058), a jurist and great judge (*Akbar quḍāt*) of the late ʿAbbāsid period, states that the qāḍī must follow the instructions contained in his decree of appointment (*ʿahd*) regarding action (*ʿamal*) and speculation (*naẓar*).[50] In his *Rasāʾil*, Ibn ʿAbbād reports the terms of the deed of appointment of *qāḍī al-quḍāt* detailing the specifications of his responsibilities in ethical and legal terms. Above all, he is asked to be devoted to God and to straighten his soul before straightening his action, then he must decide according to the text of the Qurʾan (*kitāb Allāh*), the tradition of the prophet (*sunna*), the consensus (*ijmāʿ*) and, if necessary, to use speculation (*naẓar*) and the consultation of *fuqahāʾ* (*mashūra*).[51] The main legal functions of qāḍī ʿAbd al-Jabbār concerned disputes related to personal status, in particular those relating to inheritance, marriage of widows and persons under the guardianship of the qāḍī. However, the nature of the function of qāḍī ʿAbd al-Jabbār was not exclusively judicial, since it extended, through the religious nature of the *qāḍī al-quḍāt*'s function, to administrative tasks such as the management of property, religious endowment (*waqf*), the protection of orphans and the appointment of secretaries (*umanāʾ*) to supervise coinage.[52] Regarding the close dependence of the judiciary and the executive power and according to the deed of appointment mentioning both the *ʿahd* of Muʾayyid al-Dawla and the *amr* of al-Ṭāʾiʿ li-llāh, the *qāḍī al-quḍāt* was only a delegate or a representative of both *amīr al-umarāʾ* and *amīr al-mūʾminīn*.[53] This subordination of the judiciary to the executive power hovered over the exercise of the function of ʿAbd al-Jabbār and the end of his mandate demonstrated the links of this subordination, or

48 Ibn ʿAbbād, *Rasāʾil*, 42:34.

49 Hourani, *Islamic rationalism*, 6.

50 Al-Māwardī, *Adab al-Qāḍī*, 2:397.

51 Ibn ʿAbbād, *Rasāʾil*, 34–6.

52 Ibid., 39.

53 "L'institution judiciaire ne constitue pas un pouvoir séparé et indépendant des autres pouvoirs de l'État. Elle est dans un état de dépendance étroite à l'égard du pouvoir exécutif, qui relève en principe du même titulaire." See Tyan, *Histoire de l'organisation judiciaire en pays d'Islam*, 11.

rather the consequences of what might be understood as the insubordination of *qāḍī al-quḍāt* towards the ruling power.

When Ibn ʿAbbād died in 385/995, ʿAbd al-Jabbār refused to pronounce the prayer of mercy (*taraḥḥum*) at his funeral. The vizier Abū Shujāʿ (d. 488/1095) reports that the qāḍī stated: "I refuse to pray for the one who has not shown his repentance (*lā ataraḥḥamu ʿalayh liʾannahu māta min ghayr tawba ẓaharat ʿalayh*)".[54] However, it is reported that one day Ibn ʿAbbād, then vizier, publicly repented of his sins (*innī tāʾib ilā-llāh min dhanbin adhnabtuhu*), named a house *bayt al-tawba* before writing to qāḍī ʿAbd al-Jabbār.[55] The repentance by government officials was a practice among Muʿtazilī followers but, if the event of *tawba* did occur ʿAbd al-Jabbār did not take it under account.[56] Furthermore, the *taraḥḥum* incident is crucial because, if it did take place, it was at least a turning point in the qāḍī's career.[57]

While many people showed their solidarity at the vizier's funeral, some biographers understood ʿAbd al-Jabbār's position as a lack of concern (*qillat al-riʿāya*) for those who were generous towards him, while for others it was "l'acte logique d'un esprit rigoriste".[58] Abū Shujāʿ reports that following his act Fakhr al-Dawla removed ʿAbd al-Jabbār from his judicial functions before confiscating his possessions and imprisoning him.[59] Did Fakhr al-Dawla take the

54 Abū Shujāʿ, *Dhayl tajārib al-umam*, 261–2. See also al-Ṣafadī, *al-Wāfī bi-l-wafayāt*, 18:22.

55 Yāqūt, *Kitāb Irshād al-arīb ilā maʿrifat al-adīb*, 2:312. Al-Ṣafadī, *al-Wāfī bi-l-wafayāt*, 9:78.

56 In the fourth/tenth century, the government officials perform their repentance at the end of their duties. This act of repentance has theological and doctrinal motivations. See Maurice A. Pomerantz, "Muʿtazilī Theory in Practice: The Repentance (*tawba*) of Government Officials in the 4th/10th century," in *A Common Rationality: Muʿtazilism in Judaism and Islam*, eds. Camilla Adang, Sabine Schmidtke, and David Sklare (Würzburg: Ergon Verlag, 2007), 464. Maybe it is the lifestyle of Ibn ʿAbbād that cause the problem. What al-Thaʿālibī describes as the vizier's hospitality could be taken for a waste.

57 For some scholars, the *taraḥḥum* may never have occurred. It was the position of Madelung who stated that "hostile sources attribute his dismissal to his refusal to pray for Ebn ʿAbbād, as the latter had failed to display repentance before his death." See Wilferd Madelung, "ʿAbd al-Jabbār B. Aḥmad," *Encyclopeadia Iranica*, 1/2, 116–7. See also Heemskerk, Margaretha T., *Suffering in the Muʿtazilite theology: ʿAbd al-Jabbār's teaching on pain and divine justice* (Leiden: Brill, 2000), 48.

58 Yāqūt, *Kitāb Irshād al-arīb ilā maʿrifat al-adīb*, 2:335; Monnot, *Penseurs Musulmans et religions Iraniennes: ʿAbd al-Ǧabbār et ses devanciers* (Paris: Vrin, 1974), 17.

59 Abū Shujāʿ, *Dhayl tajārib al-umam*, 262. Hourani reports other chronicler's versions about the dismissal of ʿAbd al-Jabbār: his behaviour toward the vizier, the favour of his entourage or his growing wealth. Hourani, *Islamic rationalism*, 6. Some critique sources report that ʿAbd al-Jabbār, son of a peasant had a lot of possessions (*kathīr al-māl wa-l-ʿaqār*) and became a very wealthy man (*qārūn*). See al-Ṣafadī, *al-Wāfī bi-l-wafayāt*, 18:21; al-Tawḥīdī, *al-Imtāʿ wa-l-muʾānasa*, 141. According to Reynolds after his dismissal, ʿAbd al-Jabbār's reputation has been damaged. Al-Ṣafadī claimed that ʿAbd al-Jabbār gathered

refusal of the prayer of ʿAbd al-Jabbār as an act of distrust and therefore insubordination towards him or did this opportunity allow him to settle political scores with Ibn ʿAbbād's relatives? I will consider the second hypothesis since Fakhr al-Dawla also seized all of Ibn ʿAbbād's property and imprisoned all his companions in order to dispel any competition since the vizier was close and devoted to his rival brother Mu'ayyid al-Dawla. However, after Fakhr al-Dawla's escape to Khurāsān and his refuge with the Samanids, Ibn ʿAbbād was the one who repatriated him before returning his heritage to him.[60] Nevertheless, despite the success of Ibn ʿAbbād during the reign of Fakhr al-Dawla, the latter did not have much consideration for him: not only did he make sarcastic remarks towards the vizier – in an assembly he addressed him with vindictive allegations: "You say that the doctrine is *iʿtizāl* and the coitus is with men (*al-madhhab madhhab al-iʿtizāl wa-l-nnayk nayk al-rijāl*)" – but he waited until his death to get rid of his companions and at the same time of ʿAbd al-Jabbār.[61]

Another element that point to the strategic reasons behind the eviction of ʿAbd al-Jabbār is that after the dismissal of the qāḍī, Fakhr al-Dawla appointed Abū-l-Ḥasan ʿAlī Ibn ʿAbd al-ʿAzīz al-Jurjānī (d. 392/1002) *qāḍī al-quḍāt* of Rayy.[62] Al-Jurjānī, who also followed the Shāfiʿī *fiqh* and the Muʿtazilī doctrine (*jamaʿa bayn kalām al-muʿtazila wa fiqh al-shāfiʿī*) was, according to some sources, the qāḍī of Jurjān previously appointed by Ibn ʿAbbād.[63] At first sight, this seems to contradict what is mentioned in the *Rasāʾil* of Ibn ʿAbbād extending the geographic judicial authority of ʿAbd al-Jabbār to Jurjān unless this indication informs us of the establishment of judges in different cities or provinces which were probably under the jurisdiction of the *qāḍī al-quḍāt* of Rayy. Was the question of *madhhab* decisive in the decision-making of the political elite and in its relationship with its delegates from appointment to dismissal? As

---

his fortune by being corrupt and unfair during his judgeship (*jamaʿa hādha al-māl min al-qaḍāʾ wa-l-ḥukm bi-l-ẓulm wa-l-rashā*). See al-Ṣafadī, *al-Wāfī bi-l-wafayāt*, 18:22; Yāqūt, *Kitāb Irshād al-arīb ilā maʿrifat al-adīb*, 2:335.

60 Abū Shujāʿ, *Dhayl tajārib al-umam*, 264; Yāqūt, *Kitāb Irshād al-arīb ilā maʿrifat al-adīb*, 2:275.

61 Yāqūt reports the military victories of Ibn ʿAbbād: "*fataḥa khamsīn qalʿa sallamahā ilā Fakhr al-Dawla*". Yāqūt, *Kitāb Irshād al-arīb ilā maʿrifat al-adīb*, 2:311. Pomerantz adds that these victories were due to the "careful management of affairs" of the vizier from 366/976 till his death in 385/995. See Pomerantz, "*A political*," 1. For the position of Faḫr al-Dawla against his vizier see al-Thaʿālibī, *Yatīmat al-dahr fī maḥāsin ahl al-ʿaṣr*, 3:237. Al-Ṣafadī, *al-Wāfī bi-l-wafayāt*, 9:81.

62 Abū Shujāʿ, *Dhayl tajārib al-umam*, 263.

63 See al-Jushamī, *Sharḥ al-ʿUyūn*, 380; Allen Roger, and DeYoung Terri, Edmund Lowry Joseph, Stewart Devin J. *Essays in Arabic Literary Biography: 925–1350* (Wiesbaden: Harrassowitz Verlag, 2011), 224.

some scholars note, the fourth/tenth century was the "Shīʿī century" of Islam: Imāmism extended to Baghdād and the Iranian provinces thanks to the reign of the Būyids and in certain regions of Syria and Iraq thanks to the reign of the Hamdānides, in addition to Zaydism in Yemen and Ismāʿilism in certain regions of Syria and North Africa.[64] It is in this climate that Fārs, with the exponential influence of Hamadhān, Iṣfahān, Rayy, and Shīrāz, became the cultural epicenter of this century. At a time when Būyid leaders were more inclined to Imāmism than Zaydism, pressure from the majority-Sunnī population forced Būyid leaders to combine their policies with existing Sunnī doctrines.[65]

After the ordeal of his dismissal ʿAbd al-Jabbār devoted himself to teaching and continued to travel to meet scholars until his death in 415/1025 in Rayy.[66] The professional mobility of ʿAbd al-Jabbār helped him not only to extend his knowledge but also to expand his notoriety in the Muʿtazilite milieu both among Sunnī and Shīʿi theologians.[67] Considered as one of the most prominent Muʿtazilī theologians of the fourth/tenth century, he combined Sunnism and Muʿtazilism with great wit.[68] At a time when the resurgence of the Ashʿarī and Ḥanbalī doctrines – advocating a selective interpretation of religious foundations based on the main legal schools – the Muʿtazila, with ʿAbd al-Jabbār as their fervent representative, broke the chain of the imitation and raised the debate on religious principles to the rank of rationality.[69]

64 Mohammad Ali Amir-Moezzi and Pierre Lory, *Petite Histoire de l'Islam* (Paris: Flammarion, 2007), 73.

65 On the difference between the two trends, see M.A. Amir-Moezzi and P. Lory, *Petite Histoire de l'Islam*, 60–3; Kraemer, *Humanism in the renaissance of Islam*, 60–72.

66 According to what Reynolds reports from the study of Abd al-Karīm ʿUthmān, the professional mobility of ʿAbd al-Jabbār continue with the teachings in Rayy, Iṣfahān and Qazwīn. Reynolds, "The Rise and Fall," 7. During this period ʿAbd al-Jabbār composed his books *Tanzīh al-qurʾān ʿan al-maṭāʿin* and *al-Majmūʿ fī-l-muḥīṭ bi-l-taklīf* after the year 380 AH, *Tatbīth dalāʾil al-nubuwwa* in 385 AH, *Faḍl al-iʿtizāl wa ṭabaqāt al-Muʿtazila* between the year 388 and 407 AH. See Peters, *God's created speech*, 12–3. Al-Khaṭīb al-Baghdādī reports that ʿAbd al-Jabbār died before he entered Rayy in 415 AH and states that he may have died earlier this same year. See al-Baghdādī, *Tārīkh Baghdād*, 12: 416.

67 McDermott notes that ʿAbd al-Jabbār was "the only Muʿtazilite whose theological writings are largely extant" even among Shīʿi theologians. McDermott, *The theology of al-Shaikh al-Mufīd*, 4.

68 The term Sunnism here refers to the Shāfiʿī *madhhab* of ʿAbd al-Jabbār not to his theological doctrine. Some scholars use the term Sunnī by contrast to the Mu'tazilī as some others opposed Sunnī to Shīʿī. See for example Daniel Gimaret, *Théories de l'acte humain en théologie Musulmane* (Paris: Vrin, 1980); Madelung "Imāma," *Encyclopaedia of Islam*, Second Edition, ed. P. Bearman, Th. Bianquis, C.E. Bosworth, E. van Donzel, W.P. Heinrichs, P.J. Bearman (volumes X, XI, XII).

69 See al-Jushamī, *Sharḥ al-ʿUyūn*, 365. Nyberg states that during the fifth/eleventh century the theology of ʿAbd al-Jabbār dominated in Baṣra and during his stay in Rayy he founded

Acknowledgments

I am grateful to Associate Prof. Susan Gunasti and Prof. Gabriel Said Reynolds for reading, commenting and providing valuable suggestions for the draft version of this paper. The responsibility for the content of the paper is fully my own.

Bibliography

Abdulsater, Hussein Ali. *Shiʿi Doctrine, Muʿtazili Theology: al-Sharīf al-Murtaḍā and Imami Discourse*. Edinburgh: Edinburgh University Press, 2017.

Abū Shujāʿ Muḥammad b. al-Ḥusayn. *Dhayl tajārib al-umam*. Cairo: Maṭbaʿat al-Tamaddun, 1916.

Amir-Moezzi, Mohammad Ali, and Lory Pierre. *Petite histoire de l'Islam*. Paris: Flammarion, 2007.

al-Anbārī, ʿAbd al-Razzāk ʿAlī. *Manṣib qāḍī-l-quḍāt fī-l-dawla al-ʿAbbāsiyya: mundhu nashʾatihi ḥattā nihayat al-ʿahd al-Saljūqī*. Beirut: al-Dār al-ʿArabiyya li-l-Mawsūʿāt, 1987.

al-Baghdādī, al-Khaṭīb Abū Bakr Aḥmad. *Tārīkh Baghdād*, ed. Bashshār ʿAwwād Maʿrūf, 17 vols. Beirut: Dār al-Gharb al-Islāmī, 2001.

Bosworth, C.E. "ʿAskar Mokram," *Encyclopædia Iranica* (December 1987) online at http://www.iranicaonline.org/articles/askar-mokram-lit (accessed March 10, 2019).

Bowen, Harold. "ʿAḍud al-Dawla," *Encyclopaedia of Islam*, Second Edition.

Cahen, Claude. "Buwayhids," *Encyclopaedia of Islam*, Second Edition.

Cahen, Claude. "Ibn ʿAbbād," *Encyclopaedia of Islam*, Second Edition.

Canard, Marius. "Baġdād au IVᵉ siècle de l'Hégire (Xᵉ siècle de l'ere chrétienne)," *Arabica*, T. 9, Fasc. 3 (October 1962): 267–287.

Caspar, Rudi. "Un aspect de la pensée Musulmane moderne: le renouveau du Moʿtazilisme," *Mélanges de l'Institut Dominicain d'Etudes Orientales du Caire*, 4 (1957): 141–202.

Ess, Josef van. "Abū Abdallah al-Baṣrī," *Encyclopaedia of Islam*, Second Edition.

Frye, Richard N. *The Golden Age of Persia The Arabs in the East*. London: Weidenfeld and Nicolson, 1975.

Gimaret, Daniel. "Muʿtazila," *Encyclopaedia of Islam*, Second Edition, ed. P. Bearman, Th. Bianquis, C.E. Bosworth, E. van Donzel, W.P. Heinrichs. Leiden: Brill, 1960–2004.

Gimaret, Daniel. *Théories de l'acte humain en théologie Musulmane*. Paris: Vrin, 1980.

an "influential school". See, Nyberg, H.S., "al-Muʿtazila," *Encyclopaedia of Islam*, First Edition (1913–1936).

al-Hamadhānī, ʿAbd al-Jabbār. *Tanzīh al-qurʾān ʿan al-maṭāʿin*. Beirut: Dār al-Nahda al-Ḥadītha, 1966.

al-Hamadhānī, ʿAbd al-Jabbār. *Mutashābih al-Qurʾān*. ed. ʿAdnān Zarzūr. 2 vols. Cairo: Dār al-Turāth, 1969.

al-Hamadhānī, ʿAbd al-Jabbār. *Faḍl al-iʿtizāl wa ṭabaqāt al-Muʿtazila*. ed. Fuʾād Sayyid. Tunis: al-Dār al-Tūnusiyya li-l-Nashr, 1974.

al-Hamadhānī, ʿAbd al-Jabbār. *al-Mughnī fī abwāb al-tawḥīd wa-l-ʿadl*. 10 vols. Beirut: Dār al-Kutub al-ʿIlmiyya, 2012.

Heemskerk, Margaretha T. *Suffering in the Muʿtazilite theology: ʿAbd al-Jabbār's teaching on pain and divine justice*. Leiden: Brill, 2000.

Hourani, George F. *Islamic rationalism: The Ethics of ʿAbd al-Jabbār*. Oxford: Clarendon Press, 1971.

Hourani, George F. *Reason and tradition in Islamic ethics*. Cambridge University Press, 1985.

Ibn al-Athīr, Abū-l-Ḥasan ʿAlī. *Al-Kāmil fi-l-tārīkh*. ed. ʿAbdallāh al-Qāḍī. 11 vols. Beirut: Dār al-Kutub al-ʿIlmiyya, 1995.

Ibn Ḥawqal, Abū l-Qāsim. *Kitāb Sūrat al-arḍ*. Beirut: Manshūrāt Dār Maktabat al-Ḥayāt, 1996.

Ibn al-Jawzī, Abū l-Faraj ʿAbd al-Raḥmān. *al-Muntaẓam fī tārīkh al-mulūk wa-l-umam*. 19 vols. Beirut: Dār al-Kutub al-ʿIlmiyya, 1412/1992.

Ibn al-Murtaḍā, Aḥmad Ibn Yaḥyā. *Ṭabaqāt al-Muʿtazila*. Beirut: Dār al-Muntaẓar, ed. 2, 1988.

al-Jushamī, al-Ḥākim Abū-l-Saʿd al-Muḥsin al-Bayhaqī. *Sharḥ al-ʿUyūn*. ed. Fuʾād Sayyid. Tunis: al-Dār al-Tūnusiyya li-l-Nashr, 1393/1974.

al-Khawārizmī, Abī Bakr. *Rasāʾil*. Constantinople: Maṭbaʿat al-Jawāʾib, 1297.

Kraemer, Joel. L. *Humanism in the renaissance of Islam*. Leiden: E.J. Brill, 1986.

Laoust, Henri. *Les schismes dans l'Islam: introduction à une étude de la religion Musulmane*. Paris: Payot, 1965.

Madelung, Wilferd. "Imāma," *Encyclopaedia of Islam*, Second Edition, ed. P. Bearman, Th. Bianquis, C.E. Bosworth, E. van Donzel, W.P. Heinrichs, P.J. Bearman (volumes x, xi, xii).

Madelung, Wilferd. "ʿAbd al-Jabbār B. Aḥmad," *Encyclopeadia Iranica*, i/2.

Madelung, Wilferd. "The Assumption of the Title Shāhānshāh by the Būyids and The Reign of the Daylam (Dawlat Al-Daylam)," *Journal of Near Eastern Studies*, 28, no. 3 (July, 1969): 168–183.

al-Māwardī, Abū-l-Ḥasan ʿAlī b. Muḥammad b. Ḥabīb. *Adab al-qāḍī*. Baghdād: Maṭbaʿat al-Irshād, 1391/1971.

McDermott, Martin J. *The Theology of al-Shaikh al-Mufīd*. Beirut: Dār al-Mashreq, 1978.

Mitz, Adam. *al-Ḥaḍāra al-islāmiyya fī-l-qarn ar-rābiʿal-hijrī*. Beirut: Dār al-Kitāb al-ʿArabī, 1947.

Monnot, Guy. *Penseurs Musulmans et religions Iraniennes: ʿAbd al-Ǧabbār et ses devanciers*. Paris: Vrin, 1974.

Nader, Albert N. *Le Système philosophique des Muʿtazila*. Beirut: Les lettres orientales, 1956.

Nawas, John A. "The Miḥna of 218 A.H./833 A.D. Revisited: An Empirical Study," *Journal of the American Oriental Society*, 116, no. 4 (October–December 1996): 698–708.

Nyberg, Henrik Samuel. "al-Muʿtazila," *Encyclopaedia of Islam*, Second Edition, 1913–1936.

Peters, Johannes Reinier. *God's created speech: A study in the Speculative Theology of the Muʿtazilî Qâḍî l-Quḍât Abū l-Ḥasan ʿAbd al-Jabbâr bn Aḥmad al-Hamaḏânî*. Leiden: E.J. Brill, 1976.

Pomerantz, Maurice A. "Muʿtazilī Theory in Practice: The Repentance (*tawba*) of Government Officials in the 4th/10th century." In *A Common Rationality: Muʿtazilism in Judaism and Islam*, edited by Camilla Adang, Sabine Schmidtke, and David Sklare, 463–493. Würzburg: Ergon Verlag, 2007.

Pomerantz, Maurice A. "A political biography of al-Ṣāḥib Ismāʿīl b. ʿAbbād," *Journal of the American Oriental Society*, vol. 134, no. 1 (January-March 2014): 1–23.

al-Rāfiʿī, Abū l-Qāsim ʿAbd al-Karīm. *al-Tadwīn fī akhbār Qazwīn*. ed. ʿAzīz Allāh al-ʿAṭṭāridī. 4 vols. Beirut: Dār al-Kutub al-ʿIlmiyya, 1408/1987.

Reynolds, Gabriel Said. *A Muslim theologian in the sectarian milieu: Abd al-* Jabbār *and the critique of Christian origins*. Leiden, Boston: Brill, 2004.

Reynolds, Gabriel Said. "The Rise and Fall of Qadi ʿAbd al-Jabbar," *International Journal of Middle East Studies*, vol. 37, no. 1 (February 2005): 3–18.

Roger, Allen and DeYoung Terri, Lowry Joseph Edmund, Stewart Devin J. *Essays in Arabic Literary Biography: 925–1350*. Wiesbaden: Harrassowitz Verlag, 2011.

Saʿāda, Ṣafia. *Min tārīkh Baghdād al-ijtimāʿī: Taṭayyur manṣib qāḍī al-quḍāt fī-l-fatratayn al-buwīhiyya wa al-saljūqiyya*. Beirut: Dār Amwāj, 1986.

al-Ṣābiʾ, Abū l-Ḥusayn Hilāl b. al-Muḥassin. *Tuḥfat al-umarāʾ fī tārīkh al-wuzarāʾ*. ed. Aḥmad Farrāj. Cairo: Dār Iḥyāʾ al-Kutub al-ʿArabiyya, 1958.

al-Ṣafadī, Ṣalāḥ al-Dīn. *al-Wāfī bi-l-wafayāt*. 29 vols. ed. Aḥmad al-Arnāʾūṭ and Turkī Mustafā. Beirut: Dār Iḥyāʾ al-Turāth al-ʿArabī, 2000.

al-Ṣāḥib b. ʿAbbād, Abū l-Qāsim Ismāʿīl. *Rasāʾil*. ed. ʿAbd al-Wahhāb ʿAzzām. Cairo: Dār al-Fikr al-ʿArabī, 1947.

al-Samʿānī, Abū Saʿd ʿAbd al-Karīm. *al-Ansāb*. Beirut: Dār al-Jinān li-l-Ṭibāʿa wa-l-Nashr wa-l-Tawzīʿ, 1988.

al-Subkī, Abū Naṣr Tāj al-Dīn. *Tabaqāt al-Shāfiʿiyya al-Kubrā*. ed. Maḥmūd Muḥammad al-Ṭanāhi and Abd al-Fattāḥ Muḥammad al-Ḥilw. Cairo: Maṭbaʾat ʿĪsa al-Bābī, 1964–76.

Schwarb, Gregor M. "Abū ʿAbdallāh al-Baṣrī," *Encyclopaedia of Islam*, Third Edition, eds. Kate Fleet, Gudrun Krämer, Denis Matringe, John Nawas, Everett Rowson.

Stern, S.M. "Abd Al-Djabbār B. Aḥmad," *Encyclopaedia of Islam*, Second Edition, ed. P. Bearman, Th. Bianquis, C.E. Bosworth, E. van Donzel, W.P. Heinrichs, P.J. Bearman (volumes X, XI, XII).

al-Subkī, Abū l-faḍl ʿAbd al-Rahmān. *Tabaqāt al-Shāfiʿiyya al-Kubrā*. ed. Maḥmūd Muḥammad al-Ṭanāhi and Abd al-Fattāḥ Muḥammad al-Ḥilw. Cairo: Maṭbaʿat ʿĪsa al-Bābī, 1964–76.

al-Tawḥīdī, Abū Ḥayyān. *al-Imtāʿ wa-l-muʾānasa*. 3 vols. ed. Aḥmad Amīn and Aḥmad al-Zayn. Cairo: Maṭbaʿat Lajnat al-Taʾlīf wa-l-Tarjama wa-l-Nashr, 1939–44.

al-Tawḥīdī, Abū Ḥayyān. *Akhlāq al-wazīrayn*. ed. Muḥammad al-Ṭanjī, Beirut: Dār Ṣādir, 1992.

Taymūr, Aḥmad. *Naẓra tārīkhiyya fī ḥudūth al-madhāhib al-arbaʿa*. Beirut: Dār al-Qādirī, 1411/1990.

al-Thaʿālibī, Abū Manṣūr ʿAbd al-Mālik. *Yatīmat al-dahr fī maḥāsin ahl al-ʿaṣr*. 5 vols. Beirut: Dār al-Kutub al-ʿIlmiyya, 1983.

Turner, J.P. "The end of the Miḥna," *Oriens* 38 (2010): 89–106.

Tyan, Emile. *Histoire de l'organisation judiciaire en pays d'Islam*. Leiden: E.J. Brill, 1960.

Waines, David. "The Pre-Buyid Amirate, Two views from the past," *International Journal of Middle East Studies* 8 no. 3 (July 1977): 339–49.

Yāqūt, Abū ʿAbdallāh Yaʿqūb. *Kitāb Irshād al-arīb ilā maʿrifat al-adīb*. ed. D.S. Margoliouth. 7 vols. London: Luzac, 1907–1926.

al-Zuhayrī, Maḥmūd Ghanāwī. *al-Adab fī ẓill banī buwayh*. Cairo: Maṭbaʿat al-Amāna, 1368/1949.

CHAPTER 5

Mobility and Versatility of the *ʿulamāʾ* in the Mamluk Period: The Case of Ibn Taymiyya

Mehdi Berriah

1 Introduction

Over the last three decades, Western scholarship has paid increasing attention to the study of the *ʿulamāʾ* of the Mamluk period.[1] Similarly, interest in Ibn Taymiyya has also increased, leading to the production of a considerable number of academic works. While his fatwas and positions on dogmatic, legal, philosophical and political questions have aroused the interest of researchers and are beginning to become well-known, his mobility has been less frequently investigated. Both contemporary chroniclers of the 7th/13th–8th/14th centuries and Ibn Taymiyya's own writings provide a significant amount of information concerning his life, which makes it possible to not only trace with precision his mobility but also to understand it. While this article occasionally analyses certain passages on Taymiyya's life, it is not intended to be an exhaustive biographical investigation of the *shaykh* of Damascus on which Henri Laoust, Muḥammad Abū Zahra, Caterina Bori and, more recently, Jon Hoover worked.[2] The most significant work on Ibn Taymiyya's biography remains the compilation of Muḥammad ʿAzīz Shams and ʿAlī b. Muḥammad al-ʿImrān.[3]

Why the interest in studying Ibn Taymiyya's mobility? First, by studying his mobility, we also study the types of mobility that an independent religious

1 Jonathan P. Berkey, *The Transmission of Knowledge in Medieval Cairo: A Social History of Islamic Education*, Princeton 1992, pp. 95–127; id, *The Formation of Islam: Religion and Society in the Near East, 600–1800*, Cambridge 2002, pp. 224–230; Michael Chamberlain, *Knowledge and social practice in medieval Damascus*, Cambridge 1995, pp. 69–151; Irmeli Perho, "Climbing the Ladder: Social Mobility in the Mamluk Period," *Mamluk Studies Review* 15 (2011), pp. 19–35.

2 Henri Laoust, "La biographie d'Ibn Taymîya d'après Ibn Kathîr", *Bulletin d'études orientales*, 12 (1942–1943), pp. 115–162; id, *Le Hanbalisme sous les Mamlouks bahrides (658–784/1260–1382)*, Paris, 1960, pp. 7–34; Muḥammad Abū Zahra, *Ibn Taymiyya: ḥayātu-hu wa ʿaṣru-hu wa fiqhu-hu*, Cairo 1952; Caterina Bori, *Ibn Taymiyya: una vita esemplare. Analisi delle fonti classiche della sua biografia*, Supplemento monografico alla Rivista degli Studi Orientali 1/76 (2003); Jon Hoover, *Ibn Taymiyya*, London, 2020.

3 Muḥammad ʿAzīz Shams and ʿAlī b. Muḥammad al-ʿImrān, *al-Jāmiʿ li-sīrat shaykh al-Islām Ibn Taymiyya khilāl sabʿat qurūn*, Jeddah 1422H.

 | DOI:10.1163/9789004467637_007

scholar who never integrated into the official *ʿulamāʾ*'s hierarchy of the Mamluk era could have achieved, whether professional, social or otherwise. In addition, as I argue in this article, the study of the mobility of a religious scholar, in this case Ibn Taymiyya, above all allows us to better understand his character and psychology and thus his interests and positions on theological, law, philosophical and political questions. To understand the nature of the "Ibn Taymiyya phenomenon" and the influence of his writings on the development of Islamic thought, it is necessary to begin by understanding the character of the author.[4] Studying his mobility represents a step towards achieving such an understanding.

Studying Ibn Taymiyya's mobility raises several questions: as an independent scholar, what were Ibn Taymiyya's patterns of mobility? What form(s) did they take? Were they professional, social or other? What are the reasons that allowed him to achieve such mobilities? What were the consequences thereof? Were these mobilities "normal" or atypical for a scholar of his time? For what reasons? Were these mobilities initiated by Ibn Taymiyya, or were they "imposed" on him?

To attempt to provide answers to these questions, I consult the chroniclers and contemporary biographers of Ibn Taymiyya, many of whom were his students, who provide helpful information concerning his mobility: al-Yūnīnī (726/1326), al-Birzālī (739/1339), al-Dhahabī (748/1348), Ibn ʿAbd al-Hādī (743/1344), Abū Ḥafs al-Bazzār (749/1349) and Ibn Kathīr (774/1373). In addition, certain writings of Ibn Taymiyya also provide insight into his mobility. A close examination of this *corpus* sheds light on the decisions, events and circumstances that resulted in Ibn Taymiyya's mobility.

In what follows, Ibn Taymiyya's mobility is analysed under two headings, each of which has three subsections. The first section deals with Ibn Taymiyya's mobility in the sphere of the Mamluk Sultanate, while the second section focuses on what I call voluntary mobilities. Ibn Taymiyya's spatial mobility is also of interest, and his history of moving dates back to his childhood. When he was six or seven years old (with the age varying according to the source consulted), he and his family left Ḥarrān for Damascus due to Mongol invasions.[5] This forced exile from Ḥarrān could have traumatised Ibn Taymiyya and led to

4 Donald Little, "Did Ibn Taymiyya Have a Screw Loose?," *Studia Islamica* 41 (1975), pp. 93–111.

5 Ibn ʿAbd al-Hādī, *al-ʿUqūd al-durriyya min manāqib shaykh al-Islām Ibn Taymiyya*, ed. Abū Muṣʿab Ṭalaʿat b. Fuʾād al-Ḥalwānī al-Farūq, Cairo, 2002, p. 4; al-Bazzār, *al-Aʿlām al-ʿaliyya fī manāqib shaykh al-Islām Ibn Taymiyya*, ed. Ṣalāḥ al-Dīn al-Munjid, Beirut 1976, p. 21; al-Kutubī, *Fawāt al-wafāyāt*, ed. ʿAlī Muḥammad Muʿawwiḍ and ʿĀdil Aḥmad ʿAbd al-Mawjūd, Beirut 2000, I, p. 124; Ibn Ḥajar al-ʿAsqalānī, *al-Durar al-kāmina fī aʿyān al-miʾa al-tāmina*, Beirut 1997, I/I, p. 88.

the development of what Emmanuel Sivan calls "refugee syndrome".[6] Mongol invasions and convocations of Mamluk authorities led to Ibn Taymiyya travelling back and forth between Syria and Egypt; these trips have been studied by scholars and are well-known.[7] For this reason, I address Ibn Taymiyya's spatial mobility only in relation to his other mobilities.

2 Mobility in the Sphere of the Mamluk Sultanate

2.1 *Professional Mobility: Ibn Taymiyya's First Major Mobility*

On 29 Dhū al-ḥijja 682/19 March 1284, Ibn Taymiyya's father died. This event led to Ibn Taymiyya's first major mobility given that he was appointed to succeed his father as a teacher at the *madrasa* al-Sukkariyya. Ibn Taymiyya, who was granted the honorary title (*laqab*) of *shaykh al-Islām* by some of his peers, was then 22 years old.[8] In 695/1296, he received a new teaching position at the *madrasa* al-Ḥanbaliyya, succeeding one of his teachers (*shuyūkh*), Zayn al-Dīn Abū al-Barakāt b. Munajjā, after the death of the latter in the same year.[9] As a *madrasa* teacher, Ibn Taymiyya received a salary, as a result of the professionalization of teachers. This meant that he was working for the Sultanate, as the system of *madrasas* and their funding at that time were intrinsically linked to charitable endowments (*waqfs*), sponsorship and decisions of the *amīrs*.[10] We

---

6 E. Sivan, *Radical Islam. Medieval Theology and Modern Politics*, Binghamton, 1990, p. 96.

7 The following is a non exhaustive list: Ibn Taymiyya, *Lettre à un croisé*, ed. trans. Yahya Michot, Lyon-Louvain-La-Neuve, 1995, pp. 70–82; Denise Aigle, "The Mongol Invasions of Bilād al-Shām by Ghāzān Khān and Ibn Taymīyah's Three 'Anti-Mongol' Fatwas," *Mamluk Studies Review* 11/2 (2007), pp. 89–120; id, "Ghazan Khan's Invasion of Syria. Polemics on his Conversion to Islam and the Christian Troops in His Army," in *The Mongol Empire between Myth and Reality. Studies in Anthropological History*, ed. Denise Aigle, Boston/Leiden 2016, pp. 255–282; Reuven Amitai, "The Mongol Occupation of Damascus in 1300: A Study of Mamluk Loyalities," in *The Mamluks in Egyptian and Syrian politics and society*, ed. Michael Winter and Amalia Levanoni, Leiden 2004, pp. 21–41; Laoust, *Le Hanbalisme sous les Mamlouks*, pp. 15–34.

8 Ibn Kathīr, *al-Bidāya wa-l-nihāya*, ed. ʿAbd Allāh b. ʿAbd al-Raḥmān al-Turkī, Giza 1998, XVII, pp. 592–593.

9 Ibid., XVII, pp. 684–685.

10 Georges Makdisi, *The Rise of Colleges. Institutions of Learning in Islam and the West*, Edinburgh 1981; Berkey, *The Transmission of Knowledge*, pp. 128–160; Chamberlain, *Knowledge and social practice*, pp. 95–100. See also Ira Lapidus, *Muslim Cities in the Later Middle Ages*, Cambridge, 1984, pp. 112–113; Joan E. Gilbert, "Institutionalization of Muslim Scholarship and Professionalization of the ʿulamāʾ in Medieval Damascus," *Studia Islamica* 52 (1980), pp. 105–135; Stephen Humphreys, "Politics and Architectural Patronage in Ayyūbid Damascus," in *The Islamic World from Classical to Modern Times Essays in Honor of Bernard Lewis*, ed. Bosworth *et al.*, Princeton 1989, pp. 151–174; Abdul-Latif

know that Ibn Taymiyya was criticized by other Ḥanbalīs for receiving a stipend for his teaching.[11] This first mobility of Ibn Taymiyya is doubly important because, on the one hand, he became a professional teacher despite his youth, and, on the other hand, it would be the only type of professional mobility that he would ever enjoy. Indeed, he never ascended the official hierarchy of the *ʿulamāʾ* or assumed other positions throughout the remainder of his life.

About 14 years later, in 697/1298, Ibn Taymiyya, then aged 36, was commissioned by Sultan Lājīn (d. 698/1299) to preach jihad at the Umayyad mosque on 17 Shawwāl 697/28 July 1298 to encourage volunteers to join the troops who were to be sent under the command of the *amīr* Sayf al-Dīn Qibjāq to reinforce the contingent already on the ground in Armenian territories.[12] At the time, Lājīn wanted to take advantage of the unrest that was dividing the Mongols by sending an expeditionary force to raid the kingdom of Armenia, an ally of the Ilkhanids. After initial successes, the Mamluk troops, who were led by the *amīr* ʿAlam al-Dīn al-Dawādārī, encountered difficulties, and it was necessary for the Mamluk power to send reinforcements. Ibn Taymiyya's preaching on this date was to be the first in a long series of calls to jihad.

At the beginning of Ṣafar 700/end of October 1300, news arrived *via* the *barīd* (postal system) of the progression of Ilkhanid troops towards Syria, which caused panic, the flight of a large part of the population and considerable inflation.[13] It was in this atmosphere that Ibn Taymiyya was compelled to continue teaching at the mosque, where he would present Quranic verses and *ḥadīths* on the merits of jihad to encourage people to fight, not flee, the enemy and to spend their money to protect Muslims, their land and their property, as it was considered preferable to spend money in "the path of God" than to flee.[14]

Two years later, we find Ibn Taymiyya as propagandist in the expeditionary force sent against the dwellers of the mountains of Kisrawān; the first time in Shawwāl 699/June 1300, when he addressed their chiefs who decided to

---

Tibawi, "Origin and Character of the Madras," *Bulletin of the School of Oriental and African Studies* 25 (1962), pp. 225–238; Anne F. Broadbridge, "Academic Rivalry and the Patronage System in the Fifteenth Century Egypt: al-ʿAynī, al-Maqrīzī and Ibn Ḥajar al-ʿAsqalānī," *Mamluk Studies Review* 3 (1999), pp. 85–106.

11 Abdul Hakim I. Al-Matroudi, *The Ḥanbalī School of Law and Ibn Taymiyya. Conflict or conciliation*, London/New-York 2006, p. 53.

12 Al-Birzālī, *al-Muqtafī ʿalā kitāb al-rawḍatayn*, ed. ʿUmar ʿAbd al-Salām al-Tadmurī, Beirut/Sayda 2006, I/II, p. 554; Ibn Kathīr, *al-Bidāya*, XVII, p. 704.

13 Al-Dhahabī, *Tārīkh al-Islām*, ed. ʿUmar ʿAbd al-Salām al-Tadmurī, Beirut 1990–2000, LII, p. 95; al-Birzālī, *al-Muqtafī*, II/I, pp. 131–132; Ibn Kathīr, *al-Bidāya*, XVII, p. 735.

14 Ibid., XVII, p. 736.

return the property looted from the Mamluk army following its defeat of Wādī al-Khāzindār; the second intervention in summer 704/1305.[15]

Can these propagandist and preaching activities all be considered forms of professional mobility in addition to that associated with his teaching position? First, it should be noted that the contexts in which Ibn Taymiyya fulfilled this role of propagandist differed from each other. In the second case, Ibn Taymiyya preached while fulfilling his teaching function at the mosque. For the preaching and the call to jihad at the Umayyad mosque, it is known from Ibn Kathīr that Ibn Taymiyya engaged in these activities at the request of the Mamluk Sultan Lājīn. Nevertheless, did the official character of the preaching confer the status of professional, that is to say, *khāṭib*'s (preacher) pay, to Ibn Taymiyya? Was Ibn Taymiyya paid to preach? No sources mention Ibn Taymiyya serving as an official preacher of Friday sermons.[16] The account of Ibn Baṭṭūṭa that described Ibn Taymiyya during a speech at the Umayyad mosque that God comes down (*nuzūl*) from the sky in the same way as he descended a step of the *minbar* is not clear since, at the time when the famous traveller was in Damascus, Ibn Taymiyya was in prison.[17]

Although there is no mention of remuneration for his official preaching of jihad at the Umayyad mosque on 17 Shawwāl 697/28 July 1298, it is quite possible that Ibn Taymiyya received compensation in view of the remuneration of the preachers of the time or that the Mamluk power at least proposed paying him. Another hypothesis is that Ibn Taymiyya may have sometimes received, as in the case of his pupil Ibn Qayyim al-Jawziyya (d. 751/1350), donations or gifts from certain amirs with whom he had good relations.[18] Lastly, we have also no precision concerning the nature of Ibn Taymiyya's position as a propagandist in the Mamluk expeditions against the Kisrawān population. In sum, the lack of information about Ibn Taymiyya's preaching does not permit us to state with certainty that he received money for those activities. If it is possible that Ibn Taymiyya could have been paid for that, this would concern a few

15 Ibid., XVII, p. 730; XVIII, p. 49. For more information on these expeditions see Henri Laoust, "Remarques sur les expéditions du Kasrawān sous les premiers Mamluks," *Bulletin du Musée de Beyrouth* 4 (1940), pp. 93–115; Kamal S. Salibi, "The Maronites of Lebanon under Frankish and Mamluk Rule (1099–1516)," *Arabica* 4/3 (1957), pp. 294–299; Ahmad Hutait, "Les expéditions mamloukes de Kasarwān. Critique de la lettre d'Ibn Taymiyya au sultan al-Nāṣir bin Qalāwūn," *ARAM Periodical* 9/1–2 (1997), pp. 77–84.

16 *Khāṭib* position is not well-documented or compared to others positions. Konrad Hirschler, "The Formation of the Civilian Elite in the Syrian Province: The Case of Ayyubid and Early Mamluk Ḥamāh," *Mamluk Studies Review* 12/2 (2008), p. 155.

17 Little, "Did Ibn Taymiyya Have a Screw Loose?," pp. 93–97.

18 Caterina Bori and Livnat Holtzman, "A Scholar in the Shadow," *Oriente Moderno* 1, 2010, p. 25.

cases given the very limited number of instances of official preachings that he accomplished at the Mamluk authorities' request. Due to lack of evidence, it may be difficult to speak of professional mobility in this case. The same conclusion concerns his activities as propagandist; the absence of any evidence for an official request from the Mamluk authorities leads me to think that Ibn Taymiyya did not play this propagandist role in a professional capacity but rather did so voluntarily. Indeed, Mamluk period chroniclers relate that many civilians among them *ʿulamāʾ* participated in the Mamluk army's expeditions as *mutaṭawwiʿa* (volunteers).[19]

2.2 *Ibn Taymiyya's Voluntary Tasks as Diplomat and Negotiator*

In addition to having served as propagandist (whether officially or unofficially), Ibn Taymiyya was called upon to play the role of diplomat and negotiator following the defeat of the Mamluks at the battle of Wādī al-Khāzindār on 27 Rabīʿ I 699/23 December 1299 and its sequel, the occupation of part of Syria by the Ilkhanid troops of Ghazan.[20] To best analyse this instance of Ibn Taymiyya's mobility, it is necessary to review the key facts.

After receiving the keys to the city of Homs from the city governor, *amīr* Muḥammad b. al-Ṣārim, Ghazan headed for Damascus and stopped in Ghūṭa.[21] The notables of Damascus gathered at Mashhad ʿAlī, where they decided to send a delegation to meet Ghazan and request an *amān* (guarantee of protection) for the population. Ibn Taymiyya was part of this delegation alongside other important figures, such as, among others, Badr al-Dīn b. Jamāʿa, ʿIzz al-Dīn al-Qalānisī and Wajīh al-Dīn b. Munajjā. The delegation left on Monday 3 of Rabīʿ II 699/28 December 1299.[22]

On Friday, 14 Rabīʿ II 699/8 January 700, the Friday prayer sermon at the Umayyad mosque in Damascus was delivered in the name of Ghazan. At the same time, a decree (*firmān*) declaring Sayf al-Dīn Qibshaq governor of Damascus and the *amīr* Sayf al-Dīn Baktamur governor of the fortresses in

19 Abbès Zouache, *Armées et combats en Syrie de 491/1098 à 569/1174. Analyse comparée des chroniques médiévales latines et arabes*, Damascus 2008, pp. 376–380.

20 Reuven Amitai, "The Logistics of the Mongol-Mamlūk War, with Special Reference to the Battle of Wādī ʾl-Khaznadār, 1299 C.E.," in *Logistics of Warfare in the Age of the Crusades. Proceedings of a Workshop at the Centre for Medieval Studies, University of Sydney, 30 September to 4 October 2002*, ed. John H. Pryor, Aldershot 2006, pp. 25–42; id, "The Mongol Occupation of Damascus in 1300: A Study of Mamluk Loyalities," in *The Mamluks in Egyptian and Syrian politics and society*, ed. Michael Winter and Amalia Levanoni, Leiden 2004, pp. 21–41.

21 Baybars al-Manṣūrī, *Zubdat al-fikra fī tārīkh al-hijra*, ed. Donald Richards, Berlin 1998, p. 332; Ibn Kathīr, *al-Bidāya*, XVII, p. 719.

22 Al-Dhahabī, *Tārīkh al-Islām*, LII, p. 74.

northern Syria and the Euphrates region was read in public.[23] While the inhabitants seemed more afraid than hurt, after the *firmān* promising them *amān* and declaring that Ghazan was a Muslim was read, the abuses of Ilkhanid soldiers began in the surroundings of Damascus region and elsewhere.[24] Commander Būlāy, who had pursued the remnants of the Mamluk army to Ghazza after the battle of Wādī al-Khāzindār, ravaged the region and captured many civilians.[25] At the same time, Ilkhanid troops, along with the Armenian and Georgian auxiliary forces fighting in the Ghazan army, devastated the quarters of al-Ṣāliḥiyya, Dārayyā as well as al-Mizzā, destroying and looting dwellings, mosques and *madrasas* and capturing men, women and children. Exactions and looting were also committed in other localities, such as Jerusalem and Nāblus.[26]

It is in this context that Ibn Taymiyya directly intervened on several occasions with the Ilkhanid authorities, in particular by meeting personalities close to Ghazan, including Sayf al-Dīn Qibshaq and the *shaykh al-shuyūkh* Niẓām al-Dīn Maḥmūd b. ʿAlī al-Shaybānī, who had accompanied Ghazaan and over whom he had a great influence.[27] Niẓām al-Dīn Maḥmūd had already left for al-Ṣāliḥiyya when Ilkhanid Mongols, Armenian and Georgian troops began looting the region. It seems that the *shaykh al-shuyūkh* Niẓām al-Dīn Maḥmūd was widely known and feared, since, as soon as they were informed of his arrival, the Ilkhanid soldiers left the region.[28] Niẓām al-Dīn ordered that all stolen goods be returned to the the inhabitants of the region, which was only partially done.[29] Certainly, Ibn Taymiyya got wind of this story and thought of convincing Niẓām al-Dīn to intercede with Ghazan to bring a swift end to the looting and atrocities, but his efforts were in vain. Indeed, as reported by al-Dhahabī, who paints an unflattering portrait of the *shaykh al-shuyūkh*, Niẓām al-Dīn completely changed his mind and allowed the Ilkhanid soldiers

23 Baybars al-Manṣūrī *Zubdat al-fikra*, pp. 333–344.

24 Al-Dhahabī, *Tārīkh al-Islām*, LII, p. 79; Ibn Kathīr, *al-Bidāya*, XVII, p. 720.

25 Al-Dhahabī, *Tārīkh al-Islām*, LII, p. 80. Written also "Mūlāy". See Aigle, "The Mongol Invasions of Bilād al-Shām," pp. 89–120; Ibn Taymiyya, *Lettre à un croisé*, pp. 44, 46; Mehdi Berriah, "Un aspect de l'art de la guerre de l'armée mamelouke: la pratique de la 'fausse ouverture' à la bataille de Shaqḥab (702/1303)," *Arabica* 65/4 (2018), pp. 450, 453, 463.

26 Baybars al-Manṣūrī, *Zubdat al-fikra*, p. 332; al-Dhahabī, *Tārīkh al-Islām*, LII, pp. 81–82, 86; Ibn Kathīr, *al-Bidāya*, XVII, pp. 721–722.

27 Al-Dhahabī, *Tārīkh al-Islām*, LII, p. 81.

28 Al-Yūnīnī, *Dayl mirʾāt al-zamān*, ed. Ḥamza A. ʿAbbās, Abu Dhabi 2007, p. 272; al-ʿAynī, *ʿIqd al-jumān fī tārīkh ahl al-zamān*, ed. Muḥammad Muḥammad Amīn, Cairo 2010, IV, pp. 33–34.

29 Al-Dhahabī, *Tārīkh al-Islām*, LII, p. 81.

to plunder the city of Damascus.[30] According to Wajīh al-Dīn b. al-Munajjā, Ghazan would have given him no less an amount than 600,000 dirhams from the large amount of money he managed to collect from the population.[31]

On 20 Rabīʿ II 699/14 January 1300, Ibn Taymiyya left with a group of notables to Ghazan's camp, which was in Tall Rāhit, near Damascus.[32] There, the delegation was not permitted to meet Ghazan in person; instead, Ibn Taymiyya met with his two viziers, Saʿd al-Dīn and Rashīd al-Dīn, who asked him not to complain about the Ilkhanid Mongols because they were doing what was best and that it was necessary to satisfy the soldiers, a large part of whom had received no loot until now.[33] Ibn Taymiyya also interacted with two other important Ilkhanid figures: the commanders Quṭlūshāh and Būlāy.[34]

On 2 Rajab 699/19 March 1300, Ibn Taymiyya went to the Būlāy's camp to negotiate with the Ilkhanid commander the release of the Muslim, Christian and Jewish prisoners who had been captured during the raids in the region. The negotiations seem to have been tense and lengthy; Ibn Taymiyya spent three nights in Būlāy's camp and succeeded in securing the release of several prisoners.[35] The Ilkhanids evacuated Syria and returned to Iraq in Jumādā II 699/March 1300, but the threat still loomed. On 10 Rajab/1 April, Ilkhanid riders attacked peasants who went out to work in the fields outside of Damascus.[36]

30 Ibid., LII, pp. 82–83.

31 Ibid., LII, p. 84.

32 Al-Birzālī, *al-Muqtafī*, II/1, pp. 29–34; al-ʿAynī, *ʿIqd al-jumān*, IV, pp. 29–30.

33 Al-Dhahabī, *Tārīkh al-Islām*, LII, p. 82; Ibn Kathīr, *al-Bidāya*, XVII, p. 722; al-ʿAynī, *ʿIqd al-jumān*, IV, pp. 34–35. Al-Dhahabi relates that Ibn Taymiyya met Ghazan a second time. Al-Dhahabi, *Tārīkh al-Islām*, LII, p. 90. See also Caterina Bori, "A New Source for the Biography of Ibn Taymiyya," *Bulletin of the School of Oriental and African Studies* 67/3 (2004), p. 325. Henri Laoust and Thomas Raff think there was only one meeting. Henri Laoust, *Essais sur les doctrines sociales et politiques de Tâkî-d-Dîn Aḥmad b. Taymîya, canoniste ḥanbalite né à Ḥarrân en 661/1262, mort à Damas en 728/1328*, Cairo 1939, pp. 117–120; id, "La biographie d'Ibn Taymîya d'après Ibn Kathîr," *Bulletin d'études orientales*, 12 (1942–1943), pp. 122–124; Thomas Raff, "Remarks on an anti-Mongol Fatwâ by Ibn Taimîya," Leiden 1973, pp. 20–24; Ibn Taymiyya, *Lettre à un croisé*, note 125, pp. 74–74.

34 Ibn Aybak al-Dawādārī, *Kanz al-durar wa jāmiʿ al-ġurar*, ed. Bernd Ratke *et al.*, Cairo, 1960–1994, IX, pp. 291–293. On these two personnages see Denise Aigle, "The Mongol Invasions of Bilād al-Shām," pp. 89–120. Like Ibn Taymiyya, they took part in the battle of Shaqḥab in Ramaḍān 702/April 1303. Berriah, "Un aspect de l'art de la guerre de l'armée mamelouke," pp. 450–463.

35 Al-Yūnīnī, *Dhayl mirʾāt al-zamān*, p. 299; al-Dhahabī, *Tārīkh al-Islām*, LII, p. 93; Ibn Aybak al-Dawādārī, *Kanz al-ġurar*, IX, pp. 35–36; Ibn Kathīr, *al-Bidāya*, XVII, p. 725.

36 Al-Dhahabī, *Tārīkh al-Islām*, LII, p. 94; Ibn Kathīr, *al-Bidāya*, XVII, p. 727.

Far from innovating by playing the role of diplomat and negotiator, Ibn Taymiyya followed a well-established tradition among the *ʿulamāʾ* of the Mamluk period. Previously, at the end of 657/1259, the Ayyubid sultan al-Nāṣir Yūsuf sent the *qāḍī* and historian Kamāl al-Dīn b. ʿAdīm (d. 660/1262) to ask for the assistance of the Mamluk Sultanate against Hülegü's advance, a request that was accepted by the new sultan Quṭuz.[37] Under the Mamluks, several *ʿulamāʾ* were entrusted with important diplomatic missions, such as the *qāḍī* Ibn Wāṣil (d. 697/1298), the *qāḍī* Shams al-Dīn b. Quraysh who was sent to sign the truces with the Hospitallers of Ḥiṣn al-Akrād and Marqab in 665/1266, or of the historian Ibn ʿAbd al-Ẓāhir (d. 692/1293) who was sent to negotiate with the authorities of Acre in 666/1267.[38] The examples cited above are cases of professional mobility; it is the Mamluk power which officially instructed these *ʿulamāʾ* to conduct negotiations on behalf of the sultanate, which is not the case with Ibn Taymiyya. As such, referring to the latter, professional mobility would not be appropriate in this context.

Indeed, a close reading of the sources shows that Ibn Taymiyya's intercession with the Ilkhanid authorities to negotiate the release of Muslim, Christian and Jewish prisoners have been the fruit of his personal initiative, as with the case with the other scholars mentioned above. In a certain sense, this initiative served the interests of the Mamluk Sultanate, which was encountering great difficulties at the time. Yahya Michot's use of the term "voluntary mediator" to describe Ibn Taymiyya's role has its full meaning here.[39] It is interesting to note that Ibn Taymiyya subsequently enjoyed a mobility that allowed him to advance from the status of volunteer diplomat and negotiator to that of an official envoy. At the beginning of Jumādā I 700/January 1301, Ibn Taymiyya left to meet the sultan's *nāʾib*, al-Afram, and other *amīrs*, who had withdrawn from Damascus and had set up camp for several months in the surroundings of the city. Ibn Taymiyya spent a night there encouraging the *amīrs* to hold out.[40] As the Ilkhanid danger was drawing nearer and the situation was increasingly deteriorating, al-Afram asked Ibn Taymiyya to go to the sultan and press him to send the army, a request that the *shaykh* of Damascus accepted. Therefore, Ibn Taymiyya left for Cairo with the *barīd*'s horses and arrived on

37 Al-Dhahabī, *Tārīkh al-Islām*, XXXXVIII, pp. 45–46; Ibn Kathīr, *al-Bidāya*, XVII, pp. 387–388; al-ʿAynī, *ʿIqd al-jumān*, I, pp. 218–219.

38 Konrad Hirschler, "Ibn Wāṣil: An Ayyūbid Perspective on Frankish Lordships and Crusades," in *Medieval Muslim Historians and the Franks in the Levant*, ed. Alex Mallett, Leiden/Boston 2015, pp. 142–143; Ibn ʿAbd al-Ẓāhir, *al-Rawḍ al-zāhir fī sīrat al-Malik al-Ẓāhir Baybars*, ed. ʿAbd al-ʿAzīz al-Khuwayṭir, Riyadh 1976, pp. 283, 332–333.

39 Ibn Taymiyya, *Lettre à un croisé*, p. 74.

40 Al-Birzālī, *al-Muqtafī*, II/I, p. 133.

20 Jumādā I 700/31 January 1301.[41] In Cairo, Ibn Taymiyya urged the sultan and the *amīrs* to meet the invader and not give up the jihad.[42] Ibn Taymiyya's energetic and optimistic speech inspired the Mamluk leaders and gave them free resolve.[43] Orders were given to call and prepare for the jihad throughout Cairo. Ibn Taymiyya returned to Syria on 27 Jumādā I 700/7 February 1301. His stay in Cairo had only lasted seven or eight days.[44]

At some point during the years 702–703/1303–1304, Ibn Taymiyya would again play the role of volunteer mediator. During the years 699/1299–702/1303, Muslims were captured by Ilkhanids and Armenians, as well as crusaders from Cyprus, during the temporary Ilkhanid occupation of Syria and sold as slaves, particularly in Cyprus. At approximately the same time, crusaders led several maritime raids on the coast of the Mamluk Sultanate, during which they captured many prisoners, who were also sold in Cyprus. By writing his *Risāla al-qubruṣiyya*, Ibn Taymiyya made what Yahya Michot refers to as "une démarche humanitaire".[45] In this text, Ibn Taymiyya requested of the crusader prince Sir Johan of Gibelet that he provides opportunities for the release of Muslim prisoners and their good treatment; in particular, he requested that they not be forced to change their religion.[46] This letter was also written on Ibn Taymiyya's personal initiative. It was the *shaykh* Abū al-ʿAbbās al-ʿUdusī, who was captured during a crusader attack on the Dāmūr coast in Syria and who had succeeded in paying his ransom, who informed Ibn Taymiyya of the plight of the Muslim prisoners in Cyprus.[47] Ibn Taymiyya's roles as negotiator, humanitarian and mediator were clearly not instances of professional mobility, as no sources indicate that the Mamluk authorities made him responsible for negotiating for the release of the prisoners. This voluntary mobility is due, on the one hand, to Ibn Taymiyya's religious scruples and constant concern for both Islam and Muslims and, on the other hand, his reluctance to make friends in the circles of power.

---

41 Al-Dhahabī, *Tārīkh al-Islām*, LII, p. 101; Ibn Kathīr, *al-Bidāya*, XVII, pp. 738–739.

42 Ibn Kathīr, *al-Bidāya*, XVII, p. 738.

43 Al-Dhahabī, *Tārīkh al-Islām*, LII, p. 104.

44 Ibid., 52:104; al-Birzālī, *al-Muqtafī*, II/I, p. 138; Ibn Kathīr, *al-Bidāya*, XVII, p. 739.

45 Ibn Taymiyya, *Lettre à un croisé*, pp. 70, 92.

46 Id, *al-Risāla al-qubruṣiyya*, ed. Qaṣī Muḥibb al-Dīn, Cairo 1974, pp. 31–35, 40. See also Ibn Taymiyya, *Lettre à un croisé*, pp. 90–92.

47 Id, *al-Risāla al-qubruṣiyya*, pp. 22, 40. See also Ibn Taymiyya, *Lettre à un croisé*, p. 90.

2.3 *From Political Adviser to Political Enemy: Ibn Taymiyya's Upward and Downward Mobility*

It would be incorrect to consider the relations that Ibn Taymiyya maintained with the Mamluk authorities of his time as having been poor simply because he was repeatedly condemned and imprisoned.[48] While it is true that he encountered certain difficulties and forms of opposition from *ʿulamāʾ* and *amīrs*, this should not be generalized.

Ibn Taymiyya's relations with the Mamluk power seem to have been ambivalent, as indicated by his writings on the sultanate, in which he both praises and indirectly criticises the Mamluk authorities.[49] Nevertheless, despite these criticisms, cooperation between the *ʿulamāʾ* class and Mamluks was a fundamental principle of Ibn Taymiyya's political thought.[50] As many scholars have demonstrated, the relations between *ʿulamāʾ* and Mamluks power were more "symbiotic" in nature than a simple case of the subservience of the *ʿulamāʾ* to the Mamluk *amīrs*.[51]

---

48 Chamberlain, *Knowledge and social practice*, pp. 169–173; Donald Little, "The Historical and Historiographical Significance of the Detention (miḥna) of Ibn Taymiyya," *International Journal of Middle East Studies* 4/3 (1973), pp. 311–327.

49 Mehdi Berriah, "The Mamluk Sultanate and the Mamluks seen by Ibn Taymiyya: between Praise and Criticism," *Arabian Humanities* 14, 2020.

50 Caterina Bori, "One or Two Versions of *al-Siyāsa al-sharʿiyya* of Ibn Taymiyya? And What Do They Tell Us?," *ASK Working Papers* 26, Bonn 2016, p. 17; Michael Cook, *Commanding Right Forbidding Wrong in Islamic Thought*, Cambridge 2000, p. 150. For more details on Ibn Taymiyya's political conception see Mona Hassan, "Modern Interpretations and Misinterpretations of a Medieval Scholar: Apprehending the Political Thought of Ibn Taymiyyah," in *Ibn Taymiyya and his Times*, ed. Yossef Rapoport and Shahab Ahmed, Karachi 2010, pp. 338–366; Caterina Bori, "Théologie politique et Islam à propos d'Ibn Taymiyya (m. 728/1328) et du sultanat mamelouk," *Revue de l'histoire des religions* 224 no. 1 (2007), pp. 5–46; Ovamir Anjum, *Politics Law and Community. The Taymiyyan Moment*, Cambridge 2012; Abdelsamad Belhaj, "Law and Order according to Ibn Taymiyya and Ibn Qayyim al-Jawziyya: A Re-Examination of siyāsa sharʿiyya," in *Islamic Theology Philosophy and Law. Debating Ibn Taymiyya and Ibn Qayyim al-Jawziyya*, ed. Birgit Krawietz and George Tamer, Berlin 2013, pp. 400–422; Baber Johansen, "A Perfect Law in an Imperfect Society. Ibn Taymiyya's Concept of 'Governance in the Name of the Sacred Law,'" in *The Law Applied: Contextualizing the Islamic Sharīʿa: A Volume in Honour of Frank E. Vogel*, ed. Peri Bearman, Bernard G. Weiss, and Wolfhart Heinrichs, London/New York 2008, pp. 259–294; A.K.S. Lambton, *State and Government in Medieval Islam: An Introduction to the Study of Islamic Political Theory: the Jurists*, Oxford 1981, pp. 145–149.

51 Yaacov Lev, "Symbiotic Relations: Ulama and the Mamluk Sultans," *Mamluk Studies Review* 13/1 (2009), pp. 8, 19. See also Mathieu Eychenne, *Liens personnels, clientélisme et réseaux de pouvoir dans le sultanat mamelouk (milieu XIII*e*–fin XIV*e* siècle)* Damascus-Beirut, 2013; Éric Geoffroy, *Le soufisme en Égypte et en Syrie sous les derniers mamelouks et les premiers Ottomans. Orientation spirituelles et enjeux culturels*, Damascus 1996, pp. 54–61, Broadbridge, "Academic Rivalry and the Patronage System in the Fifteenth Century

An examination of contemporary authors' chronicles and Ibn Taymiyya's writings indicate that Ibn Taymiyya enjoyed a significant increase in mobility, as he intervened in Mamluk affairs on several occasions, with the most crucial of these being in Syria, where, as discussed above, he responded to the threat of Ilkhanid invasion. Particularly well-known are the letters sent to Sultan al-Nāṣir Muḥammad encouraging him and his *amīrs* to come to Syria to fight the Ilkhanids, as these letters have been the subject of many academic works.[52]

If the Ilkhanid crisis was a major turning point for Ibn Taymiyya on the political level, it is clear from al-Nāṣir Muḥammad's victory against Baybars al-Jāshankīr and his second reign that Ibn Taymiyya enjoyed an increasing upward mobility, as his influence over the Mamluk sultan increased. How should this influence be evaluated? The following paragraphs attempt to provide some answers.

In 710/1310, Ibn Taymiyya advised Sultan al-Nāsir to name *amīr* al-Afram as governor of Tripoli instead of the minor province of Ṣalkhad.[53] On 13 Jumādā I 711/27 September 1311, a popular revolt led by Jalāl al-Dīn al-Qazwīnī and Majd al-Dīn al-Tūnisī broke out against Sayf al-Dīn Karāy's abuses, governor of Damascus, who ordered the arrest of the revolt's leaders. However, following Ibn Taymiyya's intervention, the governor was also arrested 10 days later and jailed in the Karak citadel.[54] After Tankīz's nomination as governor of Damascus in 712/1312, two letters arrived from Cairo and were read in the Umayyad mosque. The first concerned the prohibition of awarding public positions to those who attempted to obtain them by bribery (*rashwā*); the second ordered that homicides be punished according to *sharīʿa* rules. According to Ibn Kathīr, Ibn Taymiyya was the cause (*sabab*) of these two letters.[55] If there is no clearly evidence that Ibn Taymiyya was behind the two letters, they both

Egypt," p. 85; Lutz Wiederhold, "Legal-Religious Elite, Temporal Authority, and the Caliphate in Mamluk Society: Conclusions Drawn from the Examination of a 'Zahiri Revolt' in Damascus in 1386," *International Journal of Middle East Studies*, 31/2 (1999), p. 225; Jean-Claude Garcin, "Le sultan et Pharaon (le politique et le religieux dans l'Égypte mamluke)," in *Espaces, pouvoirs et idéologies de l'Égypte médiévale*, ed. J.-C. Garcin, London 1987, part IX, p. 14; Emmanuel Sivan, *L'Islam et la croisade. Idéologie et Propagande dans les Réactions Musulmanes aux Croisades*, Paris 1968, pp. 110–111.

52 Teymour Morel, "Deux textes anti-Mongols d'Ibn Taymiyya," *The Muslim World* 105/2 (2015), p. 371; Yahya Michot, "Texte spirituels d'Ibn Taymiyya. Nouvelle série XXIII. Lettre au sultan al-Nāsir concernant les Tatars", 2017.

53 Ibn Kathīr, *al-Bidāya*, XVIII, p. 109.

54 Ibid., XVIII, pp. 111–112.

55 Ibid., XVIII, p. 124.

correspond, as Henri Laoust has demonstrated, to two important chapters of his *Siyāsa al-sharʿiyya*.[56]

Lastly, Ibn Taymiyya may also have been a political adviser, as the issue Sultan al-Nāṣir Muḥammad's demand concerning *amīr* Ḥumayḍa's goods illustrates. After succeeding his brother Ghazan as the head of the Ilkhanate and converting to Shīʿism, Öljeitü (d. 716/1316) intervened in the affairs of the holy city of Makkah. Makkah's sharīf, Ḥumayḍa b. Abī Numayy al-Ḥasanī, had fought and killed his brother Abū al-Ghayth and had been chased away by Mamluk troops sent to the Ḥijāz. Ḥumayḍa came in person to seek the help and support of Öljeitü, who acceded to his request by sending 4,000 Khurāsānī fighters to accompany him to Makkah.[57] This was an opportunity for the Ilkhanids to attempt to gain control over the holy places of Islam and thus gain political legitimacy. The troops left at the end of Rajab 715/October 1315 led by the Shīʿī Ilkhanid commander, al-Dulqundī.[58] After passing Basra, the troops received news of Öljeitü's death, which prompted the majority of the soldiers to no longer wish to continue the expedition. Only 300 Ilkhanid soldiers and 400 Bedouins from Banū ʿAqīl of Basra decided to continue their journey with Ḥumayḍa and Dulqundī, but they were routed by Muḥammad b. ʿĪsā, *amīr* of Āl Faḍl, in that time the most powerful Bedouin tribe of Syria and ally of the Sultanate, and his troops.[59] After the defeat of Ḥumayda, Sultan al-Nāṣir consulted Ibn Taymiyya and asked him to issue a fatwa concerning the seizure of *sharīf* Makkah Ḥumayḍa's goods and, more generally, the property and lands of Muslims initially taken by infidels and then recovered by Muslim authorities as either *ghanīma* (spoils of war after fight) or *fay'* (spoils of war without fight). The issue concerned whether these properties should be returned to their owners or become the property of the *amwāl al-sulṭāniyya* (property of the sultanate)? This question led to differences of opinion among the *ʿulamā'*, and a host of opinions exist on the subject. For Ibn Taymiyya, the answer was affirmative:

> [...] if the Mongols attack Syria and plunder the property of Muslims and Christians and then the Muslims attack the Mongols and plunder the property of their slain, is what was taken to them lawful or not? He

---

56 Laoust, *Le Hanbalisme*, p. 27.

57 Al-Maqrīzī, *Kitāb al-sulūk li-maʿrifat duwal al-mulūk*, ed. Muḥammad ʿAbd al-Qādir ʿAṭā (Beirut: Dār al-kutub al-ʿilmiyya, 1997), II, p. 505.

58 May be also al-Dulqandī or al-Dilqandī. We find الدرفندي in Abū al-Fidā'. Abū al-Fidā', *al-Mukhtaṣar fī tārīkh al-bashar* (Cairo, s.d), II/IV, p. 81; Ibn Kathīr, *al-Bidāya*, XVIII, p. 154; al-Maqrīzī, *Kitāb al-sulūk*, II, p. 505.

59 Abū al-Fidā', *al-Mukhtaṣar*, II/IV, p. 81.

> replied: 'Everything that has been taken from the Mongols is divided into five parts, and it is allowed to profit from it.'[60]

The previous examples must not be generalized. While Ibn Taymiyya may have enjoyed upward mobility and influence in the political sphere for a time, this period was limited. His famous treaty *al-Siyāsa al-sharʿiyya*, which was likely written between 711/1311–714/1314 and which some scholars consider to be an ethical leadership treaty or an example of the "Mirrors for Princes" literature, was written for the sultan.[61] Ibn Taymiyya's goal was to advise and encourage the Mamluk authorities to practice a form of governance that was in accordance with Islamic law. However, as Caterina Bori noted regarding the misdeeds that characterized al-Nāṣir's reign, the impact of Ibn Taymiyya's *Siyāsa* must have been close to zero.[62]

Although the anti-Mongol religious stance of Ibn Taymiyya and the political interests of the Mamluks converged, this was not always the case as the Mamluk expeditions against the population of Kisrawān illustrate. According to Ibn Taymiyya's biographer and student Ibn Kathīr, the *shaykh al-Islām* of Damascus incited Mamluk authorities to severely punish the Ismāʿīlī populations of the Kisrawān region at the end of an important military expedition during summer 704/1305.[63] As Stefan Winter demonstrated, the Mamluk expeditions against the Nuṣayrī and other Kisrawān populations in 705/1305 and 718/1318 seem to have been motivated more by economic than religious reasons.[64] For Yaron Friedman, Ibn Taymiyya's anti-Nuṣayrī fatwa cannot therefore be considered as an indicator of an inquisitorial Mamluk policy against these minorities, which Ibn Taymiyya considered to be heretical.[65] Ibn Taymiyya and the Mamluks clearly had different reasons for attacking religious minorities in this region.

From 718/1318, Ibn Taymiyya experienced a downward trend in terms of his mobility, as opposed to the previous upward tendency, as a result of encountering difficulties with the Mamluk authorities. On 1 Jumādā I 718/1 July 1318, a letter

---

60 Ibn Taymiyya, *al-Jihād*, ed. ʿAbd al-Raḥmān ʿUmayra, Beirut 1997, II, p. 182.

61 Hassan, "Modern Interpretations and Misinterpretations," p. 347; Bori, "One or Two Versions", p. 23.

62 Bori, "One or Two Versions", p. 11.

63 Ibn Kathīr, *al-Bidāya*, XVIII, pp. 49–50.

64 Stefan Winter, *A History of the ʿAlawis: From Medieval Aleppo to the Turkish Republic*, Princeton 2016, pp. 58–60.

65 Yaron Friedman, "Ibn Taymiyya's Fatāwā against the Nuṣayrī-ʿAlawī Sect," *Der Islam* 82:2 (2005), pp. 349–363; id, *The Nuṣayrī – ʿAlawīs: An Introduction to the Religion, History and Identity of the Leading Minority in Syria* Leiden 2010, pp. 188–199.

from Cairo arrived in Damascus prohibiting Ibn Taymiyya from giving fatwa about the oath of divorce (*al-ḥilf bi-l-ṭalāq*).[66] After appearing three times before a *ʿulamāʾ* council, he was accused of not respecting the prohibition and was jailed for five months, with his sentence ending on 10 Muḥarram 721/9 February 1321. Four years later, he was again arrested due to his writings and positions on the matter of *ziyārat al-qubūr* in which he was opposed to the Mālikī chief judge Tāqī al-Dīn Muḥammad b. Abī Bakr al-Ikhnāʾī.[67] How can this reversal of Ibn Taymiyya's mobility be explained? How did Ibn Taymiyya go from being known as a celebrated preacher and a political adviser to being perceived as a troublemaker and a dangerous individual?

Ibn Taymiyya was always an unwavering supporter of the Mamluk power, particularly in the years 699/1299, when, under the threat of the Ilkhanids, the sultanate was in great peril. However, his positions and writings against Ashʿarism, dominant doctrines such as that of Ibn ʿArabī, popular practices such as visiting the graves (*ziyārāt*) of the Prophets and Saints as well as his fatwas opposed to the majority opinions of the legal schools, were all perceived as potentially dangerous because they had the potential to social disruption and therefore disturb the Mamluk establishment.[68] These were some *ʿulamāʾ* who were hostile to Ibn Taymiyya and close to the *amīrs* who encouraged the latter to have him tried, after which he was incarcerated. Ibn ʿAbd al-Hādī, ʿUmar b. ʿAlī al-Bazzār and Ibn Kathīr, all three of whom were students of Ibn Taymiyya, accuse, with some rather virulent remarks, certain of these scholars of having knowingly conspired against their *shaykh*.[69]

66 Carolyn Baugh, "Ibn Taymiyya's Feminism?: Imprisonment and the Divorce Fatwās," in *Muslima Theology: The Voices of Muslim Women Theologians*, ed. Ednan Aslan, Marcia Hermansen, Elif Medeni, Frankfurt 2013, pp. 181–196; Al-Matroudi, *The Ḥanbalī School of Law and Ibn Taymiyya*, pp. 171–185; Yossef Rapoport, *Mariage, Money and Divorce in Medieval Islamic Society*, Cambridge 2005, pp. 94–105; Taqī al-Dīn al-Subkī,, "Naqd al-ijtimāʿ wa l-iftirāq fī masāʾil al-aymān wa l-ṭalāq" in *al-durra al-muḍiyya fī al-radd ʿalā Ibn Taymiyya*, ed. Muḥammad Zāhid al-Kawtharī, Damacus al-Taraqī, 1348H, pp. 43–53; id, "al-Naẓar al-muḥaqqiq fī-l-ḥilf bi-l-ṭalāq al-muʿaliq" in *al-durra al-muḍiyya fī al-radd ʿalā Ibn Taymiyya*, ed. Muḥammad Zāhid al-Kawtharī, Damacus al-Taraqī, 1348H, pp. 55–58.

67 Ibn Taymiyya, *al-Radd ʿalā al-Ikhnāʾī*, ed. Aḥmad b. Munas al-Ghanzī, Jeddah 2011.

68 Caterina Bori, "Theology, Politics, Society: The Missing Link. Studying Religion in the Mamluk Period" in *Ubi Sumus? Quo Vademus? Mamluk Studies – State of the Art*, ed. Stephan Conermann, Göttingen 2013, pp. 71–73, 78–79. Caterina Bori suggests "that Ibn Taymīyah's detachment from the authority of the four *madhāhib* and his challenge to judicial authority became socially and politically inconvenient at some point, as his death in prison shows." Caterina Bori, "The Collection and Edition of Ibn Taymiyah's Works: Concerns of a Disciple," *Mamluk Studies Review* 13/2, 2009, p. 67.

69 Ibn ʿAbd al-Hādī, *al-Ṣārim al-munkī fī al-radd ʿalā al-Subkī*, ed. Badriyya bint Ḥamīd al-Rāʾiqī, Ṣafiyya bint Sulaymān al-Tawījrī, Sihām bint Aḥmad al-Muḥammadī, al-Mansura

It can therefore be said that Ibn Taymiyya's contradictory mobility – initially upward and then downward – is linked to the nature of his relations with the Mamluk power.[70] All of his fatwas against the Ilkhanid invaders were welcome and could only benefit the Mamluks politically. However, once the Ilkhanid threat had been lifted, Ibn Taymiyya's fatwas, which had the potential to create social disruption and challenge the power of certain *ʿulamāʾ*, some of whom were close to the Mamluk authorities, were no longer acceptable. As a result, the sultan issued the decree prohibiting Ibn Taymiyya from giving fatwas on divorce; alternatively, his remarks on the *ziyārāt* may have been deliberately falsified to provide a pretext by which to get rid of him.[71]

3 Voluntary Mobilities

3.1 *Was Ibn Taymiyya's Mobility within the Mamluk Army due to His Role as a Mujāhid (Warrior) or for Moral Support?*

In addition to describing him as a scholar endowed with outstanding intellectual properties and a *mujtahid* (*person capable of interpreting religious law*), a *mujaddīd* (*scholar who brings "renewal" of the religion*) and *shaykh al-Islām*, some of Ibn Taymiyya's contemporaries also referred to him as a *mujāhid*.[72] His portrayal as a *mujāhid* can be explained with reference to his numerous writings on jihad as well as his investment in jihad against the Ilkhanid Mongols. Since it is irrefutable that he fought the Ilkhanids ideologically, as Thomas Raff, Yahya Michot and Denise Aigle have clearly demonstrated, did he also fight them with the sword?

Several *ʿulamāʾ* participated alongside the Mamluk army in the fight against the Ilkhanids, and some even died doing so, such as Shams al-Dīn b. Maktūm

2014, pp. 178–179, 182–192; id, *al-ʿUqūd al-durriyya*, p. 258; al-Bazzār, *al-Aʿlām al-ʿaliyya fī manāqib shaykh al-Islām Ibn Taymiyya*, ed. Ṣalāḥ al-Dīn al-Munjad, Beirut 1976, pp. 42–43, 45–46, 66–68; Ibn Kathīr, *al-Bidāya wa-l-nihāya*, XVIII, p. 270. Al-Bazzār accuses them of having wanted to condemn him to death. Al-Bazzār, *al-Aʿlām al-ʿaliyya*, pp. 57, 68.

70 Berriah, "The Mamluk Sultanate and the Mamluks seen by Ibn Taymiyya: between Praise and Criticism," 2020.

71 Yahya Michot, "Reflections on the funeral, and the present state of the tomb, of Ibn Taymiyya in Damascus. For a Grave in Damascus", 6 http://www.interfacepublications.com/~interfa3/images/pdf/IbnTaymiyya_Tomb.pdf. Niels Olesen speaks about a "malentendu". Niels H. Olesen, *Culte des Saints et Pèlerinage chez Ibn Taymiyya* (*661/1263–728/1328*) (Paris, 1991), 50. See also Yossef Rapoport, "Ibn Taymiyya's Radical Legal Thought: Rationalism, Pluralism and the Primacy of Intention", in *Ibn Taymiyya and his Times*, ed. Yossef Rapoport and Shahab Ahmed, Karachi 2010, p. 211.

72 Ibn ʿAbd al-Hādī, *al-ʿUqūd al-durriyya*, p. 3; al-Bazzār, *al-Aʿlām al-ʿaliyya*, pp. 18, 63.

Baʿlabakkī, ʿAbd Allāh b. Muḥammad al-Yūnīnī and the *qāḍī* Tāj al-Dīn Yaḥyā al-Irbīlī during the battle of Ḥoms of 680/1281 or the chief judge of the Ḥanafīs, Ḥusām al-Dīn al-Rāzī, who was killed in Wādī al-Khāzindār.[73] What is certain is Ibn Taymiyya's presence on the battlefield. As mentioned above, he participated in two expeditions against the Nuṣayrīs and other populations of Kisrawān as well as in actions against the Ilkhanid Mongols.

During the temporary occupation of Syria by the Ilkhanids, the *barīd* announced news of the army's departure from Cairo on 9 Rajab 700/ 31 March 1300. When informed, Arjuwāsh, the commander of the citadel of Damascus, decreed a general mobilization of all men for the surveillance of the ramparts of the city.[74] Ibn Kathīr reports, quoting al-Birzālī, that Ibn Taymiyya participated in the night patrols on the ramparts, urged people to be patient and encouraged them to fight by reciting verses relating to the merits of jihad.[75]

In Rajab 702/19 February–20 March 1303, the Ilkhanids started to march again towards Syria.[76] This news forced the Mamluk forces in Syria to concentrate their forces while awaiting the arrival of reinforcements sent from Cairo. Ibn Taymiyya left to join the Mamluk troops from Hama, who had settled in al-Quṭayfa, located about 40 kilometres from Damascus, in order to join forces with the troops in the region.[77] According to Ibn Kathīr, Ibn Taymiyya played a primary moral support role for both *amīrs* and soldiers.[78]

On Thursday 29 Shaʿbān 702/18 April 1303, Ibn Taymiyya accompanied a group of volunteers who had left the city to fight the Ilkhanids alongside the Mamluk army. On leaving the city, he came under criticism from some residents, who accused him of leaving with the intention to flee not fight, which he had urged the population not to do.[79] He joined the Mamluk army, where he urged the sultan, the *amīrs* and the combatants to pursue the jihad and promising them victory over the enemy by issuing a fatwa authorizing the combatants to disregard the Ramaḍān fast while fighting in order to favour the effort of the jihad.[80] The largest and most important battle of the Mamluk-Ilkhanid

73 Al-Birzālī, *al-Muqtafī*, I/I, p. 523; al-Dhahabī, *Tārīkh*, LII, p. 74; Ibn Kathīr, *al-Bidāya*, XVII, p. 718.

74 Ibid., XVII, p. 727.

75 Al-Birzālī, *al-Muqtafī*, II/I, p. 73; Ibn Kathīr, *al-Bidāya*, XVII, p. 727.

76 Al-Nuwayrī, *Nihāyat al-arab fī funūn al-adab*, ed. N.M. Fawāz, Beirut 2004, XXXII, p. 15; Baybars al-Mansuri, *Zubdat al-fikra*, p. 367; Abū al-Fidā', *al-Mukhtaṣar*, II/IV, p. 48.

77 Al-Birzālī, *al-Muqtafī*, II/I, p. 219; Ibn Kathīr, *al-Bidāya*, XVIII, p. 23.

78 Ibid., XVIII, p. 23.

79 Ibid., XVIII, pp. 24–25.

80 Ibid., XVIII, p. 28.

conflict, took place at Shaqḥab south of Damascus. After two days of hard fighting, the Mamluks won an overwhelming victory on Ghazan's army.[81] On Monday 4 Ramaḍān/22 April, Ibn Taymiyya and the volunteers who had left to fight returned to Damascus, which they found cheering.[82]

Contemporary authors do not make it clear whether the *ʿulamāʾ* fought physically, with most writers simply noting their presence in battle. The question that arises is the following: did Ibn Taymiyya fight in the strict sense at Shaqḥab? In his *al-ʿUqūd al-durriyya*, Ibn ʿAbd al-Hādī describes Ibn Taymiyya entering Damascus 'carrying weapon [and cuirass]' (*shākan fī silāḥi-hi*) before the battle of Shaqḥab.[83] Nowhere, however, does Ibn ʿAbd al-Hādī write that Ibn Taymiyya participated in combat with arms in hand. In addition, according to Ibn ʿAbd al-Hādī, who reports the account of a Syrian *amīr* present at the same battle, Ibn Taymiyya and his companions shouted encouragement to the soldiers, urging them to fight, not flee, during the battle.[84] It would therefore seem, according to Ibn ʿAbd al-Hādī, that Ibn Taymiyya and his companions were present on the battlefield and provided essential psychological support to the combatants without taking part in combat.

Al-Bazzār, another student and biographer of Ibn Taymiyya, devotes chapter eleven of his *al-Aʿlām al-ʿaliyya* to Ibn Taymiyya's strength of heart (*quwwat qalbihi*) and courageousness (*shajāʿatihi*). This chapter provides a more martial depiction of Ibn Taymiyya's participation in jihad. While, like Ibn ʿAbd al-Hādī and Ibn Kathīr, al-Bazzār describes the psychological role played by Ibn Taymiyya on the battlefield in terms of encouraging those who were afraid by quoting verses on the merits of jihad and promising God's support against the infidel threat, he also notes that:

> When he rode a horse, he would tie his turban around his neck and manoeuvre close to the enemy with the greatest recklessness and remain firm like the greatest horsemen. He shouted 'God is the Greatest' and inflicted many losses on the enemy. He rushed at the enemy, unafraid of death.[85]

This passage indicates that Ibn Taymiyya not only provided moral support but also served as an actual warrior by fighting the Ilkhanids with his sword

81 M. Berriah, "Un aspect de l'art de la guerre de l'armée mamelouke," pp. 431–469.
82 Ibn Kathīr, *al-Bidāya*, XVIII, 27. See also al-Birzālī, *al-Muqtafī*, II/1, p. 222.
83 Ibn ʿAbd al-Hādī, *al-ʿUqūd*, p. 147.
84 Ibid., p. 148.
85 Al-Bazzār, *al-Aʿlām al-ʿaliyya*, p. 63.

in hand. Ibn Taymiyya was here depicted not only a *ʿālim* with deep knowledge of Islamic sciences, philosophy and logic but also an individual who possessed warrior skills such as riding horses, handling weapons and *furūsiyya*.[86] To my knowledge, al-Bazzār is the only source to present this information, so one may ask whether this account can be considered credible. Of course, Al-Bazzār seems to exaggerate when he relates Ibn Tayymiyya's charge against the Ilkhanid soldiers and his preeminent role in the conquest of Acre in Jumādā I 690/May 1291.[87] However, when considering the accounts of other contemporary authors, the participation of Ibn Taymiyya in the warfare not only as a provider of moral support but also as a warrior is not impossible, particularly when one considers his temperament and religious activism. Yet, among all Ibn Taymiyya's students, only al-Bazzār provides accounts of his teacher's valor in combat. Some *ʿulamāʾ* fought at Shaqhab, such as *shaykh* Najm al-Dīn Ayyūb al-Kurdī, who, according to al-Maqrīzī fought to the death.[88] Thus, Ibn Taymiyya's role as a *mujāhid* must not be understood in the literal sense but rather, as al-Bazzār suggests, that he fought in the way of God (*jāhada fī sabīli-llāh*) "with his heart, tongue and hand".[89]

We find Ibn Taymiyya again fighting the Ilkhanids in the winter of 712/1312–1313, when Öljeitü and his army laid siege to al-Raḥba. Ibn Taymiyya and other volunteers left Cairo with the army led by Sultan al-Nāṣir Muḥammad to fight the enemy. With the announcement of the arrival of the Mamluk army and in the face of al-Raḥba's resistance, the Ilkhanids decided to withdraw. Once arrived in ʿAsqalān, Ibn Taymiyya decided to leave the army and return to Damascus after seven years of absence.[90]

Ibn Taymiyya's participation in Mamluk expeditions as a provider of psychological support or fighter cannot be considered a form of professional

86 Ibid., 75. Here the word *furūsiyya* has a larger definition that horsemanship. He refers to a multicultural art of war that evaluated from the Abbasid period to the Mamluks. For more information Shihab al-Sarraf, "Évolution du concept de furûsiyya et de sa littérature chez les Abbassides et les Mamlouks," in *Chevaux et cavaliers arabes dans les arts d'Orient et d'Occident*, ed. Jean-Pierre Digard, Paris 2002, pp. 67–72; id, "Mamluk Furūsīyah Literature and Its Antecedents," *Mamluk Studies Review* 8/1 (2004), pp. 141–200; Abbès Zouache, "Une culture en partage: la *furūsiyya* à l'épreuve du temps," in "Temporalités de l'Égypte", *Médiévales* 64 (2013), pp. 57–75; Mehdi Berriah, "Le cheval arabe chez les Mamelouks baḥriyya entre pragmatisme, symboles et représentations (XIIIe–XIVe siècles)," *Arabian Humanities* 8 (2017), on line URL: http://journals.openedition.org/cy/3398.

87 "*Qālū: la-qad kāna al-sabab fī tamalluk al-muslimīn iyyāhā bi-fiʿlihi wa mashūratihi wa ḥusn naẓarihi.*" Al-Bazzār, *al-Aʿlām al-ʿaliyya*, pp. 63–64.

88 Al-Maqrīzī, *al-Sulūk*, II, p. 367.

89 Al-Bazzār, *al-Aʿlām al-ʿaliyya*, p. 63.

90 Al-Birzālī, *al-Muqtafī*, II/II, p. 89.

mobility. In addition to their professional army corps, consisting of the sultan's mamluks, *amīrs*' mamluks and the *ḥalqa* regiment, which enjoyed certain benefits and were remunerated according to their status within the *iqṭāʿ* system, the Mamluk Sultanate mobilized auxiliary forces such as Bedouins, Kurds and Turcomans.[91] This form of military mobilization is a pattern of professional mobility, which is in contrast to the case of Ibn Taymiyya and other civilians who participated in military actions alongside the army. The sources refer to them as *al-mutaṭawwiʿa*, a word that indicates that this form of mobility can be considered voluntary in nature.[92]

3.2 *Ibn Taymiyya as a Popular ʿālim and Social Actor with a Significant Degree of Social Mobility*

Close examination of the sources shows that Ibn Taymiyya enjoyed a significant degree of social mobility as a result of engaging in popular religious activism. Two main events reflect this phenomenon.

The first event is linked to the Ilkhanid invasion. On Friday 17 Rajab 699/8 April 1300, after the departure of the Ilkhanid troops, at dawn, Ibn Taymiyya and his disciples went to several taverns which had proliferated during the Ilkhanid occupation, largely due to the support and complicity of the *amīr* Sayf al-Dīn Qibshaq, who, according to Ibn Kathīr, received a thousand dirhams a day from this trade.[93] The alcohol containers were smashed, the drink spilled on the floor and those wine consumers who were caught red-handed beaten.[94] A 26 year-old and firsthand witness to these events in Syria, al-Dhahabī reports them differently providing less information than Ibn Kathīr who was not born yet at the time. Both authors don't give precise information about Ibn Taymiyya's role in these events. In Rajab 704/January 1305, Ibn Taymiyya went with his disciples and some stonemasons (*ḥajjārūn*) to the al-Nāranj mosque, also called al-Ḥajar mosque, in Damascus, to destroy a rock which they considered as the source of serious polytheistic (*shirk*) practices because people considered it sacred and visited it to make offerings.[95] The accounts of Ibn Kathīr clearly aim at emphasizing the role of his teacher.

---

91 Reuven Amitai, *Mongols and Mamluks: the Mamluk-Īlkhānid War, 1260–1281*, Cambridge/New-York 1995, pp. 64–69; David Ayalon, "The Auxiliary Forces of the Mamluk Sultanate," *Islam and the Abode of the War. Military slaves and Islamic adversaries*, London 1994, pp. 13–37.

92 See note 18.

93 Ibn Kathīr, *al-Bidāya*, XVII, p. 725.

94 Al-Dhahabī, *Tārīkh al-Islām*, LII, p. 95; Ibn Kathīr, *al-Bidāya*, XVII, p. 728.

95 Ibid., XVIII, pp. 46–47.

Ibn Taymiyya's social activism was mainly possible through his proximity and accessibility to the masses and his ability to popularise and make his thoughts accessible. These qualities made Ibn Taymiyya what one could call a popular *ʿālim*. This was the main difference between Ibn Taymiyya and other *ʿulamāʾ* occupying official functions such as *qāḍī al-quḍāt*. As Caterina Bori demonstrated, Ibn Taymiyya's accessibility and proximity to the masses, in addition to his ability to popularise and summarize complicated subjects such as the interpretation of divine Names and Attributes, allowed the *shaykh* of Damascus to spread his thought in society, thus compensating for his lack of influence on the network of *madrasas*.[96]

Here, I would like to add a few observations that demonstrate that Ibn Taymiyya's significant degree of popular activism was only possible to due to his proximity, his accessibility to the masses and his ability to popularise Islamic sciences. Ibn Taymiyya's student al-Bazzār relates information demonstrating the importance of these characteristics. While al-Birzālī's description of Ibn Taymiyya's funeral is sufficient to obtain some impression of his popularity,[97] another report by al-Bazzār gives further evidence as to the scholar's popularity:

> And certainly, all those who have seen him, in particular those who have known him for a long time, agree that they have not seen anyone show such asceticism and such abstinence vis-à-vis the life of this world (*dunyā*) to the point that it became known and stayed in the hearts of those who were close to or distant from those who have heard of its qualities. If we questioned a commoner (*ʿāmmī*) from a region distant from that of the *shaykh* (Ibn Taymiyya) who was the ascetic of that time showing the greatest detachment vis-à-vis the goods of this low world and the greater lust for the afterlife he would say: I have heard of no one like Ibn Taymiyya.[98]

Beyond the natural praise that one would expect from a student of his *shaykh* and without taking into consideration Ibn Taymiyya's *zuhd* (asceticism), the most important element in this passage is the appearance of the word *ʿāmmī*, which indicates the most prominent characteristic of Ibn Taymiyya as a scholar who was very close to the masses. Among the number of important people

96 Bori, "Theology, Politics, Society," pp. 78–80.

97 Yahya Michot, "Reflections on the funeral, and the present state of the tomb, of Ibn Taymiyya in Damascus. For a Grave in Damascus," pp. 2–4.

98 Al-Bazzār, *al-Aʿlām al-ʿaliyya*, pp. 44–45.

who attended Ibn Taymiyya's courses, al-Bazzār informs us that there were not only *ʿulamāʾ* but also *ʿawām* (commoners).[99] This last word again confirms Ibn Taymiyya's proximity and accessibility to the common people. In two other passages, al-Bazzār relates the following:

> His assembly was open to all (*ʿāmman*) ranging from the important to the common, the notable and the obscure, free people and slaves, men and women.[100]

> He never became impatient with the person who came to ask his opinion and question him. On the contrary, he accepted questions with great joy and gentleness and remained with the person until he chose to leave, regardless of whether the visitor was renowned or common, man or woman, free or slave, scholar or commoner, city dweller or Bedouin [...].[101]

Although panegyric, these two passages, which are fairly similar and complementary, give some impression of Ibn Taymiyya's close proximity to the masses and his ability to popularise and render his fatwas accessible. Another indicator is that many of these fatwas relate to question asked by commoners. Ibn Taymiyya's popularity rose to such an extent that Sultan al-Nāṣir Muḥammad summoned him, stating that he had been informed that many people heeded Ibn Taymiyya and that he wished to seize power, an accusation that Ibn Taymiyya denied.[102] Ibn Taymiyya's accessibility and ability to popularise his thoughts were also acknowledged by his opponents. Behind the criticism of Tāqī al-Dīn al-Subkī, one of Ibn Taymiyya's greatest rivals, there is a kind of recognition of Ibn Taymiyya's ability to popularise his thoughts, his accessibility and popularity and the dangers that these qualities represented for his opponents:

> As for his innovations in the branches of law (*furūʿ*), they are something which have led a to general bewilderment. Among these innovations, his fatwa on conditional divorce [...]. The commoners sought comfort and reassurance in his words and hurried to take them (as a legal opinion) [...]. Then I have been informed that he sent his propagandists to different regions to spread his awful message, and he led astray, concerning

99 Ibid., p. 30.
100 Ibid., p. 39.
101 Ibid., pp. 48–49.
102 Ibid., pp. 55–56.

> the divorce oath, groups of commoners, Bedouins, peasants, and people of other territories [...].[103]

Ibn Taymiyya's social mobility, which was reflected in his proximity to the masses, his teaching and the dissemination of his views on religion in the popular strata of society work against the notion that he sought to secure control over teaching posts in the *madrasas* of Damascus.[104] Setting up a network would have required Ibn Taymiyya to develop relations with high Mamluk authorities and other well-placed *ʿulamāʾ* close to Mamluk power; however, he does not seem to have done so given the tense relations he clearly had with several of these individuals and his character.[105]

3.3 *Between uṣūl and furūʿ: Ibn Taymiyya's Mobility and Priorities in the Islamic Sciences' Field*

Probably, one of the most important forms of mobility that Ibn Taymiyya enjoyed, and that which he was better known for, was on the intellectual field. In what follows, I argue that we can speak of Ibn Taymiyya's mobility based on his prioritization of Islamic sciences. When considering Ibn Taymiyya's works, it can be observed that almost all of his writings deal with issues related to *ʿaqīda* (creed) and *tawḥīd* (unity of God) issues, in particular *asmāʾ wa ṣifāt* (the Names and Attributes of God) and, to a lesser extent, *ziyārat al-qubūr* (visitation of tombs).[106] While it is true that Ibn Taymiyya is better known as a theologian than a jurist, this does not mean that he had no interest in the field of jurisprudence. Since the 1990s in Middle Eastern scholarship and for the two

---

103 Taqī al-Dīn al-Subkī, *al-durra al-muḍiyya fī al-radd ʿalā Ibn Taymiyya*, ed. Muḥammad Zāhid al-Kawtharī, Damascus al-Taraqī 1348H, pp. 7–8. For more information on the oppositions between al-Subkī and Ibn Taymiyya and his pupil Ibn Qayyim al-Jawziyya see Bori and Holtzman, "A Scholar in the Shadow", pp. 20–24.

104 Caterina Bori, *Ibn Taymiyya: una vita esemplare. Analisi delle fonti classichedella sua biografia*, Supplemento monografico alla Rivista degli Studi Orientali (Roma-Pisa, 2003) 1/76, pp. 145–146.

105 Little, "Did Ibn Taymiyya Have a Screw Loose?," pp. 108–109.

106 On Names and Attributes see Farid Suleiman, *Ibn Taymiyya Und Die Attribute Gottes*, Berlin/Boston 2019; Jon Hoover, *Ibn Taymiyya's theodicy of perpetual optimism*, Leiden/Boston 2007; id, "God Acts by His Will and Power: Ibn Taymiyya's Theology of a Personal God in his Treatise on the Voluntary Attributes," in *Ibn Taymiyya and his Times*, ed. Yossef Rapoport and Shahab Ahmed, Karachi 2010, pp. 55–77. On visitation of tombs see Niels H. Olesen, *Culte des Saints et Pèlerinage chez Ibn Taymiyya (661/1263–728/1328)*, Paris 1991; Christopher S. Taylor, *In the Vicinity of the Righteous. Ziyāra & the Veneration of Muslim Saints in Late Medieval Egypt*, Boston 1999, pp. 179–194; Daniella Talmon-Heller, "Historiography in the Service of the Muftī: Ibn Taymiyya on the Origins and Fallacies of Ziyārāt," *Islamic Law and Society* 26 (2019), pp. 227–251.

last decades in Western scholarship, many works have studied Ibn Taymiyya's influence in *fiqh* and *uṣūl fiqh*.[107]

How can one explain Ibn Taymiyya's mobility and priorities in the Islamic sciences? One of the most important reasons is the political and social context related to Ibn Taymiyya's physical mobility. This is not systematic, but we have several examples: his writings on the Ilkhanid Mongols were created during the period in which there was the threat of invasion; his *Minhāj al-Sunna* was a response to al-Ḥillī's book offer to Öljeitü, who had converted to Shīʿism and desired to attack the Mamluk Sultanate;[108] and it was during his stay in Egypt that Ibn Taymiyya wrote his refutation of Ibn ʿArabī's doctrine and probably his fatwa on Ibn Tumart's *Murshida*.[109] However, it seems it is the general religious context of Ibn Taymiyya's period that motivated him to focus on issues related to creed known as *uṣūl al-dīn* in the field of Islamic sciences.

It is once again his student and biographer al-Bazzār who identifies reasons for Ibn Taymiyya's mobility and priorities in Islamic sciences:

> He (Ibn Taymiyya) – May God be pleased with him – has written a great deal on the founding principles (*uṣūl*) in addition to other sciences. I asked him about the reason for this and to write me a text on law, which would group his choices and preferences so that he would serve as a support (*ʿumda*) for giving fatwas. He replied: concerning the branches (*al-furūʿ*) the matter is simple. If a Muslim follows and applies (*qallada*) the opinions of one of the *ʿulamāʾ* who is authoritative, then he is allowed to practice his religion based on his words (of the scholar) and for what he is not certain that this scholar made a mistake. As for the founding

107 Y. Rapoport, "Ibn Taymiyya's Radical Legal Thought," pp. 191–226; Al-Matroudi, *The Ḥanbalī School of Law and Ibn Taymiyya*, London/New-York 2006; Ibn Taymiyya, *al-Qawāʿid al-nūrāniyya al-fiqhiyya*, ed. Aḥmad b. Muḥammad al-Khalīl, al-Dammam 1433H; Saʿūd al-ʿUṭayshān, *Manhaj Ibn Taymiyya fī l-fiqh*, Riyadh 1999; Ismāʿīl b. Ḥasan b. Muḥammad ʿUlwān, *al-Qawāʿid al-fiqhiyya al-khams al-kubra wa-l-qawāʿid al-mundarija taḥta-ha. Jamʿ wa dirāsa min majmuʿ fatāwā shaykh al-Islām Ibn Taymiyya*, al-Dammam 2000; Muḥammad Abū Zahra, *Ibn Taymiyya*, pp. 350–365, 378–405.

108 Tariq al-Jamil, "Ibn Taymiyya and Ibn al-Muṭahhar al-Ḥillī: Shiʿi Polemics and the Struggle for Religious Authority in Medieval Islam," in *Ibn Taymiyya and his Times*, ed. Yossef Rapoport and Shahab Ahmed, Karachi 2010, pp. 229–246.

109 Henri Laoust, "Une fatwa d'Ibn Taymiyya sur Ibn Tumart", *Bulletin de l'Institut français d'archéologie orientale* 59 (1960), pp. 157–184. Concerning the dispersal of Ibn Taymiyya's writings, Caterina Bori writes: "[…] his mandatory travels and changes of residence (from Damascus to Cairo, from Cairo to Alexandria, from Alexandria back to Cairo, then finally to Damascus), combined with his ongoing intellectual activity, must have contributed to the dispersal." Bori, "The Collection and Edition of Ibn Taymiyah's Works: Concerns of a Disciple," p. 55.

> principles of religion (*uṣūl*), I have seen people of innovation, bewilderment and passions like followers of philosophy, *bāṭiniyya*, heretics (*malāḥida*), supporters of the unity of existence (*waḥdat al-wujūd*), *dahriyya, qadariyya, Nuṣayrīs, jahmiyya, ḥulūliyya*, those who refute divine Names and Attributes (*al-muʿaṭila*), anthropomorphists (*al-mujassima wa al-mushabbiha*), the supporters of al-Rawāndī, those of Kullāb, the Sulamiyya and others among the people of innovation […] and it was clear that many of them sought to nullify the sacred *sharīʿa* of Prophet Muḥammad, which prevails over all other legislations, and that they put people in doubt regarding the founding principles of their religion (*uṣūl dīnihim*). This is why from what I have heard or seen, it is rare that the one who opposes the Book and the Sunnah and is favourable to their words does not become a *zindīq* or has no longer the certainty (*yaqīn*) about his religion and belief. When I saw this situation, it seemed obvious to me that it was up to anyone who had the capacity to combat these ambiguities, these trivialities, to refute their arguments and errors, to strive to expose their vile and low character as well as the falsity of their evidence in order to defend the religion of pure monotheism delete and the authentic and illustrious prophetic tradition.[110]

This passage shows both Ibn Taymiyya's scepticism and that his principal aim was to dissuade Muslims from falling victim to what he considered heretical, philosophical and *shīʿī* beliefs.[111] Ibn Taymiyya's concern about the dangers faced by his conception of the orthodox Islamic creed may account for his significant social mobility, his greater accessibility when compared to other *ʿulamāʾ* like *qāḍī al-quḍāt*, and, in particular, his ability to popularise and to render *ʿilm al-ʿaqīda* (creedal science) and *tawḥīd* (unity of God) concepts accessible to the masses.[112] His ability to popularise his ideas served as antidote to what he considered the heretical practices and beliefs that existed and were diffused among members of society at the time.

By the end of his life, Ibn Taymiyya's awareness of his great erudition and asceticism had expanded beyond Syria's borders. Al-Bazzār, who was one of them, relates that he came from Bagdad to study with the *shaykh* of

---

110 Al-Bazzār, *al-Aʿlām al-ʿaliyya*, pp. 33–35.

111 Wael B. Hallaq, *Ibn Taymiyya Against the Greek Logicians*, Oxford 1993, pp. XXXIX–L.

112 Bori, "Theology, Politics, Society," pp. 78–80. For an example of Ibn Taymiyya's knowledge popularisation see Caterina Bori, "Religious Knowledge between Scholarly Conservatism and Commoners' Agency," in *The Wiley Blackwell History of Islam*, ed. Amando Salvatore, Oxford 2018, pp. 301–306. See also Bori, "The Collection and Edition of Ibn Taymiyah's Works: Concerns of a Disciple," pp. 55–56.

Damascus.[113] However, Ibn Taymiyya's scholarship went beyond his own time, as it was one of the major influences as well as object of refutation in *ʿulamāʾ* circles, as Khaled El-Rouyaheb, Ovamir Anjum and, more recently, Caterina Bori have demonstrated.[114] His influence on contemporary Islamic thought is such that groups with that differ significantly in ideology claim his legacy, such as Wahhabism, quietist Salafism, the Muslim Brotherhood and even extremist groups.[115]

4 Conclusion

Close analysis of relevant sources demonstrates that Ibn Taymiyya's mobilities were of multiple kinds. After his emigration to Damascus, Ibn Taymiyya's first major form of mobility was professional, which was a result of his teaching position. Beyond this, however, Ibn Taymiyya never enjoyed another form of professional mobility. Ibn Taymiyya's religious activism led him to volunteer to engage in many forms of horizontal mobility within the sphere of the Mamluk Sultanate, including as a political advisor, warrior and/or provider of moral support, mediator, negotiator and humanitarian.

Beyond his spatial mobility, Ibn Taymiyya's career underwent an upward and then downward trajectory. He joined the elite ranks of society during the second reign of al-Nāṣir Muḥammad by becoming both a political advisor and a mufti; however, this was followed by his downfall. Throughout his life, however, Ibn Taymiyya was also close to the masses, as he made his teachings and fatwas available to all. As such, he was a popular *ʿālim*. The last form of mobility that Ibn Taymiyya engaged in focus on *uṣūl al-dīn* due to doctrines that

113 Al-Bazzār, *al-Aʿlām al-ʿaliyya*, p. 6.

114 Khaled El-Rouayheb, "From Ibn Ḥajar al-Haytamī (d. 1566) to Khayr al-Dīn al-Ālūsī (d. 1899): Changing Views of Ibn Taymiyya among non-Ḥanbalī Sunni Scholars," in *Ibn Taymiyya and his Times*, ed. Yossef Rapoport and Shahab Ahmed, Karachi 2010, pp. 305–311; Ovamir Anjum, Politics, *Law, and Community in Islamic Thought: The Taymiyyan Moment*, New-York 2012, pp. 173–188; Caterina Bori, "Ibn Taymiyya (14th to 17th Century): Transregional Spaces of Reading and Reception: Transregional Spaces of Reading and Reception," *The Muslim World* 108/1 (2018), pp. 87–123.

115 Yahya Michot, *Ibn Taymiyya against extremisms, texts translated annotated and introduced by Y. Michot*, Beirut 2012, pp. XXIV–XXXII; id, *Ibn Taymiyya: Muslims under non-Muslim Rule*, London 2006, pp. 27–61; See also Jon Hoover, "Ibn Taymiyya between Moderation and Radicalism," in *Reclaiming Islamic Tradition: Modern Interpretations of the Classical Heritage*, ed. Elisabeth Kendall and Ahmad Khan, Edinburgh 2016, pp. 177–203.

he considered deviant and therefore as posing a greater danger than the Ilkhanid Mongols.[116]

Studying Ibn Taymiyya's mobility allows a better understanding of complex aspects of the personal life of this author. Was Ibn Taymiyya's mobility unique in the Mamluk period? To answer this question, an examination of other *ʿulamā*'s mobility should be undertaken. Social context, living conditions, education and other factors indicate that patterns of mobility among the *ʿulamāʾ* differed from one case to another; such research is not only valuable but necessary to achieve a better understanding of the networks of *ʿulamāʾ* during this period.

Bibliography

Sources

Abū al-Fidāʾ. *al-Mukhtaṣar fī tārīkh al-bashar*, Cairo: Maktabat al-Mutanabbī, s.d, 2 vols.

Al-ʿAynī. *ʿIqd al-jumān fī tārīkh ahl al-zamān*, ed. Muḥammad, M.A., Cairo: Dār al-wathā'iq al-qawmiyya, I, IV, 2010.

Al-Bazzār. *al-Aʿlām al-ʿaliyya fī manāqib shaykh al-Islām Ibn Taymiyya*, ed. Ṣalāḥ al-Dīn al-Munjid, Beirut: Dār al-kutub al-jadīd, 1976.

Al-Birzālī. *al-Muqtafī ʿalā kitāb al-rawḍatayn*, ed. ʿUmar ʿAbd al-Salām al-Tadmurī, Beirut/Sayda, al-Maktaba al-ʿaṣabiyya, I, II, 2006.

Al-Dhahabī. *Tārīkh al-Islām*, ed. ʿUmar ʿAbd al-Salām al-Tadmurī, Beirut: Dār al-kitāb al-ʿarabī, XXXXVIII, LII, 1990–2000.

Al-Kutubī. *Fawāt al-wafāyāt*, ed. Muʿawwiḍ, A.M. and ʿAbd al-Mawjūd, A.A., Beirut: Dār al-kutub al-ʿilmiyya, I, 2000.

Al-Maqrīzī. *Kitāb al-sulūk li-maʿrifat duwal al-mulūk*, ed. ʿAṭā, M.A., Beirut: Dār al-kutub al-ʿilmiyya, II, 1997.

Al-Nuwayrī. *Nihāyat al-arab fī funūn al-adab*, ed. N.M. Fawāz, Beirut: Dār al-kutub al-ʿilmiyya, XXXII, 2004.

al-Subkī, Taqī al-Dīn. *al-Durra al-muḍiyya fī al-radd ʿalā Ibn Taymiyya*, ed. Muḥammad Zāhid al-Kawtharī, Damacus al-Taraqī, 1348H.

al-Subkī, Taqī al-Dīn. "Naqd al-ijtimāʿ wa l-iftirāq fī masā'il al-aymān wa l-ṭalāq" in *al-durra al-muḍiyya fī al-radd ʿalā Ibn Taymiyya*, ed. Muḥammad Zāhid al-Kawtharī, Damacus al-Taraqī, 1348H, 43–53.

116 Wael B. Hallaq, *Ibn Taymiyya Against the Greek Logicians*, pp. XII, XXVII.

al-Subkī, Taqī al-Dīn. "al-Naẓar al-muḥaqqiq fī-l-ḥilf bi-l-ṭalāq al-muʿaliq" in *al-durra al-muḍiyya fī al-radd ʿalā Ibn Taymiyya*, ed. Muḥammad Zāhid al-Kawtharī, Damacus al-Taraqī, 1348H, 55–58.

Al-Yūnīnī. *Dayl mir'āt al-zamān*, ed. ʿAbbās H.A., Abu Dhabi: Abu Dhabi Authority for Culture and Heritage, 2007.

Baybars al-Manṣūrī. *Zubdat al-fikra fī tārīkh al-hijra*, ed. Richards, D., Berlin: Das Arabische Buch, 1998.

Ibn ʿAbd al-Hādī. *al-Ṣārim al-munkī fī al-radd ʿalā al-Subkī*, ed. Badriyya bint Ḥamīd al-Rā'iqī, Ṣafiyya bint Sulaymān al-Tawījrī, Sihām bint Aḥmad al-Muḥammadī, al-Mansura: Dār al-Faḍīla, 2014.

Ibn ʿAbd al-Hādī. *al-ʿUqūd al-durriyya min manāqib shaykh al-Islām Ibn Taymiyya*, ed. Abū Muṣʿab Ṭalaʿat b. Fu'ād al-Ḥalwānī al-Farūq, Cairo: al-Fārūq al-ḥadītha, 2002.

Ibn ʿAbd al-Ẓāhir. *al-Rawḍ al-zāhir fī sīrat al-Malik al-Ẓāhir Baybars*, ed. al-Khuwayṭir A., Riyadh, 1976.

Ibn Aybak al-Dawādārī. *Kanz al-durar wa jāmiʿ al-ġurar*, ed. Ratke, B. *et al.*, Cairo: al-Maʿhad al-almānī lilātār bi-l-Qāhira, IX, 1960–1994.

Ibn Ḥajar al-ʿAsqalānī. *al-Durar al-kāmina fī aʿyān al-mi'a al-tāmina*, Beirut: Dār al-kutub al-ʿilmiyya, I, 1997.

Ibn Kathīr. *al-Bidāya wa-l-nihāya*, ed. al-Turkī, A., Giza: Dār hajr, XVII, XVIII, 1998.

Ibn Taymiyya. *al-Ikhnā'iyya*, ed. Aḥmad b. Munas al-Ghanzī, Jeddah: Dār al-kharāz, 2011.

Ibn Taymiyya. *al-Jihād*, ed. ʿUmayra, A., Beirut: Dār al-Jayl, 1997.

Ibn Taymiyya. *al-Qawāʿid al-nūrāniyya al-fiqhiyya*, ed. al-Khalīl, A.M., al-Dammam: Dār Ibn Jawzī, 1433H.

Ibn Taymiyya. *al-Risāla al-qubruṣiyya*, ed. Muḥibb al-Dīn, Q., Cairo: Dār al-maṭbaʿa al-salafiyya, 1974.

Ibn Taymiyya. *Lettre à un croisé*, ed. trans. Yahya Michot, Lyon/Louvain-La-Neuve: Academia/Tawhid, 1995.

Studies

Abū Zahra, M. *Ibn Taymiyya: ḥayātu-hu wa ʿaṣru-hu wa fiqhu-hu*, Cairo: Dār al-fikr al-ʿarabī, 1952.

Aigle, D. "A Religious Response to Ghazan Khan's Invasions of Syria. The Three 'Anti-Mongol' *fatwās* of Ibn Taymiyya", in *The Mongol Empire between Myth and Reality. Studies in Anthropological History*, ed. Denise Aigle, Boston/Leiden: Brill, 2016, 283–305.

Aigle, D. "Ghazan Khan's Invasion of Syria. Polemics on his Conversion to Islam and the Christian Troops in His Army", in *The Mongol Empire between Myth and Reality. Studies in Anthropological History*, ed. Denise Aigle, Boston/Leiden: Brill, 2016, 255–282.

Amitai, R. *Mongols and Mamluks: the Mamluk-Īlkhānid War, 1260–1281*, Cambridge/New-York: Cambridge University Press, 1995.

Amitai, R. "The Logistics of the Mongol-Mamlūk War, with Special Reference to the Battle of Wādī 'l-Khaznadār, 1299 C.E.", in *Logistics of Warfare in the Age of the Crusades. Proceedings of a Workshop at the Centre for Medieval Studies, University of Sydney, 30 September to 4 October 2002*, ed. John H. Pryor, Ashgate: Aldershot, 2006, 25–42.

Amitai, R. "The Mongol Occupation of Damascus in 1300: A Study of Mamluk Loyalities", in *The Mamluks in Egyptian and Syrian politics and society*, ed. Michael Winter and Amalia Levanoni, Leiden: Brill, 2004, 21–41.

Anjum, O. *Politics Law and Community. The Taymiyyan Moment*, Cambridge: Cambridge University Press, 2012.

Ayalon D. "The Auxiliary Forces of the Mamluk Sultanate", *Islam and the Abode of the War. Military slaves and Islamic adversaries*, London: Variorum, 1994, 13–37.

Baugh C. "Ibn Taymiyya's Feminism? Imprisonment and the Divorce Fatwās", in *Muslima Theology: The Voices of Muslim Women Theologians*, ed. Ednan Aslan, Marcia Hermansen, Elif Medeni, Frankfurt: Peter Lang AG, 2013, 181–196.

Belhaj A. "Law and Order according to Ibn Taymiyya and Ibn Qayyim al-Jawziyya: A Re-Examination of siyāsa sharʿiyya," in *Islamic Theology Philosophy and Law. Debating Ibn Taymiyya and Ibn Qayyim al-Jawziyya*, ed. Birgit Krawietz and George Tamer, Berlin: De Gruyter (2013), 400–422.

Berkey, J.P. *The Formation of Islam: Religion and Society in the Near East, 600–1800*, Cambridge: Cambridge University Press, 2002.

Berkey, J.P. *The Transmission of Knowledge in Medieval Cairo: A Social History of Islamic Education*, Princeton: Princeton University Press, 1992.

Berriah, M. "Le cheval arabe chez les Mamelouks baḥriyya entre pragmatisme, symboles et représentations (XIIIe–XIVe siècles)", *Arabian Humanities* 8 (2017), on line URL: http://journals.openedition.org/cy/3398.

Berriah, M. "Un aspect de l'art de la guerre de l'armée mamelouke: la pratique de la 'fausse ouverture' à la bataille de Šaqḥab (702/1303)", *Arabica* 65/4 (2018), 431–469.

Berriah, M. "The Mamluk Sultanate and the Mamluks seen by Ibn Taymiyya: between Praise and Criticism," *Arabian Humanities* 14, 2020. DOI: https://doi.org/10.4000/cy.6491.

Bori, C. "A New Source for the Biography of Ibn Taymiyya", *Bulletin of the School of Oriental and African Studies* 67, 3 (2004), 321–348.

Bori, C. and Holtzman, L. "A Scholar in the Shadow", *Oriente Moderno* 1, 2010, 11–42.

Bori, C. *Ibn Taymiyya: una vita esemplare. Analisi delle fonti classichedella sua biografia*, Supplemento monografico alla Rivista degli Studi Orientali, Istituti Poligra ci Internazionali: Roma-Pisa, 1/76, 2003.

Bori, C. "One or Two Versions of *al-Siyāsa al-sharʿiyya* of Ibn Taymiyya? And What Do They Tell Us?" *ASK Working Papers* 26: Bonn, 2016, 1–27.

Bori, C. "Religious Knowledge between Scholarly Conservatism and Commoners' Agency", in *The Wiley Blackwell History of Islam*, ed. Amando Salvatore, Oxford: Wiley Blackwell, 2018, 291–309.

Bori, C. "The Collection and Edition of Ibn Taymiyah's Works: Concerns of a Disciple", *Mamluk Studies Review* 13/2, 2009, 47–66.

Bori, C. "Theology, Politics, Society: The Missing Link. Studying Religion in the Mamluk Period" in *Ubi Sumus? Quo Vademus? Mamluk Studies – State of the Art*, ed. Stephan Conermann, Göttingen: V&R Unipress, 2013, 57–94.

Bori, C. "Théologie politique et Islam à propos d'Ibn Taymiyya (m. 728/1328) et du sultanat mamelouk." *Revue de l'histoire des religions* 224, no. 1 (2007), 5–46.

Bori, C. "Ibn Taymiyya (14th to 17th Century): Transregional Spaces of Reading and Reception: Transregional Spaces of Reading and Reception", *The Muslim World* 108/1 (2018), 87–123.

Broadbridge, A.F. "Academic Rivalry and the Patronage System in the Fifteenth Century Egypt: al-ʿAynī, al-Maqrīzī and Ibn Ḥajar al-ʿAsqalānī", *Mamluk Studies Review* 3 (1999), 85–106.

Chamberlain, M. *Knowledge and social practice in medieval Damascus*, Cambridge: Cambridge University Press, 1995.

Cook, M. *Commanding Right Forbidding Wrong in Islamic Thought*, Cambridge: Cambridge University Press, 2000.

El-Rouayheb K. "From Ibn Ḥajar al-Haytamī (d. 1566) to Khayr al-Dīn al-Ālūsī (d. 1899): Changing Views of Ibn Taymiyya among non-Ḥanbalī Sunni Scholars", in *Ibn Taymiyya and his Times*, ed. Yossef Rapoport and Shahab Ahmed, Karachi: Oxford University Press, 2010, 305–311.

Eychenne, M. *Liens personnels, clientélisme et réseaux de pouvoir dans le sultanat mamelouk (milieu XIII*ᵉ*-fin XIV*ᵉ *siècle)*, Damascus-Beirut: Presses de l'Ifpo, 2013.

Friedman, Y. "Ibn Taymiyya's Fatāwā against the Nuṣayrī-ʿAlawī Sect", *Der Islam* 82:2 (2005), 349–363.

Friedman, Y. *The Nuṣayrī – ʿAlawīs: An Introduction to the Religion, History and Identity of the Leading Minority in Syria*, Leiden: Brill, 2010.

Garcin, J.-C. "Le sultan et Pharaon (le politique et le religieux dans l'Égypte mamluke)", in *Espaces, pouvoirs et idéologies de l'Égypte médiévale*, ed. J.-C. Garcin, London: Variorum, 1987, part IX, 261–272.

Geoffroy, E. *Le soufisme en Égypte et en Syrie sous les derniers mamelouks et les premiers Ottomans. Orientation spirituelles et enjeux culturels*, Presses de l'Ifpo: Damascus, 1996.

Hallaq, W.B. *Ibn Taymiyya Against the Greek Logicians*, Oxford: Clarendon Press, 1993.

Hassan, M. "Modern Interpretations and Misinterpretations of a Medieval Scholar: Apprehending the Political Thought of Ibn Taymiyyah", in *Ibn Taymiyya and his Times*, ed. Yossef Rapoport and Shahab Ahmed, Karachi: Oxford University Press, 2010, 338–366.

Hirschler, K. "Ibn Wāṣil: An Ayyūbid Perspective on Frankish Lordships and Crusades", in *Medieval Muslim Historians and the Franks in the Levant*, ed. Alex Mallett, Leiden/Boston: Brill, 2015,142–143.

Hirschler, K. "The Formation of the Civilian Elite in the Syrian Province: The Case of Ayyubid and Early Mamluk Ḥamāh", *Mamluk Studies Review* 12/2, 2008, 95–132.

Hoover, J. "God Acts by His Will and Power: Ibn Taymiyya's Theology of a Personal God in his Treatise on the Voluntary Attributes", in *Ibn Taymiyya and his Times*, ed. Yossef Rapoport and Shahab Ahmed (Karachi, 2010), 55–77.

Hoover, J. *Ibn Taymiyya* (London: Oneworld Academic, 2020).

Hoover, J. "Ibn Taymiyya between Moderation and Radicalism", in *Reclaiming Islamic Tradition: Modern Interpretations of the Classical Heritage*, ed. Elisabeth Kendall and Ahmad Khan, Edinburgh: Edinburgh University Press, 2016, 177–203.

Hoover, J. *Ibn Taymiyya's theodicy of perpetual optimism*, Leiden/Boston: Brill, 2007.

Hutait, A. "Les expéditions mamloukes de Kasarwān. Critique de la lettre d'Ibn Taymiyya au sultan al-Nāṣir bin Qalāwūn", *ARAM Periodical* 9/1–2 (1997), 77–84.

al-Jamil, T. "Ibn Taymiyya and Ibn al-Muṭahhar al-Ḥillī: Shiʿi Polemics and the Struggle for Religious Authority in Medieval Islam", in *Ibn Taymiyya and his Times*, ed. Yossef Rapoport and Shahab Ahmed, Karachi: Oxford University Press, 2010, 229–246.

Johansen, B. "A Perfect Law in an Imperfect Society. Ibn Taymiyya's Concept of 'Governance in the Name of the Sacred Law,'" in *The Law Applied: Contextualizing the Islamic Shariʿa: A Volume in Honour of Frank E. Vogel*, ed. Peri Bearman, Bernard G. Weiss, and Wolfhart Heinrichs, London/New York: I.B. Tauris, 2008, 259–294.

Lambton, A.K.S. *State and Government in Medieval Islam: An Introduction to the Study of Islamic Political Theory: The Jurists*, Oxford: Oxford University Press, 1981.

Laoust, H. *Essais sur les doctrines sociales et politiques de Tâkî-d-Dîn Aḥmad b. Taymîya, canoniste ḥanbalite né à Ḥarrân en 661/1262, mort à Damas en 728/1328*, Cairo: Institut français d'archéologie orientale, 1939.

Laoust, H. "La biographie d'Ibn Taymîya d'après Ibn Kathîr", *Bulletin d'études orientales*, 12 (1942–1943), 115–162.

Laoust, H. *Le Hanbalisme sous les Mamlouks bahrides (658–784/1260–1382)*, Paris: Paul Geuthner, 1960.

Laoust, H. "Remarques sur les expéditions du Kasrawān sous les premiers Mamluks", *Bulletin du Musée de Beyrouth* 4 (1940), 93–115.

Laoust, H. "Une fatwa d'Ibn Taymiyya sur Ibn Tumart", *Bulletin de l'Institut français d'archéologie orientale* 59 (1960), 157–184.

Lev, Y. "Symbiotic Relations: Ulama and the Mamluk Sultans", *Mamluk Studies Review* 13/1 (2009), 1–26.

Little, D. "Did Ibn Taymiyya Have a Screw Loose", in *History and Historiography of the Mamluks*, ed. Donald Little, Londres: Variorum, 1986, part VIII, 93–111.

Little, D. "The Historical and Histriographical Significance of the Detention (miḥna) of Ibn Taymiyya", *International Journal of Middle East Studies*, 4/3, 1973, 311–327.

Makdisi, G. *The Rise of Colleges. Institutions of Learning in Islam and the West*, Edinburgh: Edinburgh University Press, 1981.

al-Matroudi, A.I. *The Ḥanbalī School of Law and Ibn Taymiyya. Conflict or conciliation*, London/New-York: Routledge, 2006.

Michot, Y. *Ibn Taymiyya against extremisms, texts translated annotated and introduced by Y. Michot*, Beirut: Albouraq, 2012.

Michot, Y. *Ibn Taymiyya: Muslims under non-Muslim Rule*, London: Interface, 2006.

Michot, Y. "Reflections on the funeral, and the present state of the tomb, of Ibn Taymiyya in Damascus. For a Grave in Damascus", 1–10 http://www.interfacepublications.com/~interfa3/images/pdf/IbnTaymiyya_Tomb.pdf.

Michot, Y. "Textes spirituels d'Ibn Taymiyya. Nouvelle série XXIII. Lettre au sultan al-Nāṣir concernant les Tatars", 2017. https://www.academia.edu/34853690/Yahya_Michot_Textes_spirituels_d_Ibn_Taymiyya._Nouvelle_série_XXIII._Lettre_au_sultan_al-Nāṣir_concernant_les_Tatars_.

Morel T. "Deux textes anti-Mongols d'Ibn Taymiyya", *The Muslim World* 105/2 (2015), 368–397.

Niels, H.O. *Culte des Saints et Pèlerinage chez Ibn Taymiyya (661/1263–728/1328)*, Paris: Geuthner, 1991.

Perho, I. "Climbing the Ladder: Social Mobility in the Mamluk Period", *Mamluk Studies Review* 15 (2011), 19–35.

Raff, T. *Remarks on an anti-Mongol Fatwâ by Ibn Taimîya*, Leiden, Brill, 1973.

Raḥāl, A. Ḥ. *Maʿāmil wa ḍawābiṭ al-ijtihād ʿin shaykh al-Islām Ibn Taymiyya*, Amman: Dār al-nafāʾis, 2002.

Rapoport, Y. "Ibn Taymiyya's Radical Legal Thought: Rationalism, Pluralism and the Primacy of Intention", in *Ibn Taymiyya and his Times*, ed. Yossef Rapoport and Shahab Ahmed, Karachi: Oxford University Press, 2010, 191–228.

Rapoport, Y. *Mariage, Money and Divorce in Medieval Islamic Society*, Cambridge: Cambridge University Press, 2005.

Salbi, K.S. "The Maronites of Lebanon under Frankish and Mamluk Rule (1099–1516)", *Arabica* 4/3 (1957), 294–299.

al-Sarraf, S. "Évolution du concept de furûsiyya et de sa littérature chez les Abbassides et les Mamlouks", in *Chevaux et cavaliers arabes dans les arts d'Orient et d'Occident*, ed. Jean-Pierre Digard, Paris: Gallimard/Institut du Monde Arabe, 2002, 67–72.

al-Sarraf, S. "Mamluk Furūsīyah Literature and Its Antecedents", *Mamluk Studies Review* 8/1 (2004), 141–200.

Shams, M.A. and al-ʿImrān, A.M. *al-Jāmiʿ li-sīrat shaykh al-Islām Ibn Taymiyya khilāl sabʿat qurūn*, Dār ʿālam al-fawāʾid: Djeddah, 1422H.

Sivan, E. *L'Islam et la croisade. Idéologie et Propagande dans les Réactions Musulmanes aux Croisades*, Paris: Librairie d'Amérique et d'Orient, 1968.

Sivan, E. *Radical Islam. Medieval Theology and Modern Politics*, Binghamton: Yale University Press, 1990.

Suleiman, F. *Ibn Taymiyya Und Die Attribute Gottes*, Berlin/Boston: De Gruyter, 2019.

Talmon-Heller, D. "Historiography in the Service of the Muftī: Ibn Taymiyya on the Origins and Fallacies of Ziyārāt", *Islamic Law and Society* 26 (2019), 227–251.

Taylor, C.S. *In the Vicinity of the Righteous. Ziyāra & the Veneration of Muslim Saints in Late Medieval Egypt*, Leiden: Brill, 1999.

ʿUlwān, I.H. *al-Qawāʿid al-fiqhiyya al-khams al-kubra wa-l-qawāʿid al-mundarija taḥta-ha. Jamʿ wa dirāsa min majmuʿ fatāwā shaykh al-Islām Ibn Taymiyya*, al-Dammam: Dār Ibn Jawzī, 2000.

al-ʿUṭayshān S. *Manhaj Ibn Taymiyya fī l-fiqh*, Maktaba al-ʿUbaykān: Riyadh, 1999.

Wiederhold L. "Legal-Religious Elite, Temporal Authority, and the Caliphate in Mamluk Society: Conclusions Drawn from the Examination of a 'Zahiri Revolt' in Damascus in 1386", *in International Journal of Middle East Studies*, 31/2 (1999), 203–235.

Winter, S. *A History of the ʿAlawis: From Medieval Aleppo to the Turkish Republic*, Princeton: Princeton University Press, 2016.

Zouache A. *Armées et combats en Syrie de 491/1098 à 569/1174. Analyse comparée des chroniques médiévales latines et arabes*, Ifpo: Damascus, 2008.

Zouache A. "Une culture en partage: la *furūsiyya* à l'épreuve du temps", in "Temporalités de l'Égypte", *Médiévales*, 64 (2013), 57–75.

CHAPTER 6

Mobility among the Andalusī *quḍāt*: Social Advancement and Spatial Displacement in a Professional Context

Adday Hernández López

The *qaḍā'* (judicature) is a legal-religious magistracy that traditionally played a central role in the legal dynamics of Islamic societies. Judges belonged to the *'ulamā'* (religious scholars), who, although not officially institutionalised, were selected by the central power and therefore acted as the link between rulers and scholars.[1] The dependence of the judiciary on the rulers was not always accepted by the *'ulamā'*, and in the biographical dictionaries we find some scholars who refused to be appointed as judges, such as 'Uthmān b. 'Alī b. Da'mūq (d. 709/1309).[2] Starting in the 8th c. CE, the formation of a concrete corpus of legal doctrine that judges had to apply (Mālikī doctrine in the case of al-Andalus) granted them a certain degree of independence,[3] and in some periods judges themselves even wielded great power.[4] In short, although judges provided the rulers with moral, legal and religious legitimacy before the people, at certain times their proximity to the latter constituted a threat to the power structure.[5]

---

1 According to Juan Martos, the activities and attributions of the Andalusī *qāḍīs* are not exactly the same as those of their Eastern counterparts. See Martos, *El mundo jurídico en al-Andalus*, 43–45.

2 The refusal of appointments is a frequent way to demonstrate a pious attitude, but according to Ahmad Chafic Damaj, the sources contain few cases of refusal in relation to the post of judge; see Damaj, "Punto de vista del intelectual," 106–107.

3 See Martos, "Poder central Omeya."

4 The use of *taqlīd* (imitation of the legal precedents of the *madhhab*) and the restriction of *ikhtilāf* (legal divergence) – through the composition of *mukhtaṣar*s which gathered the preferred opinion of the school, or the most famous opinion (*al-qawl al-mashhūr*) – have been seen by some scholars as an attempt to establish a fixed set of rules which limited the intervention of the political leaders in the creation of legal norms, and eased the practical application of those rules. For more information on this topic see Fadel, "Rules, judicial discretion, and the rule of law in Naṣrid Granada," 49–86; "The Social Logic of Taqlīd," 193–233.

5 For more information on the different attitudes of rulers towards scholars see Fierro, "Ulemas en las ciudades andalusíes."

 | DOI:10.1163/9789004467637_008

My aim in this paper is to show how the different forms of mobility (social or vertical mobility, horizontal mobility,[6] spatial mobility), when associated with the appointment of scholars to remunerated posts – and especially the post of *qāḍī* – was often used by rulers as a means of controlling the religious scholars. For instance, the consecutive appointment of the same *ʿulamāʾ* to the judicature in different cities made them dependent on the state. Judges came to be treated as public employees, and were constantly sent off to distant locations in order to prevent them from developing personal connections to a particular place that might enable them to gain popular support against the rulers.

The main resource employed here for the study of judges' professional mobility is the relational database "Prosopografía de los Ulemas de al-Andalus" (PUA), created at the Escuela de Estudios Árabes in Granada (EEA-CSIC) under the direction of María Luisa Ávila.[7] The judicature is well represented in the biographical sources dealing with scholars, and there were even biographical dictionaries specifically devoted to judges. In the specific case of al-Andalus, we have Ibn Ḥārith al-Khushanī's (d. 361/971)[8] *Kitāb akhbār quḍāt Qurṭuba* for the early period, and ʿAlī b. ʿAbd Allāh al-Bunnāhī's (d. 792/1389)[9] *al-Marqabat al-ʿulyā fī-mān yastaḥiqq al-qaḍāʾ wa-al-futyā*,[10] the contents of which have been included in the PUA database. Although these sources offer information that might be considered partial or biased, we can get a more complete picture of the Andalusī judicature thanks to other biographical data sources for PUA, such as Ibn al-Faraḍī's *Taʾrīkh ʿulamāʾ al-Andalus*, al-Ḍabbī's *Bughyat*

6 By "horizontal mobility" I mean mobility from legal-religious posts to administrative-political posts.

7 It contains information about more than 11,600 *ʿulamāʾ* from al-Andalus, extracted from different editions of more than 175 bio-bibliographical dictionaries and historical chronicles and 348 related studies. This electronic resource, which is still being developed, is freely accessible at https://www.eea.csic.es/pua/.

8 He was a scholar born in Ifrīqiya who was an expert in jurisprudence and history. He lived in Ceuta and later in Cordoba. All of his roughly fourteen works were devoted to Islamic law and the lives and opinions of the Mālikī jurists, both in al-Andalus and North Africa. See Zomeño, "Al-Jušanī," *BA* 3, pp. 290–296, [548].

9 He was also known as al-Nubāhī until the publication by Bencherifa, "al-Bunnāhī, lā al-Nubāhī," see Calero Secall, "Al-Bunnāhī, Abū al-Ḥasan," *BA* 1, 282–286, [85].

10 Ibn Ḥārith al-Khushanī, *Historia de los jueces de Córdoba*, Julián Ribera (ed. and tr.) Madrid: 1914; al-Bunnāhī, *al-Marqaba al-ʿulyā*, ed. Lévi-Provençal (Cairo: 1948); al-Bunnāhī, *al-Marqaba al-ʿulyā fī-mān yastaḥiqq al-qaḍāʾ wa-l-futyā* (*La atalaya suprema sobre el cadiazgo y el muftiazgo*), ed. and tr. A. Cuellas Marqués (Granada: 2005).

al-multamis fī ta'rīkh rijāl ahl al-Andalus or Qāḍī 'Iyāḍ's *Tartīb al-madārik wa-taqrīb al-masālik li-ma'rifat a'lām madhhab Mālik*, among others.[11]

While the history of the Andalusī judicature[12] and the mobility of the Andalusī *'ulamā'*[13] – especially spatial mobility – have been studied extensively, the professional mobility of Andalusī judges in its different facets, which depended on the will of the rulers, has yet to receive the same attention.[14]

1 Vertical Mobility

Regarding social/vertical mobility in al-Andalus, Manuela Marín has stated that the study of the Islamic sciences was one of the main channels for social advancement.[15] Although in the category of Andalusī urban notables (*a'yān*) we find scholarly families most often in charge of legal activities as jurists, notaries, professional witnesses, judges, etc., becoming an *'ālim* was not part of a specific professional career. This allowed, at least in theory, for people from what were considered the "inferior strata" of Andalusī society, such as artisans, to ascend to the ranks of the scholarly class. In the biographical sources, for instance, we find examples of merchants and artisans who became interested in legal issues related to their activity in the market, and then went on

11 I would like to thank Jo Vansteenbergen for his comments on the agency and involvement of the authors of the biographical collections and on the fact that the information extracted from them responds to a textual reality in need of contextualization. Al-Bunnāhī, for example, is said to have composed his *Marqaba* with the aim of making a reflection on the judiciary for doctrinal purposes. Al-Bunnāhī only includes objective data with no personal additions, but since the complete title refers to those "*who deserve the judicature*" (*man yastaḥiqq al-qaḍā'*) one can infer that some names may have been excluded from his work. In addition, his primary aim in writing the *Marqaba* was apparently to demonstrate the nobility of his own lineage (banū al-Ḥasan), many members of which were judges, and to include mainly his own relatives, teachers and related scholars; see Calero Secall, "Al-Bunnāhī, Abū al-Ḥasan," *BA* 1, 282, 285; "Los Banū al-Ḥasan al-Bunnāhī," 53–76.

12 Since the beginning of the twentieth century there have been studies on different aspects of the Andalusī judicature in diverse periods. The pioneer was Julián Ribera, and more recently we find studies by Ridha Hadi Abbas, María Arcas Campoy, Jacinto Bosch Vilá, María Isabel Calero, Pedro Cano, Alfonso Carmona, Juan Castilla, Maribel Fierro, Francisco Franco, Rachid el Hour, Vincent Lagardère, Mercedes Lucini, Manuela Marín, Juan Martos, Christian Müller, Fernando Velázquez Basanta, etc.

13 See for instance the works by María Luisa Ávila, Sam Isaac Gellens, Bárbara Boloix, François Clément, Jorge Lirola, Mahmud Ali Makki, Manuela Marín, etc.

14 By "professional mobility" I mean mobility related to performing remunerated positions within the magistracy, especially the appointment as *qāḍī*.

15 Marín, "Movilidad social y ciencias islámicas," 26.

to specialize in Islamic law.[16] However, in such cases becoming a scholar did not necessarily entail greater wealth so much as an increase in social prestige. Thus, the question is, were scholars from humble backgrounds actually appointed to the *qaḍāʾ*, with all the material and social benefits associated with such a position?

The biographies of the Andalusī *ʿulamāʾ* do not usually tell us much about their social origins, but names themselves can provide us with valuable information on the professional activities performed by the *ʿulamāʾ* outside the educational, legal, and religious sphere. I have therefore carried out an analysis on the 745 judges recorded[17] in the PUA database to identify *laqab*s (nickname) related to professional activities,[18] modeled on Marín's study "El oficio de la ciencia y otros oficios." The search has revealed that only 40 of the 745 judges (5.5%) had this kind of profession-based *laqab*,[19] 34 of them with "Ibn"[20] and only 7 without "Ibn,"[21] all of whom lived from the 11th c. CE onwards. Among

16 Marín, "El oficio de la ciencia y otros oficios," 380.

17 Since the database is under development and new data can still be introduced, the numbers are approximate and may vary.

18 To the professions included by Manuela Marín, in my search I have added the following: *ḥallā* (jeweler), *khallās* (dyer), *khayyāṭ* (tailor), *labbān* (bricklayer), *maqbarī* (cemetery keeper, grave digger), *mawwāz* (banana grower/seller), *nakhkhās* (male slave trader), *qābila* (midwife), *saqāṭ* (junk dealer), *shaqqāq* (wood cutter), *ṭallāʾ* (juice seller), *ṭayyāb* (masseur), *tayyān* (fig seller) and *zajjāj* (glazier).

19 These are the professional *laqab*s found among the judges: al-Abbār (needle maker); Ibn al-ʿAssāl (honey seller); Ibn al-ʿAṭṭār, Ibn al-Bannāʾ (mason, architect, builder); Ibn al-Daqqāq (cereal grinder, flour merchant); al-Ghāsil (corpse washer); al-Ghazzāl (yarn merchant, spinner); Ibn al-Farrāʾ (furrier) (2); Ibn al-Ḥadhdhāʾ (shoemaker) (2); Ibn al-Ḥaddād (ironsmith); Ibn al-Ḥammāmī (keeper of the *ḥammām*); Ibn al-Ḥannāt (grain merchant); Ibn al-Ḥashshāʾ (dress liner); Ibn al-Ḥaṣṣār (mat maker); Ibn al-Jannān (gardener); al-Kattānī (flax merchant); Ibn al-Kharrāṭ (glass/wood worker/seller); Ibn al-Kharrāz (leather worker); Ibn al-Khashshāb (lumber merchant); Ibn al-Labbān (bricklayer); Ibn al-Laḥḥām (butcher); Ibn al-Mashshāṭ (flax comber); al-Mawwāq (junk seller) (2); Ibn al-Qaṭṭān (cotton spinner/seller); Ibn al-Raffāʾ (garment mender); Ibn al-Ṣabbāg (garment and leather dyer, textile dyer); Ibn al-Ṣaffār (brass smith/coppersmith) (3); Ibn al-Ṣannāʿ (craftsman in the mint); Ibn al-Sarrāj (saddler); Ibn al-Saqāṭ (junk dealer); al-Ṣaydalānī (druggist or medicine seller); Ibn al-Ṣayqal (burnisher); Ibn al-Shaqqāq (wood cutter) (2); and Ibn al-Tayyān (fig seller).

20 In her study, Marín divided the *laqab*s into two groups because she considered that some of the *nisba*s preceded by "Ibn" could be seen as a historical petrification with no real meaning. See Marín, "El oficio de la ciencia y otros oficios."

21 *Laqab*s without "Ibn" indicate that, in many cases, these scholars had parallel occupations, probably because their intellectual activities were unpaid. As Marín points out, some others abandoned these activities at some point but retained the *laqab*. In this sense, if we are looking for information about vertical mobility, perhaps the *nisba*s preceded by "Ibn" are actually more meaningful because they might indicate someone who originally came

the 34 whose *laqab*s are preceded by "Ibn," 16 belong to families of *ʿulamāʾ*,[22] and of these 16, there are 7 who have other family members that held legal-religious positions.

Apart from these seven, the Banū al-Jannān ("sons of the gardener") are also said to have been appointed to different posts in Xativa.[23] In these cases, social advancement does not seem to have taken place through individual merit. Indeed, studies on Andalusī *ʿulamāʾ* families conducted by scholars such as María Luisa Ávila, Luis Molina and Maribel Fierro have shown that it was easier for the members of such families to become *ʿālim*s themselves than for someone without such family ties.[24] Although it may seem that the judicature cannot be learned as in the case of hadith, *fiqh* and other Islamic sciences, in fact being a judge involved not only legal knowledge, but also a set of social practices and behaviors that could be acquired through family connections. Thus, just as we find families of hadith scholars or Qurʾan readers, we also find families of *quḍāt*,[25] such as the Banū Simāk,[26] the Banū al-Ṣaffār, the Banū Abī ʿĪsā,[27] etc.

Among the 7 scholars without "Ibn" in the *laqab* we find:

- Saʿīd b. Muḥsin al-Ghāsil, Abū ʿUthmān (d. 401/1011). He was a *ghāsil* (corpses' washer). Judge in Medinaceli.
- Muḥammad b. Wahb b. Bukayr al-Kattānī,[28] Abū ʿAbd Allāh (d. 461/1068). Judge in Calatrava la Vieja.
- Yaḥyā b. ʿAbd al-Jabbār b. Yaḥyā b. Yūsuf b. Masʿūd b. Saʿīd al-Anṣārī al-Abbār, Abū Bakr (d. 590/1193). Judge of Malaga. He was an *abbār* (needle maker) according to the sources.[29]

---

from a family of craftspeople, but who did not need to carry on with the family profession himself. But, of course, it also depends on the time elapsed since quitting the activity; see Marín, "El oficio de la ciencia y otros oficios," 378–382.

22 We do not have information about the families of the other 17 scholars.

23 In the PUA database we have only found up to now: Khalaf b. Mufarrij b. Saʾīd al-Kinanī, Ibn al-Jannān Abū al-Qāsim (n.d.).

24 See Molina, "Familias andalusíes"; Fierro, "Familias en el Taʾrij iftitāḥ al-Andalus"; de la Torre, "Familias andalusíes."

25 See Ávila, "Cargos hereditarios."

26 Bosch Vila, "Los Banū Simāk de Málaga y Granada."

27 Among the members of this family there is Yaḥyā b. Yaḥyā b. Kathīr, who was never a judge, but was an important figure in the introduction of Malikism in al-Andalus, see Marín, "Una familia de ulemas cordobeses"; Fierro, "El alfaquí beréber Yaḥyā b. Yaḥyā al-Laythī."

28 Flax merchant, linen seller, see Shatzmiller, *Labour*, 132.

29 Documentación, "Al-Abbār/al-Labbār, Abū Bakr" *BA*, A, 15, [1897].

- Abū Bakr b. Khalaf al-Anṣārī al-Faqīh, al-Mawwāq[30] (al-Muwāfiq), Abū Yaḥyā (d. 599/1203). He was at the service of the sultan of Marrakech and afterwards he was appointed as judge in Fes.
- Yūsuf b. Muḥammad b. ʿAlī b. Mūsā al-Anṣārī, al-Ghazzāl,[31] Abū al-Ḥajjāj (d. 620/1223). Judge of Algeciras born in Jerez whose family was apparently from the North of Africa.[32]
- ʿAbd al-Ghanī b. Muḥammad b. ʿAbd al-Ghanī b. Salama b. Ḥakam al-Umawī al-Gharnāṭī (d. 627/1229). He was a *ṣaydalānī* (druggist or medicines seller). Judge in Mallorca.
- Muḥammad b. Yūsuf b. Abī al-Qāsim b. Yūsuf al-ʿAbdarī, al-Mawwāq al-Gharnāṭī (d. 894/1492). He was *qāḍī* in Malaga and *qāḍī al-jamāʿa* in Granada. At some point he left to Jerusalem and he also managed to be appointed as a judge there.[33]

Only three of these judges with a *laqab* not preceded by "Ibn" have been proven to have actually carried out the mentioned activity (a corpse washer, Saʿīd b. Muḥsin; a needle maker, Yaḥyā b. ʿAbd al-Jabbār; and a druggist or medicine seller, ʿAbd al-Ghanī b. Muḥammad). Moreover, as none of them was an artisan or other type of manual laborer,[34] which were not well considered,[35] we cannot ensure that these scholars actually represent social advancement from the lower classes, due to a lack of information in the sources. In fact, one case that we do have information about is that of ʿAbd al-Ghanī b. Muḥammad al-Umawī al-Gharnāṭī al-Ṣaydalānī, who was appointed *qāḍī* on the *kuttāb*'s recommendation to the ruler. Even though he turned out to be a terrible judge, he was maintained in his position, which indicates that his proximity to the ruler's administration afforded him protection, probably because as judge he also protected the interests of the ruler and his men.

---

30 Manuela Marín includes "*al-Mawwāq*" without a translation among the professional activities in Marín, "El oficio de la ciencia y otros oficios", p. 394, but it is not found in the list of activities in PUA and Maya Shatzmiller does not list it among her index of professions. The root M-W-Q is translated as "being cheap" so it could be inferred that "*al-mawwāq*" is the one who elaborates or sells cheap things, see Corriente, *Diccionario Árabe-Español*, 735.

31 Yarn merchant, spinner, see Shatzmiller, *Labour*, 131.

32 Marín; Fierro, *Sabios*, 140, no. 147.

33 See Damaj, "Punto de vista del intelectual", 105–106.

34 Although a needle maker can also be considered as an artisan, as it happens with goldsmiths and the like, the fact that their work implies care and delicacy seems to have granted them a special status.

35 In any case, according to Manuela Marín the preservation of such *laqab*s as family names seems to have endowed them with a prestige that does not correspond with that of the activity in question. See Marín, "El oficio de la ciencia y otros oficios," 381.

In relation to ethnicity, three of the *quḍāt* have the *nisba* al-Anṣārī: Yaḥyā b. ʿAbd al-Jabbār, Abū Bakr b. Khalaf and Yūsuf b. Muḥammad al-Ghazzāl, all of whom lived in the 12th c. CE. According to Maribel Fierro, this *nisba* could have been adopted by Muslims of non-Arab origin beginning in the 5th/11th century[36] as a result of the "*growing importance of the Islamic identity over and against an Arabic identity*."[37] If we analyze the presence of non-Arabs in the judicature from the times of the *amīr* Muḥammad (r. 238/852–273/886), considering the ethnic division of labor proposed by Maya Shatzmiller,[38] it is possible to draw a connection between ethnicity and social advancement at the end of the Umayyad Emirate. According to Shatzmiller, "*Muslim Spain was one of the regions where ethnicity and religion were an active differentiating factor, as dominant in labour as in the political, social and economic life*."[39] The Andalusī Arabs, who were part of the elites, tended to provide professional and public services, mainly those related to the educational/legal/religious sector, while Berbers, and Jews and Ibero-Romans *mawālī* (clients) who had converted to Islam, worked in the extractive sector (mainly mining and agriculture), as well as in the different industries.[40] There was a limited participation of the Arab sector in cottage industries and some food trading and, in general, we can infer that most of the *ʿulamāʾ* who passed from manual to legal or religious professions and moved up the social ladder had a non-Arab origin. Among the 10 confirmed cases of commoners who became *ʿulamāʾ* studied by Manuela Marín, we also find six scholars with the *nisba* al-Anṣārī, and at least another two of demonstrable north-African origin.[41] Therefore, while the *quḍāt* appointed during the first years of Islamic expansion were Arabs, by the end of the Umayyad Emirate of Cordoba the Arab elites had grown weaker and the Islamization of the population had reached its peak.[42]

Finally, belonging to a specific school of law is another of the aspects considered by the rulers when choosing a *qāḍī*. After the introduction in al-Andalus of Mālikism, the main school of law followed by the Andalusī *fuqahāʾ*, the positions within the judicature were reserved for *Mālikī ʿulamāʾ* until the arrival of ʿAbd al-Raḥmān III, who appointed as judges *ʿulamāʾ* with different doctrinal inclinations, such as Aḥmad b. Baqī b. Makhlad, son of Baqī b. Makhlad, who introduced al-Shāfiʿī's *Risāla* and Ibn Abī Shayba's *Muṣannaf* in

36 On this topic see Fierro, "La nisba al-Anṣārī en al-Andalus," 233–237.
37 See Fierro, "Mawālī and muwalladūn in al-Andalus."
38 Shatzmiller, *Labour*, 327–346.
39 Shatzmiller, *Labour*, 329; she is referencing Pérès, "Les éléments ethniques," 2: 717–733.
40 Shatzmiller, *Labour*, 336–337.
41 Marín, "Movilidad social y ciencias islámicas," 21–25.
42 Fierro, "Los Cadíes de Córdoba de ʿAbd al-Raḥmān III," 85.

al-Andalus.[43] According to Juan Martos, we can also find the influence of other doctrines in the legal mainstream,[44] as in the case of ʿAbd Allāh b. Muḥammad b. al-Qāsim, who was expert in *Mālikī* doctrine but also studied with the *Ḥanbalī* masters Abū Isḥāq al-Hājimī (d. 351/962), Ibn al-Ṣawwāf (d. 359/969) and Abū Bakr b. Hamdān (d. 368/978). Likewise, ʿAbd Allāh b. Ibrāhīm al-ʿAṣīlī (d. 392/1002), although himself a *Mālikī*, studied with the *Ḥanafī* masters Abū al-Ḥasan al-Naysabūrī al-Miṣrī (d. 366/976), Abū Zayd Muḥammad al-Marwāzī (d. 371/981) and Aḥmad b. Yūsuf b. Khallād (d. 359/969).[45] Given the "anti-*madhhab*" inclinations of the Almohads, according to Fierro they made some attempts to give prominence to Ẓāhirism; however, the Mālikī scholars were so powerful that the Almohads finally settled for a "reformed Mālikism."[46]

To summarize, notwithstanding the cases of judges appointed due to their piety, righteousness or knowledge, lineage[47] and social contacts tended to be crucial factors, and other aspects such as one's ethnicity and whether one was a Mālikī were also considered when choosing a judge.

Under Almoravid rule there is a notable increase in the percentage of judges who did not belong to a renowned family of Andalusī *aʿyān*. For example, this period saw two Maghrebi families loyal to the Almoravids appointed to the judicature: the Banū Samajūn,[48] a family studied by Mercedes Lucini and Rachid el-Hour,[49] and the Banū Ḥammād. The first member of the Banū Samajūn, ʿAbd Allāh b. ʿAlī b. ʿAbd al-Malik b. Samajūn (524/1130), was also the first Maghrebi scholar appointed by the Almoravids to the *qaḍāʾ* in al-Andalus, but among the Banū Samajūn we find another three judges after ʿAbd Allāh. For

43 See Fierro, "Los Cadíes de Córdoba de ʿAbd al-Raḥmān III," 78–79; María Luisa Ávila. "Baqī b. Makhlad." *Encyclopaedia of Islam*. Third Edition, online. (= *EI*3). Ed. Kate Fleet; Gudrun Krämer; Denis Matringe; John Nawas y Everett Rowson. http://dx.doi.org/10.1163/1573-3912_ei3_COM_24530 [consulted 13/03/2018]; "Ibn Majlad Bāqī."

44 See Martos, "Poder central Omeya," 137–138.

45 Marín and Fierro, *Sabios*, 105, n. 7.

46 Fierro, "The religious policy of the Almohads," 687.

47 See for instance the case of Abū Jaʿfar Aḥmad b. Barṭāl, who despite lacking the required knowledge for the position, became *qāḍī al-jamāʿa* in Granada simply because he was the member of a well-situated family related to notables in Malaga. See Velázquez Basanta, "Ibn Barṭāl (s. XIV)," 271–276.

48 Of the members that Mercedes Lucini mentions in her article on this family, only one served as *qāḍī* during the Almohad period; see Lucini, "Los Banū Samaŷūn."

49 Rachid El Hour has specialized in the study of the Andalusī judicature during the Almoravid period. See for instance El Hour, *La administración judicial almorávide en al-Andalus*; "Algeciras, ciudad magrebí en al-Andalus"; "Reflexiones acerca del desarrollo de la justicia"; "El cadiazgo de Granada bajo los almorávides"; "El cadiazgo en Jaén en época Almorávide"; "Córdoba frente a los almorávides"; "The Andalusian qāḍī in the Almoravid period."

instance, ʿAlī b. b ʿAbd al-Raḥmān b. Samajūn (d. 539/1144) was first appointed to the judicature in Tlemcen, apparently travelling back and forth between North Africa and al-Andalus, while the other two members of the family were actually born in al-Andalus.

The first member of the Banū Ḥammād included in the biographical sources is Mūsā b. ʿAbd al-Raḥmān b. Ḥammād al-Ṣanhājī, Abū ʿImrān (535/1141). In the next century we find Muḥammad b. ʿAlī b. Ḥammād, Abū ʿUbayd Allāh (629/1231), possibly a grandson of the aforementioned Mūsā who was appointed to the *qaḍāʾ* in Murcia, Algeciras, Rabat and Saleh.

The famous ʿIyāḍ b. Mūsā from Ceuta was appointed to the judicature of Granada under Almoravid rule, and his descendants, the Banū ʿIyāḍ, continued to serve as judges under Almohad rule. Other renowned Maghrebi families whose members were appointed as judges under the Almohads were the Banū ʿImrān, the Banū al-Khaṭīb al-Tamīmī, the Banū Yakhluftān, the Banū al-Muʾminānī, the Banū al-Jumayyil, and the Banū Marwān al-Hamdānī.

In the Almohad period, by contrast, the number of judges who did not hail from families of notables is much higher, applying to 25 out of the 57 judges recorded for this period (nearly 44%). Only 7, however, were Andalusīs, and among these 7 we find special cases, such as that of Aḥmad b. ʿAbd Allāh b. ʿAmīra al-Makhzūmī (d. 656/1257), whose genealogy is not clear, some sources claiming he was of Jewish descent.[50] This is a consequence of the education system established by the Almohads, who recruited clever young men regardless of their social provenance with the aim of instructing them as scholars loyal to their cause.[51] These scholars, the *ṭalaba*, spread the Almohad doctrine in exchange for a salary. This seems to be the case, for example, of ʿAbd al-ʿAẓīm b. Yazīd b. Yaḥyā b. Hishām al-Khawlānī (d. 576/1180), who went to North Africa with his master Abū ʿImrān Mūsā b. Ḥammād (d. 535/1141), probably to receive instruction, eventually becoming a judge in Dukkala and Sijilmasa.

2 Horizontal Mobility

Because legal-religious and administrative-political posts fall into different spheres of state power, we wanted to determine the extent to which judges were also involved in administrative tasks. It appears that out of the 745 *quḍāt*

50 See Ávila, "id. 1255," PUA, http://eea.csic.es/pua/personaje/consulta_personaje.php?id=1255.

51 See Fierro, "Ulemas en las ciudades andalusíes," 145; Fricaud, "Les *Ṭalaba* dans la société Almohade."

recorded, only 18 held a parallel administrative or political position. Three held the position of *amīn*,[52] two of them *ṣāḥib al-wathāʾiq al-sulṭāniyya*,[53] one *ʿāmil*,[54] two *wālī*,[55] and 10 *wazīr*.[56] Also of note is that all of them lived between the 8th c. CE and the middle of the 12th c. CE.

1. Saʿīd b. Abī Hind al-Aṣbāḥī al-Ṭulayṭūlī, Abū ʿUthmān (d. 200/815): *wazīr*, *qāḍī*. The date of death is not clear, he could have died earlier.
2. Naḍar b. Salama b. Walīd b. Abī Bakr b. ʿUbayd b. Balj b. ʿUbayd b. ʿAlī al-Kilābī al-Qaysī, Abū Muḥammad (d. 302/914): *wazīr*, *ṣāḥib al-ṣalāt* and *qāḍī*. He was appointed by the *amīr* ʿAbd Allāh b. Muḥammad (r. 274/888–299/912).
3. Mūsā b. Muḥammad b. Ziyād b. Yazīd b. Ziyād b. Kathīr b. Yazīd b. Ḥabīb al-Judhamī, Abū al-Qāsim (d. 307/919): *wazīr*, *ṣāḥib al-radd*, *ṣāḥib al-shurṭa*, *ṣāḥib al-shurṭa al-ʿulyā*, *ṣāḥib al-ṣalāt*, *qāḍī al-jamāʿa*. Appointed by the *amīr* ʿAbd Allāh.
4. Aḥmad b. ʿAbd Allāh b. Ghuṣn Abī Ṭālib b. Ṭālib v. Ziyād b. ʿAbd al-Ḥamīd b. al-Ṣabbāḥ b. Yazīd b. Ziyād b. Malīḥ b. Khayr al-Aṣbaḥī, Abū ʿAbd Allāh (d. 326/938): *amīn*, *ṣāḥib al-sūq*, *qāḍī al-jamāʿa*, *qāḍī*. Appointed by ʿAbd al-Raḥmān III (r. 299/912–349/961).
5. ʿAbd Allāh b. al-Ḥasan, Ibn al-Sindī, Abū Muḥammad (d. 335/947): *wazīr* and three times *qāḍī*. Appointed by ʿAbd al-Raḥmān III.
6. Muḥammad b. ʿAbd Allāh b. Yaḥyā b. Yaḥyā b. Yaḥyā al-Laythī, Ibn Abī ʿĪsā, Abū ʿAbd Allāh (d. 339/950): *amīn*, 3 times *qāḍī* and *qāḍī al-jamāʿa*. Appointed by ʿAbd al-Raḥmān III.
7. Muḥammad b. ʿAmr b. Muḥammad b. Ayyūb b. ʿAmr al-Bakrī, Abū al-Qāsim (d. 366/976): *wazīr*, *qāḍī*. Appointed by Muḥammad b. Abī ʿĀmir (Almanzor), who sent him to sign the peace with the Christian kings and counts during the rule of Hishām II (r. 365/976–399/1009).
8. Saʿīd b. Muḥammad b. Maslama b. Muḥammad b. Saʿīd b. Butrī, Abū Bakr (d. 386/996): *amīn*, *qāḍī*. Appointed under the rule of Hishām II.
9. Muḥammad b. Zakariyyāʾ b. Yaḥyā al-Tamīmī, Ibn Barṭāl, Abū ʿAbd Allāh (d. 394/1004): *wazīr*, *ṣāḥib al-ṣalāt*, *qāḍī al-jamāʿa* and two times *qāḍī*. Uncle of Almanzor, he was appointed as vizier by his nephew when he was old, under the rule of Hishām II.

52 Administrator.
53 Person in charge of the chancery documents.
54 Governor.
55 Governor.
56 Vizier.

10. ʿAbd al-Raḥmān b. Muḥammad b. Aḥmad b. ʿUbayd Allāh al-Ruʿaynī, Ibn al-Mashshāṭ, Abū al-Muṭarrif (397/1007): *ṣāḥib al-wathāʾiq al-sulṭāniyya, ṣāḥib al-sūq, ṣāḥib al-shurṭa, ṣāḥib al-shūrā* and 3 times *qāḍī*. He was appointed in times of Almanzor, under the rule of Hishām II.
11. ʿAbd Allāh b. Aḥmad b. Qand al-Lughawī, al-Ṭayṭal, Abū Muḥammad (d. 400/1009): *wazīr, ṣāḥib al-aḥkām* and two times *qāḍī*. Probably appointed under the rule of Hishām II. He died during the battle of al-Baqar, on the side of Sulaymān al-Mustaʿīn.
12. Muḥammad b. ʿĪsā b. Zawbiʿ, Abū Bakr (d. 401/1010): *ʿāmil, ṣāḥib al-shurṭa al-ʿulyā* and 3 times *qāḍī*. Probably appointed under the rule of Hishām II and killed by ʿAlī b. Ḥammūd for being faithful to the caliph Sulaymān al-Mustaʿīn during the *fitna*.
13. Al-Ḥusayn b. Ḥayy b. ʿAbd al-Malik b. Ḥayy b. ʿAbd al-Raḥmān b. Ḥayy al-Tujībī, al-Ḥuzuqqa, Abū ʿAbd Allāh (d. 401/1011): *ṣāḥib al-wathāʾiq al-sulṭāniyya* and 3 times *qāḍī*. Appointed by al-Muẓaffar ʿAbd al-Malik b. Abī ʿĀmir probably under the rule of Hishām II.
14. ʿAbd al-Raḥmān b. Muḥammad b. ʿĪsā b. Fuṭays b. Aṣbagh b. Fuṭays (ʿUthmān) b. Sulaymān el *qāḍī*, Abū al-Muṭarrif (d. 402/1012): *wazīr, ṣāḥib al-ṣalāt, ṣāḥib al-khuṭba, ṣāḥib al-maẓālim* and *qāḍī al-jamāʿa*. Member of the Banū Fuṭays, family that was close to the Umayyads.
15. ʿAbd Allāh b. Saʿīd b. ʿAbd Allāh (Muḥammad) al-Umawī, Ibn al-Shaqqāq, Abū Muḥammad (d. 426/1035): *wazīr, ṣāḥib al-radd, qāḍī*. Appointed by Hishām II. His *nisba* al-Umawī indicates that he comes from a family of *mawālī* of the Umayyads.[57]
16. ʿAbd al-Raḥmān b. Ibrāhīm b. Muḥammad, Ibn al-Sharafī (d. 438/1047): *wālī* and *qāḍī*. Appointed at the end of the Caliphate.
17. ʿAlī b. ʿUmar b. Muḥammad b. Musharraf b. Muḥammad b. Aḍḥā b. ʿAbd al-Laṭīf (ʿAbd Allāh) b. al-Gharīb (b. Khālid) b. Yazīd b. al-Shamir b. ʿAbd al-Shams b. al-Gharīb al-Hamadānī, Abū al-Ḥasan (d. 539/1144): *wālī, qāḍī* and *qāḍī al-quḍāt*.[58] He became governor of Granada after the fall of the Lamtūnī (Almoravid) state, but he died soon after his appointment.

---

57 See Fierro, "Los mawālī de ʿAbd al-Raḥmān I", 87.

58 Rachid el Hour states that this figure was introduced in al-Andalus in the final stage of the Almoravid rule, although it was only applied in *Sharq al-Andalus* (mainly Murcia). See El Hour, "El Levante de al-Andalus en época Almorávide", 54. In the PUA database there are only 5 scholars holding this post, three between the late 11th and the early 6/12th c. (one in *Sharq al-Andalus*, another one in Murcia and the last one in Granada), one in the 7/13th c. in the Maghreb, and another one in the 8/14th–9/15th c., but this one was appointed somewhere in the East. According to Juan Castilla, this post was similar to

18. ʿAbd Allāh b. Aḥmad (b. Ismāʿīl b. ʿĪsā b. Aḥmad b. Ismāʿīl) b. Simāk al-ʿĀmilī, Abū Muḥammad (540/1146): *wazīr* and *qāḍī* in Granada before the entrance of the Almohads.

The judges dating from the first period of Andalusī history were soldiers who sometimes carried out various types of responsibilities, so it is not unusual for two of them to have acted as viziers as well. The later cases – dating from the end of the Emirate to the end of the Caliphate, and in particular from the rule of the *amīr* ʿAbd Allāh to the rule of caliph Hishām II (through his vizier Almanzor) – might respond to a political strategy whereby trusted men were appointed both to the judicial magistracy and to administrative posts.[59]

While these data indicate that it was not commonplace for judges to be appointed to positions in the state administration, we also know that during the 11th and 12th c. CE some judges in al-Andalus even acted as rulers, a phenomenon that has been studied by Maribel Fierro.[60] According to Fierro, in the face of the power vacuums both after the collapse of the Umayyad Caliphate and between the fall of the Almoravids and the Almohad conquest, many judges belonging to families of urban notables took charge of political affairs to maintain order in their societies. The famous Qāḍī ʿIyāḍ, for example, was both *qāḍī* and leader of Ceuta during the fall of the Almoravids. In her article, Fierro identifies the origin of this phenomenon as the crisis of the imamate in al-Andalus, because in this context the *quḍāt* were recognized as "*a source of authority for knowing what was licit and, as interpreters of the* sharīʿa, *a source of legitimization.*"[61] In all cases, the context of political crisis and the absence of other figures of authority (such as a powerful military leader) meant that the judges were the only remaining option.

First period of Taifas:
- Yaʿīsh b. Muḥammad (registered as *ṣāḥib al-aḥkām* in PUA, not *qāḍī*): Toledo.
- Muḥammad b. Ismāʿīl b. ʿAbbād al-Lakhmī (d. 433/1042): Sevilla.
- ʿĪsā b. Abī Bakr Muḥammad b. Saʿīd b. Muzayn (ʿĪsā b. Muzayn, Abū al-Aṣbagh, registered only as *faqīh*): Silves.
- Jaʿfar b. ʿAbd Allāh b. Jaḥḥāf al-Maʿāfirī (d. 488/1095): Valencia.

---

the one of *qāḍī al-jamāʿa*, although apparently the functions of the *qāḍī al-jamāʿa* were slightly more restricted. See Castilla, "El primer qāḍī l-quḍāt de al-Andalus", 47–57.

59 See for instance the case of Muḥammad b. ʿAbd Allāh b. Yaḥyā b. Yaḥyā b. Yaḥyā al-Laythī (sixth position of the list), appointed by ʿAbd al-Raḥmān III as *amīn*. He was a descendant of Yaḥyā b. Yaḥyā al-Laythī; see Fierro, "El alfaquí beréber Yaḥyā b. Yaḥyā al-Laythī."

60 See Fierro, "The qāḍī as ruler."

61 Fierro, "The qāḍī as a ruler," 105.

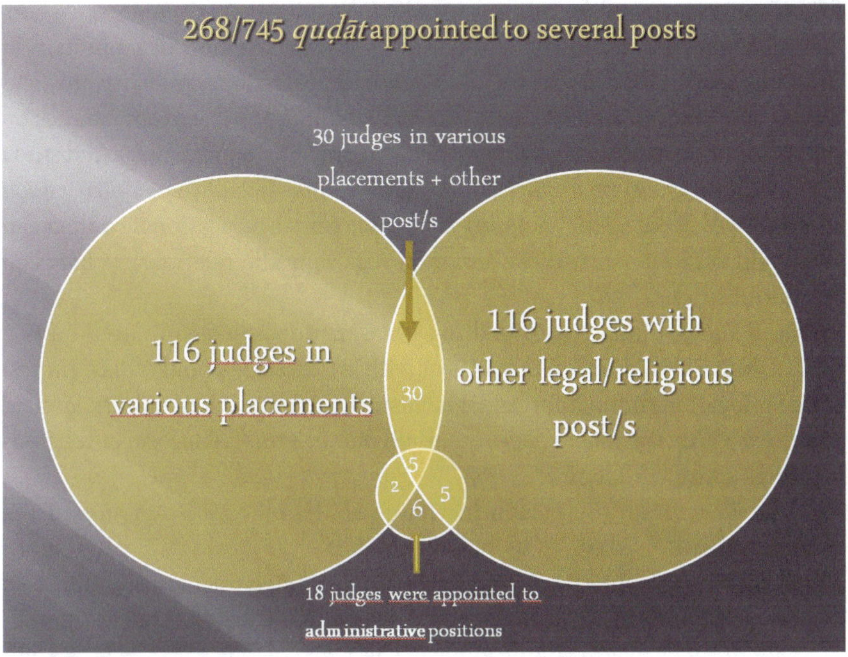

FIGURE 6.1 Judges appointed to several posts

Second period of Taifas:
- Ḥamdīn b. Muḥammad b. ʿAlī b. Ḥamdīn al-Thaʿlabī, Abū Jaʿfar (d. 546/1151): Cordoba.
- Ibn Juzayy (not clear), possibly Yūsuf b. ʿAbd al-Raḥmān b. Juzayy (d. 589/1193): Jaen.
- Ibn Ḥassūn, al-Ḥusayn b. al-Ḥusayn b. ʿAbd Allāh b. al-Ḥusayn al-Kalbī, Abū al-Ḥakam (d. after 538/1143): Malaga.
- Ibn Abī Jaʿfar, Abū Muḥammad ʿAbd al-Raḥmān b. Jaʿfar b. al-Ḥājj al-Lurqī (d. 550/1155): Murcia.
- Ibn ʿAbd al-ʿAzīz, Marwān b. ʿAbd Allāh (d. 578/1182): Valencia.

3 Spatial Mobility

Another type of mobility that will be examined here is spatial mobility. Was spatial mobility significant in the judges' careers?

In order to answer this question, we must first distinguish between the different types of spatial mobility. Mahmud Ali Makki has classified the different motivations for the trips carried out by Andalusī scholars, among which we find (1) pilgrimage, (2) learning, (3) trade, (4) espionage, (5) political asylum, and (6) embassies. He does not mention, however, the kind of mobility that most interests us for the purpose of this article: professional mobility linked to the specific posts to which the judges were appointed.[62] The extant studies on the mobility of the Andalusī *ʿulamāʾ* focus mainly on the pilgrimage and study trips because "*traveling to the Islamic East was an essential step in their period of formation*,"[63] but spatial mobility stemming from a professional context can shed light on other sorts of information regarding the relationship between rulers and scholars.

262 of the 745 judges recorded in PUA were appointed to more than one post in their lifetime, which provides us with information about judges' professional relocation throughout Andalusī history. 146 out of these 262 *quḍāt* held positions within the magistracy other than that of *qāḍī*.[64] The legal or religious positions considered here are:[65]

- *Ṣāḥib al-wathāʾiq*: the person in charge of the official documents of the judicature.
- *Ṣāḥib al-maẓālim*: judicial post devoted to investigating cases of abuse of power and to trying appeals against the sentence of another judge.
- *Ṣāḥib al-radd*: magistrate of appeal. The tasks of this magistrate are not clear, but it seems that he was in charge of appealed sentences and doubtful cases.
- *Ṣāḥib al-sūq*: This position would later be known as *ṣāḥib al-ḥisba* or *muḥtasib*, in charge of supervising that the market was functioning properly.
- *Ṣāḥib al-shurṭa*: Chief of police.
- *Nāʾib*: Substitute judge.
- *Ṣāḥib al-manākiḥ*: Magistrate specialized in marriage contracts.
- *Ṣāḥib al-ḥisba*: See *ṣāḥib al-sūq*. According to Martos, the *muḥtasib*, unlike the *ṣāḥib al-sūq*, was not a public employee, but rather acted independently to supervise peoples' moral conduct in the daily activities of the market.[66]
- *Ṣāḥib al-aḥkām*: Secondary judge. He ensured compliance with the *qāḍī*'s sentences.
- *Khaṭīb*: Person in charge of the sermon (*khuṭba*).

---

62 See Ali Makki, *Ensayo sobre las aportaciones orientales en la España musulmana*, 5–23.

63 Ávila, "The search for knowledge," 125–139.

64 Among them we find 30 judges who were appointed to both the judicature of other places and to an additional position (or several additional positions).

65 For further information on these posts see Lévi-Provençal, "3. La organización judicial", *Historia de España de Menéndez Pidal* (*HEMP*) V, 72–98; Martos, *El mundo jurídico en al-Andalus*, 57–63, 112.

66 See Chalmeta, *El zoco medieval*.

- *Ṣāḥib al-khuṭba*: Person in charge of the sermon (chief of the *khuṭṭāb*).
- *Ṣāḥib al-shūrā*: Chief of the Judicial Advisory Board.
- *Ṣāḥib al-ṣalāt*: Person in charge of prayer in the mosque.
- *Qāḍī al-jamāʿa*: Judge of the community. Slightly different from the eastern term *qāḍī al-quḍāt* because the *qāḍī al-jamāʿa* does not represent the top of the judicial hierarchy. He was the direct delegate of the supreme head of the Andalusī community for the purpose of executing justice, an intermediate appointment between the political power and the judicial magistracy.

Among the judges[67] who held other positions within the magistracy others than that of *qāḍī*:

- 42 profiles of *qāḍī* + *ṣāḥib al-ṣalāt*: 31/42 stayed in the same place (73.8%), only 11/42 moved (26.2%).
- 37 profiles of *qāḍī* + *qāḍī al-jamāʿa*: 14/37 stayed in a single place (37.8%), while 23/37 moved (62.2%).
- 21 profiles of *qāḍī* + *khaṭīb*: 14/21 stayed in a concrete place (66.6%), 7/21 moved (33.3%).
- 15 profiles of *qāḍī* + *ṣāḥib al-khuṭba*: 10/15 stayed in a place (66.6%), 5/15 moved (33.3%).
- 14 profiles of *qāḍī* + *ṣāḥib al-shurṭa*: 4/14 stayed in a single place (28.6%), 10/14 moved (71.4%).
- 12 profiles of *qāḍī* + *ṣāḥib al-aḥkām*: 4/12 stayed in a single place (33.3%), 8/12 worked in different places (66.6%).
- 9 profiles of *qāḍī* + *ṣāḥib al-shūrā*: 2/9 stayed in the same place (22.2%), 7/9 moved (77.8%).
- 6 profiles of *qāḍī* + *ṣāḥib al-sūq*: 2/6 stayed in a concrete place (33.3%), 4/6 moved (66.6%).
- 5 profiles of *qāḍī* + *nāʾib*: All of them moved (100%).
- 5 profiles of *qāḍī* + *ṣāḥib al-maẓālim*: 4/5 stayed in a single place (80%), 1/5 moved (20%).
- 4 profiles of *qāḍī* + *ṣāḥib al-radd*: 2/4 stayed in a place (50%), 2/4 moved (50%).

The results show that some of these positions implied a high degree of mobility, for example *ṣāḥib al-shurṭa*, *ṣāḥib al-sūq*, *nāʾib*, *ṣāḥib al-aḥkām*, *ṣāḥib al-shūrā*, and *qāḍī al-jamāʿa*, while others seem to be linked to specific places, as with *ṣāḥib al-maẓālim*, *khaṭīb*, *ṣāḥib al-khuṭba*, and especially *ṣāḥib al-ṣalāt*. In my opinion, the explanation for this phenomenon is that the second group is made up of positions which can be carried out simultaneously by the judge,

67 Discrepancies in the total number are caused by one individual with more than one charge of those included in the list.

which is confirmed by the information provided in some of the biographies. The interim nature of the *nā'ib* and *ṣāḥib al-aḥkām*, who were basically substitute judges, explains their high degree of mobility.

On the other hand, if we look at the percentage of mobility among the total number of *quḍāt* appointed to several posts of *qāḍī*,[68] we see that mobility levels were highest during the Caliphate and the Almohad period, with almost the same percentage in both cases.

- Emirate (756–929 CE):[69] Single place: 12/31 (38.7%), mobility: 19/31 (61.2%).
- Caliphate (929–1031 CE): Single place: 8/57 (14%), mobility: 49/57 (86%).
- Taifas (1031–1091 CE): Single place: 6/13 (46.2%), mobility: 7/13 (53.8%).
- Almoravids (1091–1142 CE): Single place: 7/27 (25.9%), mobility: 20/27 (74.1%).
- Taifas (2) (1142–1170 CE): Single place: 5/16 (31.25%), mobility: 11/16 (68.75%).
- Almohads (1145–1229 CE): Single place: 11/80 (13.75%), mobility: 69/80 (86.25%).
- Taifas (3) (1229–1270 CE): Single place: 6/12 (50%), mobility: 6/12 (50%).
- Naṣrid kingdom (1232–1492 CE): Single place: 5/26 (19.2%), mobility: 21/26 (80.8%).

According to these data, spatial mobility was more common in some periods than in others, namely from the beginning of the 10th c. CE to the beginning of the 11th c. CE, during the Umayyad Caliphate, and especially during the second half of the 10th c. CE; and then from the middle of the 12th c. to the beginning of the 13th c. CE, during the Almohad Empire. Thus, the information likewise indicates that after the fall of the Umayyads, during the subsequent *fitna* (sedition, disorder) and the division of the territory into the *Taifa* kingdoms, local families tended to hold onto power by staying put. In consequence, mobility partially ceased, although there are some cases of *'ulamā'* moving around with different appointments, such as Abū al-Aṣbagh 'Īsā b. Sahl (d. 486/1093), who acted as *qāḍī* in various cities, including Tangier and Granada. Interestingly, when the Almoravids reached Granada they dismissed him from his post, perhaps precisely because he had worked in different locations serving multiple rulers, which in their eyes made him untrustworthy. The information extracted from the PUA database indicates that professional mobility resumed during the Almoravid period, this time logically extending to the Maghreb.

68 146 judges.

69 These are approximate dates, but the case of every *qāḍī* has been individually analyzed considering the place where the position was held and the year in which he was appointed if the information was available.

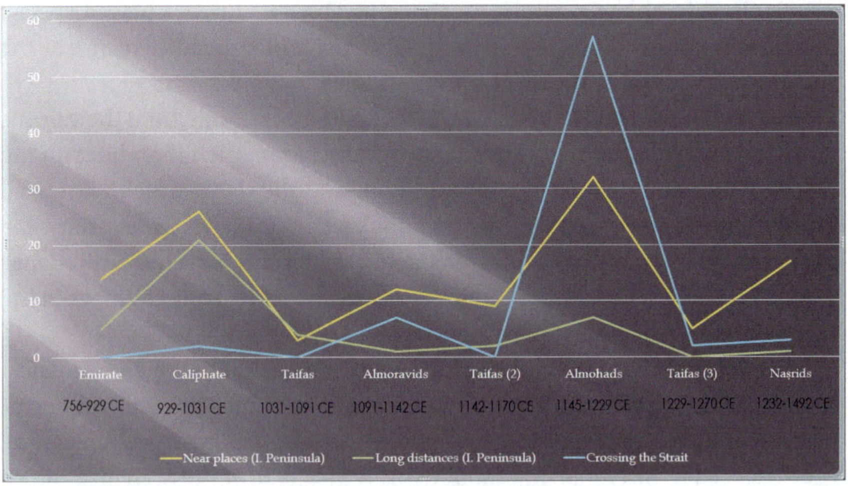

FIGURE 6.2 Types of mobility along the different periods

Because the Berber rulers were well aware of the great power that the *ʿulamāʾ* had amassed in al-Andalus during the years of political instability, they started using spatial mobility as a strategy to keep them under control, appointing Andalusīs to posts in the Maghreb and sending a handful of Maghrebis loyal to their cause to posts in al-Andalus. A search in PUA turns up 78 judges who crossed the Strait of Gibraltar in either direction throughout all the periods of Andalusī history: 36 from the Iberian Peninsula to the Maghreb, and 42 in the opposite direction. Of the latter, only six were sent by the Almoravids from the Maghreb to al-Andalus in a feeble bid to take over the Andalusī judicature.

The Almoravids had originally been called in by the Andalusīs for help in fending off the advancing Christian armies, but once they entered the Peninsula they took over al-Andalus themselves. However, their timid attempts to control the local institutions were not successful, as they had to contend with the powerful Andalusī urban notables,[70] in many cases allowing the members of the previous judicial elite to stay on in their posts.

We find exceptional cases of Maghrebi judges in cities such as Sevilla under the Almoravid government, but they seem to have consistently held the position of *qāḍī* only in Granada, while in places like Cordoba it is more frequent to find judges who were members of local families of notables such as the Banū al-Munāṣif, the Banū Wājib, the Banū Rushd, the Banū Furtish, the Banū Shurayḥ, the Banū Fatḥūn al-Anṣārī and the Banū ʿAbd al-Waḥīd. In this

70 Rodríguez Mediano, "Instituciones judiciales," 172–173.

respect, Rachid el Hour points out that the Almoravid rulers placed special emphasis on controlling the judicature of the city of Granada because at the time it was regarded as the capital of al-Andalus.[71]

The Almoravids tried to make the Andalusī judges relocate from their towns of origin to other cities in al-Andalus in order to strengthen their hold on the region. They believed that this policy, alongside the deals struck with local families in other cities, could prevent popular uprisings. On the contrary, the last years of Almoravid rule were characterized by revolts across al-Andalus, headed by various local judges hailing from the most important families in the biggest cities, such as Cordoba, Valencia, Jaen, Malaga and Murcia.[72]

Although the Almohads were also forced to negotiate with the Andalusī notables in some cases, they enjoyed a greater degree of legitimacy, and managed to create their own elites and control the *ʿulamāʾ* and the judicature. They succeeded in employing mobility as a means of professionalization of the judgeship, as confirmed unambiguously by the data extracted from PUA. Indeed, we find a dramatic increase in the number of judges sent from one side of the Strait to the other during this period.[73] The Almohad rulers increased the appointments of Maghrebi judges in different cities of the Iberian Peninsula such as Granada, Murcia, Sevilla, Valencia or Cordoba, but also the appointments of Andalusī judges in the Maghreb, especially in Ceuta, Marrakesh and Aghmat. In this way, the Almohads developed a kind of judicial network that allowed them to control the judicature across the various regions of their vast domain.

In the next period, the loss of territories would set in motion a third type of mobility: the emigration of scholars out of the Iberian Peninsula without a direct academic or professional purpose. After the definitive fall of the Almohads in 1229, for example, two judges are recorded as having moved to Hafsid Tunis:[74] Muḥammad b. ʿAbd al-Raḥmān al-Khazrajī al-Anṣārī al-Shāṭibī, Abū ʿAbd Allāh (d. 691/1292) and Aḥmad b. Muḥammad b. Ḥasan (al-Ḥasan) b. Muḥammad b. ʿAbd al-Raḥmān b. Saʿd b. Saʿīd b. Muḥammad al-Anṣārī al-Khazrajī al-Andalusī al-Qāḍī, Ibn al-Ghammāz, Abū al-ʿAbbās (693/1293).[75]

71 See El Hour, "El cadiazgo de Granada bajo los almorávides," 14–15.

72 Plazas Rodríguez, "Los ulemas andalusíes y el poder Almorávide," 1081–1110, 1102–1103.

73 57 of the 78 judges crossed the Strait under Almohad rule.

74 On this kind of migration see Manzano, "De cadíes y fuentes históricas," 188–190.

75 On the scholars who left al-Andalus fearing the end of Muslim rule in the territories see Boloix, "Viajes con retorno y sin retorno," 71–87.

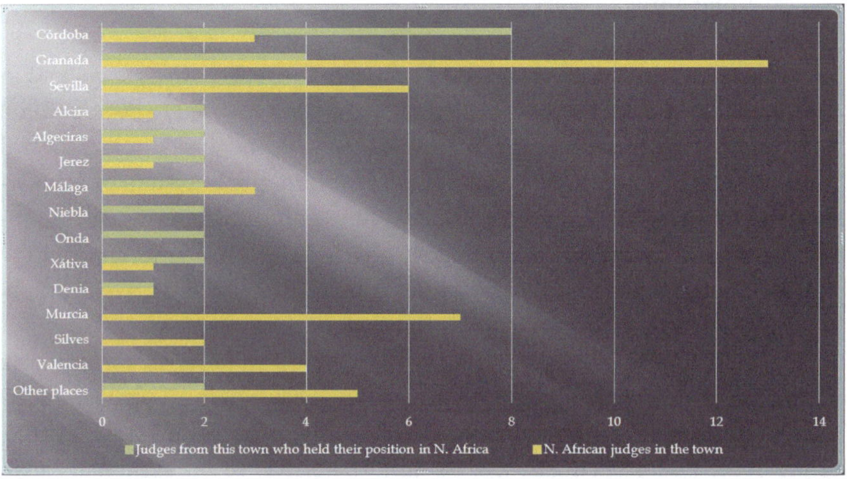

FIGURE 6.3 Judges appointed in Andalusī cities

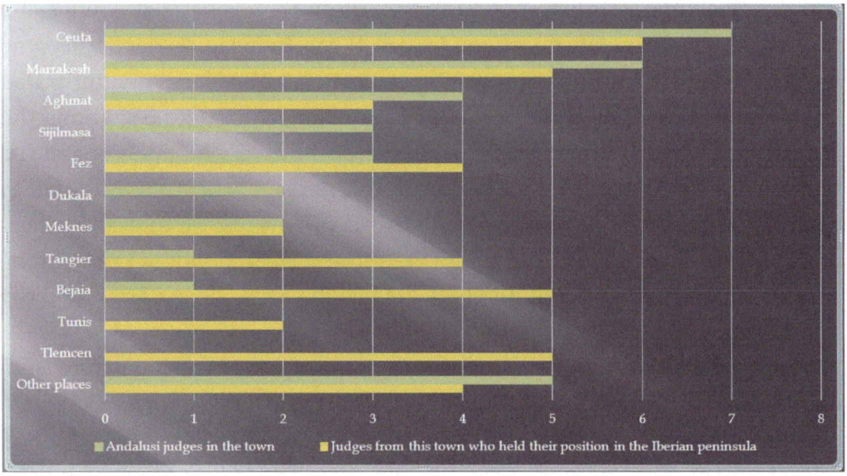

FIGURE 6.4 Judges appointed in Maghrebi cities

This kind of definitive emigration, whose motivation Mahmud Ali Makki has described as "*political asylum*," characterized not only the last period of Almohad rule, but also the Naṣrid period, when Andalusī territory was ultimately restricted to Granada and its surroundings. Three such cases have been detected from the thirteenth c. CE onwards: Muḥammad b. ʿUmar b. Muḥammad al-Fihrī, Ibn Rashīd (d. 721/1321), Husayn b. Yūsuf b. Yaḥyā b. Aḥmad al-Ḥusaynī al-Sabtī, Abū ʿAlī (d. 753/1352) and Muḥammad b. Yūsuf, Abū al-Qāsim al-ʿAbdarī, al-Mawwāq al-Gharnāṭī (d. 894/1492).

4 Concluding Remarks

As we have seen, there was not a legal or religious career path as such, and in consequence there was no established route to follow in order to be appointed to the judicature. In spite of the intense mobility of Andalusī scholars toward the East and their active participation in the international system of scholarship, the Andalusī system of learning developed on its own terms. For example, the *madrasa* system was completely absent from al-Andalus up until the Naṣrid period. In consequence, the professionalization of the *ʿulamāʾ*, and specifically of the *quḍāt*, follows a totally different course.

Apart from those who were appointed by the rulers to remunerated posts within the magistracy and/or the administration, scholars always depended on additional sources of income, whether another paid job, a family fortune, or pay received for teaching, at least until the arrival of the Almohads, who did provide scholars with salaries. Accordingly, the *ʿulamāʾ* recorded as judges in PUA do not share a specific profile;[76] some of them eventually held administrative positions or other appointments within the magistracy, while some others seem to have only ever been judges. It was indeed possible to become an *ʿālim* regardless of one's family or social origin, as has been demonstrated by Manuela Marín.[77] However, it is equally true that, with some exceptions, the attested cases of commoners exercising the position of *qāḍī* are few, and the highest posts within the judicature were reserved for scholars from families of urban notables, and even under Almohad rule, when we find a significative increase of social mobility in the magistracy, we find judges from among the 'old' Andalusī families of notables such as the Banū al-Munāṣif[78] and the Banū Makhlad.[79]

The results of this study indicate that appointments to the judicature were employed by some rulers, especially during the Umayyad and the Almohad caliphates, as a safeguard against the threat that these families of the scholarly establishment represented for the central power. The three different kinds of

76 For instance, in relation to the specific case of the *quḍāt* appointed by ʿAbd al-Raḥmān III, the sources reveal very different profiles; all of them were well educated in the Islamic sciences, but each in different subjects. See Fierro, "Los cadíes de Córdoba de ʿAbd al-Raḥmān III," 77.

77 For example Abū ʿAlī ʿUmar b. Muḥammad al-Azdī al-Shalawbīnī (d. 645/1247–8 or 646/1248–9), see Marín, "Movilidad social y ciencias islámicas," 20–27.

78 The brothers Muḥammad b. ʿĪsā b. Muḥammad b. Aṣbagh al-Azdī, Ibn al-Munāṣif, Abū ʿAbd Allāh (d. 620/1223), judge in Murcia and Valencia, and Ibrāhīm b. ʿĪsā b. Muḥammad b. Aṣbagh al-Azdī, Ibn al-Munāṣif, Abū Isḥāq (d. 627/1229), judge in Denia and Sijilmasa.

79 For instance, Aḥmad b. Yazīd b. ʿAbd al-Raḥmān al-Umawī al-Baqawī al-Qurṭubī al-Mālikī, Ibn Baqī, Abū al-Qāsim (d. 625/1227), who was *qāḍī al-quḍāt* in the Maghreb.

mobility analyzed here seem to have been used in different moments as strategies for gaining control over the notables and religious scholars in general. During Almohad times, the professionalization of the *ʿulamāʾ* was accompanied by an attempt at codifying the law and avoiding legal divergence (*ikhtilāf*), undermining the authority of the religious scholars.[80]

Horizontal mobility was not frequent, but occurred more often in periods in which the scholars were more powerful, for example right after the Islamic conquest and during the *fitna* and subsequent *Taifa* kingdoms. However, it seems to have been avoided under the two caliphates, when social and spatial mobility peaked, pointing to a relative loss of power by the *ʿulamāʾ*. Regarding social advancement, the first Andalusī judges, for instance, had been soldiers, but starting at the end of the Umayyad Emirate a group of scholars well educated in the Islamic sciences emerged,[81] and in consequence the new candidates appointed to the judicature would then be experts in qurʾanic sciences and *fiqh* (jurisprudence). Thus, Berbers and *muwalladūn* (converts to Islam) started to be included in the judicial magistracy.[82] Likewise, most of the scholars from families engaged in manual trades were non-Arabs who had converted to Islam, some of whom ended up as magistrates. The same happened in the 13th c. CE, when the Almohads recruited and instructed scholars regardless of their social provenance.[83] As for spatial mobility, judges were appointed to the judicature of different and distant locations in what seems to be a strategy aimed to prevent them from becoming powerful in their own right. As an example, several members of Andalusī families of judges, such as the previously mentioned Banū al-Munāṣif, the Banū Makhlad, and the Banū ʿUfayr, were sent off by the Almohads to exercise the judicature in Maghrebi cities.

The professionalization of the judicature is therefore outlined here as a logical consequence of the control exerted by the rulers over the judges. This process turned them into state employees who depended on the central power, thus depriving them of their authority as popular religious leaders.

80 Fierro, "Codifying the law," 112–114.

81 They lent legitimacy to the conquest and the Umayyad dynasty. See Manzano, *Conquistadores, emires y califas*, 36–39.

82 The Umayyad dynasty probably did not want to be associated with the Arab minority, since Andalusī society was ethnically heterogeneous. The inclusion of non-Arabs in official institutions may have sought to secure greater support among the population; see Fierro, "Genealogies of power in al-Andalus."

83 While the emergence of scholars usually follows a bottom-up process, meaning that students interested in the Islamic sciences first studied with reputed masters, after which some were selected by the rulers for different posts, the Almohads created a top-down system in which scholars received a salary from the state.

Acknowledgments

This work has been elaborated thanks to a postdoctoral contract Juan de la Cierva – incorporación (IJCI-2017–31351) funded by the Spanish Ministry of Science, Innovation and Universities (2019–2021). English review by Nicholas Callaway.

Bibliography

Ávila, María Luisa. "Cargos hereditarios en la administración judicial y religiosa de al-Andalus", in *Saber religioso y saber político en el Islam* (Madrid: Agencia Española de Cooperación Internacional, 1994), 27–37.

Ávila, María Luisa. "The search for knowledge: Andalusi scholars and their travels to the Islamic East". *Medieval Prosopography: History and Collective Biography* 23 (2002): 125–139.

Ávila, María Luisa. "Baqī b. Makhlad". *Encyclopaedia of Islam*. Third Edition, online. (= *EI*³). Ed. Kate Fleet; Gudrun Krämer; Denis Matringe; John Nawas y Everett Rowson. http://dx.doi.org/10.1163/1573-3912_ei3_COM_24530 [consulted 13/03/2019].

Bencherifa, Muhammad. "Al-Bunnāhī, lā al-Nubāhī". *Académia: Revue de l'académie du Royaume du Maroc* 8 (1998): 17–89.

Boloix, Bárbara. "Viajes con retorno y sin retorno: Andalusíes hacia la *Dār al-Islam* en el s. XIII", in *Entre Oriente y Occidente: Ciudades y viajeros en la Edad Media*, eds. Juan Pedro Monferrer Sala and Dolores Rodríguez Gómez (Granada: Universidad de Granada, 2005), 71–101.

Bosch, Vila. "Los Banū Simāk de Málaga y Granada: una familia de cadíes". *Miscelánea de Estudios Arabes y Hebraicos: Sección Arabe-Islam* 11 (1962): 21–37.

Calero Secall, María Isabel. "Los Banū l-Ḥasan al-Bunnāhī: una familia de juristas malagueños (ss. X–XV)", in *Estudios árabes dedicados a D. Luis Seco de Lucena. (En el XXV aniversario de su muerte)*, ed. C. Castillo Castillo, I. Cortés Peña, J.P. Monferrer Sala (Granada: Universidad de Granada, 1999), 53–76.

Calero Secall, María Isabel. "Al-Bunnāhī, Abū al-Ḥasan", *Biblioteca de al-Andalus. De al-ʿAbbādīya a Ibn Abyaḍ* (BA) 1, ed. Jorge Lirola and José Miguel Puerta Vílchez (Almería: Fundación Ibn Tufayl de Estudios Arabes, 2012), 282–286, [85].

Castilla Brazales, Juan. "El primer qāḍī l-quḍāt de al-Andalus". *Miscelánea de Estudios Arabes y Hebraicos: Sección Arabe-Islam* 48 (1999): 47–57.

Chalmeta, Pedro. *El zoco medieval: contribución al estudio de la historia del mercado* (Almería: Fundación Ibn Tufayl de Estudios Árabes, 2010).

Clément, François. "Catégories socioprofessionnelles et métiers urbains dans l'Espagne musulmane", in *Regards sur al-Andalus (VIIIe–XVe siècle)*, ed. François Géal (Madrid: Casa de Velázquez, 2006), 95–128.

Corriente, Federico. *Diccionario Árabe- Español*, 3rd ed. (Barcelona: Herder, 1991).

Damaj, Ahmad Chafic. "Punto de vista del intelectual sobre su relación del poder político en la época nazarí". *Anaquel de Estudios árabes e Islámicos*, no. 15 (2004): 97–121.

Documentación, "Al-Abbār/al-Labbār, Abū Bakr". *Biblioteca de al-Andalus. Apéndice*, 8, ed. Jorge Lirola y José Miguel Puerta Vílchez (Almería: Fundación Ibn Tufayl de Estudios Árabes, 2012), 15, [1897].

Fadel, Mohammad. "The Social Logic of Taqlīd and the Rise of the Mukhtaṣar," *Islamic Law and Society* 3, no. 2 (1996): 193–233.

Fadel, Mohammad. "Rules, judicial discretion, and the rule of law in Naṣrid Granada: an analysis of al-Ḥadīqa al-mustaqilla al-naḍra fī al-fatāwā al-ṣādira ʿan ʿulamāʾ al-ḥaḍra." In *Islamic Law: theory and practice*, ed. R. Gleave and E. Kermeli (London/New York: Tauris, 1997), 49–86.

Fierro, Maribel. "Familias en el Taʿrij al-iftitāḥ al-Andalus de Ibn al-Qūṭiyya", in *Estudios Onomástico-Biográficos de al-Andalus* 4 (Madrid: CSIC, 1990): 41–70.

Fierro, Maribel. "The qāḍī as ruler", in *Saber religioso y poder político en el Islam. Actas del Simposio Internacional (Granada, 15–18 octubre 1991)* (Madrid: Agencia Española de Cooperación Internacional, 1994), 71–116.

Fierro, Maribel. "El alfaquí beréber Yaḥyā b. Yaḥyā al-Laythī (m. 234/848), 'El inteligente de al-Andalus'", in *Estudios Onomástico-Biográficos de al-Andalus* 8 (Madrid: CSIC, 1997), 269–344.

Fierro, Maribel. "Los mawālī de ʿAbd al-Raḥmān I". *Al-Qanṭara: Revista de Estudios Arabes* 20, no. 1 (1999): 65–97.

Fierro, Maribel. "La nisba al-Anṣārī en al-Andalus y el Cadí Munḏir b. Saʿīd". *Al-Qanṭara: Revista de Estudios Arabes* 25, no. 1 (2004): 233–237.

Fierro, Maribel. "Mawālī and muwalladūn in al-Andalus (second/eighth-fourth/tenth centuries)", in *Mawālī in the Islamic World*, eds. J. Nawas and M. Bernanrds (Leiden: Brill, 2005), 195–245.

Fierro, Maribel. "Genealogies of Power in al-Andalus. Politics, Religion and Ethnicity during the Second/Eighth-Fifth-Eleventh Centuries". *Annales Islamologiques* 42 (2008): 29–55.

Fierro, Maribel. "Ulemas en las ciudades andalusíes: religión, política y prácticas sociales", in *Escenarios Urbanos de al-Andalus y el Occidente musulmán*, ed. Virgilio Martínez Enamorado (Málaga: Ayuntamiento de Vélez-Málaga, 2011), 137–167.

Fierro, Maribel. "Los Cadíes de Córdoba de ʿAbd al-Raḥmān III al-Nāṣir, Umayyad Amīr/Caliph of Cordoba", in *Cadíes y cadiazgo en al-Andalus y el Magreb medieval,* ed. Rachid el Hour, *Estudios Onomástico-Biográficos de al-Andalus* 18 (Madrid: CSIC, 2012), 69–98.

Fierro, Maribel. "Codifying the law: the case of the medieval Islamic West", in *Diverging paths? The shapes of power and institutions in medieval Christendom and Islam*, ed. John Hudson, Ana Rodríguez (Leiden: Brill, 2014), 98–118.

Fierro, Maribel. "The religious policy of the Almohads", in *The Oxford handbook of Islamic theology*, ed. Sabine Schmidtke (Oxford: Oxford University Press, 2016), 679–692.

Fricaud. "Les *Ṭalaba* dans la société Almohade (Le temps d'Averroès)". *Al-Qanṭara: Revista de Estudios Arabes* 18, no. 2 (1997): 331–387.

Gellens, Sam Isaac. *Scholars and Travellers: The social History of early Muslim Egypt*. PhD diss., Columbia University, 1986.

El Hour, Rachid. "Córdoba frente a los almorávides: familias de cadíes y poder local en al-Andalus". *Revista del Instituto Egipcio de Estudios Islámicos en Madrid* 29 (1997): 181–210.

El Hour, Rachid. "The Andalusian qāḍī in the Almoravid period: political and judicial authority". *Studia Islamica* 90 (2000): 67–83.

El Hour, Rachid. *La administración judicial almorávide en al-Andalus. Élites, negociaciones y enfrentamientos* (Helsinki: Academia Scientiarum Fennica, 2006).

El Hour, Rachid. "Algeciras, ciudad magrebí en al-Andalus. Una reflexión acerca de su administración de justicia". *Quaderni Di Studi Arabi* 1 (2006): 69–79.

El Hour, Rachid. "El cadiazgo de Granada bajo los almorávides: negociaciones y enfrentamientos". *Al-Qanṭara: Revista de Estudios Árabes* 27, no. 1 (2006): 7–24.

El Hour, Rachid. "Reflexiones acerca del desarrollo de la justicia en Alcalá la Real en época almorávide", in *Islam y cristiandad. Siglos XI–XVI*, eds. Ceballos and Molina (Jaén: Diputación Provincial de Jaén, 2008), 249–256.

El Hour, Rachid. "El cadiazgo en Jaén en época Almorávide: una propuesta de interpretación", in *Cadíes y cadiazgo en al-Andalus y el Magreb medieval*, ed. Rachid el Hour, *Estudios Onomástico-Biográficos de al-Andalus* 18 (Madrid: CSIC, 2012), 169–185.

Lévi-Provençal, Évariste. "3. La organización judicial", in *Historia de España de Menéndez Pidal*, 30 vols. (Madrid: Espasa-Calpe, 1958–2000), V, 72–98.

Lirola, Jorge. "Los viajes de los autores andalusíes a Oriente y al-Magreb", in *Homenaje al Dr. Jaafar Ben El haj Soulami. Semblanzas y Estudios*, ed. Mohamed Reda Boudchar (Tetuán: Asociación Tetuán Asmir, 2015), 100–110.

Lucini, Mercedes. "Los Banū Samaŷūn, una familia de cadíes", in *Estudios Onomástico-Biográficos de al-Andalus* 5 (Madrid: CSIC, 1992): 171–199.

Makki, Mahmud Ali. *Ensayo sobre las aportaciones orientales en la España musulmana y su influencia en la formación de la cultura hispano-árabe* (Madrid: Instituto Egipcio de Estudios islámicos, 1968).

Manzano, Eduardo. *Conquistadores, emires y califas: los omeyas y la formación de al-Andalus* (Barcelona: Crítica, 2006).

Manzano, Miguel Ángel. "De Cadíes y fuentes históricas: apuntes en el Kitāb al-ʿibar", in *Cadíes y cadiazgo en al-Andalus y el Magreb medieval*, ed. Rachid el Hour, *Estudios Onomástico-Biográficos de al-Andalus* 18 (Madrid: CSIC, 2012), 188–190.

Marín, Manuela. "Una familia de ulemas cordobeses: los Banū Abī ʿĪsā". *Al-Qanṭara: Revista de Estudios Árabes* 6 (1985): 291–320.

Marín, Manuela. "El oficio de la ciencia y otros oficios: En torno a la onomástica de los ulemas Andalusíes", in *Estudios Onomástico-Biográficos de al-Andalus* 7 (Madrid: CSIC, 1995): 377–435.

Marín, Manuela. "Movilidad social y ciencias islámicas: ejemplos biográficos andalusíes de la Baja Edad Media (siglos XII–XIV)", in *Categorias sociais e mobilidade urbana na Baixa Idade Média: Entre o Islão e a Cristandade*, ed. Hermínia Vasconcelos Vilar and maría Filomena Lopes de barros (Évora: Publicações do Cidehus, 2012), 11–34.

Marín, Manuela; Fierro, Maribel. *Sabios y santos musulmanes de Algeciras* (Algeciras: Fundación municipal de Cultura José Luis Cano, 2004).

Marlow, Louise. *Hierarchy and Egalitarianism in Islamic thought* (Cambridge: Cambridge University Press, 1997).

Martos, Juan. *Introducción al mundo jurídico de la España musulmana* (Madrid: Ediciones G. Martín, 1999).

Martos, Juan. *El mundo jurídico en al-Andalus* (Madrid: Delta, 2004).

Martos, Juan. "Poder central Omeya y poder judicial en al-Andalus", in *Cadíes y cadiazgo en al-Andalus y el Magreb medieval*, ed. Rachid el Hour, *Estudios Onomástico-Biográficos de al-Andalus* 18 (Madrid: CSIC, 2012), 121–145.

Molina, Luis. "Familias andalusíes: los datos del Taʿrij al-ʿulamaʾ al-Andalus de Ibn al-Faradi", I, *Estudios Onomástico-Biográficos de al-Andalus* (EOBA) 2 (Granada: CSIC, 1989), 19–99; EOBA 3 (Granada: CSIC, 1990), 13–58; EOBA 4 (Granada: CSIC, 1990), 13–40.

Müller, Christian. "Administrative tradition and civil jurisdiction of the Cordoban Ṣāḥib al-aḥkām". *Al-Qanṭara: Revista de Estudios Árabes* 21, no. 1 (2000): 57–84.

Pérès, Henri. "Les éléments ethniques de l'Espagne musulmane et la langue arabe au Xe/XIe siècle", *Études d'Orientalisme dédiés à la mémoire de Lévi-Provençal* 2 (Paris: Maisonneuve et Larose, 1962): 717–733.

Perho, Irmeli. "Climbing the ladder: social mobility in the Mamluk period". *Mamlūk Studies Review* 15 (2011): 19–35.

Plazas Rodríguez, Teresa. "Los ulemas andalusíes y el poder almorávide (ss.XI–XII)". *Estudios sobre Patrimonio, Cultura y Ciencias Medievales* 19, no. 3 (2017): 1081–1110.

Rodríguez Mediano, Fernando. "Instituciones judiciales: cadíes y otras magistraturas", El retroceso territorial de al-Andalus: Almorávides y Almohades, siglos XI al XII.

Coord. María Jesús Viguera Molíns, *Historia de España de Menéndez Pidal,* VIII/2 (Madrid: Espasa Calpe, 1997), 172–173.

Rozi, Abdulghafour Ismail. *The social role of Scholars* (*ʿulamāʾ*) *in Islamic Spain: A study of medieval Biographical Dictionaries* (*Trajim*). PhD diss., Boston University, 1983.

Shatzmiller, Maya. *Labour in the Medieval Islamic world* (Brill: Leiden, 1994).

Torre, Concepción de la. "Familias andalusíes: bibliografía comentada", in *Estudios Onomástico-Biográficos de al-Andalus* 5 (Madrid: CSIC, 1992): 349–371.

Velázquez, Basanta, Fernando Nicolás. "Ibn Barṭāl (s. XIV): un malagueño "iletrado" en el cadiazgo supremo de Granada", in *Estudios árabes dedicados a D. Luis Seco de Lucena.* (*En el XXV aniversario de su muerte.*), eds. C. Castillo Castillo, I. Cortés Peña, J.P. Monferrer Sala (Granada: Universidad de Granada, 1999), 271–276.

Viguera, María Jesús. "Fuentes de al-Andalus (siglos XI y XII). I: Crónicas y obras geográficas", in *Actas I Curso sobre la Península Ibérica y el Mediterráneo durante los siglos XI y XII*, ed. Fernando Valdés Fernández (Aguilar de Campoo: Fundación Santa maría la Real, 1998), 9–32.

Zomeño, Amalia. "Al-Jušanī", *Biblioteca de al-Andalus. De Ibn al-Dabbāg a Ibn Kurz* (BA) 3, ed. Jorge Lirola and José Miguel Puerta Vílchez (Almería: Fundación Ibn Tufayl de Estudios Arabes, 2004), 290–296, [548].

PART 3

Power, Politics, and Mobility

CHAPTER 7

Imām al-Ḥaramayn al-Juwaynī's Mobility and the Saljūq's Project of Sunnī Political Unity

M. Syifa Amin Widigdo

The success of the Saljūq political dynasty in ruling and uniting the majority of the Muslim world, ranging from the Mediterranean Sea to Central Asia in the fifth/eleventh century, was in part due to a network of *madrasas*.[1] The Saljūq supported logistically and politically these *madrasas* through endowment.[2] Under the influential vizier Niẓām al-Mulk (d. 486/1093), the Saljūqs were largely successful in uniting the shattered Muslim world under "Sunnī Islam"[3] and gradually ending the Shīʿa political domination through building *madrasas* while congruently patronizing religious scholars.[4] One of the scholars that the vizier Niẓām al-Mulk patronized and appointed as the director of the *madrasa* that he founded was Imām al-Ḥaramayn al-Juwaynī (d. 478/1085). With the support and collaboration of Niẓām al-Mulk, Imām al-Ḥaramayn, who was the first director of *madrasa Niẓāmīya* in Nishapur, was influential for his contribution to the construction of the Saljūq's political ideology through his scholarly careers and writings. He attempted to formulate a new understanding of Sunnī orthodoxy, which then became the Saljūqs' political ideology.[5]

1 Richard N. Frye, *The Golden Age of Persia* (USA: Harper & Row Publishers Inc., 1975), 226.

2 Daphna Ephrat, *A Learned Society in a Period of Transition: The Sunni 'Ulama' of Eleventh-Century Baghdad* (Albany: State University of New York Press, 2000), 103.

3 The term "Sunnī Islam" is used here with an assumption that a sense of unity of non-Shīʿa community (or Sunnī-oriented community) is present under the Saljūqs and the vision of "Sunnī orthodoxy" is formulated.

4 Frye, *The Golden Age of Persia*, 226–28; Marshall G.S. Hodgson, *The Venture of Islam 2* (Chicago: The University of Chicago Press, 1974), 46–48; Massimo Campanini, "In Defence of Sunnism: Al-Ghazīlī and The Seljuqs," in *The Seljuqs: Sociaety, Society and Culture*, ed. Christian Lange and Songul Mecit (Edinburgh: Edinburgh University Press, 2011), 230.

5 The orthodoxy of proto-Sunnī Muslims in the tenth and early eleventh century, especially within traditional and legal-minded people, was associated with creed of Aḥmad b. Hanbal and his followers regarding "uncreatedness" of the Qur'an. See Christopher Melchert, "Sectaries in the Six Books: Evidence for their exclusion from the Sunnī orthodoxy," in *Orthodoxy and Heresy in Islam: Critical Concepts in Islamic Studies*, ed. Maribel Fierro

 | DOI:10.1163/9789004467637_009

However, despite the pivotal role and position of Imām al-Ḥaramayn in the formation of Sunnī doctrines in the eleventh century, the study of the development of his intellectual and professional career and his scholarly contribution is still limited. Among the few studies that address Imām al-Ḥaramayn's scholarly works are the translation of the book *al-Irshād* by Paul E. Walker and a dissertation written by Mohammad Moslem Adel Saflo entitled *Al-Juwaini's Thought and Methodology, with A Translation and Commentary on Luma' al-Adilla*, and Sohaira Z.M. Siddiqui's book *Law and Politics under the Abbasids: An Intellectual Portrait of al-Juwayni.*[6] While Walker provides a short discussion of Imām al-Ḥaramayn's biography in the introduction of his translation, Saflo elaborates not only his biography but also his legal and theological thoughts. Siddiqui studies Imām al-Ḥaramayn's life and contribution more comprehensively by elaborating on his larger historical background and his intellectual and political project.

Nevertheless, each of these studies has its merit and deserves a scholarly appreciation, yet, still leaves some lacunas. Walker's presentation of Imām al-Ḥaramayn's biography relies heavily on a traditional narrative and excludes some alternative accounts, for example, about Imām al-Ḥaramayn's reason for leaving Nishapur. The traditional account claims that the reason is the persecution of the Saljūq vizier, al-Kundurī, of Ash'arī scholars.[7] Some alternative narratives report that the reason is Imām al-Ḥaramayn's deliberation with the help and permission of the Saljūq regime to widen his influence beyond Nishapur.[8]

(London and New York: Routledge Taylor & Francis Group, 2014), 137. However, a more established "Sunnī orthodoxy" was not formulated during this period since a rational theology, like *kalām* of al-Ash'arī, was largely considered heretic.

6 Imām al-Ḥaramayn al-Juwaynī, *Kitāb al-Irshād Ilā Qawaṭi' al-Adilla fī Uṣūl al- I'tiqād* (*A Guide to Conclusive Proofs for The Principles of Belief*), ed. and trans. Paul E. Walker (UK: The Center for Muslim Contribution to Civilization/Garnet Publishing, 2000); Mohammad Moslem Adel Saflo, *Al-Juwaini's Thought and Methodology, with A Translation and Comentary on Luma' al-Adilla* (Berlin: Klaus Schwarz Verlag, 2000); Sohaira Z.M. Siddiqui, *Law and Politics under the Abbasids: An Intellectual Portrait of al-Juwayni* (Cambridge: Cambridge University Press, 2019).

7 Tāj al-Dīn Abū Naṣr 'Abd al-Wahhāb b. 'Alī al-Subkī, *Ṭabaqāt al-Shāfi'īyah al-Kubrā 3*, ed. Maḥmūd Muḥammad and 'Abd al-Fattāḥ Muḥammad al-Ḥalw al-Ṭanāḥī, vol. 3 (Cairo: Maṭba'ah 'Īsā al-Bābī al-Halbī, 1386/1967), Vol. 3., 391–92.

8 See Abū al-Faraj 'Abd al-Raḥmān b. 'Alī Ibn al-Jawzī, *al-Muntaẓam fī tārīkh al-mulūk wa al-umam*, vol. 9 (Hyderabad: Dā'irah al-Ma'ārif al-'Uthmānīyah, 1359/1940); Abū 'Abbās Shams al-Dīn Aḥmad b. Muḥammad b. Abū Bakr Ibn Khallikān, *Wafayāt al-a'yān wa anbā' abnā' al-zamān 3*, ed. Iḥsān 'Abbās, vol. 3 (Beirut: Dār al-Thaqāfah, 1968). Siddiqui notices the record in the biographical dictionaries of Ibn Khallikān and Ibn al-Jawzī, which mentions

This alternative narrative is absent from Walker's presentation of Imām al-Ḥaramayn's biography. Similarly, Saflo's elaboration of Imām al-Ḥaramayn's life and thoughts suffers from some noticeable flaws, such as translating *adillat al-ʿuqūl* as "mental arguments", which should be rendered as "rational proofs." In addition to the problems of accuracy and consistency in making claims, translations, and the bibliographical quotations, I concur with Frank Griffel who criticizes Saflo for not looking beyond Imām al-Ḥaramayn's writings or trying to discuss Imām al-Ḥaramayn's role in shaping the Saljūq Empire.[9] Meanwhile, Siddiqui's study argues that Imām al-Ḥaramayn al-Juwaynī's intellectual and political career is dedicated to searching legal-theological certainty and maintaining a Muslim political continuity. Imām al-Ḥaramayn's early study in Nishapur, his departure from to Nishapur to Baghdad and Ḥijāz, and his return to Nishapur accepting the directorship appointment in the Niẓāmīya *madrasa* are inseparably linked with his intellectual project of finding certainty and preserving Muslim socio-political sustainability.[10] While this article agrees with Siddiqui's argument in general, Siddiqui's explanation of how Imām al-Ḥaramayn gained a credential within Shāfiʿī and Ashʿarī schools and a good reputation in Niẓām al-Mulk's Saljūq administration underestimates Imām al-Ḥaramayn's intentionality and the role of his intellectual mobility. She provides a different information from biographical dictionaries on why Imām al-Ḥaramayn left Nishapur, what he did in Baghdad and Ḥijāz, and what made him return to Nishapur. Nevertheless, a coherent explanation on what Imām al-Ḥaramayn's intention and aspiration in his departure from Nishapur is not provided.

In this regard, this paper attempts to present a coherent interpretation of Imām al-Ḥaramayn's intention leaving Nishapur, his subsequent mobility, and the consequence of this mobility in the Sunnī orthodoxy formation. This study offers an explanation of how Imām al-Ḥaramayn's intellectual network and mobility established his credentials in both Shāfiʿī legal and Ashʿarī theological scholarship, which in turn enabled him to have an authority to offer a new understanding of Sunnī orthodoxy through the integration of *kalām* and *fiqh*.

---

that Imām al-Ḥaramayn's reason to leave was to continue his studies with scholars beyond Nishapur. See Siddiqui, Law and Politics under the Abbasids: An Intellectual Portrait of al-Juwayni 57.

9 Frank Griffel, "A Review of al-Juwayni's Thought and Methodology by Mohammad Moslem Adel Saflo," *Journal of the American Oriental Society* 122, no. 4 (2002).

10 Siddiqui, *Law and Politics under the Abbasids: An Intellectual Portrait of al-Juwayni* 36–37.

1 Imām al-Ḥaramayn al-Juwaynī: Religious Credential and Intellectual Mobility

Imām al-Ḥaramayn al-Juwaynī lived in a time when medieval religious, social, and political landscape transformed, and Nishapur became one of the centers where such transformation occurred. He was born in Muḥarram 419/ February 1028 and died in the village named Bushtaniqān (Bashtaniqān), about a half league (approximately 1.5 miles) from the city of Nishapur, in the year 478/1085.[11] His father, Abū Muḥammad ʿAbdullāh b. Yūsuf al-Juwaynī (d. 439/1047), was a leading jurist (*faqīh*), legal theorist (*uṣūlī*), Arabic grammarian (*naḥwī*), and Quran exegete (*mufassir*).[12] His full genealogical name (*ism*) is ʿAbd al-Malik b. al-Shaykh Abū Muḥammad ʿAbdullāh b. Abū Yaʿqūb Yūsuf b. ʿAbdullāh b. Yūsuf b. Muḥammad b. Hayyūyah al-Juwaynī.[13] Although he was born in the city of Nishapur, his more popular appellation (*nisbah*) was al-Juwaynī. He got this name as an inheritance from his father because, after the death of his father, he took his position and duty of teaching religious lessons.[14] More frequently, however, he was addressed by his well-known

11 Ibn Khallikān recorded that Imām al-Ḥaramayn was born on Muḥarram 18, 419/ February 17, 1028, Abū Isḥāq al-Shīrāzī wrote that his date of birth was Muḥarram 2nd, 419/ February 1st, 1028, and according to ʿAbd al-Ghāfir al-Fārisī, it was Muḥarram 19, 419/ February 18, 1028. Although there were some differences on the precise date of the Imām's birth, it is a general agreement that it was on Muḥarram 419/February 1028. Ibn Khallikān in this edition mentions this village as Bashtaniqān, but he also cited Yāqūt al-Ḥamawī (d. 626/1229) who preferred to Bushtaniqān. See Abū ʿAbbās Shams al-Dīn Aḥmad b. Muḥammad b. Abū Bakr Ibn Khallikān, *Wafayāt al-aʿyān wa anbāʾ abnāʾ al-zamān*, ed. Iḥsān ʿAbbās, vol. 3 (Beirut: Dār al-Thaqāfah, 1968), 169. See also Tāj al-Dīn Abū Naṣr ʿAbd al-Wahhāb b. ʿAlī al-Subkī, *Ṭabaqāt al-Shāfiʿīya al-kubrā*, ed. Maḥmūd Muḥammad and ʿAbd al-Fattāḥ Muḥammad al-Ḥalwī al-Ṭanāḥī, vol. 5 (Cairo: Maṭbaʿat ʿĪsā al-Bābī al-Halabī, 1386/1967), 184.

12 Abū'l-Ḥasan ʿAbd al-Ghāfir b. Ismāʿīl al-Fārisī, *Tārīkh Nīsābūr al-muntakhab min al-siyāq* (Qum: Jamāʿah al-Mudarrisīn, 1362 H/1943), 435.

13 Ibn Khallikān, *Wafayāt al-aʿyān wa anbāʾ abnāʾ al-zamān*, 3, 167.

14 Dr. Fawqīyah Ḥusayn Maḥmūd, *al-Juwaynī: Imām al-Ḥaramayn* (Egypt: al-Muʾassasah al-Miṣrīyah al-ʿĀmmah, 1964), 14. However, he was sometimes called by his patronymic name (*kunyah*), namely "Abū al-Maʿālī (Father of the Noble)," and some other times by his honorific names (*laqab*) such as "*Ḍiyāʾ al-Dīn* (Light of Religion)" and "*Fakhr al-Islām* (The Pride of Islam)." He was also called "Abū al-Maʿālī" as an honor and praise, among other things, for his excellent works in generating knowledge (*ʿilm*), inviting people to the call of religion (*daʿwah*), refuting the (arguments of the) adversary, and being right in the debates and argumentations. Another name, "*Ḍiyāʾ al-Dīn* (The Light of Religion)," was also associated with him because of his ability to be "a beacon of the defenders of the faith." "*Fakhr al-Dīn*" was sometimes attributed to him as well because his exemplary

honorific name "Imām al-Ḥaramayn (The Imām of the Two Noble Sanctuaries: Mecca and Medina)." Therefore, in this article, the name of Imām al-Ḥaramayn al-Juwaynī is used to refer to "ʿAbd al-Malik b. al-Shaykh Abū Muḥammad ʿAbdullāh al-Juwaynī."[15]

At an early age, Imām al-Ḥaramayn studied a number of basic religious sciences under his father, Abū Muḥammad al-Juwaynī (d. 439/1047), ranging from the Qurʾān, *ḥadīth*, *fiqh* (Islamic law), *khilāf* (the art of disagreement), *uṣūl al-fiqh* (Islamic legal theory), to Arabic grammar (*naḥw*) and its eloquence (*balāgha*).[16] He even read and mastered all of his father's writings, such as *al-Tafsīr al-kabīr*, *al-Tabṣirah*, *al-Tadhkirah*, *Mukhtaṣar al-mukhtaṣar*, *Sharḥ al-Muzanī*, and *Sharḥ uṣūl al-Shāfiʿī*.[17] Under the tutelage of his father, Imām al-Ḥaramayn was exposed to the study of Qurʾān, *ḥadīth*, *fiqh*, *uṣūl al-fiqh*, and Arabic grammar. He was grounded within the Shāfiʿī legal tradition. He was well-established within Shāfiʿī circles in Nishapur because, first, his father was a prominent Shāfiʿī scholar (which means Imām al-Ḥaramayn had a good genealogical and intellectual lineage), second, his understanding of Shāfiʿī legal tradition through his father's legal works was comprehensive to the extent that he could provide his *ijtihād* (independent legal judgment based on one's intellectual discretion).[18] Moreover, after the death of his father in 439/1047, Imām al-Ḥaramayn, who was early in his twenties, took over his father's position to teach at home. At the same time, he also started his intellectual mobility through studying with Abū al-Qāsim al-Isfarāʾīnī in the *madrasa* of al-Bayhaqī when not occupied with teaching activities.[19]

---

works in education and knowledge production. See al-Ḥāfiẓ Ibn Kathīr, *Ṭabaqāt al-fuqahāʾ al-shāfiʿiyīn*, ed. Anwār al-Bāz, vol. 2 (Egypt: Dār al-Wafāʾ, 2004), 866; al-Fārisī, *Tārīkh Nīsābūr al-muntakhab min al-siyāq*, 1090; Dr. Muḥammad al-Zuḥaylī, *al-Imām al-Juwaynī: Imām al-Ḥaramayn* (Damascus: Dār al-Qalam, 1986), 45–46; Maḥmūd, *al-Juwaynī: Imām al-Ḥaramayn*, 14–15; Ibn Khallikān, *Wafayāt al-aʿyān wa anbāʾ abnāʾ al-zamān*, 3, 168.

15 This name is used by Abū Isḥāq al-Shīrāzī's *Ṭabaqāt*, Abū Ghafir al-Fārisī's *Siyāq al-Nīsābūr*, Ibn Khallikān's *Wafayāt al-aʿyān*, al-Subkī's *Ṭabaqāt*, and also Ibn Kathīr's *Ṭabaqāt*. This name was given to him because he used to live in Mecca and Medina for four years, during which he was teaching, giving *fatāwa* (non-binding religious legal opinions), and combining different methodologies of legal thoughts.

16 Maḥmūd, *al-Juwaynī: Imām al-Ḥaramayn*, 23–24.

17 Dr. ʿAbd al-ʿAẓīm al-Dīb, *Imām al-Ḥaramayn Abū al-Maʿālī ʿAbd al-Malik b. ʿAbdullāh al-Juwaynī* (Kuwait: Dār al-Qalam, 1981), 34.

18 Maḥmūd, *al-Juwaynī: Imām al-Ḥaramayn*, 23.

19 al-Subkī, *Ṭabaqāt al-Shāfiʿīya al-kubrā*, 5, 169; Ibn Khallikān, *Wafayāt al-aʿyān wa anbāʾ abnāʾ al-zamān*, 3, 168.

In addition to studying with his father and Abū al-Qāsim al-Isfarāʾīnī, Imām al-Ḥaramayn took lessons in Arabic grammar further from Abū al-Ḥasan ʿAlī b. Faḍl b. ʿAlī al-Majāshī (d. 479/1086) and the science of the Qurʾān from Abū ʿAbdullāh al-Khabbāzī (d. 447/1055).[20] As for the science of *ḥadīth* and its transmission, Imām al-Ḥaramayn learned and received from different teachers. Besides learning from his father, he received *ḥadīth* transmission form scholars such as Abū Bakr Aḥmad b. Muḥammad al-Tamīmī, Abū Saʿd ʿAbd al-Raḥmān b. Ḥamdān al-Naḍrawī, Abū Ḥassān Muḥammad b. Aḥmad al-Muzakkī, and Abū ʿAbdullāh Muḥammad b. Ibrāhīm al-Ṭarrāzī, Abū Naʿīm al-Iṣbahānī (d. 430/1039), and Abū Muḥammad al-Jawharī.[21]

After having acquired a solid ground in the foundational sciences of Islamic studies, Imām al-Ḥaramayn started to extend his intellectual mobility in the context of establishing stronger religious credentials within the Shāfiʿī legal school and Ashʿarī theological school. In the field of the Shāfiʿī legal school, besides learning *fiqh* and *uṣūl al-fiqh* from his father, Imām al-Ḥaramayn also took some legal lessons from al-Qāḍī Abū ʿAlī Ḥusayn b. Muḥammad b. Aḥmad al-Marw al-Rūdhī (mistakenly written, al-Marwazī) (d. 462/1070) and Abū al-Qāsim al-Fūrānī, the leader of Shāfiʿīs in Marw (d. 463/1071).[22] Then, when he traveled to Isfahan, Baghdad, and the Ḥijāz and met scholars in these regions, he used that opportunity to study *fiqh* and *uṣūl al-fiqh* as well.[23] By studying *fiqh* and *uṣūl al-fiqh* at least under the three above mentioned teachers (i.e., his father Abū Muḥammad al-Juwaynī, al-Qāḍī Abū ʿAlī Ḥusayn Marwarūdhī, and Abū Qāsim al-Fūrānī), Imām al-Ḥaramayn not only gained knowledge of legal sciences but also established a strong intellectual and educational lineage in the Shāfiʿī legal tradition. This lineage was recorded to have an unbroken chain of scholarly connection with the originator of the Shāfiʿī legal school itself, Muḥammad b. Idrīs al-Shāfiʿī (d. 204/820). This whole teacher-student relationship that shows Imām al-Ḥaramayn's intellectual genealogy within Shāfiʿī legal tradition can be described in the following table:

20 al-Subkī, *Ṭabaqāt al-Shāfiʿīya al-kubrā*, 5, 170.
21 al-Dīb, *Imām al-Ḥaramayn Abū al-Maʿālī ʿAbd al-Malik b. ʿAbdullāh al-Juwaynī*, 35.
22 al-Zuḥaylī, *al-Imām al-Juwaynī: Imām al-Ḥaramayn*, 74.
23 al-Zuḥaylī, *al-Imām al-Juwaynī: Imām al-Ḥaramayn*, 75.

TABLE 7.1 The intellectual genealogy of Imām al-Ḥaramayn al-Juwaynī in Shāfiʿī legal school

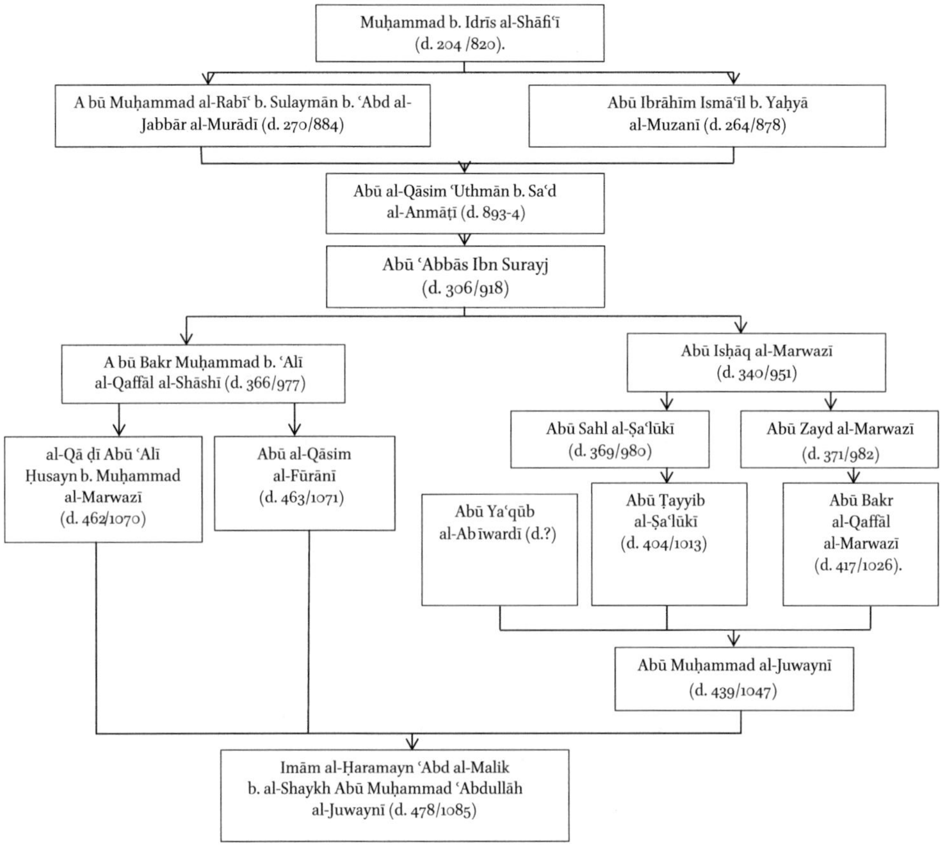

⟶ = This arrow indicates the intellectual lineage in the Shāfiʿī legal school through a teacher-student relationship.

As can be seen from the above table, the first intellectual line was from his father, Abū Muḥammad al-Juwaynī. He took legal training from three primary teachers: Abū Yaʿqūb al-Abīwardī (the date of his death is not recorded), Abū Ṭayyib al-Ṣuʿlūkī (d. 404/1013), and Abū Bakr al-Qaffāl al-Marwazī (d. 417/1026) (al-Shīrāzī 1356/1937).[24] The legal teacher of Abū Yaʿqūb al-Abīwardī was

24 Abū Isḥāq al-Shīrāzī, *Ṭabaqāt al-Shāfiʿīya* (Baghdād: al-Maktabah al-ʿArabīyah, 1356/1937), 48.

unknown so that the intellectual lineage from his side will not be further discussed.

Abū Ṭayyib al-Ṣuʿlūkī studied *fiqh* under his father, Abū Sahl al-Ṣuʿlūkī (d. 369/980), who was the leader of the Shāfiʿīs in Nīshāpūr at that time.[25] Abū Sahl al-Ṣuʿlūkī got legal training from one of the leading Shāfiʿī scholars who lived in Egypt, namely Abū Isḥāq al-Marwazī (d. 340/951).[26] Abū Isḥāq al-Marwazī himself obtained his Shāfiʿī legal teachings from the leading Shāfiʿī scholar in Baghdad, namely Ibn Surayj (d. 306/918).[27] Meanwhile, another teacher of Abū Muḥammad al-Juwaynī, Abū Bakr al-Qaffāl ʿAbdullāh b. ʿAbdullāh al-Marwazī was trained in *fiqh* by Abū Zayd al-Marwazī (d. 371/982).[28] The latter was also one of Abū Isḥāq al-Marwazī's students in Egypt. As mentioned above, Abū Isḥāq al-Marwazī studied *fiqh* under Ibn Surayj. Therefore, both Abū Ṭayyib al-Ṣuʿlūkī and Abū Bakr al-Qaffāl al-Marwazī's intellectual genealogy first met at Abū Isḥāq al-Marwazī, whose main teacher was Ibn Surayj.

The second lineage of Imām al-Ḥaramayn in Shāfiʿī legal tradition strengthened his intellectual and religious credential within the Shāfiʿī legal scholarship. It was a bit shorter than the lineage drawn from his father's side. The second intellectual lineage was drawn from his two other teachers: al-Qāḍī Abū ʿAlī Ḥusayn al-Marw al-Rūdhī (d. 462/1070) and Abū Qāsim al-Fūrānī (d. 463/1071). Both of them were students of Abū Bakr Muḥammad b. ʿAlī al-Qaffāl al-Shāshī (d. 366/977).[29] The latter, interestingly, had the same teacher as Abū Isḥāq al-Marwazī because he also studied the Shāfiʿī legal theory and tradition from the main Shāfiʿī scholar in Baghdad, Ibn Surayj.[30] Eventually, Imām al-Ḥaramayn's intellectual lineages in the Shāfiʿī legal tradition, whether drawn from Abū Muḥammad al-Juwaynī or his two other teachers, met at the figure of Abū ʿAbbās Ibn Surayj, who was known as Ibn Surayj. In fact, to some modern scholars, Ibn Surayj (along with his students) was regarded as the central figure responsible for the formation of the Shāfiʿī legal school through his introduction of a more refined *uṣūl al-fiqh* (Islamic legal theory).[31] He got his Shāfiʿī legal certificate from Abū al-Qāsim ʿUthmān b. Saʿd al-Anmāṭī

25 al-Shīrāzī, *Ṭabaqāt al-Shāfiʿīya*, 40–41.

26 Abū Zakarīyā al-Nawawī, *Tahdhīb al-asmāʾ wa al-lughāt*, vol. 1 (Beirut: Dār al-Kutub al-ʿIlmīyah 1977), 242.

27 al-Shīrāzī, *Ṭabaqāt al-Shāfiʿīya*, 19.

28 al-Nawawī, *Tahdhīb al-asmāʾ wa al-lughāt*, 1, 234.

29 al-Shīrāzī, *Ṭabaqāt al-Shāfiʿīya*, 56–57; Ibn Khallikān, *Wafayāt al-aʿyān wa anbāʾ abnāʾ al-zamān*, 3, 132.

30 al-Nawawī, *Tahdhīb al-asmāʾ wa al-lughāt*, 1, 282.

31 See Wael B Hallaq, *The Origins and Evolution of Islamic Law* (Cambridge: Cambridge University Press, 2005), 127–28; Christopher Melchert, *The Formation of the Sunni Schools of Law, 9th–10th Century C.E.* (Leiden: Brill, 1997), 87–102.

(d. 280–1/893–4).[32] Al-Anmāṭī had two main teachers, Abū Muḥammad al-Rabīʿ b. Sulaymān b. ʿAbd al-Jabbār al-Murādī (d. 270/884) and Abū Ibrāhīm Ismāʿīl b. Yaḥyā al-Muzanī (d. 264/878), who were direct students of Imām al-Shāfiʿī.[33]

In addition to obtaining Shāfiʿī legal authority through his intellectual mobility, Imām al-Ḥaramayn also gained a solid credential within the Ashʿarī theological school through an analogous intellectual strategy. This theological credential was initially built as soon as he went to the *madrasa* of al-Bayhaqī and attended sessions of Abū al-Qāsim al-Iskāf al-Isfarāʾīnī (d. 452/1060) on the subjects of *kalām* and *uṣūl* – both *uṣūl al-dīn* (principles in Islamic theology) and *uṣūl al-fiqh* (principles in Islamic law). He mastered these subjects very well.[34] Imām al-Ḥaramayn graduated from the *madrasa* with full mastery of both theoretical and practical aspects of Abū al-Qāsim al-Iskāf's methodology.[35] He used to reflect regarding this learning period saying: "I gave a commentary on several chapters of his *uṣūl* and studied on my own a hundred volumes (of books)."[36]

The study with Abū al-Qāsim was not only Imām al-Ḥaramayn's first serious encounter with the discourse of Islamic theology (*kalām*). His student-teacher relationship with Abū al-Qāsim, who was the director of *madrasa* or *duwayrah* (convent) of al-Bayhaqī, also established and ensured his chain of authority within Ashʿarī theological scholarship.[37] By studying *kalām* under Abū al-Qāsim, Imām al-Ḥaramayn was linked to the intellectual pedigree of Ashʿarism that can be traced back to the founder of the school, Abū al-Ḥasan al-Ashʿarī (d. 324/936).

It had been well recorded that Abū al-Qāsim al-Iskāf al-Isfarāʾīnī was a student of Abū Isḥāq al-Isfarāʾīnī (d. 418/1027), the Ashʿarī scholar in Nishapur.[38] Then, there are some differing accounts on how Abū Isḥāq al-Isfarāʾīnī

32 Tāj al-Dīn Abū Naṣr ʿAbd al-Wahhāb b. ʿAlī al-Subkī, *Ṭabaqāt al-Shāfiʿīyah al-Kubrā*, ed. Maḥmūd Muḥammad and ʿAbd al-Fattāḥ Muḥammad al-Ḥalw al-Ṭanāḥī, vol. 3 (Cairo: Maṭbaʿah ʿĪsā al-Bābī al-Halbī, 1386/1967), 21.

33 al-Shīrāzī, *Ṭabaqāt al-Shāfiʿīya*, 5–6.

34 See Jamāl al-Dīn ʿAbd al-Raḥīm b. al-Ḥasan al-Isnawī, *Ṭabaqāt al-Shāfiʿīyah*, ed. ʿAbdullāh al-Jabūrī (Baghdad: al-Jumhūrīyah al-Irāqīyah Riʾāsah Dīwān al-Awqāf, 1390 H), 91; Taqī al-Dīn Abū Bakr b. Aḥmad Ibn Qāḍī Shuhbah, *Ṭabaqāt al-Fuqahāʾ al-Shāfiʿīyah*, ed. Muḥammad ʿUmar ʿAlī, vol. 1 (Cairo: Maktabah al-Thaqāfah al-Dīnīyah, 1990), 237.

35 al-Fārisī, *Tārīkh Nīsābūr al-muntakhab min al-siyāq*, 522.

36 See the account of ʿAbd al-Ghāfir al-Fārisī that was recoded in al-Subkī, *Ṭabaqāt al-Shāfiʿīya al-kubrā*, 5, 175.

37 al-Subkī, *Ṭabaqāt al-Shāfiʿīya al-kubrā*, 5, 99.

38 al-Fārisī, *Tārīkh Nīsābūr al-muntakhab min al-siyāq*, 522; Ibn Kathīr, *Ṭabaqāt al-fuqahāʾ al-shāfiʿīyīn*, 2, 49.

received authority and credential in Ashʿarī theology. Al-Subkī recorded that Abū Isḥāq al-Isfarāʾīnī together with two other prolific theologians Abū Bakr Ibn Fūrak (d. 406/1015) and al-Qāḍī Abū Bakr al-Bāqillānī (d. 403/1013) studied Ashʿarī *kalām* from the direct student of Abū al-Ḥasan al-Ashʿarī, namely Abū al-Ḥasan al-Bāhilī.[39] The following testimony of al-Qāḍī Abū Bakr al-Bāqillānī regarding their togetherness in the Ashʿarī theology class affirms this scenario. Al-Bāqillānī used to say: "I used to be in the study session of al-Shaykh al-Bāhilī together with Abū Isḥāq al-Isfarāʾīnī and Ibn Fūrak. Shaykh al-Bāhilī taught us once every Friday …"[40] However, al-Subkī and Ibn Kathīr also mentioned that the trio Ashʿarī scholars were the direct students of Abū al-Ḥasan al-Ashʿarī, without the intermediary of Abū al-Ḥasan al-Bāhilī.[41] This account mentioned that they lived in the same period in their scholarly career (*mutaʿāṣirīn*) and al-Bāhilī attended al-Ashʿarī's *kalām* sessions together with them.[42] In short, despite these different accounts, the intellectual linkage of Imām al-Ḥaramayn al-Juwaynī is still connected to Abū Ḥasan al-Ashʿarī, with or without the intermediation of Abū al-Ḥasan al-Bāhilī.

In addition to the above direct linkage of Imām al-Ḥaramayn with the Ashʿarī scholars, he also established an indirect linkage of authority. It happened because, in the *madrasa* of al-Bayhaqī, he had access to the works of al-Qāḍī Abū Bakr al-Bāqillānī.[43] Therefore, he could learn not only *kalām* in person with Abū al-Qāsim al-Iskāf al-Isfarāʾīnī but also acquired knowledge of Ashʿarī *kalām* through reading Abū Bakr al-Bāqillānī's work. Reflecting on this moment, he used to say: "I did not say a word in *kalām* until I memorized twelve thousand pages of the *kalām* of Abū Bakr al-Bāqillānī."[44]

In other words, his encounter with al-Bāqillānī's works was also another formative period to the extent that al-Bāqillānī's theological ideas are influential in Imām al-Juwaynī's writings. In this respect, his affiliation with the Ashʿarī theological tradition was not only strengthened through direct and personal training with Abū al-Qāsim al-Iskāf al-Isfarāʾʾīnī, but also using the indirect

39 The exact date of Abū al-Ḥasan al-Bāhilī's death is unavailable. However, knowing the fact that he was one of Abū al-Ḥasan al-Ashʿarī's students together with Abū Bakr al-Bāqillānī and at the same time used to teach Abū Bakr al-Bāqillānī and his colleagues on *kalām*, his life was most probably contemporaneous to al-Qāḍī Abū Bakr al-Bāqillānī who died in 404/1013. See al-Subkī, *Ṭabaqāt al-Shāfiʿīyah al-Kubrā*, 3, 368–69.

40 al-Subkī, *Ṭabaqāt al-Shāfiʿīyah al-Kubrā*, 3, 369.

41 al-Subkī, *Ṭabaqāt al-Shāfiʿīyah al-Kubrā*, 3, 367–68.

42 Ibn Kathīr, *Ṭabaqāt al-fuqahāʾ al-Shāfiʿiyīn*, ed. Anwār al-Bāz, vol. 1 (Egypt: Dār al-Wafāʾ, 2004), 323.

43 Saflo, *Al-Juwaini's Thought and Methodology, with A Translation and Comentary on Lumaʿ al-Adilla*, 19.

44 al-Zuḥaylī, *al-Imām al-Juwaynī: Imām al-Ḥaramayn*, 60.

intellectual encounter and association through an autodidact study of Abū Bakr al-Bāqillānī's works. Therefore, Imām al-Ḥaramayn's theological authority lineage can be described in the following table:

TABLE 7.2 The scheme of Imām al-Ḥaramayn's intellectual pedigree in Ashʿarī theology

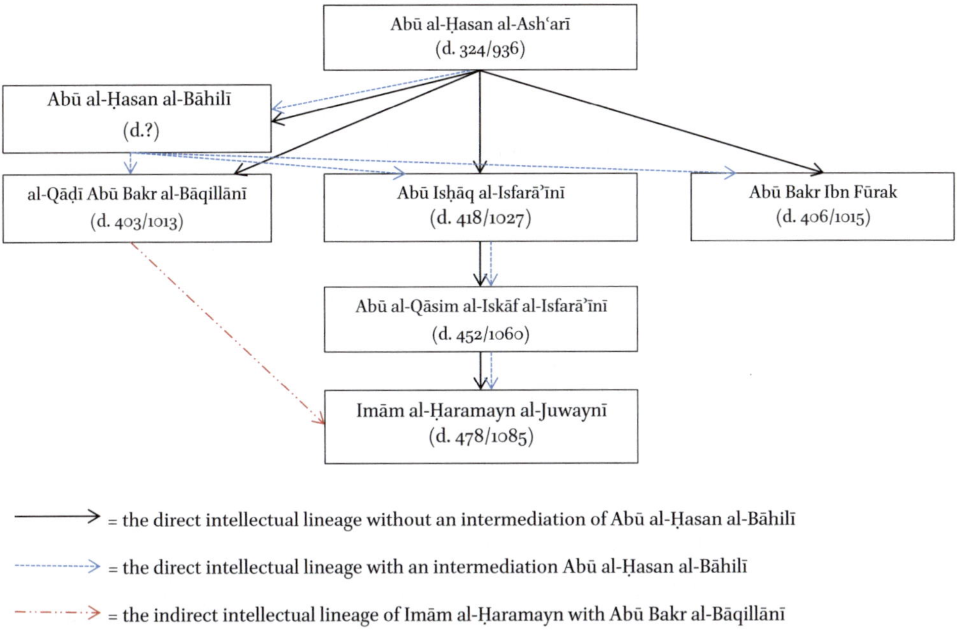

2 Mobility Beyond Nishapur

After studying for four years in al-Bayhaqī's *madrasa*, Imām al-Haramayn was encountering an escalation in sectarian tensions in Nishapur between 443/1051 and 448/1056 among the Ḥanafī-Muʿtazilī and the Shāfiʿī-Ashʿarī groups. They were the main patricians and players in Nishapur who often competed for political posts or social recognition. This sectarian conflict was worsened by a political policy of the Saljūq vizier at that time, ʿAmīd al-Mulk al-Kundurī (d. 456/1064). According to a traditional account by Ibn al-Athīr, al-Kundurī was a fanatic vizier who persecuted his opponents based on their different religious and sectarian affiliations. In the year of 446/1054, al-Kundurī persecuted Shīʿa as well as Shāfiʿī-Ashʿarī scholars and cursed them from the pulpit.[45] He

45 ʿIzz al-Dīn Ibn al-Athīr, *The Annals of the Saljuq Turks: Selections from al-Kāmil fī'l Ta'rīkh of ʿIzz al-Dīn Ibn al-Athīr*, trans. D.S. Richards (London: RoutledgeCurzon, 2002), 148.

used the authority of the Saljūq Sultan, Tughril Beg (d. 453/1063) to order the imprisonment of the four Shāfiʿī-Ashʿarī scholars – Abū al-Qāsim al-Qushayrī (d. 465/1072), Abū al-Faḍl Aḥmad al-Furātī (d. 446/1054), Imam al-Ḥaramayn al-Juwaynī, and Abū Sahl al-Muwaffaq (d. 456/1064). As a result, al-Qushayrī and al-Furātī were sent to jail, Abū Sahl al-Muwaffaq revolted, and only Imām al-Ḥaramayn managed to leave Nishapur.[46]

When the *fitnah* (strife due to sectarianism) broke up, and the political persecution took place, Imām al-Ḥaramayn was about twenty-six years old. Unlike al-Qushayrī and al-Furātī, he was not old enough to pose a threat to the vizierate office or Ḥanafī religious establishment. That was why the Saljūq administration did not immediately imprison him. Moreover, unlike Abū Sahl al-Muwaffaq, who was young but holding a position as the chief of Shāfiʿī scholars in Nishapur, Imām al-Ḥaramayn was not holding any leadership position in Nishapur. Although he was already an influential Shāfiʿī-Ashʿarī scholar, he still studied in the *madrasa* of al-Bayhaqī and in the house of al-Khabbāzī in addition to teaching in his own home. There existed no motivation for Imām al-Ḥaramayn to join a violent revolt since he did not lose any of his posts in Nishapur. However, he still aimed to flee to Baghdad and the Ḥijāz instead of other cities as a haven.[47] Baghdad was a central city in which prominent Shāfiʿī and Ashʿarī scholars lived and flourished.

At the age of twenty-six, he traveled to Baghdad. Siddiqi observes conflicting accounts in the biographical dictionaries on why Imām al-Ḥaramayn left Nishapur for Baghdad. On the one hand, as Siddiqui explains, al-Subkī, Ibn ʿImad, and ʿAbd Ghāfir al-Fārisī maintained that Imām al-Ḥaramayn's reason was the anticipation of the intensification of political oppression of Ashʿarī-Shāfiʿī scholars by the Saljūq administration. On the other hand, as Siddiqui describes, Ibn Khallikān and Ibn al-Jawzī recorded that the main reason was to continue his studies with scholars outside Nishapur.[48] Although Siddiqui cannot ascertain the exact reason, she leans toward al-Fārisī's account on the fact that he was Imām al-Ḥaramayn's student for four years.[49]

46 al-Subkī, *Ṭabaqāt al-Shāfiʿīyah al-Kubrā*, 3, 391–92.

47 Most of the historical accounts mentioned that he went to Baghdad first and then travelled to the Ḥijāz. Only al-Subkī who mentioned in his *Ṭabaqāt* that Imām al-Ḥaramayn left Nishapur through Kirmān without entering Baghdad, and finally arrived at the Ḥijāz. See al-Subkī, *Ṭabaqāt al-Shāfiʿīyah al-Kubrā*, 3, 392. However, al-Subkī contradicted himself regarding this event by quoting and confirming ʿAbd al-Ghāfir al-Fārisī's account that Imām al-Ḥaramayn was conditioned to leave Nishapur for Baghdad. See al-Subkī, *Ṭabaqāt al-Shāfiʿīya al-kubrā*, 5, 170.

48 Siddiqui, *Law and Politics under the Abbasids: An Intellectual Portrait of al-Juwayni* 57.

49 Siddiqui, *Law and Politics under the Abbasids: An Intellectual Portrait of al-Juwayni* 58.

However, considering that Imām al-Ḥaramayn learned, met, and engaged in a scholarly disputation in Baghdad, the above biographical dictionaries' accounts are not contradictory as they seemed to be.[50] Imām al-Ḥaramayn's departure from Nishapur to Baghdad was motivated by a coherent intention and purpose. It was not only to avoid sectarian conflict and political oppression in Nishapur, but more importantly, to widen his intellectual networking and strengthen his Shāfiʿī and Ashʿarī credential. In Baghdad, he met, studied, and had disputations (*munāẓarāt*) with prominent scholars to the extent scholars in the city and beyond widely recognized his name.[51] He was indeed a tough, smart, and skillful debater after studying this science and skill in the *madrasa* of al-Bayhaqī with Abū al-Qāsim al-Iskāf al-Isfarāʾīnī. This widening recognition beyond Nishapur was not possible without Imām al-Ḥaramayn leaving Nishapur and traveling to the capital city of the ʿAbbasid Caliphate and interacting with scholars in the city. In this regard, Siddique's observation of Imām al-Ḥaramayn's impact of his travel to Baghdad noted:

> … His travel to the intellectual epicenter of the ʿAbbasid Empire and engagement with prominent scholars no doubt further raised his stature and recognition within the Muslim community … his time in the capital of the caliphate would have extended his reputation beyond Nishapur and connected whom he would not have encountered otherwise.[52]

In other words, Imām al-Ḥaramayn's intellectual mobility to Baghdad is not only intended to anticipate the worsening political condition in Nishapur but, more importantly, to extend his network, strengthen his credential and authority, and eventually raise his intellectual reputation.

After spending time in Baghdad and accumulating a good reputation there, Imām al-Ḥaramayn traveled to the Ḥijāz. He performed and completed the last pillar of Islam, *Ḥajj* (the Muslim Pilgrimage), and resided in the Ḥijāz land, Mecca and Medina, for four years. During his sojourn in these two holy cities, he gave lectures, issued fatwas, exerted *ijtihād* in law, and spread religious knowledge.[53] He moreover started writing the book of *Nīhayat al-maṭlab fī dirāyat al-madhhab* in this period. According to al-Subkī, he was primarily occupied with teaching, worship, and spiritual cultivation to the extent that

50 al-Subkī, *Ṭabaqāt al-Shāfiʿīya al-kubrā*, 5, 170.

51 al-Subkī, *Ṭabaqāt al-Shāfiʿīya al-kubrā*, 5, 170.

52 Siddiqui, *Law and Politics under the Abbasids: An Intellectual Portrait of al-Juwayni* 59.

53 al-Subkī, *Ṭabaqāt al-Shāfiʿīya al-kubrā*, 5, 170.

when he talked about spirituality, he would shed in tears.[54] In short, these intellectual and religious activities in Ḥijāz further raised his stature. They extended further his reputation as a prominent Shāfiʿī-Ashʿarī scholar in the Muslim world at that time.

Therefore, it can be inferred that his intellectual-professional mobility to the Ḥijāz (just as his travel to Baghdad) was not being forced or accidental but intentional and based on careful calculation. He wanted to add some more weights to his authority in religious scholarship by, first, completing the last pillar of Islam by performing *ḥajj*, and second, cultivating a reputation as the Imām of the two holy places (Mecca and Medina) through teaching, intellectual exertion, and spiritual cultivation. He met his goal because scholars in his time and beyond recognized him as the leading authority in religious scholarship and awarded him the famous honorific name, *Imām al-Ḥaramayn* (The Imām of The Two Holy Places).

3 Returning to Nishapur: Supporting the Saljūq's Project of Sunnī Political Unity

After staying four years in Mecca and Medina, the political constellation in Nishapur had changed. Sultan Tughril Beg and his vizier, al-Kundurī, were no longer in power. The Saljūq ruler was now the Sultan Alp Arslan (d. 465/1072) and his vizier, Niẓām al-Mulk (d. 486/1093), starting in the year of 455/1063 (although both were already appointed respectively as the governor of Nishapur and his secretary in 450/1058). Under the leadership of Alp Arslan, the role of the vizier Niẓām al-Mulk was very important and influential to the extent that he was regarded as the government of Saljūq administration, instead of merely a government official.[55] The new Saljūq administration, under its influential vizier, pursued a new political ideal and ambition. The new Saljūq vizier wanted, first, to restore the balance and order in a society that had been destroyed by the previous vizier, ʿAmīd al-Mulk al-Kundurī.[56] Second, he also aimed to continue the mission of the previous Sultan (Tughril Beg) to bring the rich regions of ancient Persia under Saljūq control as well as recreate a centralized bureaucratic government like that of Sassanian or

54 al-Subkī, *Ṭabaqāt al-Shāfiʿīya al-kubrā*, 5, 133.

55 Omid Safi, *The Politics of Knowledge in Modern Islam* (Chapel Hill: The University of North Carolina Press, 2006), 44.

56 Richard Bulliet, *The Patricians of Nishapur, A Study in Medieval Islamic History* (Cambridge: Harvard University Press, 1972), 73–75. See also Safi, *The Politics of Knowledge in Modern Islam*, 94.

Ghaznavid governments.[57] Third, he wanted to unite the Muslim world under Sunnī-Islam by building a network of *madrasas*, which not only became competitors of Fatimid learning institutions but also contributed to the unity of the Muslim world under Sunnī-Islam.[58]

In this purpose, Niẓām al-Mulk issued three critical policies to turn his political ideals into reality. First, in order to bring social balance and order, Niẓām al-Mulk put the political persecution of Shāfiʿī-Ashʿarī scholars in Nishapur to an end and invited the exiled scholars to come back to Nishapur, including Imām al-Ḥaramayn al-Juwaynī.[59] He knew Imām al-Ḥaramayn's intellectual reputation and religious authority and appointed him as the director of the first *madrasa* Niẓāmīya in Nishapur. Imām al-Ḥaramayn assumed this position and responsibility for about thirty years until his death in 478/1085.[60] Second, in addition to restoring the order of society in Nishapur and other conflicting cities like Baghdad, Niẓām al-Mulk continued to launch military expeditions, especially in the lands of Khurasan, Jibal, and Fars, and other lands into the Mediterranean Sea and Central Asia.[61] These military expeditions were launched not only to hamper the spread of Shīʿa political force, which was dominantly ruling the Muslim world in the fourth/tenth century.[62] More importantly, the military campaigns were waged to unite the lands of Islam that had been shattered after the fall of the caliph al-Ma'mūn (d. 218/833) under "Sunnī-Islam".[63] Third, Niẓām al-Mulk as a military commander was a significant beneficiary of the *iqṭāʿ* (land grant) system.[64] He was the recipient

57 Hodgson, *The Venture of Islam* 2, 44–46; C.E. Bosworth, "The Political and Dynastic History of the Iranian World (A.D. 1000–1217)," in *The Cambridge History of Iran 5: The Saljuq and Mongol Periods*, ed. J.A. Boyle (New York: Cambridge University Press, 1968), 22. While Hodson suggests that Niẓām al-Mulk was aiming to rebuild the bureaucratic structure of the late Sassanian and Ghaznavid administration for the Saljūq, Bosworth here identifies the vizier Niẓām al-Mulk's goal in *Siyāsat Nāma* when the vizier lamented the Saljūq's leaders for not following "the wise administrative followed by the Ghazdavids and other former rulers". See also A.C.S. Peacock, *The Great Seljuk Empire* (Edinburgh: Edinburgh University Press, 2015), 52–53.

58 Frye, *The Golden Age of Persia*, 226–28.

59 Safi, *The Politics of Knowledge in Modern Islam*, 94–95.

60 See ʿAbd al-Ghāfir al-Fārisī's account in al-Subkī, *Ṭabaqāt al-Shāfiʿīya al-kubrā*, 5, Vol. 5, 171.

61 Bosworth, "The Political and Dynastic History of the Iranian World (A.D. 1000–1217)," 45; Frye, *The Golden Age of Persia*, 226.

62 Hodgson, *The Venture of Islam* 2, 36.

63 Frye, *The Golden Age of Persia*, 226.

64 Nizalm al-Mulk granted *amīrs* (military commanders) who played an important role in military expeditions a system of payment called *iqṭāʿ* (land-grant), instead of a fixed salary. This system, which is translated well by Hodgson as "revenue assignment" or "land grant,"

of one-tenth of the produce of the whole Saljūq lands as the *iqṭāʿ* in addition to the grant given directly by Alp Arslan.[65] Through the funds that he collected, he was able to provide a *waqf* (endowment) to build learning institutions for religious scholars (*ʿulamāʾ*) in many cities. These cities include Nishapur, Balkh, Herat, Merv, Tabaristan, Āmūl, Baghdad, Basra, and Mawsil.[66] According to Richard Bulliet, the establishment of *madrasas*, especially for the Shāfiʿī scholars, was not because he was a fanatic follower of Shāfiʿī *madhhab*, but rather, in the midst of dominant Ḥanafī and Ḥanbalī institutions of learning in Khurasan and Baghdad respectively.[67] The establishment of *madrasas* for the Shāfiʿīs was aimed "to restore and maintain a balance between patrician factions of every stripe."[68]

The balance of different factions in society was essential for maintaining social order and unity. Moreover, the *madrasas* that were built by Niẓām al-Mulk were spread throughout the Saljūq territories at that time. This network of *madrasas* across the lands of Sunnī-Islam, along with their relatively common and standardized curriculum, allowed the religious scholars to foster a spirit of unity among the Sunnī-minded scholars and to engender a degree of homogeneity in the Muslim community.[69] In other words, the establishment of *madrasas* was crucial for reuniting the Muslim community in the Saljūq territory under Sunnī-Islam through a sense of homogeneity in religious teachings and *esprit de corps* among the Sunnī-minded scholars, who were in charge of running those *madrasas*.

Therefore, the return of Imām al-Ḥaramayn al-Juwaynī to Nishapur in the early leadership of Sultan Alp Arslan and his vizier Niẓām al-Mulk was not only instrumental in restoring the social balance in Nishapur but also to support the project of the vizier Niẓām al-Mulk in terms of uniting the Islamic

---

on the one hand, made the *amīrs* (as the land-grant assignees) relatively independent from any local civilian ruler because they received revenues directly from the land-grant (*iqṭāʿ*) without an intervention of local civilian administration; while on the other hand, they were directly controlled by central Saljūq bureaucracy which was responsible for assessing the yield of their land-grants and making sure that they were loyal and accountable to the central government. See Safi, *The Politics of Knowledge in Modern Islam*, 88–89; Hodgson, *The Venture of Islam* 2, 49–50.

65 Omid Safi cites Ibn Khallikān's bibliographical dictionary. See Safi, *The Politics of Knowledge in Modern Islam*, 88.

66 Tāj al-Dīn Abū Naṣr ʿAbd al-Wahhāb b. ʿAlī al-Subkī, *Ṭabaqāt al-Shāfiʿīyah al-Kubrā*, ed. Maḥmūd Muḥammad and ʿAbd al-Fattāḥ Muḥammad al-Ḥalw al-Ṭanāḥī, vol. 4 (Cairo: Maṭbaʿah ʿĪsā al-Bābī al-Halbī, 1386/1967), 314.

67 Bulliet, *The Patricians of Nishapur, A Study in Medieval Islamic History*, 73–74.

68 Bulliet, *The Patricians of Nishapur, A Study in Medieval Islamic History*, 74.

69 Hodgson, *The Venture of Islam* 2, 47–48; See also Frye, *The Golden Age of Persia*, 228.

world under Sunnī-Islam. With his authority and credential in the Shāfiʿī legal school and Ashʿarī theological school as well as his leadership as the director of *madrasa Niẓāmīya* in Nishapur, Imām al-Ḥaramayn provided an intellectual foundation for the new Saljūq administration. He made *kalām* (theology) harmonious with *fiqh* (law) and integrated it into the body of Sunnī-oriented scholarship in addition to jurisprudence (*fiqh* and *uṣūl al-fiqh*). This integration provided Niẓām al-Mulk with an intellectual and ideological basis for the project of uniting the Muslim world under "Sunnī Islam." Imām al-Ḥaramayn even wrote a theological book dedicated explicitly to Niẓām al-Mulk, *al-ʿAqīda al-Niẓāmīya*.[70] In other words, one of the consequences of Imām al-Ḥaramayn's intellectual mobility is the reformulation of a more mature orthodoxy of Sunnīsm.

4 Toward a "New" Sunnī Orthodoxy

At this time, however, the definition of the term "Sunnī" was still unsettled. Used as a shortened term for "*Ahl al-Sunna wa al-Jamāʿa* (People of the Tradition and Community)," this name had been used loosely to denote people or communities who did not belong to *Shīʿa* (the loyalist party of the ʿAlīds) or to *Khawārij* (considered by other Muslims to be deserters of ʿAlī and the Muslim community in general). The terms were mentioned in either legal or theological texts.[71] The term became more crystallized in the third/ninth century when the tension between Muʿtazilī theologians and the People of Tradition (*Asḥāb al-ḥadīth*) was at its apex. The term "Sunnī" in this period was initially associated with, among others, the People of Tradition who opposed speculative theology (*kalām*). Marshal G.S. Hodgson calls them the "*Sharīʿah*-minded people."[72] They called themselves Sunnī because they based their religious opinions on the Sunna of the Prophet instead of speculative reasoning, which was commonly employed by theologians (and philosophers).

The orthodoxy of these traditional and legal-minded people was, according to Christopher Melchert, primarily centered on the creed of Aḥmad b. Hanbal

70 Imām al-Ḥaramayn al-Juwaynī, *Al-ʿAqīdah al-niẓāmīyah*, ed. Muḥammad al-Zubaydī (Beirut: Dār al-Sabīll al-Rashād and Dār al-Nafāʾis, 1424/2003), 122.

71 See the scholars that used the term Sunnī and its variations in Montgomery Watt, *The Formative Period of Islamic Thought* (Edinburgh: Edinburgh University Press, 1973), 268–72.

72 Marshall G.S. Hodgson, *The Venture of Islam 1: Conscience and History in a World of Civilization*, vol. 1: The Classical Age of Islam (Chicago: The University of Chicago Press, 1974), 278.

and his followers.[73] They opposed the doctrine of the "created Qur'ān" held by the Muʿtazilī scholars and supported by the Abbasid caliph al-Ma'mūn (d. 218/833) during the period of inquisition (*miḥna*). After the death of al-Ma'mūn and the subsequent ʿAbbāsid caliphs who supported the Inquisition, al-Muʿtaṣim (d. 228/842) and al-Wāthiq (d. 233/847), the Inquisition eventually ended in the late third/ninth century. The traditionalist religious groups started to gain momentum and claimed to be the Sunnīs, representing Islamic orthodoxy. Their movements and doctrines reached the peak of victory, according to George Makdisi, when the ʿAbbāsid caliph al-Qādir (d. 422/1031) issued a creed (*al-Iʿtiqād al-Qādirī*) condemning theological doctrines of Muʿtazila and Ashʿarīya in the first half of the fifth/eleventh century.[74] Ashʿarī *kalām* was particularly condemned because it was viewed as falling into *tashbīh* (anthropomorphism) and abandoning the supremacy of the Qur'ān and Sunna.[75] As a result, according to George Makdisi, the Ashʿarīs' attempt to gain recognition as a part of the greater Sunnī orthodoxy was unsuccessful, and traditionalism reigned supreme as the contemporary orthodoxy.[76] In addition to the Ḥanbalī legal school, the traditionalist groups during this period were also represented by three other primary legal schools: Mālikī, Shāfiʿī, and Ḥanafī.[77]

However, instead of signifying the failure and the defeat of Ashʿarī theology to be a part of the Sunnī-minded scholarly community and the victory of traditionalism, as Makdisi suggests, the Qādirī creed in principle only reflected the rejection of legal-traditionalism over rational theology, including Ashʿarī theology. The creed was not a reflection of the defeat or elimination of theology. The legal-traditionalists were not the only representation of Sunnī orthodoxy since theologians, including Ashʿarī scholars, among others, also had the same

---

73 Melchert, "Sectaries in the Six Books: Evidence for their exclusion from the Sunnī orthodoxy," 137.

74 George Makdisi, "Tabaqat-Biography: Law and orthodoxy in classical Islam," in *Orthodoxy and Heresy in Islam: Critical Concepts in Islamic Studies*, ed. Maribel Fierro (London and New York: Routledge Taylor & Francis Group, 2014), 122.

75 Watt, *The Formative Period of Islamic Thought*, 295.

76 George Makdisi also makes an assertion that the failure of the Ashʿarī's bid in the eleventh century can be seen from the fact that Ashʿarī-minded scholars, namely Ibn ʿAsākir (d. 571/1175) and Tāj ad-Dīn as-Subkī (d. 771/1369), still needed to convince the traditionalists of Ashʿarī theology in the twelfth and fourteenth century through their *tabaqāt* works. See George Makdisi, "Ashʿarī and The Ashʿarites in Islamic Religious History Part I," in *Religion, Law, and Learning in Classical Islam* (Vermont, USA: Voriourum, 1991), 50–80. This assertion was challenged by the observation of other scholars like Marshal G.S. Hodgson and Richard Martin (and Abbas Barzegar). They argue that the term Sunnī is later associated with Ashʿarī theology as well, not attributed to the legal-traditionalists. See the footnote 85 and 86 below.

77 Makdisi, "Tabaqat-Biography: Law and orthodoxy in classical Islam," 122.

claim.[78] The formation of Sunnī orthodoxy in the eleventh century was still far from complete, with the theologians and the legal-minded people continuing to have debate and contestation over the claim of Sunnī orthodoxy.[79]

In this period of rivalries and tensions, Imām al-Ḥaramayn attempted to bridge the gap between the traditional legal-minded scholars and theologians through his conciliatory intellectual mobility within the Shāfiʿī school of law and the Ashʿarī school of theology across the medieval Muslim world. He tried to appeal and convince Shāfiʿī legal scholars that Ashʿarī theology was complementary to Shāfiʿī legal scholarship not only in obtaining knowledge of God and His laws with certainty but also to face the challenges from external religious doctrines, especially the Muʿtazila's rational theology. At the same time, he also tried to make *kalām* grounded within legal orthodoxy, while convincing theologians to respect traditional sources and proofs.[80] As a result, Ashʿarī theology gradually gained recognition. Ashʿarī theologians who were subject to the persecution during the early Saljūq ruling in Nishapur under the vizier al-Kundurī obtained their freedom after the later vizier, Niẓām al-Mulk, rescinded the policy of persecuting Ashʿarīs. Eventually, these theologians were also recognized as members of the Sunnī-minded scholarly community.[81]

Based on this kind of historical information, Marshal Hodgson observes that the term Sunnī was later not only attributed to the anti-*kalām* and legal-minded people led by Ḥanbalīs but also to orthodox theologians represented

78 The theological creed in Abū al-Ḥasan al-Ashʿarī's *Ibāna* was considered to be that of *Ahl al-Ḥaqq wa al-Sunnah* (People of the Truth and Sunnah), which is a variation of the term Sunnī. Al-Ashʿarī also mentions a lot of names and terms associated with the idea Sunnī in *Maqālāt al-islāmiyyīn*. See Watt, *The Formative Period of Islamic Thought*, 269.

79 Watt, *The Formative Period of Islamic Thought*, 317.

80 In this regard, I agree with Siddique who views that Imām al-Ḥaramayn's usage of the Ashʿarī theological method of speculative reasoning is to attain epistemological certainty. This is an important step of Imām al-Ḥaramayn to gain a recognition from his fellow Ashʿarī theologians. However, Siddique misses to notice that Imām al-Ḥaramayn as a Shāfiʿī legal scholar also attempted to convince his fellow theologians to respect more legal-traditional sources, which led him to gain a good reputation among his fellow Shāfiʿī legal scholars. See Siddiqui, *Law and Politics under the Abbasids: An Intellectual Portrait of al-Juwayni* 131–32.

81 The later biographical dictionaries (*tabaqāt*) include their names in their list of the "Sunnī" scholarly community. In this regard, Ibn ʿAsākir's *Tabyīn* and al-Subkī's *Tabaqāt* are not seen as attempts of Ashʿarī scholars to infiltrate legal schools as Makdisi suggests. Instead, their works are viewed as a proof of the success of previous Ashʿarī scholars to persuade legal scholars and biography writers like both of them to include Ashʿarī theologians as parts of Shāfiʿī-legal school in particular and Sunnī orthodoxy in general.

by Ashʿarī (or Māturīdī) theological school that opposed the Muʿtazilī school.[82] Richard Martin and Abbas Barzegar also notice that, after undergoing a particular repression and persecution, the popular Ashʿarī theological movement was "synonymous with orthodox Sunnī Islam" by the fifth/eleventh to sixth/twelfth century.[83] Ashʿarī Sunnī theology was regarded as part of "a new Sunnī orthodoxy" that came out of the contestation between Muʿtazilī rational theology and Ḥanbalī traditional-legal view.[84]

5 Conclusion

As can be seen in the discussion above, Imām al-Ḥaramayn al-Juwaynī started a scholarly and professional career by building intellectual credentials within Shāfiʿī and Ashʿarī intellectual circles through his intellectual mobility by studying under Shāfiʿī and Ashʿarī authoritative teachers. His intellectual lineage can be traced back to the originator of each school, Muḥammad b. Idrīs al-Shāfiʿī for the legal school and Abū Ḥasan al-Ashʿarī for the theological school. This credential made him well placed to continue his father's teaching position after his passing. Furthermore, his intellectual mobility through studying with different teachers made him connected with a broader network of Shāfiʿī and Ashʿarī scholars in Nishapur and beyond, especially Baghdad, Mecca, and Medina (Ḥijāz). This mobility engendered his intellectual recognition and religious authority grew stronger and broader.

Imām al-Ḥaramayn's intellectual and religious stature attracted the attention of the Saljūq vizier, Niẓām al-Mulk. The vizier was convinced that Imām al-Ḥaramayn was the right person to help him in reviving and uniting the Sunnī world in the eleventh century. He then requested Imām al-Ḥaramayn to return to Nishapur to become the chair of the first Muslim learning institution, the Niẓāmīya *madrasa*. Imām al-Ḥaramayn agreed and accepted the teaching and directorship position of the Niẓāmīya *madrasa*. He served there until his death in 478/1085. This religious and professional position could not be achieved without his intellectual mobility through learning from different teachers in Nishapur and his intellectual-professional journey to interact with scholars in Baghdad and Ḥijāz. His mobility can be regarded as a conciliatory

82 Hodgson, *The Venture of Islam 1: Conscience and History in a World of Civilization*, 1: The Classical Age of Islam, 278.

83 Richard C. Martin and Abbas Barzegar, "Formations of Orthodoxy," in *Rethinking Islamic Studies: From Orientalism to Cosmopolitanism*, ed. Carl W. Ernst and Richard C. Martin (South Carolina: The University of South Carolina Press, 2010), 189.

84 Martin and Barzegar, "Formations of Orthodoxy," 197.

intellectual mobility since Imām al-Ḥaramayn was then grounded within both the Shāfiʿī school and Ashʿarī theology and able to build harmony between the two opposing camps.

In his position as the scholar and director of the Niẓāmīya *madrasa*, he could support Niẓām al-Mulk's project to restore the order of the medieval Muslim world under "Sunnī" Islam through his scholarship, authority, and reputation. Imām al-Ḥaramayn had the necessary confidence and credentials to provide the intellectual, ideological, and theological foundations for the Sunnī world through his reformulation of Sunnī orthodoxy. He reformulated certain doctrinal aspects within the Shāfiʿī legal and Ashʿarī theological scholarship and dealt with his contemporary religious colleagues and adversaries. He penned books using *jadal* (disputation) method in the field of law and theology to appeal to his fellow Shāfiʿī legal scholars about the importance of the adoption of Ashʿarī theology to withstand challenges from intellectual and religious adversaries. Therefore, for him, Ashʿarī theology, with some revisions and modifications, was to be adopted. As a result, Sunnī orthodoxy, which was initially only associated with traditionalism and legal schools, now included theological schools, especially the Ashʿarī one, owing to the efforts of Imām al-Ḥaramayn al-Juwaynī.

Bibliography

al-Dīb, Dr. ʿAbd al-ʿAẓīm. *Imām Al-Ḥaramayn Abū Al-Maʿālī ʿabd Al-Malik B. ʿabdullāh Al-Juwaynī*. Kuwait: Dār al-Qalam, 1981.

al-Fārisī, Abū'l-Ḥasan ʿAbd al-Ghāfir b. Ismāʿīl. *Tārīkh Nīsābūr Al-Muntakhab Min Al-Siyāq*. Qum: Jamāʿah al-Mudarrisīn, 1362 H/1943.

al-Isnawī, Jamāl al-Dīn ʿAbd al-Raḥīm b. al-Ḥasan. *Ṭabaqāt Al-Shāfiʿīyah*. Edited by ʿAbdullāh al-Jabūrī. Baghdad: al-Jumhūrīyah al-Irāqīyah Riʾāsah Dīwān al-Awqāf, 1390 H.

al-Juwaynī, Imām al-Ḥaramayn. *Al-ʿaqīdah Al-Niẓāmīyah*. Edited by Muḥammad al-Zubaydī. Beirut: Dār al-Sabīll al-Rashād and Dār al-Nafāʾis, 1424/2003.

al-Juwaynī, Imām al-Ḥaramayn. *Kitāb Al-Irshād Ilā Qawaṭiʾ Al-Adilla Fī Uṣūl Al-Iʿtiqād (a Guide to Conclusive Proofs for the Principles of Belief)*. Edited and Translated by Paul E. Walker. UK: The Center for Muslim Contribution to Civilization/Garnet Publishing, 2000.

al-Nawawī, Abū Zakarīyā. *Tahdhīb Al-Asmāʾ Wa Al-Lughāt*. Vol. 1, Beirut: Dār al-Kutub al-ʿIlmīyah 1977.

al-Shīrāzī, Abū Isḥāq. *Ṭabaqāt Al-Shāfiʿīya*. Baghdād: al-Maktabah al-ʿArabīyah, 1356/1937.

al-Subkī, Tāj al-Dīn Abū Naṣr ʿAbd al-Wahhāb b. ʿAlī. *Ṭabaqāt Al-Shāfiʿīya Al-Kubrā*. Edited by Maḥmūd Muḥammad and ʿAbd al-Fattāḥ Muḥammad al-Ḥalwī al-Ṭanāḥī. Vol. 5, Cairo: Maṭbaʿat ʿĪsā al-Bābī al-Halabī, 1386/1967.

al-Subkī, Tāj al-Dīn Abū Naṣr ʿAbd al-Wahhāb b. ʿAlī. *Ṭabaqāt Al-Shāfiʿīyah Al-Kubrā*. Edited by Maḥmūd Muḥammad and ʿAbd al-Fattāḥ Muḥammad al-Ḥalw al-Ṭanāḥī. Vol. 4, Cairo: Maṭbaʿah ʿĪsā al-Bābī al-Halbī, 1386/1967.

al-Subkī, Tāj al-Dīn Abū Naṣr ʿAbd al-Wahhāb b. ʿAlī. *Ṭabaqāt Al-Shāfiʿīyah Al-Kubrā*. Edited by Maḥmūd Muḥammad and ʿAbd al-Fattāḥ Muḥammad al-Ḥalw al-Ṭanāḥī. Vol. 3, Cairo: Maṭbaʿah ʿĪsā al-Bābī al-Halbī, 1386/1967.

al-Subkī, Tāj al-Dīn Abū Naṣr ʿAbd al-Wahhāb b. ʿAlī. *Ṭabaqāt Al-Shāfiʿīyah Al-Kubrā 3*. Edited by Maḥmūd Muḥammad and ʿAbd al-Fattāḥ Muḥammad al-Ḥalw al-Ṭanāḥī. Vol. 3, Cairo: Maṭbaʿah ʿĪsā al-Bābī al-Halbī, 1386/1967.

al-Zuḥaylī, Dr. Muḥammad. *Al-Imām Al-Juwaynī: Imām Al-Ḥaramayn*. Damascus: Dār al-Qalam, 1986.

Bosworth, C.E. "The Political and Dynastic History of the Iranian World (A.D. 1000–1217)." In *The Cambridge History of Iran 5: The Saljuq and Mongol Periods*, edited by J.A. Boyle. New York: Cambridge University Press, 1968.

Bulliet, Richard. *The Patricians of Nishapur, a Study in Medieval Islamic History*. Cambridge: Harvard University Press, 1972.

Campanini, Massimo. "In Defence of Sunnism: Al-Ghazīlī and the Seljuqs." In *The Seljuqs: Sociaety, Society and Culture*, edited by Christian Lange and Songul Mecit. Edinburgh: Edinburgh University Press, 2011.

Ephrat, Daphna. *A Learned Society in a Period of Transition: The Sunni 'Ulama' of Eleventh-Century Baghdad*. Albany: State University of New York Press, 2000.

Frye, Richard N. *The Golden Age of Persia*. USA: Harper & Row Publishers Inc., 1975.

Griffel, Frank. "A Review of Al-Juwayni's Thought and Methodology by Mohammad Moslem Adel Saflo." *Journal of the American Oriental Society* 122, no. 4 (2002).

Hallaq, Wael B. *The Origins and Evolution of Islamic Law*. Cambridge: Cambridge University Press, 2005.

Hodgson, Marshall G.S. *The Venture of Islam 1: Conscience and History in a World of Civilization*. Vol. 1: The Classical Age of Islam, Chicago: The University of Chicago Press, 1974.

Hodgson, Marshall G.S. *The Venture of Islam 2*. Chicago: The University of Chicago Press, 1974.

Ibn al-Athīr, ʿIzz al-Dīn. *The Annals of the Saljuq Turks: Selections from Al-Kāmil Fīʾl Taʾrīkh of ʿizz Al-Dīn Ibn Al-Athīr*. Translated by D.S. Richards. London: RoutledgeCurzon, 2002.

Ibn al-Jawzī, Abū al-Faraj ʿAbd al-Raḥmān b. ʿAlī. *Al-Muntaẓam Fī Tārīkh Al-Mulūk Wa Al-Umam*. Vol. 9, Hyderabad: Dāʾirah al-Maʿārif al-ʿUthmānīyah, 1359/1940.

Ibn Kathīr, al-Ḥāfiẓ. *Ṭabaqāt Al-Fuqahā' Al-Shāfi'iyīn*. Edited by Anwār al-Bāz. Vol. 2, Egypt: Dār al-Wafā', 2004.

Ibn Khallikān, Abū 'Abbās Shams al-Dīn Aḥmad b. Muḥammad b. Abū Bakr. *Wafayāt Al-A'yān Wa Anbā' Abnā' Al-Zamān*. Edited by Iḥsān 'Abbās. Vol. 3, Beirut: Dār al-Thaqāfah, 1968.

Ibn Khallikān, Abū 'Abbās Shams al-Dīn Aḥmad b. Muḥammad b. Abū Bakr. *Wafayāt Al-A'yān Wa Anbā' Abnā' Al-Zamān 3*. Edited by Iḥsān 'Abbās. Vol. 3, Beirut: Dār al-Thaqāfah, 1968.

Ibn Qāḍī Shuhbah, Taqī al-Dīn Abū Bakr b. Aḥmad. *Ṭabaqāt Al-Fuqahā' Al-Shāfi'īyah*. Edited by Muḥammad 'Umar 'Alī. Vol. 1, Cairo: Maktabah al-Thaqāfah al-Dīnīyah, 1990.

Kathīr, Ibn *Ṭabaqāt Al-Fuqahā' Al-Shāfi'iyīn*. Edited by Anwār al-Bāz. Vol. 1, Egypt: Dār al-Wafā', 2004.

Maḥmūd, Dr. Fawqīyah Ḥusayn. *Al-Juwaynī: Imām Al-Ḥaramayn*. Egypt: al-Mu'assasah al-Miṣrīyah al-'Āmmah, 1964.

Makdisi, George. "Tabaqat-Biography: Law and Orthodoxy in Classical Islam." In *Orthodoxy and Heresy in Islam: Critical Concepts in Islamic Studies*, edited by Maribel Fierro. London and New York: Routledge Taylor & Francis Group, 2014.

Makdisi, George "Ash'arī and the Ash'arites in Islamic Religious History, Part I." In *Religion, Law, and Learning in Classical Islam* 37–80. Vermont, USA: Voriourum, 1991.

Martin, Richard C., and Abbas Barzegar. "Formations of Orthodoxy." In *Rethinking Islamic Studies: From Orientalism to Cosmopolitanism*, edited by Carl W. Ernst and Richard C. Martin. South Carolina: The University of South Carolina Press, 2010.

Melchert, Christopher. *The Formation of the Sunni Schools of Law, 9th–10th Century C.E.* Leiden: Brill, 1997.

Melchert, Christopher. "Sectaries in the Six Books: Evidence for Their Exclusion from the Sunnī Orthodoxy." In *Orthodoxy and Heresy in Islam: Critical Concepts in Islamic Studies*, edited by Maribel Fierro. London and New York: Routledge Taylor & Francis Group, 2014.

Peacock, A.C.S. *The Great Seljuk Empire*. Edinburgh: Edinburgh University Press, 2015.

Safi, Omid. *The Politics of Knowledge in Modern Islam*. Chapel Hill: The University of North Carolina Press, 2006.

Saflo, Mohammad Moslem Adel *Al-Juwaini's Thought and Methodology, with a Translation and Comentary on Luma' Al-Adilla*. Berlin: Klaus Schwarz Verlag, 2000.

Siddiqui, Sohaira Z.M. *Law and Politics under the Abbasids: An Intellectual Portrait of Al-Juwayni* Cambridge: Cambridge University Press, 2019.

Watt, Montgomery. *The Formative Period of Islamic Thought*. Edinburgh: Edinburgh University Press, 1973.

CHAPTER 8

Iran's State Literature under Afghan Rule (1722–1729)

M.A.H. Parsa

1 Introduction

In the early twelfth/eighteenth century, the Ghaljāy Afghans rose up in Qandahar, declaring independence from the Ṣafavid empire. They followed up their rebellion with the capture of the Ṣafavid capital, terminating its resident dynasty. No longer merely a rebel on the imperial periphery, the Afghan leader, Maḥmud Hotak, was the first sovereign in the new Hotakid dynasty of Iran. The official investiture of imperial authority meant that the Hotakids were expected to govern Iran's subject territories and peoples. As the Hotakids' control over the realm grew, so did their need for reviving advanced government functions. Accordingly, they took steps to consolidate administrative control over their conquests; the Afghan kings commissioned manuals of state administration, and their civil servants succeeded in producing for them edicts, seals, coinage, diplomatic correspondence and foreign treaties. It is the inter-dynastic mobility of this group of bureaucratic professionals, particularly those involved in composing state literature, that is the focus of this present study.

This chapter investigates the epistolary practices of the Secretariat as it changed its allegiance from the Ṣafavids to the Hotakids, in other words, the professional mobility of civil servants as they passed from the employ of one dynasty to another. It asks whether the scribes and secretaries were tasked with formulating a new approach to their profession, or whether they adhered to Ṣafavid precedence? And if so, then in which functions, and to what extent? The answer will be sought by consulting what remains of the period's state literature, that is, the literature produced by the Chancellery's Secretariat; The Chancellery (*Divān*), or to give it its official name, the Supreme Chancellery (*Divān-e Aʿlā*), was the central administrative body of the imperial state. It consisted of two institutions: The Secretariat (*Dār ol-Enshā'*, lit. Abode of Epistles) and the Supreme Records Office (*Daftarkhāneh-ye Homāyun-e Aʿlā*). The Secretariat composed edicts, royal letters, diplomatic correspondence, treaties, appointment/assignment letters, land/revenue grants, deeds of endowment,

 | DOI:10.1163/9789004467637_010

and so on, while the Records Office conducted tax assessments, registered tax records, and archived other fiscal documents. Needless to say, it is the former institution which will receive the primary focus in this chapter.

Examining the Secretariat's output in the political and cultural context of early eighteenth-century Iran will yield valuable insights on the nature of political and religious legitimacy in the post-Ṣafavid era, particularly since the Hotakids were Sunni conquerors, standing on the corpse of a Shi'i dynasty which had ruled the country for almost a quarter millennium. An in-depth and contextualised analysis of the Secretariat's output will lead into the kinds of interesting questions which this chapter hopes to address. What discourses did the Hotakid Secretariat devise in order to legitimate the new order? What conceptual models were used to express the Hotakid ruler's authority? To which literary tradition did these concepts belong (Persianate/Turco-Mongol/Islamic)?

2 Historical Background and Chronology (1120–1141/1709–1729)

Ṣafavid Iran saw a great deal of turmoil in the first two decades of the eighteenth century. Raked by economic crises dating back several decades, the Ṣafavids were increasingly challenged by numerous clients in the peripheries of their empire.[1] To the east, the Ghaljāy Afghans of Qandahar revolted against the Ṣafavids in 1120/1709 after suffering an extended period of misrule. The repeated attempts to resubjugate Qandahar in the following years were not only unsuccessful, but laid bare the impotence of the Ṣafavid state for all onlookers. Soon, the Abdāli Afghans joined the revolt, and so Herāt was also lost. The eastern provinces, though perhaps the most pressing, were far from the only ones to oust Ṣafavid garrisons. The Caucasus in the north, the Persian Gulf in the south, Ardalān in the west, 'Arabestān in the south-west,[2] and

1 The chronological narrative that follows in this section largely draws upon Father Krusinski, *The History of the Late Revolutions of Persia*, Vol. II (London, 1733); Moḥsen, Moḥammad, *Zobdat ol-Tavārikh*, ed. Behruz Gudarzi (Tehran, 1996), pp. 118–154; Astarābādi, Moḥammad Mehdi, *Jahāngoshā-ye Nāderi*, ed. 'Abdollāh Anvār (Tehran, 1962), pp. 5–16, 20–21, in consultation with the following three studies; Laurence Lockhart, *The Fall of the Safavi Dynasty and the Afghan Occupation of Persia* (London, 1958); Rudi Matthee, *Persia in Crisis: Safavid Decline and the Fall of Isfahan* (London, 2012); Willem Floor, *The Afghan Occupation of Persia 1721–1729* (Paris, 1998).

2 Ardalān and 'Arabestān roughly correspond to Iran's modern-day provinces of Kordestān and Khuzestān respectively.

Baluchestān in the south-east were all in open rebellion by 1132/1720. Not one of these met with an effectual response from Isfahan.

The chief of the Ghaljāy, Maḥmud Hotak, began raiding Ṣafavid territories to his west. In 1132/1720 Kermān was sacked. The subsequent year saw Maḥmud return to besiege the city once more. But by 1134/1722, he lifted the siege and marched toward Isfahan, the Ṣafavid capital. The king's army confronted Maḥmud a short distance from the city. Despite a clear disadvantage in numbers, the Afghans carried the day.[3] The ensuing siege of Isfahan lasted six months, ending in the surrender of the city by the Ṣafavid king himself, Shāh Solṭān Ḥoseyn, who abdicated his crown by personally placing it on Maḥmud's head. On 10 Moḥarram 1135/21 October 1722 Iran had a new ruling dynasty; the Hotakids. Yet, the Afghan's newly established rule was a tenuous one at best. The famine which had gripped the city so mercilessly during the siege persisted even after Isfahan's handover to the Afghans. This was due to the fact that none of the surrounding towns and villages submitted to Maḥmud for months, who struggled in pacifying Isfahan's surrounding countryside. Several villages remained independent through the summer of 1135/1723. Beyond Isfahan's immediate environs, no pledges of loyalty were forthcoming. For the first few years of Afghan rule in Iran, Maḥmud's authority hardly extended beyond the capital.

The fall of Isfahan proved to be a beckoning call all too sweet to resist for Iran's two expansionist neighbours, the Ottoman Empire to the West, and the Russian Empire to the north. The former occupied the Caucasus, most of Āẕarbāijān, Kordestān, and West Iran as far as Hamedān, while Russia's Peter I marched his army through the Darband Pass and occupied the Caspian littoral, taking all of Iran's northern provinces. Faced merely with local resistance, both empires found their military incursions unchecked by any serious challenge. However, they faced great difficulty in finding a legitimate authority in Iran with which to conclude a peace treaty, ratifying their substantial territorial gains.[4] The Afghan newcomers were one possibility, but the Ottomans and Russians were sceptical on their staying power. There was also the option of choosing from among the Ṣafavid pretenders. One of the more promising of these was Ṭahmāsb II, the eldest son of the overthrown Ṣafavid king. Ṭahmāsb had been slipped passed the Afghan besiegers at Isfahan in the vain hope that he would return in good time at the head of a relief army. Instead, he escaped

3 Michael Axworthy, *The Sword of Persia: Nader Shah, from Tribal Warrior to Conquering Tyrant* (London, 2006), pp. 47–49 contains a detailed description of the battle.

4 See Ernest Tucker, *Nadir Shah's Quest for Legitimacy in Post-Safavid Iran* (Gainesville, 2006) for the Ottomans' diplomatic concerns regarding the lack of legitimate entities in Iran.

to the north-west, but was chased away by an Ottoman army. His brief sojourn in the north was equally ignominious. Unable to establish his authority due to the presence of Russian troops, Ṭahmāsb eventually travelled to Khorāsān in the north-east. The Russians hedged their bets by signing treaties with both the Afghans and Ṭahmāsb II. The Ottomans were at first obstinately in favour of a Ṣafavid restoration which would acknowledge their considerable territorial acquisitions. Taking a much bolder stance than Moscow, Istanbul even planned to directly intervene in settling the matter of Iran's kingship, hoping to install a pliant Ṣafavid candidate on the throne in Isfahan by expelling the Afghans.

By 1136/1724 Maḥmud had expanded his control of central Iran by taking Shirāz. The next year however, he was dethroned by a clique of leading Ghaljāy commanders. Maḥmud's cousin, Ashraf Hotak, was crowned as king on 8 Shaʿbān 1137/22 April 1725.[5] After the coronation, Qandahar refused to submit to the newly appointed Ashraf, placing the late Maḥmud's brother on the throne. From 1137/1725 onwards, these two branches of the Hotakid dynasty ruled separate kingdoms, one based in Qandahar, the other in Isfahan. Though even after 1137/1725, many Afghans continued to travel westward to Ashraf's nascent kingdom,[6] seeking to share in its promising expansion and consolidation. At least initially, they were not to be disappointed. Ashraf set out neutralising any direct threats to his seat of power in Isfahan, hunting down and defeating Ṣafavid pretenders which might directly threaten his capital.[7] He issued an edict (analysed herein) aimed at achieving a rapprochement between his Afghan warriors and the inhabitants of his capital Isfahan who had suffered so tremendously under their occupation. When the Ottoman army marched against him to reinstall the former Ṣafavid king as their puppet, Ashraf had the imprisoned king beheaded. He sent the Ottomans the severed head of the hapless former monarch and checked their advance near Hamedān in early Rabiʿ ol-Avval 1139/November 1726. Ashraf won a great victory over the mutinous Ottoman army, convincing Istanbul that he was a formidable candidate capable of asserting his authority in Iran. In a major diplomatic coup, Ashraf was acknowledged by the Ottoman sultan as the legitimate king of Iran. In exchange, Ashraf confirmed the Ottomans' extensive territorial annexations.

5 Floor, *Afghan Occupation*, p. 196.

6 Ibid., p. 228.

7 Among these was the unfortunate Seyyed Aḥmad Ṣafavi, a cousin of Ṭahmāsb II, who declared himself king in Kermān and endeavoured to take Shirāz on several occasions before being utterly crushed by the Afghans. See Moḥammad Khalil Marʿashi Ḥoseyni, *Majmaʿ ol-Tavārikh*, ed. ʿAbbās Eqbāl (Tehran, 1983), pp. 66–74 for his career as unsuccessful claimant to the mantle of kingship in Iran.

As Ashraf further consolidated his rule, Ṭahmāsb allied himself with a talented and charismatic warlord from Khorāsān by the name of Nāder. After Ṭahmāsb had imposed control over Khorāsān with Nāder's help, the latter began a far-reaching programme of military reform, fashioning a formidable army by the late 1130s/1720s. Ashraf responded to these developments too late. The Afghan and Iranian armies formed up in the field at Mehmāndust on 6 Rabiʿ ol-Avval 1142/29 September 1729. For the very first time since the Afghan uprising in 1120/1709, they suffered a defeat in a major pitched battle. On his march to Isfahan, Nāder routed the Afghans twice more. Isfahan was recaptured, and Ṭahmāsb finally rode back into Isfahan in triumph, seven years late. Nāder vigorously pursued Ashraf to Shirāz. In a last desperate battle near Zaraqān, Ashraf's remaining forces fought valiantly before being ultimately vanquished. This marked the end of the ephemeral Hotakid dynasty of Iran.

3 Imperial Conquest and the Ensuant Need for Bureaucracy

As Maḥmud lay siege to Kermān in 1134/1721, the governor of the city wrote a letter to his besiegers, instructing them that if their intention was to seize the mantle of kingship (*molk-giri*), then they ought to lift the siege and march directly upon the Ṣafavid capital.[8] This letter constitutes one of the earliest associations made between the Afghan uprising, and the idea of their imperial conquest of Iran through the establishment of a new dynasty. It is unclear whether it was this letter that planted the idea of dynastic rule over Iran in Maḥmud's mind, or, as is more likely, it merely encouraged ambitions he already held. In any case, Isfahan's siege ended with the Ṣafavid monarch passing the mantle of Iran's kingship to Maḥmud. In the words of an Isfahanian treasurer who attended the king during the siege, 'the owner of the realm called for his diadem, then placed it upon Maḥmud's head, surrendering his crown and throne'.[9]

As former provincial chieftains who operated under Qandahar's centrally appointed governor-general, the Ghaljāy leaders were ill-equipped to staff the decimated Chancellery.[10] The Pashtun-speaking tribesmen of the Ghaljāy made for superb cavalrymen, but overwhelmingly lacking in the professional skills required of civil servants, they of course could not be expected to staff an intricate imperial bureaucracy. This predicament was of no critical

8 Ḥoseyni, *Majmaʿ*, pp. 55–56; Astarābādi, *Jahāngoshā*, p. 13.

9 Ḥoseyni, *Majmaʿ*, p. 132.

10 V. Minorsky, *Tadhkirat Al-Mulūk: A Manual of Ṣafavid Administration* (London, 1943), p. 10.

importance at the beginning of the Afghan's rule, after all, Maḥmud controlled little other than Isfahan itself. The acuity of the challenge must truly have made itself known when the Afghans began expanding their control of central Iran. Indeed, there is evidence that the Hotakids sought out and even commissioned manuals for state administration in the late 1130s/mid-1720s. The *Dastur ol-Moluk* (lit. Order of Kings) was compiled by Mirzā Rafiʿā, a state-treasurer (*mostowfi ol-mamālek*), sometime during Maḥmud's reign.[11] It might be possible that this manual was originally written after the Ṣafavids came to power in the early tenth/sixteenth century, and that it was continually added to and updated, with its preface dedicated anew to each successive monarch.[12] Mirzā Rafiʿā's *Dastur* was initially begun under the reign of Shāh Solṭān Ḥoseyn. The manuscript of the *Dastur* is explicitly dedicated to this king, the *Dastur* also makes recurrent references to the end of his reign.[13] However, there are several strong indications that the *Dastur* manuscript, was meant to be presented to Shāh Solṭān Ḥoseyn's Afghan replacement, Maḥmud. Most revealing is the respect and reverence paid to the four Rightly Guided Caliphs of Islam in the preface. This is completely at odds with the zealously Shi'i rhetorical discourse of the Ṣafavid Chancellery. A common couplet imprinted on Shāh Solṭān Ḥoseyn's coins was

> Coin was struck in his name by the grace of God,
> In this world, Solṭān Ḥoseyn is the dog of ʿAli.[14]

The reverse side listed the names of the Prophet and the twelve Imams of Shi'ism. A number of his imperial seals, as well as some of his coins, contained phrases such as 'Solṭān Ḥoseyn, the lowest dog of ʿAli' or similar devotional protestations to Shi'i Imams.[15] As will be demonstrated below, the veneration of the Four Caliphs became a strong motif in the Hotakids' discourse on legitimacy. The imperial seal of Ashraf contained a couplet expressing deep reverence for them (see Appendix below). Therefore, the contents of the *Dastur*

11 For a near-exhaustively detailed look at this manual's date of composition see Muhammad Ismail Marcinkowski, *Mīrzā Rafīʿā's Dastūr Al-Mulūk: A Manual of Later Ṣafavid Administration* (Kuala Lumpur, 2002), pp. 46–50, who concludes that a 'composition date between 1722 and 1725' is the most plausible.

12 Moḥammad Rafiʿ Anṣāri, Dastur ol-Moluk, intro., ed. Moḥammad Taqi Dāneshpaĵuh, in *Majalle Dāneshkadeh-ye Adabiāt va ʿOlum-e Ensāni-ye Dāneshgāh-e Tehrān*, Vols. 63 and 64, Nos. 5–6 (1968), p. 484.

13 Marcinkowski, *Mirzā Rafiʿā's Dastūr*, p. 48.

14 Ṣoghrā Esmāʿili, *A Study on Seals and Coins of the Safavids* (Tehran, 2006), pp. 112–113.

15 Ibid., pp. 115, 160–161.

ol-Moluk's preface strongly suggest that, in its final form, it was intended for presentation to an Afghan overlord. In fact, as Marcinkowski has acknowledged, the *Dastur ol-Moluk* may have had several contributors.[16] What may have begun as the latest edition of an administrative manual for the final Ṣafavid king, might have been continued or at least added to by subsequent scribes after the Afghan takeover. It seems to have finally been edited and presented to Maḥmud as his territories grew together with his need for a practical handbook on imperial government.

After Maḥmud's overthrow in 1137/1725, Ashraf not only came to rule a polity which now extended far beyond Isfahan, but he also harboured ambitions to consolidate administrative control over his holdings. To this end, Ashraf ordered a new manual for state administration, the *Taẕkerat ol-Moluk* (lit. Memorial for Kings). The urgency with which it was commissioned is made clear by the anonymous author's admission that his work was 'hurriedly compiled … by the supreme order'.[17] Indeed, Ashraf displayed a clear drive to repair and re-establish the Chancellery, in particular the Secretariat. After his unexpected victory over the Ottomans in Rabiʿ ol-Avval 1139/November 1726, Ashraf sent Istanbul a preliminary draft of the peace treaty, wherein the second clause requests that the Ottomans send an example of past Ṣafavid diplomatic correspondence to Isfahan,

> Because the likes [of such documents] are all lost and missing from the records and archives of Iran, [we request that] a seal-bearing letter hitherto dispatched by any one of the Ṣafavid kings to the [Ottoman] Sultan's Grand Viziers, be sent to the Royal Abode of Isfahan.[18]

This underlines the dearth of surviving archival material in the wake of the Afghan conquest, and consequently, the difficulties involved in resuming normal Secretariat functions. Although the archives of the Records Office are not mentioned here – understandably so, since its holdings would never have been shared with a foreign entity, least of all the Ottomans – they were unlikely to have fared any better than those of the Secretariat. One can only surmise, for example, the impediments to revenue collection in the absence of tax-assessment records. This unusual clause also reveals that Ashraf did not wish to uproot and replace epistolary practices in his badly raked Secretariat, at least when it came to diplomatic correspondence. In fact, the request strongly

16 Marcinkowski, *Mirzā Rafīʿā's Dastūr*, pp. 47–48.

17 Minorsky, *Tadhkirat*, p. 10.

18 ʿAbdolḥoseyn Navāʾi, *Nāder Shāh va Bāzmāndegānash* (Tehran, 1989), p. 36.

implies that the Secretariat was expected to produce documents which were, at least in part, based on the template of past Ṣafavid-Ottoman correspondence.

Prior to setting off on his successful campaign against the Ottomans in November, Ashraf had issued a reconciliatory edict in Ẕu ol-Qaʿdeh 1138/ July 1726, addressed to his subjects in the 'Royal Abode of Isfahan'. This document is the only surviving edict from Iran's Hotakid period.[19] It is highly illuminating regarding the epistolary traditions of the Chancellery's Secretariat, and how the professional secretaries and scribes working therein, either preserved or changed their literary practices as they transitioned from Ṣafavid to Hotakid service. This in turn, can proffer insights on several matters; the composition of the Secretariat's staff and how it may have differed from the Ṣafavid era; Ashraf's discourse on legitimacy as preserved in state literature; Hotakid perceptions and policies on collective identities in post-Ṣafavid Iran; The re-calibration of these collectives into new socio-political hierarchies; Efforts to reinstitute the state's fiscal procedures and taxation; and many other topics beyond the scope of this chapter. The edict, drafted by (presumably what remained of) the Chancellery's scribes, is now preserved in the archives of Iran's National Library. Its facsimile has been published by Ḥamideh Khodā-Bakhshi, who also included a transcript of its contents.[20] It is translated here for the first time in English (see Appendix).

4 Secretariat Literature under Ashraf's Reign

As the new king of a burgeoning polity beset by fundamental challenges to its legitimacy, the assay facing Ashraf was considerable. Perhaps most pressing of all, Ashraf's Isfahanian subjects – mostly settled Persian-speaking Shi'a – were of a fundamentally different social, cultural, linguistic, and religious makeup than his own Ghaljāy Afghan soldiers, who were mostly organised along tribal lines, Pashtun-speaking, and Sunni. The brutal siege of Isfahan and the harsh treatment of its (surviving) inhabitants could not have endeared them to their

19 There is a decree on a religious endowment (*vaqf*) dated 1728, tied to the shrine of Shāh ʿAbdolʿaẓim in the northern city of Rey. See Seyyed ʿAbdollāh ʿAqili, 'Farmān-e Ashraf-e Afghān va Mowqufāt-e Āstāneh-ye Ḥażrat-e ʿAbdolʿaẓim', in *Mirāṡ-e Jāvidān*, Vol. & No. 4 (2002), pp. 71–86. Though ʿAqili is mistaken in referring to the document as a *farmān*, for although it bears Maḥmud's imperial seal, the beginning of the document, where the initium is placed, is completely illegible. Without an initium to prove it, the document cannot assumed to be a *farmān* as a matter of course.

20 Ḥamideh Khodā-Bakhshi, 'Bāzkhʷāni-ye Farmāni az Ashraf-e Afghān pas az Residan beh Ḥokumat dar Isfahan', in *Ganjineh-ye Asnād*, No. 64 (2007), 31–39.

Afghan overlords.[21] Ashraf was keen in effecting a rapprochement, and took a number of steps to ingratiate himself with the Isfahanians. These included an insincere offer of abdication in favour of restoring Shāh Solṭān Ḥoseyn to the throne; marrying the latter's daughter, thereby promising to introduce Ṣafavid blood into future generations of Hotakid rulers; and the massacre or imprisonment of a number of Maḥmud's well-known lieutenants, many of whom were strongly associated with the brutality of Afghan rule.[22] As the political centre of Ashraf's dominion however, Isfahan was in dire need of having the rights and status of its inhabitants addressed in a binding and institutional manner. The natural means to achieve this would be the issuance of an edict. This would afford Ashraf the opportunity to legitimate his rule, using the epistolary skills of the Secretariat's scribes to formulate a Persianate discourse on his kingship and construct a narrative in which he would be portrayed as the just law-giver, and ultimately, rightful sovereign of Iran. It was to this end that in Ẕu ol-Qaʿdeh 1138/July 1726 Ashraf issued an official edict, declaring the rights, privileges, and obligations of all Isfahanians.[23]

The first striking feature of the edict is the imperial seal above the text. Upon close inspection, it bears a striking similarity to Ṣafavid seals. All Ṣafavid kings at one time or another in their rule had a pear-shaped seal. The bottom half was circular, atop which rested an upward-pointed cap, forming a droplet-like figure overall. The cap's left and right contours were each dented, not smooth. The cap and the circle each bore messages. 'In the Name of God' (*Bi-smi llāh*) was conventionally found in the cap. The circle would usually bear a couplet of poetry, or sometimes a quatrain. Ashraf's seal bore a couplet. Not uncommonly, the Ṣafavid seals would also contain the names of all the Twelve Shi'i Imams – something which the Hotakid seals never imitated of course. The near-identical appearance of Ashraf's seal with those of the Ṣafavid dynasty is unlikely to be mere coincidence.

Bear in mind that the second clause of Ashraf's draft of the peace treaty with the Ottomans was a request for an example of a Ṣafavid letter bearing a seal. Given the fact that Ashraf's edict predates the drafting of the peace treaty, it would seem that even after settling on an imperial seal for himself, Ashraf

21 For an overall account of the cruelties suffered by the Isfahanians, see the reports of the Dutch East India Company's staff who were resident in the city at the time, compiled by Floor, *Afghan Occupation*, pp. 81–196.

22 See J. Hanway, *A Historical Account of British Trade*, Vol. III (London, 1753), pp. 215–221 for Ashraf's charm offensive.

23 See Colin P. Mitchell, *The Practice of Politics in Safavid Iran: Power, Religion and Rhetoric* (London, 2009), pp. 11–16.

and his Chancellery were still seeking out examples belonging to past Ṣafavid kings, perhaps to be used as templates for a new seal? Alas, it cannot be said with certainty for what purpose. The Afghans evidently possessed a firm grasp of what Ṣafavid seals looked like already. Since the edict was published months prior to Ashraf's request for seal-bearing letters from the Ottomans, it must be the case that Ashraf's Chancellery already had access to either Ṣafavid seals, or at least to former Ṣafavid civil servants knowledgeable on such matters.

In contrast, the seal's text cannot be said to strongly align with Ṣafavid precedent, particularly on religious ideology. The couplet reads:

> By God's decree, Ashraf became the greatest among the kings of the world,
> The servant of righteousness, the dust under the feet of the Four Companions.[24]

Ashraf is not only a divinely-ordained king, but he is the superior of all his peers, subtly pointing to notions of Persianate imperial rule (*shāhanshāhi*). Due to a play on words, the first line can be read another way; 'Ashraf [the name means "greatest"] is the king of the world', expressing universal kingship. This is remarkably similar to the couplets found on Ashraf's royal mints:

> Due to the blessings of the king, who is the greatest (Ashraf) pursuer of justice,
> The coin of the Four Companions has been struck upon gold.[25]

While the same literary construction is used in Ashraf's first seal from 1137/1725:

> The king has been given God's blessing to disseminate the faith,
> Among the kings of the world, his moniker became the greatest (Ashraf).[26]

Serving to identify Ashraf as the superlative of kings. One can clearly see how Ashraf's new seal in 1138/1726 reiterated his coinage's affirmation of Sunni state identity, while also retaining the image of Ashraf as the superlative sovereign

24 I.e. the four Rightly Guided Rāshedun Caliphs who succeeded the Prophet; Abu Bakr, 'Oṡmān, 'Omar, 'Ali.

25 Moḥammad Shafi' Ṭehrāni, *Merāt-e Vāredāt*, ed. Manṣur Ṣefat-gol (Tehran, 2004), p. 165.

26 Ibid., p. 165.

from his first seal. These imperial characterisations of Ashraf as being king *over* all kings is not limited to Hotakid mints and sigillography. Indeed, the Secretariat drafted several diplomatic letters, in which Ashraf is portrayed as a Persianate emperor (*shāhanshāh*, lit. king of kings). In a letter to Ebrāhim Pāshā, the Ottoman Grand Vizier, Ashraf is introduced as the 'Illustrious Jamshid', one of the *Shāhnāmeh*'s renowned mythological kings of pre-Islamic Iran, Jamshid belonged to the Pishdādiān dynasty, the first to rule the country. Ashraf is also claimed to be the 'inheritor of the Kayāniān – [the dynasty succeeding the Pishdādiān] – crown and throne', and in possession of 'imperial *glory*' (***farr***-*e homāyun*).[27] The scribes' use of the term *farr* is noteworthy here, infusing Ashraf's reign with an unambiguously Persianate conception of divinely-ordained legitimacy. *Farr*, which also could be thought of as 'divine favour', is a very ancient concept, and was used by many of Iran's pre-Islamic kings, including the Sāsānids. It goes as far back as the Zoroastrian Avestā, in which it is a magical force or power, being luminous and fiery in nature.[28] Ṣafavid kings also made use of *farr* in expressing their divine mandate for sovereignty.[29] The use of such Persianate exemplars and motifs demonstrates that the Secretariat were in the process of constructing an imperial persona for Ashraf based on long established notions of cultural-political legitimacy in Iran. Ṣafavid precedents in courtly rhetoric and Chancellery literature guided the Hotakids in their pursuit of such notions, underscoring the professional mobility at play in the Secretariat, at least in terms of the conceptual models implemented, if not necessarily in terms of personnel.

In religious discourse, the Hotakids took an entirely different approach from their predecessors. Ṣafavid seals venerated the Twelve Imams, almost without exception. These were pious yet forceful affirmations of the king's Shi'ism. Ashraf was intent on making an equally forceful affirmation of his devotion to Sunnism. After all, the humble reference to Ashraf being the dust under the feet of the four Rightly Guided Caliphs is in deliberate contrast to numerous Ṣafavid seals containing verses such as

27 Navā'i, *Nāder va Bāzmāndegānash*, p. 59.

28 A full examination of the concept of *farr* is beyond the scope of this chapter. For an in-depth study, see *Encyclopaedia Iranica*, s.v. 'Farr(ah)', by Gherardo Gnoli, accessed April 3, 2020, http://www.iranicaonline.org/articles/farrah.

29 For the Ṣafavids approach to divine legitimacy refer to Sāsān Ṭahmāsbi, 'Taqaddos va Qodrat dar Dowreh-ye Ṣafaviyeh', in *Faṣlnāmeh-ye 'Elmi-Pajuheshi Shi'eh-Shenāsi*, Vol. 13, No. 3 (2015), pp. 65–85.

Whoever is not acquiescent to ʿAli, I have no affection for him whatever his standing,
He who is not as humble as *dust* at his [ʿAli's] threshold, even if he be an angel, may his head be as lowly as *dust*.[30]

And being the 'servant of righteousness' was a subversion of Shāh Solṭān Ḥoseyn's seal professing him to be the 'servant of the Lord's [*mowlā*, i.e. ʿAli's] righteousness'.[31] The imagery used by the Ṣafavids to underline their reverence for the Shi'i Imams was repurposed to underline Ashraf's reverence for the Four Caliphs. Observing Ṣafavid precedents in sigillography, the Hotakid Chancellery ironically appropriated them to drive home the reversal in state religious identity. Though the literary and sigillographic tools used here are recognisably derived from Ṣafavid practices, they are used to construct a Sunni, as opposed to a Shi'i, discourse on legitimacy.

The Ṣafavid heritage of the Secretariat is made evident even in the epistolary conventions followed in drafting the edict, which begins with a four-worded initium (*ṭoghrā*) stating 'The universal decree has become obeyed' (*Ḥokm-e jahān moṭāʿ shod*), the exact same as in many late Ṣafavid edicts.[32] The edict of Ẕu ol-Qaʿdeh 1138/July 1726 begins with a tacit acknowledgement of the privations visited upon Isfahanians and calls on them to 'accept … the evil of alternating fortune and misfortune', and reconciling themselves with their current state [of subjecthood to Ashraf] 'in the interest of friendship (*tavallā*)'. The term *tavallā* has connotations with a sort of religious/theological friendship, and is strongly associated with the first Shi'i Imam, ʿAli. This could be considered as Ashraf having extended an olive branch, a reconciliatory gesture based on the high regard in which ʿAli was held by both Sunnis and Shi'a. Ashraf's imperial realm, Iran, is described as an 'incendiary, fire-sifting garden' which he is prophesised to extinguish, then revive according to God's will. The manner in which the edict expresses this divine will is the following Qur'anic verse: 'so observe the results of God's mercy, how He gives life to the earth after its lifelessness' [Q 30:50]. The seamless inclusion of Qur'anic verses to enhance the legitimacy of a claim or an idea, was a common feature of Persianate state-literature, not just under the Ṣafavids, but throughout much of the Medieval

30 Esmāʿili, *Seals and Coins*, p. 149, the Persian is '*khāk bar sar*' (lit. dust upon head).

31 Seyyed Maḥmud Sādāt, 'Taḥlil-e Farmān-e Amānnāmeh-ye Ashraf-e Afghān beh Ahāli-ye Isfahan', in *Ganjineh-ye Asnād*, Vol. 19, No. 4 (2009), pp. 35–36.

32 ʿAbdolḥoseyn Navā'i, *Asnād va Mokātebāt-e Siāsi-ye Irān: Az Sāl-e 1105 tā 1135 H.Q.* (Tehran, Mow'aseseh-ye Moṭāleʿāt va Taḥqiqāt-e Farhangi, 1984), pp. 75–116 for just some of Shāh Solṭān Ḥoseyn's edicts bearing the same initium.

and Early Modern Islamicate world.[33] The edict makes extensive and consummate use of Qur'anic passages to imbue its arguments and narratives with Qur'anic authority. In this case, Ashraf is cast as the saviour of a scorched Iran, come to raise her from the ashes by 'God's will' as attested to by the Qur'an.

The 'intended addressees' are identified as all the residents of Isfahan. Ashraf's accession to Iran's kingship is framed as the establishment of a new and 'exalted dynasty' in the capital Isfahan, the traditional 'seat of Iran's sultans'. This transition in ruling dynasties is to be understood to be God's design, as he himself commands the Isfahanians to 'Say, "O God, owner of sovereignty, You give sovereignty to whom You will, and You take sovereignty away from whom You will. You honour whom You will, and You humble whom You will. The good is in Your hand. Indeed, You hold power over all things"' [Q 3:26]. The sentence which immediately follows – 'It is imperative to obey only their authority [the Hotakids'], and to reconcile oneself with their progeny' – is not a Qur'anic passage, but it is still written in Arabic. Even the script is changed back to *naskh* – a common script used for transcribing the Qur'an – as opposed to the *nastaʿliq*. While the Qur'anic passages all appear in *naskh*, the remainder of the text is written in *nastaʿliq*. By switching from Persian to Qur'anic Arabic, and from *nastaʿliq* to *naskh*, the Secretariat's scribes were doubtless attempting to linguistically and visually create Qur'anic associations for their demand for submission to Hotakid rule. In addition to the Qur'an, the edict makes use of several hadiths. The first of these comes from a Shi'i *hadith* compendium written by the famous tenth-century theologian Ibn Bābaway, Sheykh Ṣaduq.[34] This could be considered another olive branch the new Sunni ruling class extended to their Shi'i subjects, particularly those residents of Isfahan who were theologically literate, such as Isfahanian clerics.

A recurring theme of the edict of 1138/1726 is Ashraf's devotion to justice as the sovereign law-giver of the land. In fact, the edict self-designates as a 'charter of justice' (*manshur ol-ʿedāleh*). This discourse can be traced back to the very beginning of Ashraf's reign; recall his designation from the first royal mint; 'the greatest (Ashraf) pursuer of justice'.[35] In the edict, Ashraf's pursuit of justice and aversion to bloodshed is made to look like a natural corollary following a series of three Qur'anic verses. 'Whoever kills a soul, unless it be

33 Navā'i's *Asnād va Madārek* contains a great many examples from the Ṣafavid era, including edicts, royal letters, treaties, diplomatic and ambassadorial correspondence.

34 Moḥammad b. 'Ali Ṣaduq, *ʿIlal al-Sharāyaʿ* (Najaf, 1385/1965–1966), Vol. 1, p. 26.

35 Ṭehrāni, *Merāt-e Vāredāt*, p. 165.

in exchange for a soul [i.e. executing murderers] or for corruption in the land [meaning other criminal acts worthy of capital punishment], it is as if he had slain all of humanity' [Q 5:32]. Ashraf's pious observance of the Islamic creed is what leads him to 'the creed of justice', putting an end to any unlawful aggression against his subjects. Thus, Ashraf's bestowal of 'sanctuary and refuge' to the Isfahanians is understood to be driven by Qur'anic guidance. The edict declares that the 'Persian-speaking community' (*jamāʿat-e Farsi-zabān*) are to be given protection from any kind of molestation on their life or property, in accordance with 'religious law, and the custom of justice'.

A parallel Persianate discourse on Ashraf as the just ruler can be found in the Hotakid-Ottoman diplomatic correspondence beginning from 1139/1727. Ashraf is given the same epithet as the famous Sāsānid emperor Khosrow I: Anushiravān.[36] It is derived from the Middle Persian original, *anushag-rowān*, meaning 'the Immortal Soul'.[37] This is meant to instil Ashraf with those qualities which Anushiravān exemplifies in the Persian literary tradition; regal justice, wisdom, and righteousness.[38] In one letter addressed to the Ottoman Grand Vizier, Ashraf is described as 'the singular royal pearl of the *two seas* (*baḥrayn*) of justice and beneficence'.[39] The 'two seas' is a Qur'anic reference to Surat al-Firqān's 'And it is He [God] who has released [simultaneously] the two seas', emphasising that Ashraf's justice and beneficence were released through divine will. The letter to the Grand Vizier not only conveys such themes in prose, but also in verse:

> Due to his beneficence, the world has been overcome,
> By Anushiravān's chain (*selseleh*) of justice.[40]

The *selseleh*, meaning chain is here a reference to Anishirevān's legendary chain of justice (*zanjir-e ʿadl*) and also to Ashraf's 'chain', i.e. the Hotakid dynasty. The scribe's interplay between these two concepts continues in the prose; 'Anushiravān's chain of justice' serving as an allegory for 'this justice-serving Emperor's dynasty'.[41] Another piece of poetry continues,

---

36 Navā'i, *Nāder Shāh*, pp. 59–60.

37 Touraj Daryaee, *Sasanian Persia: The Rise and Fall of an Empire* (London, 2014), p. xvii.

38 See ʿAbolqāsem Ferdowsi, *Shāhnāmeh-ye Ferdowsi* (Tehran, 2002), pp. 461–509 for one of the most influential portrayals of Khosrow Anushiravān in Classical Persian literature.

39 Navā'i, *Nāder Shāh*, p. 59.

40 Ibid., p. 59.

41 Ibid., p. 60.

> I likened his might to Afrāsiāb's sword, though I admit Ashraf to be even stronger,
> They likened him to the Anushiravān of justice, yet they too admit him to be more righteous.[42]

A legendary hero and king of Turān in the *Shāhnāmeh* tradition, Afrāsiāb is used here to underline Ashraf's martial prowess. This embodiment of military glory is then tempered with Ashraf's epithet, Anushiravān, shared with Khosrow I, an archetype of imperial justice. This interplay lasted all the way up to the very end Ashraf's rule in Iran, for we find it revisited in a letter sent to the Ottoman sultan, dated to mid-1142/Autumn of 1729.[43] Therefore, the Secretariat used both Qur'anic as well as Persianate models of imperial rule across a range of different genres of state literature, including epistolary, sigillographic and even numismatic genres. The Persianate and Qur'anic approaches were not employed distinctly from one another, but were integrated into a discursive portrayal of Ashraf as a Persianate king, administering justice with divine sanction.

The edict also holds some information on the Chancellery staff. Apart from former Ṣafavid bureaucrats, the Hotakid Chancellery was staffed with newcomers from the region of Darjazin in North-West Iran. According to Father Krusinski, a contemporary resident of Isfahan, the Darjazinians were brought to the capital in Rajab or Shaʿbān 1137/April 1725 by Ashraf's predecessor, Maḥmud. Apparently, the Afghans relied on them since the Darjazinians were also Sunni.[44] The literate among them, being Persian speaking Sunnis, would indeed make for ideal trainee scribes, particularly in a Chancellery which sought to integrate a Sunni religious discourse with Persianate notions of imperial legitimacy. The edict not only reveals that there were 'Chancellery staff drawn from the Darjazinians', but that they also supplied the Hotakids with 'soldiers, retainers, and servants'. Thus, the composition of the Chancellery, alongside other state institutions, changed in line with the state's religious identity. It is unclear wether there was a sufficient number of literate and qualified Darjazinians for the Hotakids to begin replacing the (former Ṣafavid) Shi'i Chancellery staff to any great extent. The experience and skill of this latter group would have been indipesnable to the Hotakid Chancellery. Nonetheless, the addition of fellow Sunni Darjazinians, though maybe limited, served to underline the changing religious loyalty of this institution going from Ṣafavid

---

42 Ibid..
43 Ibid., pp. 62–72.
44 Judas T. Krusinski, *The History*, p. 197.

to Hotakid rule. This shows professional mobility to be a process which went beyond the mere transition of bureaucrats from Ṣafavid to Hotakid service. The Hotakids' introduction of new cadres into the Chancellery from previously unutilised recruitment pools was also an integral part of the process, and seems to have been carried out along religious lines.

5 A Note on the Records Office in Ashraf's Reign

In 1140/1728, Ashraf issued a royal decree on the ʿAbdolʿaẓim Shrine's religious endowments (*owqāf*), in the northern city of Rey. It bears Ashraf's personal seal on the reverse. It seems that the Ṣafavid seal(s) which Ashraf had requested the Ottomans send to his Chancellery, might have become the basis of a new imperial seal after all. Unlike the seal marking the edict of 1138/1726, this one is shaped as a perfect square. The only Ṣafavid king who had a perfect square seal was Shāh Ṣafi (r. 1038–1052/1629–1642). Ṣāfi's seal shared similar dimensions with Ashraf's, 1.8 cm^2 and 2 cm^2 respectively.[45] Is it possible that the seal-bearing diplomatic letter that the Ottomans sent to Ashraf's Chancellery was from Shāh Ṣafi's period? In any case, the couplet contained in the seal was modified to

> So long as the greatest (Ashraf) of kings possesses the crown and seal,
> Whoever is grateful to his state (*dowlat*) is ennobled.[46]

Comparing this to the seal from 1138/1726, one can infer that Ashraf's Chancellery in 1140/1728 no longer felt the need to articulate the emperor's religious legitimacy in contradistinction with Ṣafavid norms. Indeed, there are no explicit or implicit religious references. What remains, and is expanded upon, is the king's status as supreme sovereign, which appropriately parallels the consolidation of his rule during this period. The king's dedication to justice and beneficence is no longer a theme, though the term *dowlat* refers not exclusively to 'state', but also to 'beneficence', meaning those who were grateful (read: obedient) to his majesty, were assured of his continued munificence. Justice *per se* however, is absent from the seal. Putting aside sigillographic analysis, the decree of 1140/1728 is a detailed endowment mostly composed of fiscal calculations and figures. As such, it can be quite instructive in understanding some aspects of fiscal administration in the Hotakid Chancellery's Records Office; For example,

45 Esmāʿili, *Coins and Seals*, p. 150.
46 ʿAqili, 'Farmān-e Ashraf', p. 74.

in what ways it resembled or differed from previous fiscal practices under the Ṣafavid Records Office. As this study has chosen to focus on the Chancellery's Secretariat, rather than its Records Office, this topic will have to be relegated to another dedicated study for a sufficiently thorough examination.

6 Concluding Remarks

It is clear that epistolary practices in the Hotakid Secretariat followed many precedents set by its Ṣafavid predecessor. The tools and the methods used by Iran's scribes and secretaries did not undergo a fundamental change in this transitional period, there being a relatively frictionless mobility in professional Chancellery practices. Even where a reversal in the state's religious identity was required, the Secretariat used Ṣafavid discourses and sigillographic customs to effect this reversal. Drawing upon Iran's long-established literary traditions, the edicts and diplomatic correspondence composed by the Secretariat bore an unmistakably Persianate depiction of Ashraf as the imperial sovereign, and head of Iran's new ruling dynasty.

Given the brutality of the occupation the Isfahanians had been subject to in Maḥmud's reign, Ashraf was anxious to propagate an image of himself as a just law-giver. Indeed, Ashraf's dedication to justice is near-ubiquitous in the Secretariat's output at the time. Furthermore, this discourse on justice had two parallel streams which not unfrequently flowed into one another. One was concerned primarily with justice as exemplified by models of Persianate kingship; the other engaged with notions of justice as couched in Qur'anic verses. The aggregate result was Ashraf's portrayal as a new Anushiravān, upholding the 'chain of justice' through following, even sometimes fulfilling, Qur'anic dictums. The Secretariat's message was transparent; to uphold the Qur'an and Anushiravān's 'chain of justice', was to uphold the Hotakid 'chain' or dynasty.

The emphasis on the Qur'an seems to be no coincidence. The inclusion of Qur'anic verses in state literature was far from new, but few edicts from Ṣafavid times make use of the Qur'an as extensively as Ashraf's edict of 1138/1726. In order to bridge the gap between the ruling and subject classes in terms of religious identity, the Secretariat was far from reticent in using commonalities between the two Islamic denominations, such as a strong mutual reverence for the Qur'an. The 'Alid-inflected friendship (*tavallā*) which is proposed between the Hotakids and the Isfahanians is part of this Shi'i-Sunni bridging effort, as is the use of hadiths held to be authentic by both sects. This is also reflected in the professional mobility bestowed upon the Sunni Darjazinians who were brought to Isfahan to work alongside their Shi'i colleagues in the Chancellery.

Finally, and although this somewhat exceeds the scope of the present study, there is the matter of collective identities as they appear in Hotakid state literature. That Ashraf identified as the *king of Iran*, is beyond any doubt given the above evidence. Nor was it new. The Ṣafavids were one of many dynasties whose kings identified their imperial realm with Iran. But did Ashraf and his Ghaljāy Afghans collectively identify as being *Iranian*? This would be new. No post-Islamic dynasty produced state literature referring to a people as Iranian. This only changed in the post-Ṣafavid period, and under Nāder Shāh (r. 1148–1160/1736–1747) in particular. The edict of 1138/1726 clearly delineates Afghans from 'Persian-speaking' Isfahanians, and the Afghans also distinguish themselves from their Darjazinian allies who were fellow Sunnis. It seems collective identities in the Hotakid period cannot be simply understood as isomorphisms of religious denominations. Curiously, the edict ends with imploring the sultans of 'Iran, and the Iranians (*Irānián*)' to abide by the dictums and decrees set down therein. While it is easy to see that future Hotakid sovereigns are understood to be rulers of Iran, does the 'Iranian' collective include the Ghaljāy Afghans themselves, or does it refer to 'Persian-speaking' non-Afghan subjects. Given its singular appearance here in the edict, it is impossible to know precisely what the Hotakid Chancellery meant by 'Iranians'. After all, this demonym is never used in any Ṣafavid edict or royal document. It would seem that the first reference to 'Iranians' in the country's post-Islamic Chancellery literature was made during the Afghan occupation. The irony is that running counter to the Hotakid narrative, was the post Safavid discourse on Iranian identity which categorically rejected the inclusion of Afghans, and deemed them unfit for taking up the mantle of Iran's kingship.[47]

Appendix

The following is an edict (*farmān*) from Ashraf (r. 1137–1142/1725–1729), the second and last Afghan ruler of Iran. It is now preserved in the collections of the Islamic Republic of Iran's National Library and Archives. In the interests of authenticity and accuracy, the excessively florid style and inherent textual ambiguities of the original edict have been retained in this translation. It is my hope that this might also benefit scholars that are (insufficiently) familiar with the abstruse language of early modern epistolary

47 For the emergence of a cultural-political discourse on Iranian identity, steeped in militant Shi'ism, and deeply hostile to the Afghans, see the author's forthcoming 'Iran's Last Emperor: State Formation and Fragmentation in Naderid Iran', PhD diss. (School of Oriental and African Studies, University of London, 2021).

Persian, but are nonetheless interested in comparative analysis, or, are engaged in a study tangentially related to Persianate history. The underlined sections indicate that the corresponding section in the original edict is in Arabic, not Persian.

> The universal decree has become obeyed,
>
> [This edict is addressed to] Those who are privy to the finer truths of veiled knowledge, and the Parousia of the universe of creation and corruption; those who know of those blinded by the illuminating rays of the many dawns of darkness and light's absence, and the revelation of both birth and the return [to the spiritual realm for moral judgement], which is the source for all of the anxieties; those [Isfahanians] which walk the streets of secrecy, hidden in the cloisters of concealment, and [yet] to be enlightened with luminous skies so that they may accept the various forms in which wisdom's virtue appears and [accept] the evil of alternating fortune and misfortune, and [accept] the destiny's varicoloured visage, revealed to be light and dark.
>
> They [Isfahanians] ought to rid their knowing hearts of rust, brightening them with all the brilliance of a world-reflecting mirror, and in the interest of friendship (*tavallā*),[48] to surrender themselves to virtue, directing their clairvoyant eyes and discerning vision upon the hallowed mirror of divinely-ordained reality, and consenting to it. As surely as daylight pursues night's darkness, and as the smile of a rose and the teardrop of rosewater chase upon each other in tandem, so too do gaiety and grief. Existence and oblivion, light and darkness, day and night, life and death are all connected. What spring does not entail the slicing open of flower buds, the scattering of colourful petals and blood-shedding of carmine and rubicund blossoms on the garden floor? What fate under this star-lit dome does not include the onset of the sun's bloody dusk, portending life's harmonious line being swept away by the tumultuous river waves?
>
> Thus it is that in this rose garden [world], both severity and abundance reconcile themselves to the other, and all the flowers and buds bloom together, each with their own bedazzling colour. Therefore, even though a gardener – virtuous or evil – may burn this incendiary, fire-sifting garden with his false gardening or due to ill fate [referring to the Ṣafavids or Ashraf's predecessor, Maḥmud?], a boundlessly merciful one [Ashraf] will bring forth water, putting out the flames which engulf the inhabitants of this garden. He will revive life anew with ceaseless

48 This has connotation of religious/theological friendship and association with the first Shi'i Imam.

munificence, and impart the merry message 'so observe the results of God's mercy, how He gives life to the earth after its lifelessness' [Q 30:50].

The intended addressees of this letter are the residents of the Royal Abode of Isfahan, its people, its peasants, its strong and weak, the honourable as well as the dishonourable. From the very dawn of this immortal sultanship [Ashraf's], the aforementioned Royal Abode, having been the seat of Iran's sultans and caliphal rulers, has become the abode of this exalted dynasty's auspicious-fated and ever-shining sun. This has been eternally ordained by the compulsory command; 'Say, "O God, owner of sovereignty, You give sovereignty to whom You will, and You take sovereignty away from whom You will. You honour whom You will, and You humble whom You will. The good is in Your hand. Indeed, You hold power over all things"' [Q 3:26]. *It is imperative to obey only their authority, and to reconcile oneself with their progeny.* They [Isfahanians] ought to merrily take up the joyous role of peasants and subjects, eschewing insurrection or rebellion against the interests of this caliphal dynasty and those beholden to it. Having lived blissfully under [Ashraf's] benevolent banner, [the Isfahanians] ought to recognise that when clairvoyance and wisdom engulf their sight, they will doubtless [see the right path and] consent to God's design by obeying our blessed imperial sovereign.

As there is no deterrent facing the ignorant and conceited unconscious in their quest to bring forth terrifying nightmares of calamity in this age, the natter of these corrupt evildoers caused the ignition of royal wrath and a world-scorching wildfire, which is the bullet upon the shrapnel [i.e. assured] proof of 'it is hit by a whirlwind of fire, and is burnt' [Q 2:266]. This fire engulfed the lives of the vulnerable in that country [Iran]. Through God's grace, the strike of flood-inducing clouds released the merciful deluge which quenched the wildfire gnawing at the world-harvest of the vulnerable and weak. This springtide downpour became the arrayer of the everlasting garden, bestowing life upon all in this dominion [referring to the Afghan overthrow of the Ṣafavids, or the replacement of Maḥmud by Ashraf].

The owner and absolute ruler of all the realms across the expanses of both heaven and earth [God], has rendered dust – from which humankind are moulded – into an emblem of mysteries; 'The mud from which Adam was created, gestated for forty days'.[49] From this abject baseness He raised [humankind] to the pinnacle of prestige, magnanimously interweaving the components of this rotten

49 Written in Arabic, hadith taken from Sheykh Ṣaduq's *ʿIlal al-Sharāyaʿ* (see above).

dust, and with a mere gesture, He interlaced the senses into one another and formed the skeletal pillars of this majestic curtain, creating the body. He raised the restless soul [of humans] to the zenith of grandeur, 'so blessed is God, the supreme creator' [Q 23:14] demonstrating through his power that 'We have certainly created man in the best of stature' [Q 95:4]. Without the emergence of the sabre's flood-inducing faults [i.e. outside the context of war], the wise have been warned that 'whoever kills a soul, unless it be in exchange for a soul or for corruption in the land, it is as if he had slain all of humanity' [Q 3:32], and [killing] is far from both the righteous path of cultivating subjects and the creed of justice.

Therefore, all the peasants, subjects, decent tradesmen, and people of the aforementioned Royal Abode, from men and women, great and small, are given refuge from massacre and rape, as we have forgiven them their lives. This is excluding murderers of Muslims and highwaymen whose guilt has been proven by religious law (*sharʿi*). In line with the organisation of the state and order of the provinces, the punishment of these criminals will be the responsibility of judges practicing customary law (*ʿorf*). This state of affairs is permanently set in order for the security of the lands and tranquillity of the people.

Not a single one of the great commanders, khans, royal retainers, agents, slaves, or warriors among the Afghans, or the chancellery's staff drawn from the Darjazinian [?] and others, is permitted to abuse, rape, despoil, molest, or shed the blood of a single inhabitant or resident among the Persian-speaking community (*jamāʿat-e Farsi-zabān*), no matter their status. Whether they be honourable or dishonourable, weak or strong, knowing or ignorant, artisans or men of the pen, decent tradesmen or any guildsmen, workers of the estates or the royal mint, weavers, tailors, engravers, jewellers, chancellery staff, or the peasants, farmers, serfs, and private land-owners in the surrounding towns and villages of the Royal Abode, you are not to molest them so that they may confidently return to their labours.

Regarding marriage, not a single one of the women and daughters of deceased or redundant commanders, and or nobility of the previous [Ṣafavid era] or current times is to be wed [by an Afghan] without notifying the caliphate-destined (*khelāfat-maṣir*) throne.[50] Whenever the intention should arise to take a wife from among the Persian-speaking community, you are free to do so, as is permitted by holy law (*shariʿat-e moqaddaseh*). From now onwards, if Afghan and

50 Ashraf is ensuring that no other Afghan can stake a royal claim by marrying a former Ṣafavid noble or grandee.

Darjazinian soldiers, retainers, and servants wish to marry any Persian-speaker, be they honourable or dishonourable, they are not permitted to do so until they have made known their design to the caliphate-destined throne and been granted a dismissal.

Without the order of our blessed majesty, no individual has the authority to confiscate houses, estates, properties, assets in kind or in cash, for to do so would be opposed to religious law, and the custom of justice. Whenever a decree is issued [for expropriation], you are not to seize any more or other than that which is specified therein. Any individual, whether a former resident or a newcomer, intending to establish a residence in any of the neighbourhoods of the Royal Abode must have his residence reported to Isfahan's tax magistrate (*kalāntar*) by the local neighbourhood chief (*kadkhoda*). This will be recorded in a logbook, examined by wardens of this august state each day. The logbook will detail whether the new resident is a grandee, former nobleman, aristocrat, warrior, litterateur, artisan, impoverished, scum, or rabble. In this manner, their movement or settlement can be controlled based on royal authority. If the need should arise for our exemplary banners to march upon a given region [around Isfahan], the state's wardens ought to evict some of the original residents [to make room], and the residents are not to return to their estates or properties until after our glorious army has departed the Abode of Caliphate [Isfahan].

The community-chiefs of the Jews, Hindus, and Christians are not to intervene in any quarrel involving a Muslim. Disputes involving a Muslim must be adjudicated according to the religious and customary laws (*sharʿ va ʿorf*) of the core of Islam,[51] so that a just and righteous ruling may be reached. If these chiefs fail to heed this command henceforth, a considerable fine will be imposed upon them for adjudicating Muslim disputes. Jurists, judges of customary law, and upright administrative agents are to perform their duties in the usual manner, according to the command of their just sultans. They are to investigate and invigilate the truth in administering the province, upholding righteousness, the law, and the order of government. Deeming disobedience and transgression as unworthy, they are to give prayer for our holy majesty.

Any man from the community of the Darjazinians or the Muslim people who wishes to enter into business with guildsmen and artisans from other communities, whether they be Hindu, Zoroastrian, Christian, or the *mokhālefin* [lit. 'those who are opposed'; meaning Jews? Or the Shi'a?], are bound by the old

51 Does the 'core (*beyżeh*) of Islam' mean Sunni (Ḥanafi) jurisprudence? It is unclear.

regulations; Meaning that they [Darjazinians/Muslims] are still required to pay their allotted share of local taxes based on their stake [in the business] to the tax magistrate who oversees all the guilds and workshops, thereby fulfilling their chancellery [tax] obligations. They are not to pass on their share of these taxes to the guildsmen and artisans they have entered into business with. The strong are not to oppress the weak, harassing their lives and livelihoods, and ought not to draw the sultanic ire and champion-like wrath of our blessed highness. The entirety of our obedient subjects and God's worshippers are given sanctuary in this redoubtable fortress of security. The hopeful blessings of the threshold of God's creation has taken form in this document by order of the shadow of God, the just sultan [Ashraf]. Our blessed majesty will not take a single life without legitimate proof of transgression.

All the sultans of the coming centuries, from the gallant sons and judicious caliphs of Iran and the Iranians – *may God illuminate for them the path of guidance*,[52] are bound to this justice-embracing covenant. For *a single hour of justice is superior to seventy years of worship*,[53] and according to the true hadith, *the good of humanity rests upon prayer for the greatest sovereign, God, and goodness comes from what benefits the people*.[54] [Future sultans] must observe the justice found in the verse 'Indeed, God orders justice and good conduct and giving to relatives and forbids immorality and bad conduct and oppression. He admonishes you that perhaps you will be reminded' [Q 16:90], and turn it into an image of your righteous endeavour and virtuous intentions. Under the divine commandment 'fulfil your vows' [Q 16:91], you must abjure any change or alteration to the tenets and principles agreed herein, heeding the promise 'upon them is God's wrath, and a great punishment awaits them' [Q 16:106]. Act according to this treaty and charter of justice (*manshur al-ʿedāleh*) so that you may 'fulfil the covenant of God when you have taken it, [O believers], and do not break oaths after their confirmation while you have made God, over you, a witness. Indeed, God knows what you do' [Q 16:91]. 'Then whoever alters the bequest after he has heard it – the sin is only upon those who have altered it' [Q 2:181].

The Royal Abode's peasants and subjects ought to consider this written charter as their prayers' answer, granting them safety and sanctuary. Completely hopeful

52 Written in Arabic.

53 Written in Arabic, this is a modification of a hadith actually taken from a Shia Imam, Imam Ṣādeq. See the Moḥammad Reyshahri, *Mizān al-Ḥikma*, Vol. 7 (Tehran), p. 543.

54 Written in Arabic, this is a hadith taken from Reyshahri, *Mizān al-Ḥikma*, Vol. 3, p. 1934.

and assured, they must now be forthright in demonstrating their loyal service and subjection, awaiting and supplicating to his holiness [Ashraf]. They are to pray for and work towards the unceasing extension of this everlasting state. Written in Ẕu ol-Qaʿdeh 1138/July 1726.

[The seal affixed to the top of the edict contains the following couplet:] By God's decree, Ashraf became the greatest among the kings of the world, I am the servant of righteousness, the dust under the feet of the four companions.

Bibliography

ʿAqili, Seyyed ʿAbdollāh. ʿFarmān-e Ashraf-e Afghān va Mowqufāt-e Āstāneh-ye Ḥażrat-e ʿAbdolʿaẓim', in *Mirāṡ-e Jāvidān*, Vol. & No. 4 (2002), pp. 71–86.

Astarābādi, Moḥammad Mehdi. *Jahāngoshā-ye Nāderi*, ed. ʿAbdollāh Anvār (Tehran, 1962).

Axworthy, Michael *The Sword of Persia: Nader Shah, from Tribal Warrior to Conquering Tyrant* (London, 2006).

Daryaee, Touraj. *Sasanian Persia: The Rise and Fall of an Empire* (London, 2014).

Esmāʿili, Ṣoghrā. *A Study on Seals and Coins of the Safavids* (Tehran, 2006).

Ferdowsi, ʿAbolqāsem. *Shāhnāmeh-ye Ferdowsi* (Tehran, 2002).

Floor, Willem. *The Afghan Occupation of Persia 1721–1729* (Paris, 1998).

Gnoli, Gherardo. *Encyclopaedia Iranica*, s.v. 'Farr(ah)', accessed April 3, 2020, http://www.iranicaonline.org/articles/farrah.

Hanway, Jonas. *A Historical Account of British Trade*, Vol. III (London, 1753).

Khodā-Bakhshi, Ḥamideh. 'Bāzkhʷāni-ye Farmāni az Ashraf-e Afghān pas az Residan beh Ḥokumat dar Isfahan', *Ganjineh-ye Asnād*, no. 64 (2007), pp. 31–39.

Krusinski, T. *The History of the Late Revolutions of Persia*, Vol. II (London, 1733).

Lockhart, Laurence. *The Fall of the Safavi Dynasty and the Afghan Occupation of Persia* (London, 1958).

Marcinkowski. *Mīrzā Rafīʿā's Dastūr Al-Mulūk: A Manual of Later Ṣafavid Administration* (Kuala Lumpur, 2002).

Matthee, Rudi. *Persia in Crisis: Safavid Decline and the Fall of Isfahan* (London, 2012).

Minorsky, V. *Tadhkirat Al-Mulūk: A Manual of Ṣafavid Administration* (London, 1943).

Mitchell, Colin P. *The Practice of Politics in Safavid Iran: Power, Religion and Rhetoric* (London, 2009).

Moḥammad Rafiʿ Anṣāri, Dastur ol-Moluk. Intro, ed. Moḥammad Taqi Dāneshpaĵuh, in *Majalle Dāneshkadeh-ye Adabiāt va ʿOlum-e Ensāni-ye Dāneshgāh-e Tehrān*, Vols. 63 and 64, Nos. 5–6 (1968), pp. 475–504.

Moḥsen, Moḥammad. *Zobdat ol-Tavārikh*, ed. Behruz Gudarzi (Tehran, 1996).

Navā'i, ʿAbdolḥoseyn. *Nāder Shāh va Bāzmāndegānash* (Tehran, 1989).

Parsa, M.A.H. 'Iran's Last Empire and the Emergence of Iranian identity', PhD diss. (School of Oriental and African Studies, University of London, 2021).

Sādāt, Seyyed Maḥmud. 'Taḥlil-e Farmān-e Amānnāmeh-ye Ashraf-e Afghān beh Ahāli-ye Isfahan', in *Ganjineh-ye Asnād*, Vol. 19, No. 4 (2009), pp. 27–40.

Ṣaduq, Moḥammad b. ʿAli. *ʿIlal al-Sharāyaʿ* (Najaf, 1385/1965–1966), Vol. 1.

Ṭahmāsbi, Sāsān. 'Taqaddos va Qodrat dar Dowreh-ye Ṣafaviyeh', in *Faṣlnāmeh-ye ʿElmi-Paĵuheshi Shiʿeh-Shenāsi*, Vol. 13, No. 3 (2015), pp. 65–85.

Ṭehrāni, Moḥammad Shafiʿ. *Merāt-e Vāredāt*, ed. Manṣur Ṣefat-gol (Tehran, 2004).

Tucker, Ernest. *Nadir Shah's Quest for Legitimacy in Post-Safavid Iran* (Gainesville, 2006).

CHAPTER 9

Islamic Political Thought and Professional Mobility: The Intellectual and Empirical Worlds of Ibn Ṭalḥa and Ibn Jamāʿa

Mohamad El-Merheb

1 Introduction

This article examines the interrelatedness between professional mobility and the production of Islamic political thought based on two case studies from the late Ayyubid and Mamluk periods. It argues that the diverse professional careers of the two Shāfiʿī-Ashʿarī jurists, judges, and Sufis, Ibn Ṭalḥa (582/1186 or 87–652/1254) and Ibn Jamāʿa (639/1241–733/1333), helped shape the political ideas and stylistic features of their extant treatises. The article aims to highlight how the life and career of Ibn Ṭalḥa and his service to the Ayyubids and Artuqids shaped the structure and content of his political treatise and how Ibn Jamāʿa's advancing service in the Mamluk sultanate altered his conceptions of the highest political authority of Islam. These findings will be situated within the period's professionalisation and *adab*isation of scholars (*ʿulamaʾ*), and the rising influence of scholars within the judiciary and the administrative structures of Military Patronage States, and their Sufism, personal intellectual interests, and legal and theological affiliations.[1]

Professional mobility has not hitherto been considered a factor in the history of pre-modern Islamic political thought. While loyalty or service to a

1 Professionalisation refers to the emergence of the *ʿulamaʾ* as a class of bureaucrats during the twelfth and thirteenth centuries as described in Joan E. Gilbert "Institutionalization of Muslim Scholarship and Professionalization of the ʿUlamaʾ in Medieval Damascus," *Studia Islamica* 52 (1980): 105–34. *Adab*isation refers to the fusion of literary culture with religious sciences amongst scholars who studied in *madrasas* and staffed the Mamluk administration as explained in Thomas Bauer, "Mamluk Literature: Misunderstandings and New Approaches," *Mamlūk Studies Review* 9, no. 2 (2005): 105–32. For more on the Ayyubids, Artuqids, and Mamuks as Military Patronage States, refer to Michael Chamberlain, "Military Patronage States and the Political Economy of the Frontier, 1000–1250", in Y.M. Choueiri (ed.), *A Companion to the History of the Middle East* (2005), 135–53 and Jo Van Steenbergen, "The Mamluk Sultanate as a Military Patronage State: Household Politics and the Case of the Qalāwūnid bayt (1279–1382)," *Journal of the Economic and Social History of the Orient* 56 (2013): 189–217.

 | DOI:10.1163/9789004467637_011

monarch, lord, dynasty, or regime is generally accepted to have inspired jurists and other writers to author political treatises, the impact of their movement between various posts on their ideas has received little or no treatment. Indeed one can effortlessly cite instances where loyalty and service were entangled with the production of advice literature including al-Jāḥiẓ (d. 868/869) and the ʿAbbāsid; pseudo-Niẓām al-Mulk (408/1018–485/1092) and the Seljuq sultans Alp Arslān and Malikshāh; and Ayyubid vizier al-Shayzarī (d. 589/1193) and Ṣalāḥ al-Dīn. Some treatises were even named after their dedicatees such as al-Juwaynī's *Ghiyāthī* (*Ghiyāth al-umam fī iltiyāth al-ẓulam*) and al-Ghazālī's *Mustaẓhirī* (*Faḍāʾiḥ al-bāṭiniyya wa-faḍāʾil al-Mustaẓhiriyya*).[2] Not only were al-Juwaynī (d. 478/1085) and al-Ghazālī (450/1058–505/1111) motivated by securing the longevity of their dedicatees' rule, but also by the apprehension of their absence.[3] A further relevant case is Sibṭ Ibn al-Jawzī (c. 582/1186–654/1256) whose inconsistent reactions to the two surrenders of Jerusalem to the Crusaders in 1229 and 1244 seem to have merely reflected the political considerations of his patron, Ayyubid sultan al-Ashraf (r. 626/1229–635/1237).[4] Even Ibn Taymiyya's (661/1263–728/1328) well-known treatise *al-Siyāsa al-sharʿiyya*, which is often incorrectly depicted as the work of an outsider to the Mamluk political system, is now accepted to be partly the product of its author's alignment within intra-Mamluk factionalism.[5] Such cases, however, did not prompt researchers to accommodate professional mobility as an influence in the history of Islamic political thought.

2 These titles are often translated respectively as "Aid to nations shrouded in darkness" and "The scandals of the esoterics and the virtues of the party of al-Mustaẓhir".

3 Continuity, political stability, and the preservation of religion were major concerns of the *Ghiyāthī* and *Mustaẓhirī* as dictated by the Shāfiʿī-Ashʿarī juristic and theological background of al-Juwaynī and al-Ghazālī; refer to Ovamir Anjum, *Politics, Law and Community in Islamic Thought: The Taymiyyan Moment* (Cambridge University Press, 2012), pp. 126–127; and for a more comprehensive discussion on this topic to Sohaira Siddiqui, *Law and Politics under the Abbasids: An Intellectual Portrait of Al-Juwayni* (Cambridge University Press, 2019), especially Part 4 (chapters 9 and 10), which treats the political thought articulated in the *Ghiyāthī*.

4 The "handing over of Jerusalem in 1244, according to terms much worse than the treaty of 1229, was not even mentioned" by Sibṭ Ibn al-Jawzī; refer to Suleiman Mourad, "A Critique of the Scholarly Outlook of the Crusades: The Case for Tolerance and Coexistence," in *Syria in Crusader Times: Conflict and Coexistence*, ed. Carole Hillenbrand (Edinburgh University Press, 2020), p. 148.

5 Caterina Bori challenged "the common idea that Ibn Taymīyah was at odds with the Mamluk authorities" in, "The Collection and Edition of Ibn Taymīyah's Works: Concerns of a Disciple," *Mamlūk Studies Review* 13, no. 2 (2009), p. 48. For a related and useful study refer to Caterina Bori, "Thélogie politique et Islam, à propos d'Ibn Taymiyya [d. 728/1328] et du sultanat mamelouk," *Revue de l'Histoire des Religions* 224, no. 1 (2007), p. 10.

This study encompasses not just an author's mere service and allegiance to his dedicatee, but also his movement between different posts. Fortunately, the careers of Ibn Ṭalḥa and Ibn Jamāʿa provide original and direct correlations between professional mobility, on the one hand, and the thematic and stylistic traits of the tradition of authoring political treatises, on the other. The first case study is Ibn Ṭalḥa's *al-ʿIqd al-farīd li-al-malik al-saʿīd* (The unique necklace for a content king), which offers clues on the impact of his professional mobility under the Artuqids and late Ayyubids on his original and eclectic style. As such, this case study will show that Ibn Ṭalḥa's work was an amalgamation of genres of advice literature that reflected the diversity of his professional background. The second case study relies on Ibn Jamāʿa's three extant political treatises to examine the expansion of the author's political theory alongside his thriving career and professional mobility under the Mamluks. This examination, which additionally covers two treatises that predate his well-known *Taḥrīr al-aḥkām fī tadbīr ahl-al-Islām* (Drafting ordinances towards running the affairs of the people of Islam), allows the shift in Ibn Jamāʿa's postulations on the ultimate political authority in Islam to be traced.

The choice of Ibn Ṭalḥa and Ibn Jamāʿa is not arbitrary. Both jurists belonged to and flourished in nearly identical empirical and intellectual worlds and, as such, provide two comparable and successive case studies that connect professional mobility to the history of Islamic political thought.[6] The choice of this pair is therefore dictated by geographical, political, legal, and theological considerations, in addition to other perceptible resemblances between the two authors, their works, and their dedicatees. Both Ibn Ṭalḥa and Ibn Jamāʿa were jurists and statesmen whose careers emerged and flourished in Syria: under the Ayyubids and Artuqids in the case of the former, and in Syria and Egypt under the Mamluks in the case of the latter. The two jurists served at the highest echelons of the judiciary and the administrative apparatus of these Military Patronage States and played relatively significant roles at critical junctions of the political histories of these polities. Both Ibn Ṭalḥa and Ibn Jamāʿa adhered to the Shāfiʿī legal school and the Ashʿarī philosophical theology, and were known to be Sufis. Lastly and as will be discussed below, Ibn Jamāʿa knew the work of Ibn Ṭalḥa and drew from it in at least two of his extant political treatises. Accordingly, the best starting point for this study is chronological and begins with Ibn Ṭalḥa, his career, and treatise.

6 I greatly benefit here from the works of Quentin Skinner, especially his advice to focus on "the writer's mental world, the world of his empirical beliefs" as a prerequisite to interpreting a political text in, "Motives, Intentions and the Interpretation of Texts," *New Literary History* 3, no. 2 (1972), p. 407.

2 Ibn Ṭalḥa

Abū Sālim Kamāl al-Dīn Ibn Ṭalḥa al-Nuṣaybīnī was a Shāfiʿī expert in jurisprudence (*fiqh*), speculative theology and jurisprudence (*uṣūl*), and the study of legal divergence between schools or disputation (*khilāf*).[7] Ibn Ṭalḥa was furthermore a litterateur and a statesman who served Ayyubid and Artuqid rulers, participated in diplomatic missions, held the judgeship of his northern Syrian hometown Nuṣaybīn, and served as preacher (*khaṭīb*) of the Umayyad Mosque in Damascus.[8] In 648/1250, Ayyubid sultan al-Nāṣir Ṣalāḥ al-Dīn Yūsuf (r. 634/1237–658/1260) entered Damascus and appointed him vizier (*wazīr*); after holding the post for two days, he removed himself and disappeared.[9] It is said that during this period Ibn Ṭalḥa wore the cotton garment of the Sufis and became an ascetic. Later, he reappeared in Aleppo where he died in 652/1254. Ibn Ṭalḥa had a passion for *ʿilm al-ḥurūf* and *ʿilm al-awfāq*, the occult sciences of the numerical values of Arabic letters, often of verses in the Qurʾān, and their use to learn the esoteric significance of creation; such sciences were often connected to the Sufi belief in the unity of creation (*waḥdat al-wujūd*), but also associated with the practice of astrology.[10] Some stories claimed that Ibn Ṭalḥa predicted the date of his own death on the basis of his study of the letters of a verse recited by a wandering Sufi (*faqīr*).[11] Ibn Ṭalḥa is said to have later renounced such interests and composed the following verses in retrospect:

---

7 Tāj al-Dīn al-Subkī, *Ṭabaqāt al-Shāfiʿiyya al-kubrā*, 6 vols. (Beirut, 1999), vol. 4, pp. 272–273; al-Ṣafadī, *al-Wāfī bi-al-wafayāt*, 29 vols. (Beirut, 2000), vol. 3, p. 146; Abū Shāma, *al-Dhayl ʿalā al-rawḍatayn* (Beirut, 1974), p. 188; al-Yāfiʿī, *Mirʾāt al-jinān*, 4 vols. (Beirut, 1997), vol. 4, pp. 99–100; Ibn Taghrībirdī, *al-Nujūm al-zāhirah*, 16 vols. (Beirut, 1992), vol. 7, p. 30.

8 Stephen Humphreys mentioned that Ibn Ṭalḥa was the preacher of the Umayayd mosque in *From Saladin to the Mongols: The Ayyubids of Damascus, 1193–1260* (Albany, 1977), p. 247. Ibn Taghrībirdī, *Nujūm*, vol. 17, p. 30 uses *muftī* to describe Ibn Ṭalḥa.

9 In 648/1250 al-Nāṣir Yūsuf entered Damascus during a politically volatile situation in Egypt and Syria; Humphreys, *From Saladin to the Mongols*, p. 306.

10 During the Mamluk period, this "science that had formerly been the reserve of small and discreet communities of practitioners" was now being made available to a "much wider audience of literate and devout readers, as well as Turkish military-political elites" in Noah Gardiner, "The Occultist Encyclopedism of ʿAbd Al-Raḥmān Al-Bisṭāmī" (The Middle East Documentation Center (MEDOC), 2017), p. 29. For a comprehensive study that covers various aspects of Ibn Ṭalḥa's occultism refer to A.C.S. Peacock, "Politics, Religion and the Occult in the Works of Kamal Al-Din Ibn Talha, a Vizier, ʿAlim and Author in Thirteenth-Century Syria," in *Syria in Crusader Times: Conflict and Coexistence*, ed. Carole Hillenbrand (Edinburgh, 2020), pp. 34–60.

11 al-Yāfiʿī gives a detailed account of this in *Mirʾāt al-jinān*, vol. 4, p. 99.

> Never trust the prediction of an astrologer; all matters are attributed to God
> A true Muslim should not suppose that planets could influence the occurrence of events.[12]

Advice literature was also one of Ibn Ṭalḥa's fields of enquiry. He dedicated the same political treatise to two different rulers under different titles.[13] Ibn Ṭalḥa dedicated *Nafāʾis al-ʿanāṣir li-majālis al-Malik al-Nāṣir* (Precious subjects for the council of al-Malik al-Nāṣir) to the Ayyubid sultan al-Nāṣir Ṣalāḥ al-Dīn Yūsuf and later as *al-ʿIqd al-farīd li-al-malik al-saʿīd* (The unique necklace for a content king) to the Artuqid ruler of Mardin, al-Saʿīd Najm al-Dīn Ghāzī (r. 637/1239–658/1260). As clearly established by Andrew Peacock, these two treatises were nearly identical except for some minor differences such as the dedicatee's name and one passage in the *Nafāʾis* hailing sultan al-Nāṣir's victory over the Khwarazmians in 644/1246.[14] Peacock also noted that it "was as *al-ʿIqd al-farid* that the work became popular, surviving in numerous manuscripts".[15] *Nafāʾis al-ʿanāṣir* clearly predated *al-ʿIqd al-farīd* as Ibn Ṭalḥa did not trouble himself with removing the Ayyubid sultan's name from the copy he dedicated later to the Artuqid ruler where, for instance, he interestingly discussed the merit of the Ayyubid sultan's first name, Yūsuf, using the numerical values of letters.[16]

Some aspects of Ibn Ṭalḥa's professional and spatial mobility can be discerned even before attempting to examine the political thought in his treatise. Firstly, these above-mentioned two versions of the same work reflect that Ibn Ṭalḥa was a professional statesman content to serve two different dynasties, the Ayyubids and Artuqids; that is in addition to what is known about him mediating between different Ayyubid potentates.[17] Secondly, he was a professional courtier who authored works of political advice and other subjects such as the numerical value of letters both to instruct and entertain his different patrons at their courts. Thirdly, the extent of the author's spatial

12 Ibn Ṭalḥa, *al-ʿIqd al-farīd li-al-malik al-Saʿīd*, ed. Yūsuf bin ʿUthmān al-Ḥazīm (Riyadh: Ibn al-Azraq center for political studies, 2013), p. 21.

13 Peacock, "Politics, Religion and the Occult", p. 43.

14 Ibid., p. 43.

15 Ibid., p. 43. Peacock also complained of the unsatisfactory state of available editions; the edition I used was unsatisfactory and confusing with no serious effort to ascertain the dedicatee's identity.

16 Refer to Ibn Ṭalḥa, *al-ʿIqd al-farīd*, p. 328 and pp. 340–341. This suggests that the author renounced his interest in *ʿilm al-ḥurūf* after dedicating the book to two rulers or – probably – that he never did renounce it.

17 Peacock, "Politics, Religion and the Occult," p. 34.

mobility was rather limited and concentrated geographically in relative proximity to his Syrian hometown Nuṣaybīn, as he moved between Aleppo, Damascus, and Mardin.

Yet the principal question this article seeks to answer is whether Ibn Ṭalḥa's professional mobility influenced his political thought. I argue that the author's background of judge, Shāfiʿī jurist, staunch Ashʿarī-Sufi, statesman and courtier of Ayyubid and Artuqid polities, *khaṭīb*, and occultist influenced the thematic and stylistic features of his political treatise. This intricate professional and intellectual background was reflected in the variety of subjects that were covered in *al-ʿIqd al-farīd* (or *Nafāʾis al-ʿanāṣir*), which attested to the elaboration, during the late Ayyubid period, of a blended genre for works of political advice. Ibn Ṭalḥa's treatise merged classical legalistic discussions, such as al-Māwardī's (364/974–450/1058) *al-Aḥkām al-sulṭāniyya*, with other genres of advice literature including: administrative and statecraft handbooks such as al-Shayzarī's (d. 589/1193) *al-Nahj al-maslūk fī siyāsat al-mulūk* dedicated to Ṣalāḥ al-Dīn (532/1138–589/1193); mirrors for princes, such Ibn al-Ḥaddād's *al-Jawhar al-nafīs fī siyāsat al-raʾīs* dedicated to Badr al-Dīn Luʾluʾ (r. 631/1234–657/1259), ruler of Mosul; Sufi political treatises such as the anonymous *Miṣbāḥ al-hidāya fī ṭarīq al-imāma*, which was probably dedicated to al-Ẓāhir Baybars (r. 658/1260–676/1277); ethical and homiletic writings, such as al-Māwardī's *Tashīl al-naẓar wa taʿjīl al-ẓafar fi akhlāq al-malik wa-siyāsat al-mulk* and his *Adab al-dunyā wa-al-dīn*, and the anonymous *Baḥr al-fawāʾid*, composed in mid-twelfth-century Syria; and other forms of courtly didactic works, such as Ibn al-Waḥīd's (647/1249 or 50–711/1311 or 12) *al-Urjūza al-maʿrūfa bi-Niṣf al-ʿaysh fī tadbīr hādhihi al-ḥayāt* dedicated to al-Ashraf Khalīl Ibn Qalāwūn (r. 689/1290–693/1293).[18] In a nutshell, Ibn Ṭalḥa attempted to synthesise in one treatise what al-Māwardī had expressed in different works that treated the origins of political authority, the duties and rights of a ruler, senior administrative functions, and the virtues that a ruler should possess. Additionally, Ibn Ṭalḥa, aimed to entertain at court and impress his dedicatee using his knowledge of the numerical values of letters. Peacock spotted aspects of this amalgamation in Ibn Ṭalḥa's work and noted

> To a degree then, one may see Ibn Talha's project as successfully weaving together two disparate strands in the Mirrors for Princes tradition,

18 Such categorisations are in no way mutually exclusive and only serve to illustrate aspects of Ibn Ṭalḥa's blending of genres. For more on some of the treatises mentioned here and the limitations of these classifications, refer to the seminal article by Louise Marlow, "Advice and advice literature," *Encyclopaedia of Islam THREE*.

> the more homiletic, religiously motivated works with the legalistic and normative.[19]

The chapterisation of *al-ʿIqd al-farīd* mirrored Ibn Ṭalḥa's professional mobility and his amalgamation of literary genres of advice literature. The author divided his work into four main "foundations" (*qawāʿid*), the content of which resembled a mirror for princes, followed by a juristic political treatise, an administrative manual spreading over the second and third foundations, and finally an addendum:[20]

1. Noble character and attributes (*al-akhlāq wa-al-ṣifāt*)
2. The sultanate and [the main] functions (*al-salṭana wa-al-wilāyāt*)
3. Law and religious matters (*al-sharīʿa wa-al-diyānāt*)
4. An addendum consisting of assorted themes

This structure secured the treatment of nearly all themes of Islamic advice literature including: the virtues and temperament of the ruler often found in mirrors for princes authored by Ashʿarī-Sufis; followed by a discussion of the constitutional, legal, and religious foundations of the sultanate typical of juridical treatises of Shāfiʿī jurists; the main administrative and religious offices found in statecraft manuals of Ayyubid statesmen and judges; and lastly a selection of anecdotes that resembled mere *adab* works and aimed to instruct and entertain the ruler and his court, and reflect the author's varied literary and administrative proficiencies, and his occultism.

The first section (foundation) of *al-ʿIqd al-farīd* reads like works that are commonly referred to as mirrors for princes. This is manifest in this section's structure, content, and sources and the author's ideological influences. In terms of structure, the first foundation resembled a standalone mirror featuring the usual ten sub-sections as per the customary literary practice of the time.[21] Ibn

---

19 Peacock, "Politics, Religion and the Occult", p. 54.

20 Ibn Ṭalḥa, *al-ʿIqd al-farīd*, p. 28.

21 Louise Marlow noted that similar works of advice literature displayed "expected" and "generic" features that included the use of stylistic techniques like rhyming prose or pairing of synonymous words, systematic gathering from anthologies, and most noticeably the common use of ten chapters divided by usual themes; in "The Way of Viziers and Lamp of Commanders (Minhāj Al-Wuzarāʾ Wa Sirāj Al-Umarāʾ) of Aḥmad Al-Iṣfahbādhī and the Literary and Political Culture of Early Fourteen-Century Iran," in *Writers and Rulers: Perspectives on Their Relationship from Abbasid to Safavid Times*, ed. Beatrice Gruendler and Louise Marlow (Wiesbaden, 2004), pp. 177–184. For a relevant discussion on Anatolia, refer to A.C.S. Peacock, "Advice for the Sultans of Rum: The 'Mirrors for Princes' of Early Thirteenth-Century Anatolia," in *Turkish Language, Literature, and History: Travelers' Tales, Sultans, and Scholars since the Eighth Century*, ed. Bill Hickman, Gary Leiser, and Robert Dankoff (Routledge, 2016) pp. 276–307.

Ṭalḥa thus adhered to the global tradition of Islamic advice literature of the thirteenth and fourteenth centuries and treated its expected themes including the merits of justice, consultation, liberality, and moderation. Furthermore, the mirror for princes embedded in *al-ʿIqd al-farīd* is edifying with regard to Ibn Ṭalḥa's sources and his professional, theological, and intellectual background. It confirms that he was an *adab*ised jurist who relished writing in high chancery language and that he was acquainted with court interests and etiquette. This section also reflects that he was an ardent Ashʿarī, Shāfiʿī, and Sufi, as is evident from his sources and deployment of some parables and discussions. For instance, Ibn Ṭalḥa's Sufism and Ashʿarism were evident when he quoted al-Qushayrī (d. 465/1072) and included a creedal paragraph laden with anti-anthropomorphism evocative of the Shāfiʿī-Ashʿarī rhetoric that was directed against traditionalist-Ḥanbalīs in thirteenth century Damascus.[22] In terms of sources, the indications that Ibn Ṭalḥa benefited from al-Māwardī's works are easy to discern. To name one, *al-ʿIqd al-farīd*'s first sub-section on reason (*ʿaql*), in its treatment of instinctive and acquired reason, relied on the first section of al-Māwardī's *Adab al-dunyā* entitled "Regarding the merits of reason and the dispraise of passion".[23]

Following the mirror-like part of *al-ʿIqd al-farīd*, Ibn Ṭalḥa went on to treat the sultanate. The second section (foundation) resembled, structurally and thematically, classical juristic and constitutional treatises, although with a strong Sufi flavour. Ibn Ṭalḥa divided it into two sub-sections as follows:[24]

- The sultanate, the qualities of the chosen sultan, and what is required to uphold its provisions
- The [principal] offices that administer the realm and control the affairs of the state, and the description of various supervisory ranks

Like juristic treatises, the second section started with an extensive discussion on the need for the sultanate. The first sub-section listed several rationalisations for the sultanate that stressed the divine legitimacy of the sultan. Ibn Ṭalḥa stated that: the sultanate was a divine secret (*sirr min asrār al-rubūbiyya*);

---

22 For al-Qushayrī's quotations refer to Ibn Ṭalḥa, *al-ʿIqd al-farīd*, p. 71. For more on the debate on divine attributes and its context see to al-Subkī, *Ṭabaqāt al-Shāfiʿiyya al-kubrā*, vol. 4, 6 vols. (Beirut: Dār al-Kutub al-ʿIlmiyya, 1999), pp. 360–368 for a case against anthropomorphism; Konrad Hirschler, "Pre-Eighteenth-Century Traditions of Revivalism: Damascus in the Thirteenth Century," *Bulletin of the School of Oriental and African Studies* 68, no. 2 (2005), p. 197, 201, 202, and 213; George Makdisi, "Ashʿarī and the Ashʿarites in Islamic Religious History I," *Studia Islamica* 17 (1962): 44–67; and Louis Pouzet, *Damas au VIIe–XIIIe siècle: vie et structures religieuses d'une métropole islamique*, 2 (Beyrouth: Dar el-Machreq, 1991), pp. 88–93.

23 Al-Māwardī, *Adab al-dunyā wa-al-dīn*, pp. 6–33.

24 Ibn Ṭalḥa, *al-ʿIqd al-farīd*, pp. 231–276.

the sultan was needed to "tend to the people of God, protect the land of God, guard the religion of God, uphold the legal punishments (*ḥudūd*) of God, and safeguard the laws of God"; the sultan was sanctioned (*irṭaḍāhu*) by God for this task and, as such, total obedience was due to him; and he was the reflection of God on earth.[25] The sultan thus became a necessity, since without him, the author explained, there was no safety, no ritual prayer, no cultivation of land, no trade, no craftsmanship and no transmission of knowledge.[26] In return, God required the sultan to uphold the true creed and the rightful Sufi way (*ṭarīqa*), maintain virtuous conduct, achieve honorable deeds, and be effective and dedicated in carrying out his duties.[27]

Ibn Ṭalḥa then discussed the qualities of the chosen sultan and listed the traits that must be avoided. This discussion and, more generally, the ethical system proposed by *al-ʿIqd al-farīd* were influenced by works on ethical qualities including al-Māwardī's *Tashīl al-naẓar*.[28] Arrogance (*kibar*), pride (*ʿajab*), vanity (*ghurūr*), avarice (*shiḥḥ*), and deceit (*kadhib*) were five dangerous attributes that the sultan should avoid. There were very similar discussions in the *Tashīl*, especially on arrogance and pride. Furthermore, Ibn Ṭalḥa mentioned the need for the sultan to be a careful listener, measure his words, avoid rage and obstinacy, be discreet, allot and manage his time efficiently, and use capable aides and deputies, in addition to further advice, some of which seemed to derive verbatim from the *Tashīl*.[29]

The influence of ethical works like the *Tashīl* on *al-ʿIqd al-farīd* made perfect sense. Although Ibn Ṭalḥa imitated the thematic and stylistic features of juristic treatises, the essence of his conception and legitimation of supreme Islamic political authority was Sufi. This was evident in *al-ʿIqd al-farīd*'s original treatment of the sultan's ten duties, which resembled al-Māwardī's *Aḥkām* yet echoed the concerns of mirrors for princes and works of Sufi political

25 Ibid., pp. 235–236. I use reflection instead of shadow as a more meaningful translation that was suggested to me by Suzanne Ruggi.

26 Ibid., p. 236.

27 Ibid., p. 236. Ibn Ṭalḥa proclaims subsequently that the sultan is the vice-regent of God (see pp. 246 and 248).

28 The five traits are discussed in Ibn Ṭalḥa, *al-ʿIqd al-farīd*, pp. 238–242. Refer to al-Māwardī, *Tashīl al-naẓar wa taʿjīl al-ẓafar fī akhlāq al-malik wa-siyāsat al-mulk* (Beirut, 1981), pp. 50–52 where al-Māwardī treated arrogance (*kibar*) and pride (*ʿajab*). For further similar discussions refer to pp. 67–70 and pp. 112–114.

29 Ibn Ṭalḥa, *al-ʿIqd al-farīd*, p. 242. For more similarities with al-Māwardī refer to *Tashīl al-naẓar* for a discussion on rage pp. 72–73, obstinacy p. 75, and especially on the merits of being discreet pp. 89–93 where it seems that Ibn Ṭalḥa benefited from the *Tashīl*. Ibn Ṭalḥa resorted to thematic treatment and made it difficult to spot this reuse, as it was not always verbatim. It is also possible that both works benefited from the same sources.

ethics.[30] As such, the treatment of the ten duties mirrored Ibn Ṭalḥa's life and career since elements of his background as a statesman, jurist, judge, Sufi, and courtier marked his list.[31] This is manifest in that Ibn Ṭalḥa does not refer to the list as ten "duties", but rather as ten "matters" that required the sultan's attention as they were "pivotal" to running the realm.[32] Furthermore, the longevity of the sultanate appeared to be one of the author's main concerns; Ibn Ṭalḥa stated that should the sultan observe these rules (*uṣūl*) in his various decisions, he would secure the preservation of his dominion (*ḥamā ḥawzat mamlakatihi*).[33] Ibn Ṭalḥa's discussion also reflected a tendency to assert additional sultanic powers in the judicial sphere by upholding the roles of *siyāsa* and *maẓālim* courts, as the third duty called for the need for swift sultanic justice in the realm. Most noticeably, Ibn Ṭalḥa reinforced the divine origin of the sultan's legitimacy by mentioning that the sultan "was bequeathed by God the bliss of the sultanate", was God's "deputy in protecting the realm and attending to the people", and was the vice-regent of God (*inna al-sulṭān nā'ib-Allāh fī khalīqatihi*).[34] In summary, Ibn Ṭalḥa's treatment of the ten duties of the ruler was quite unique since it transformed a classical juristic discussion that was supposed to remind the sultan of his duties into one that reinforced his divine rights, political and judicial powers, and aimed to prolong his rule.

The administrative manual spreads over the second and third sections (foundations) of *al-ʿIqd al-farīd*. Al-Māwardī's works strongly influenced these sections, but careful adaptations made by Ibn Ṭalḥa reflect his background in the administration of two Military Patronage States. He first treated the principal functions (*wilāyāt*) of the state in the second sub-section of the second foundation.[35] Ibn Ṭalḥa discussed five ranks of appointments: viziers, the chancery of the state (*al-inshā'*), the inspectorate of the army (*dīwān al-jaysh*), the state treasury (*dīwān al-amwāl*), and the rest of the sultan's retinue. The discussion of the etymology of *wizāra* (vizierate) pointed clearly to al-Māwardī's *Qawānin al-wizāra* and, more significantly, the *Aḥkām*.[36] Likewise,

30 I am not suggesting in any way whatsoever that Sufi and jurist conflict. The two authors covered in this article are both jurists and Sufis. For more on the overlap between Sufis and jurists, refer to the seminal work of Nathan Hofer, *The Popularisation of Sufism in Ayyubid and Mamluk Egypt, 1173–1325* (Edinburgh, 2015).

31 Ibn Ṭalḥa, *al-ʿIqd al-farīd*, pp. 246–248.

32 Ibn Ṭalḥa mentioned "*madār quṭb al-salṭana*" in *al-ʿIqd al-farīd*, p. 246; for the full discussion see pp. 246–248.

33 Ibid., p. 248.

34 Ibid., pp. 246 and 248.

35 Ibid., p. 251.

36 Ibid., pp. 248–253. Refer to al-Māwardī, *Qawānin al-wizāra wa siyāsat al-mulk* (Beirut, 1979), pp. 137–138 and *al-Aḥkām al-sulṭāniyya wa-al-wilāyāt al-dīnīyya*, 2 vols. (Kuwait,

this influence was manifest in the discussion of the vizierate of full delegation (*wizārat al-tafwīḍ*) and special delegation (*al-tanfīdh*), where Ibn Ṭalḥa adapted the relevant text of al-Māwardī's *Aḥkām* to the Ayyubid and Artuqid contexts by removing any reference to the *imām* or caliph and restricting the discussion to the sultan.[37] Similarly, Ibn Ṭalḥa's discussion of the army's *dīwān* was based on passages from al-Māwardī's *Aḥkām*.[38] As for the author's interest in *dīwān al-inshāʾ*, it reflected his personal administrative background and his adherence to the writing style of the chancery, as is manifest throughout the treatise.

The third section (foundation) treated *sharīʿa*-related appointments and was, accordingly, a continuation of the administrative manual within *al-ʿIqd al-farīd*. Ibn Ṭalḥa, himself a Shāfiʿī jurist and judge in his Syrian hometown Nuṣaybīn, delimited the scope of four religious functions: the muftiship (*fityā*), judgeship (*qaḍāʾ*), market inspection (*ḥisba*), and supervision of charitable endowments (*wilāyat al-awqāf*).[39] As the author explained, this section covered the necessary qualifications for appointees to the above-mentioned offices.[40] Similarly, this section clarified the scope of each of these functions and Ibn Ṭalḥa even narrated, in the case of the *qaḍāʾ*, ten relevant anecdotes from the ʿAbbāsid era that exemplified the finest conduct of judges.

The fourth and final section (foundation) of *al-ʿIqd al-farīd* is an *addendum* authored by Ibn Ṭalḥa the courtier, *adīb*, and occultist. It reads like a work of *adab* designed to educate, benefit, and entertain at court and impress the dedicatee.[41] In this section, Ibn Ṭalḥa included uncomplicated problems of mathematics, fiddly legal cases, and an assortment of prayers (*duʿāʾ*) for his dedicatee, which he introduced in the rhyming prose used by chancery secretaries.[42] The author included, moreover, an additional collection of aphorisms and parables that related to earlier caliphs on the need to be just, the need to accept and seek advice, the need to abide by the teachings of the Qurʾān, and the need to fear God, and highlighted the merits of self-restraint, honesty, equability, piety, compassion, and accountability.[43] Throughout this

1989), vol. 2, pp. 30–31. For instance, note the commonality in relating caliph al-Ma'mūn's criteria for selecting his vizier.

37 Refer to Ibn Ṭalḥa, *al-ʿIqd al-farīd*, pp. 254–256 and al-Māwardī, *Aḥkām*, vol. 2, pp. 34–35.

38 Ibn Ṭalḥa, *al-ʿIqd al-farīd*, pp. 264–270 and al-Māwardī's *Aḥkām*, vol. 2, pp. 259–284.

39 Ibn Ṭalḥa, *al-ʿIqd al-farīd*, pp. 279–306. There are verbatim similarities with Ibn Jamāʿa's *Taḥrīr* here that will be discussed subsequently.

40 Ibid., p. 280.

41 Peacock considered it as the "most distinctive section of *al-ʿIqd al-farid*" in "Politics, Religion and the Occult", p. 49.

42 Ibn Ṭalḥa, *al-ʿIqd al-farīd*, pp. 342–346.

43 Ibid., pp. 347–365.

section, Ibn Ṭalḥa left some strong clues as to his occultism, such as the above-mentioned use of numerical values of letters to highlight the merits of sultan al-Nāṣir's first name, Yūsuf.[44]

Ibn Ṭalḥa's professional mobility and varied intellectual interests were reflected in *al-ʿIqd al-farīd* (and consequently *Nafāʾis al-ʿanāṣir*) in a mixed genre that merged classical normative treatises with other modes of advice literature, including mirrors for princes, administrative and statecraft manuals, Sufi and ethical writings, and homiletic works. On the one hand, Ibn Ṭalḥa treated themes of advice literature often stressed in mirrors for princes, and Sufi and ethical writings including justice, consultation, forbearance, compassion, and generosity; the author even upheld the mirrors' concern for the longevity of his patron's reign and their entertaining *adab* style, which was strengthened by his occultism. On the other hand, *al-ʿIqd al-farīd* reflected the concern of juridical treatises for the need for the sultan, his duties, the origin of his authority, and its limitations, albeit with a strong Sufi flavour. The fusion of genres was equally apparent in the administrative themes that *al-ʿIqd al-farīd* treated, like the ranks of main offices, their jurisdiction, and the qualities required of their appointees. This fusion may account for why *al-ʿIqd al-farīd* was such a popular work, influencing later thinkers in style and content including Ibn Jamāʿa.

3 Ibn Jamāʿa

The second case study examines the political thought of Mamluk-period Syrian jurist Badr al-Dīn Ibn Jamāʿa as expressed in his three extant and consecutive political treatises. It highlights the effect of Ibn Jamāʿa's professional mobility and personal scholarly interests on molding his views on government and authority. The study traces the author's changing conceptions of the functions of caliph and sultan throughout his different appointments in prominent offices before, during, and after the reign of the Mamluk sultan al-Ashraf Khalīl Ibn Qalāwūn (r. 689/1290–693/1293). Similar to Ibn Ṭalḥa's case, the political treatises of Ibn Jamāʿa will be examined in tandem with his career as a Shāfiʿī-Ashʿarī jurist, chief Sufi, chief judge, statesman trusted by the Mamluk ruling elite, and holder of other administrative offices.

44 Refer to footnote 16 above.

Ibn Jamāʿa was forty-seven years of age when he received his first important appointment as *khaṭīb* of the Aqṣā Mosque of Jerusalem in 687/1288.[45] This belated and major breakthrough came after he had befriended the powerful Mamluk *amīr* ʿAlam al-Dīn Sanjar al-Dawadārī (d. 699/1300) and the ambitious bureaucrat Shams al-Dīn Ibn al-Salʿūs (d. 693/1294). When the latter became vizier of sultan al-Ashraf Khalīl Ibn Qalāwūn, he swiftly appointed Ibn Jamāʿa in 690/1291 as chief judge in Cairo, albeit in questionable circumstances.[46] The remarkable favours of these two influential supporters continued as Ibn Jamāʿa was appointed to the prestigious *khuṭba* (Friday prayer sermon) of al-Azhar Mosque, the professorship of the Ṣāliḥiyya school, and the post of chief Sufi (*shaykh al-shuyūkh*). He was also given the *khuṭba* of the Citadel Mosque, which signalled his trustworthiness amongst the Mamluks.

Despite his proximity to the ruling circles, Ibn Jamāʿa often succeeded in disentangling his career from political changes at the top.[47] His career displayed an extraordinary resilience to perilous setbacks triggered by competition among Mamluk households. When his patron and friend Ibn al-Salʿūs died under torture following the assassination of sultan al-Ashraf Khalīl, Ibn Jamāʿa was removed from the chief judgeship in Cairo but succeeded in preserving his professorship. Ibn Jamāʿa quickly gained the favour of the new regime and was appointed chief judge of Damascus and, in 694/1295, *khaṭīb* of the Umayyad Mosque. Subsequently when sultan al-Manṣūr Lājīn (r. 696/1296–698/1299) assumed power, Ibn Jamāʿa lost the chief judgeship but retained the *khuṭba* in Damascus and the professorship of the Qaymariyya *madrasa*, which he was to keep for the next three consecutive years. Moreover, his career outlived the Il-Khānid victory over the Mamluks at Wādī al-Khaznadār in 699/1299; after playing a leading role in negotiating the safety of the Damascene populace with Il-Khān Ghāzān (r. 694/1295–713/1304), Ibn Jamāʿa was reinstated in 699/1299 by the Mamluks as chief judge of Damascus and *khaṭīb* of the Grand Mosque in 699/1300.[48] His career continued to flourish in Damascus and in 701/1301 the Sufis of the Sumaysāṭī Sufi hospice (*khānqāh*) appointed him as their chief. This led the Syrian historian Ibn Kathīr (c. 700/1300–774/1373) to

45 The summary of Ibn Jamāʿa's life is drawn from Mohamad El-Merheb, *Ibn Jamāʿa and Family, Encyclopaedia of Islam THREE*.

46 Ibid.

47 Ibid.

48 Ibn al-Dawādārī mentioned that Ibn Jamāʿa was one of the leaders of the delegation that met Ghāzān in *Kanz al-durar wa-Jāmiʿ al-ghurar*, 9 vols. (Cairo, 1960), vol. 9, p. 19. Refer also to al-Yūnīnī, *Dhayl mirʾāt al-zamān*, 3 vols. (Abu Dhabi, 2007) vol. 1, pp. 253–254.

note, rather enviously, that only Ibn Jamāʿa managed to hold the positions of chief judge, *khaṭīb*, and chief Sufi in Damascus simultaneously.[49]

Following his appointment as chief judge in Cairo in 702/1302, Ibn Jamāʿa's Egyptian career similarly displayed success and resilience in parallel. This renewed proximity to the main centre of Mamluk power brought him closer to the dangers of political scheming, especially during the period between the second and third reigns of sultan al-Nāṣir Muḥammad (r. 693/1293–694/1294, 698/1299–708/1309, and 709/1310–741/1341). In these perilous times, Ibn Jamāʿa initially survived and benefitted from the assumption of the sultanate by Baybars al-Jāshankīr (r. 708/1308–709/1309), since he retained his judgeship and was appointed to supervise Cairo's important *khānqāh* of Saʿīd al-Suʿadāʾ.[50] However, as soon as al-Nāṣir Muḥammad returned to power, Ibn Jamāʿa was reprimanded and in 710/1310 lost the chief judgeship of Cairo. Nevertheless, Ibn Jamāʿa survived the wrath of the returning sultan and quickly regained his confidence. Under al-Nāṣir Muḥammad's third and long reign, Ibn Jamāʿa's career flourished for many of the remaining years of his life. In 711/1311, he was appointed to the chief judgeship, and several other teaching and administrative posts at various religious institutions.[51] Ibn Jamāʿa's power, prominence, and sway over the administrative apparatus of the Mamluk sultanate continued until his death in Cairo in 733/1333.

The study of this jurist's mobility has further uses for this volume. Beyond the connection between his political thought and professional mobility, Ibn Jamāʿa's career developed concurrently along different spatial, horizontal, and vertical axes as will be discussed below.[52] Spatially, his effective career started in Jerusalem and then oscillated between Cairo and Damascus, eventually ending in the former. Horizontally, Ibn Jamāʿa assumed judicial posts including the chief judgeship, administrative roles, various religious and educational jobs such as chief Sufi, *khaṭīb*, and professor, and other unofficial yet critical political missions such as mediating between competing Mamluk *amīrs*. Vertically, his career witnessed recurrent rises and falls that coincided with every major change at the seat of the sultanate and with his service to different patrons. Although these changes and movements could be the object of a dedicated

---

49 Ibn Kathīr, *al-Bidāya wa-al-nihāya*, 20 vols. (Damascus, 2010), vol. 16, pp. 13–14. The editor mentions the names of other jurists who later held the three posts together.

50 Al-Yūnīnī, *Dhayl mirʾāt al-zamān*, vol. 2, p. 1264; *Ibn Jamāʿa and Family*, EI3.

51 Al-Yūnīnī, *Dhayl mirʾāt al-zamān*, vol. 2, p. 1434; al-Suyūṭī, *Ḥusn al-muḥāḍara fī akhbār Miṣr wa-al-Qāhira*, 2 vols. (Cairo, 1968), vol. 2, p. 171; and al-ʿAynī, *ʿIqd al-jumān fī taʾrīkh ahl-al-zamān*, 5 vols. (Cairo, 2009), vol. 5, p. 249.

52 Spatial, horizontal, and vertical mobility as defined in the introductory chapter of this volume.

study, the present one is only concerned with the interrelatedness between the elaboration of Ibn Jamāʿa's political thought and his impressive professional mobility.

To investigate the impact of this mobility, one has to examine his three consecutive treatises in tandem with the progress of his career. While *Taḥrīr al-aḥkām fī tadbīr ahl-al-Islām* (Drafting ordinances towards running the affairs of the people of Islam) was Ibn Jamāʿa's main political treatise and contained his crystallised and all-encompassing political theory, it was the result of a sequence of hitherto unexplored political works, namely *Mustanad al-ajnād fī ālāt al-jihād* (The soldiers' guide to war engines) and *Mukhtaṣar fī faḍl al-jihād* (A compendium of the virtues of *jihād*).[53] A close examination of these three consecutive treatises shows that their sequence mirrors the progress of Ibn Jamāʿa's mobility in the judicial, educational, political, and administrative spheres of the Mamluk sultanate.

This sequence also reflects the cumulative elaboration of Ibn Jamāʿa's political thought. It indicates that his political thought was continuously evolving according to his empirical world, observations, and the ideas that he came across as he moved between various appointments in the Syro-Egyptian lands.[54] The first treatise, the *Mustanad*, comprised the beginnings of his ideas on government and an idealised Islamic political authority and was couched in a pseudo-military manual. In the second and more practical treatise, the *Mukhtaṣar*, Ibn Jamāʿa offered his vision of the sultan's rights and duties towards his subjects. The *Mukhtaṣar* was authored during Ibn Jamāʿa's service under Ibn al-Salʿūs and sultan al-Ashraf Khalīl Ibn Qalāwūn and, arguably, reflected his emerging conceptualisation of a legitimate sultanic authority. The third and final treatise, the *Taḥrīr*, was Ibn Jamāʿa's *magnum opus* and contained well-elaborated political thought. It resembled a proto-constitution that regulated various aspects of the process of running a government in any political contingency, but predominantly under a coercive and legitimate sultan.

The first treatise, the *Mustanad*, was a piece of *adab* that comprised very basic political theory and no beneficial military knowledge. It was an embryonic version of Ibn Jamāʿa's later political ideas and his self-imposed duties of

53 Ibn Jamāʿa, *Taḥrīr al-aḥkām fī tadbīr ahl-al-Islām*, ed. Fuʾād ʿAbd al-Munʿim Aḥmad (Qatar, 1985); this is the edition I used but others are available. The two other treatises are published in one edition: *Mustanad al-ajnād fī ālāt al-jihād wa-Mukhtaṣar fī faḍl al-jihād wa faḍāʾil al-ramī fī sabīl Allāh*, ed. Usāmah Nāṣir al-Naqshabandī (Damascus, 2008).

54 Here I also benefit from Skinner's advice to focus on "the writer's mental world, the world of his empirical beliefs" as a prerequisite to interpreting a political text in his seminal work, "Motives, Intentions and the Interpretation of Texts," *New Literary History* 3, no. 2 (1972), p. 407.

educating and benefiting, as an ordinary scholar holding no prominent official appointment. All the *Mustanad*'s discussions on topics such as weaponry, the involvement of Muslim women in battles, or the Prophet's horses were practically reproductions of anecdotes from the early Islamic conquests (*futūḥ*) genre. This treatise was far from a beneficial military manual that would be consulted by or bring any benefit to highly trained and elite soldiers like the Mamluks. Rather, the *Mustanad* was reminiscent of *furūsiyya* works from the ʿAbbāsid period.[55] This suggests the survival of this literary genre into the Mamluk period and, accordingly, the persistence of an earlier self-imposed duty of the *ʿulamāʾ* and Sufis, like Ibn Jamāʿa, to complement the ʿAbbāsid caliphal role in edifying new military elites. This genre emerged from within the ʿAbbāsid courtly concept of noble *furūsiyya* (*al-furūsiyya al-nabīla*), which was closely associated with the *futūwwa* movement.[56]

In the *Mustanad*, nonetheless, Ibn Jamāʿa briefly treated the theme of duties and rights of the ruler. The author's chief concern was justice (*ʿadl*) and his proposal to rulers was straightforward, just rule in exchange for obedience.[57] In a section of the *Mustanad* entitled, *Regarding the leaders of the community: caliphs, sulṭāns, and amīrs, their obligation* [*to act with*] *justice and their right in* [*commanding*] *obedience*, Ibn Jamāʿa discussed the duties and rights of the ruler as conceived by an ordinary scholar devoid of any major appointment or official rank.[58] He posited that the ideal Islamic ruler was required to attend to his subjects, protect Islamic lands, preserve faith, dispense justice, and uphold prescribed punishments (*ḥudūd*).[59] In exchange for upholding these duties, the ruler was entitled to obedience from his subjects, unless he was making

---

55 'Chivalry' and 'equestrian knowledge' are lacking as translations of the concept of *furūsiyya*. For a very useful study that makes a distinction between *furūsiyya* manuals and the wider *furūsiyya* literature and its roots, refer to Shihāb al-Ṣarrāf, "Mamluk Furūsīyah Literature and Its Antecedents," *Mamlūk Studies Review* 8, no. 1 (2004), p. 142. Other Mamluk *ʿulamāʾ* who wrote on *furūsiyya* included Ibn Qayyim al-Jawzīya, al-Sakhāwī, and al-Suyūṭī, on p. 153. For more on this topic, refer to Abbès Zouache, "Une culture en partage: la *furūsiyya* à l'épreuve du temps," *Médiévales* 64, 2013, pp. 57–75; and Mehdi Berriah, "Le cheval arabe chez les Mamelouks baḥriyya entre pragmatisme, symboles et représentations (XIIIe–XIVe siècles)," *Arabian Humanities* 8, April 2017 and "Représentations, sunnanisation et sacralisation de la furūsiyya à l'époque mamelouke (XIIIe–XVIe siècle)," Bulletin d'études orientales, Presses de l'Ifpo, Beyrouth, 2020, pp. 229–246.

56 Ibid., pp. 144–146.

57 "In his emphasis on justice, Ibn Jamāʿa's theory is in line with the literary theory put forward in many mirrors for princes and other literary works"; Ann K.S. Lambton, *State and Government in Medieval Islam: An Introduction to the Study of Islamic Political Theory: The Jurists* (Oxford: Oxford University Press, 1981), p. 140.

58 Ibn Jamāʿa, *Mustanad*, pp. 32–35.

59 Ibid., p. 33.

sinful decisions. The *Mustanad* employed well-known maxims very common in earlier works of Islamic political advice including "A single day of just rule by a just *imām* is superior to sixty years of [ritual] worship" and "No rank is higher than that of a just *sulṭān*, except that of a Prophet or favoured angel."[60] Ibn Jamāʿa developed further such basic political ideas in his subsequent treatises.

The second treatise, a milestone in this sequence, was the *Mukhtaṣar fī faḍl al-jihād* (A compendium of the virtues of *jihād*). It marked a major shift in Ibn Jamāʿa's conception of Islamic political authority, as he now postulated that the *imāmate* was accorded to the powerful and just sultan.[61] This study argues that it is no coincidence that this major transformation discerned in the *Mukhtaṣar*, which equates sultan with *imām*, followed the author's appointment by sultan al-Ashraf Khalīl and his vizier Ibn al-Salʿūs to the highest-level judicial, religious, and administrative roles. Unlike in the *Mustanad*, where references to the ruler could have applied to a caliph, sultan, or even an *amīr*, in the *Mukhtaṣar* the supreme political authority of Islam was now firmly bestowed on the sultan. Throughout the *Mukhtaṣar*, which was dedicated by Ibn Jamāʿa to his patrons on the occasion of the sultan's victories against the Crusader lordships, the author used the terms just *imām* (*al-ʿādil*) and sultan interchangeably while the function of the caliph was simply ignored.[62] To take just one example, this was unmistakable in the subsection to which he gave the title *Regarding the duties and rights of the sultan*; this showed that the fundamentals of Ibn Jamāʿa's conceptualisation of the sultanate as the highest political authority had more or less crystallised by the time he authored the *Mukhtaṣar*.[63]

The daily requirements of serving as chief justice dictated fundamental dispensations in the *Mukhtaṣar*. As a high-ranking official in the Mamluk sultanate who must have witnessed at firsthand the need for coercive power to enforce swift justice, Ibn Jamāʿa could no longer afford the theorisation of an idealistic scholar. Notwithstanding that the *Mukhtaṣar* (like its precursor the *Mustanad* and most works of Islamic political advice) reflected a prime concern for the ideal of justice (*ʿadl*) and restated the *dictum* of justice in exchange for obedience, order occasionally superseded justice and oppression was preferred to

---

60 Ibid. According to the editor of the *Mustanad* they are quoted from al-Ṭurṭūshī's (c. 451/1059–c. 520/1126) *Sirāj al-mulūk*. Ibn Jamāʿa would reiterate some of these maxims in the *Taḥrīr*; see Lambton, *State and Government*, p. 140.

61 Refer to Ibn Jamāʿa, *Mukhtaṣar*, pp. 101–103; the first section of the *Mukhtaṣar* entitled, *Regarding the sultan, his benevolence, and the esteem he acquires through justice*, equates the just *imām* with the sultan.

62 Ibn Jamāʿa, *Mukhtaṣar*, pp. 99–100.

63 Ibid., pp. 104–107.

chaos or vacuum.[64] The *Mukhtaṣar* explained that the sultan was bestowed upon his people by God to "manage their affairs (*siyāsatuhum*), protect them, uphold justice for the oppressed, deter the unjust among them, and this is why it was said 'forty years of tyrannical rule is preferable to [the affairs of] people being neglected for a single hour'".[65] This view resembled – and was rooted in – the works of earlier Shāfiʿī-Ashʿarī thinkers who held prominent offices, most notably al-Māwardī, al-Juwaynī, and al-Ghazālī, whose theological, legal, and political writings displayed paramount concern for the political, social, and religious continuity of the community.[66] This same concern for continuity would develop into a central tenet of Ibn Jamāʿa's theory.

The closing treatise of the trilogy was *Taḥrīr al-aḥkām fī tadbīr ahl-al-Islām* (Drafting ordinances towards running the affairs of the people of Islam). The *Taḥrīr* was a coherent and all-encompassing *summa* of Ibn Jamāʿa's political thought that resembled a proto-constitution of the state. It aimed at securing the running of the Mamluk sultanate and preserving the continuity of the state by guaranteeing delegation at the highest levels of political authority, setting criteria for selecting candidates for leading posts in the judiciary and administration, and regulating various other areas such as taxation, dispensing justice, or conducting war.[67] The *Taḥrīr* marked the final phase of a sequence of elaborations in Ibn Jamāʿa's political thought, which were moulded by his professional mobility between high-ranking offices, his role in political events, and his wide-ranging knowledge of various judicial and administrative branches of government. Although he completed this treatise under the third reign of al-Nāṣir Muḥammad, Ibn Jamāʿa did not dedicate the *Taḥrīr* to his generous patron specifically; he wanted it to be consulted by those who wished to benefit from it.[68]

---

64 Refer to footnote 57 above.

65 Ibn Jamāʿa, *Mukhtaṣar*, p. 101.

66 Erwin I.J. Rosenthal spotted some aspects of this influence in what he termed "the principle of acquiescence in bad rule"; refer to in *Political Thought in Medieval Islam: An Introductory Outline* (Cambridge, 1958), p. 44. The recent work of Sohaira Siddiqui, *An Intellectual Portrait of Al-Juwayni*, makes a direct link between epistemology and political thought thus highlighting the concern for continuity and political stability. Although this present study is not the place to treat this important theme in detail, it suffices to say that there existed deeper theological and legal roots behind what is often seen as mere justification of usurpation. Refer to footnote 3 above.

67 Refer to the titles of the seventeen chapters in Ibn Jamāʿa, *Taḥrīr*, pp. 46–47.

68 Ibid., p. 45; the *Taḥrīr* was dedicated to any ruler "who was entrusted by God the affairs of the Muslims, so he arranges his ordinances in the finest manner and the best arrangement, and strives in the finest manner for the interest of his subjects ..."

One of the main contributions of this treatise was its novel conception of supreme political authority.[69] In a departure from earlier juristic treatises, the *Tahrīr* distinguished between the functions of the *imām* and caliph, deemed it permissible for the sultan to be the *imām*, and accordingly ended the normative need for the caliphate. In his brief discussion of the coercive *imāmate* (*al-imāma al-qayriyya*), Ibn Jamāʿa postulated that the usurper or wielder of coercive power, i.e. the Mamluk sultan, could be the *imām* of the Muslims.[70] This differed drastically from al-Māwardī's *Ahkām* and other earlier juristic works in that the *Tahrīr* did not merely argue that the wielder of coercive power (the sultan) could be delegated the full authorities of the *imām*, that is the powerless yet still indispensable Qurashī caliph.[71] On the contrary, the *Tahrīr* asserted that the sultan *might be* the *imām* even in the presence of a caliph.[72] This was a theory that departed from classical treatises and resulted in major consequences for Islamic constitutional thought.

Effectively, the *Tahrīr* negated the need for the caliphate without calling for an end to it. Ibn Jamāʿa conceived of the *imāmate*, caliphate, and sultanate as three distinct functions; while the sultanate and *imāmate* were indispensable for the continuity of the state, the caliphate was not. In this conception and in order to preserve Muslim unity, Ibn Jamāʿa explained that it was legitimate for a sultan, as the holder of coercive military power (*ṣāḥib al-shawka*), to seize power and become *imām*.[73] If he does so, his *imāma* becomes effective and legitimate and obedience to him mandatory from all Muslims. The *Tahrīr* even added that in case the usurper did not possess knowledge (*ʿilm*) or was of questionable moral standing (*fāsiq*), his *imāma* was still valid and obedience was due to him.[74] Accordingly, any sultan lacking knowledge or Qurashī pedigree could legitimately and effectively hold the coercive *imāmate* (*qahriyya*). To prevent any ambiguity as to whether he was referring to the Mamluk sultan, Ibn Jamāʿa stated that the full delegation from *imām* to sultan, "was as per the custom of kings and sultans in our time" (*ka-ʿurf al-mulūk wa-al-salāṭīn fī zamāninā*).[75]

---

69 Ibid., pp. 48–57: *Fī wujūb al-imāma, wa shurūṭ al-imām wa aḥkāmuhu.* For relevant discussions refer to Lambton, *State and* Government, pp. 138–142 and Rosenthal, *Political Thought*, pp. 43–50.

70 Ibn Jamāʿa, *Taḥrīr*, p. 55.

71 For more on al-Māwardī refer to Lambton, *State and Government*, pp. 83–102 and Rosenthal, *Political Thought*, pp. 27–37.

72 This is in contradistinction with Lambton's interpretation who argued that Ibn Jamāʿa believed that the sultan might be the caliph; in Lambton, *State and Government*, p. 142.

73 Ibn Jamāʿa, *Taḥrīr*, p. 55.

74 Ibid.

75 Ibid., p. 60.

These sequential transformations in Ibn Jamāʿa's political thought, from the *Mustanad* to the *Tahrīr*, are better understood within the context of the author's professional mobility. Ibn Jamāʿa's service to various Mamluk sultans, his proximity to influential viziers and *amīrs*, his involvement as chief judge in the politics and competitions of Mamluk households, and his wide-ranging experience in various branches of government motivated him to revise his views on the sultanate, *imāmate*, and caliphate. Ibn Jamāʿa was dangerously close when al-Ashraf Khalīl was murdered and his patron and friend Ibn al-Salʿūs killed under torture. As chief judge in Cairo and Damascus, he was involved – voluntarily or not – in the removal of al-ʿĀdil Kītbughā from power, in attesting to the resignation of al-Nāṣir Muḥammad and the confirmation of Baybars al-Jāshankīr, and finally, in the confirmation of al-Nāṣir's third reign.[76] This highly varied career, which was full of rises, falls, and valuable political and constitutional experiences, greatly influenced Ibn Jamāʿa's political thought as can be traced throughout his three treatises the *Mustanad, Mukhtaṣar*, and *Taḥrīr*.

4 Concluding Remarks

Tracing the influence of professional mobility on political treatises challenges existing assumptions in the history of Islamic political thought and provides valuable proof as to the evolving nature of Islamic political theory. It reflects how authors like Ibn Ṭalḥa and Ibn Jamāʿa continuously transformed and adapted their postulations and the stylistic traits of their treatises based on intellectual principles and, additionally, empirical observations that became available to them due to their professional mobility. However, historians of Islamic political thought have rarely, if at all, traced such developments beyond religiosity and allegiance to the ruler. Fortunately, the wealth of biographical information available on Ibn Ṭalḥa and Ibn Jamāʿa and their extant treatises provide additional proof to support scholarly views, like that of the present article, that no longer consider Islamic political thought to be perennially centred on a limited set of themes such as the preservation of the caliphate, the duty of *jihād*, or the implementation of ritual prayer. Examining the development of the treatises of Ibn Ṭalḥa and Ibn Jamāʿa identifies a different cluster of predominant political concerns, which were focused on the proper functioning of the state and administration, dispensation of justice, moderation of

76 *Ibn Jamāʿa and Family*, EI3.

the ruler, stability of the regime, continuity and delegation, and just taxation and distribution of wealth.

The examination of the lives and careers of Ibn Ṭalḥa and Ibn Jamāʿa serve other purposes in the study of mobility. It shows the futility of framing professional mobility of pre-modern Islamic societies in just one of three basic patterns: horizontal, spatial, and vertical, as originally envisioned when this research project was first conceived.[77] Although Ibn Ṭalḥa's career was limited spatially to Syria for the most part, he served two different dynasties, the Ayyubids and Artuqids. Furthermore, the benefits of conceptualising mobility along a vertical axis are not so evident in the case of Ibn Ṭalḥa who voluntarily refused to assume the Ayyubid vizierate and decided instead to wander as a Sufi. Similarly, the life and career of Ibn Jamāʿa provides further proof of the widespread social and professional mobility throughout the Syro-Egyptian lands, which cannot be simply studied from one of three perspectives. Spatially, Ibn Jamāʿa moved between Jerusalem, Damascus, and Cairo, back to Damascus, and then back to Cairo for a long period until his death. Vertically, his career progressed upwards and downwards between professorship, chief judgeship, and Sufi chieftainship, at one point holding the three posts simultaneously. Furthermore, the vertical axis fails to fully gauge Ibn Jamāʿa's invisible sway over the administration, which was dictated by his proximity to the Mamluk elites. Horizontally, Ibn Jamāʿa's movement between the judicial, administrative, and educational spheres can be clearly defined unlike his role in the political sphere, which is not clearly understood, including his roles as mediator between various Mamluk contenders for power, and between them and the populace. There is still a long way to go to fully comprehend mobility in pre-modern Islamic societies, but hopefully this article makes a contribution towards this end.

Bibliography

Abū Shāma. *Tarājim rijāl al-qarnayn al-sādis wa-al-sābiʿ al-maʿrūf bi-al-dhayl ʿalā al-rawḍatayn.* Edited by ʿIzzat al-ʿAṭṭār al-Ḥusaynī. Beirut: Dār al-Jīl, 1974.

Al-ʿAynī. *ʿIqd al-jumān fī taʾrīkh ahl-al-zamān.* Edited by Muḥammad Muḥammad Amīn. 5 vols. Cairo: Dār al-Kutub wa-al-Wathāʾiq al-Qawmiyya, 2009.

Anjum, Ovamir. *Politics, Law and Community in Islamic Thought: The Taymiyyan Moment.* Cambridge Studies in Islamic Civilization. Cambridge/New York: Cambridge University Press, 2012.

77 Refer to the introduction chapter of this volume.

Bauer, Thomas. "Mamluk Literature: Misunderstandings and New Approaches." *Mamlūk Studies Review* 9, no. 2 (2005): 105–32.

Berriah, Mehdi. "Le cheval arabe chez les Mamelouks baḥriyya entre pragmatisme, symboles et représentations (XIIIe–XIVe siècles)." *Arabian Humanities*, April 2017. URL: http://journals.openedition.org/cy/3398; DOI: https://doi.org/10.4000/cy.3398.

Berriah, Mehdi. "Représentations, sunnanisation et sacralisation de la furūsiyya à l'époque mamelouke (XIIIe–XVIe siècle)", *Bulletin d'études orientales* (2020): 229–246.

Bori, Caterina. "The Collection and Edition of Ibn Taymīyah's Works: Concerns of a Disciple." *Mamlūk Studies Review* 13, no. 2 (2009): 47–67.

Bori, Caterina. "Théologie politique et Islam à propos d'Ibn Taymiyya (m. 728/1328) et du sultanat mamelouk." *Revue de l'histoire des religions*, no. 1 (2007): 5–46.

Chamberlain, Michael. *Knowledge and Social Practice in Medieval Damascus, 1190–1350*. Cambridge Studies in Islamic Civilization. Cambridge: Cambridge University Press, 1995.

El-Merheb, Mohamad. "Ibn Jamāʿa and Family." *Encyclopaedia of Islam, Three*, 2021.

Gardiner, Noah. "The Occultist Encyclopedism of ʿAbd Al-Raḥmān Al-Bisṭāmī." *The Middle East Documentation Center* (MEDOC), 2017.

Gilbert, Joan E. "Institutionalization of Muslim Scholarship and Professionalization of the ʿUlamaʾ in Medieval Damascus." *Studia Islamica* 52 (1980): 105–134.

Hirschler, Konrad. "Pre-Eighteenth-Century Traditions of Revivalism: Damascus in the Thirteenth Century." *Bulletin of the School of Oriental and African Studies* 68, no. 2 (2005): 195–214.

Hofer, Nathan. *The Popularisation of Sufism in Ayyubid and Mamluk Egypt, 1173–1325*. Edinburgh Studies in Classical Islamic History and Culture. Edinburgh: Edinburgh University Press, 2015.

Humphreys, R. Stephen. *From Saladin to the Mongols: The Ayyubids of Damascus, 1193–1260*. Albany: State University of New York Press, 1977.

Ibn al-Dawādārī. *Kanz al-durar wa-jāmiʿ al-ghurar*. 9 vols. Deutsches Archäologisches Institut, 1960.

Ibn Jamāʿa. *Mustanad al-ajnād fī ālāt al-jihād wa-mukhtaṣar fī faḍl al-jihād wa-faḍāʾil al-ramī fī sabīl Allāh*. Edited by Usāma Nāṣir al-Naqshbandī. Damascus: Dār al-Wathāʾiq li-al-Dirāsāt wa-al-Ṭabʿ wa-al-Nashr wa-al-Tawzīʿ, 2008.

Ibn Jamāʿa. *Taḥrīr al-aḥkām fī tadbīr ahl-al-Islām*. Edited by Fuʾād ʿAbd al-Munʿim Aḥmad. Qatar: Riʾāsat al-Maḥākim al-Sharʿiyya wa-al-Shuʾūn al-Dīniyya, 1985.

Ibn Kathīr. *Al-Bidāya wa-al-nihāya*. Edited by Muḥyī al-Dīn Dīb Mistū. 20 vols. in 11 vols. Damascus/Beirut: Dār Ibn Kathīr li-al-Ṭibāʿa wa-al-Nashr wa-al-Tawzīʿ, 2010.

Ibn Taghrībirdī. *Al-Nujūm al-zāhira fī mulūk Miṣr wa-al-Qāhira*. Edited by Muḥammad Ḥusayn Shams al-Dīn. 17 vols. Beirut: Dār al-Kutub al-ʿIlmiyya, 1992.

Ibn Ṭalḥa. *Al-ʿIqd al-farīd li-al-malik al-saʿīd*. Edited by Yūsuf bin ʿUthmān al-Ḥazīm. Riyadh: Ibn al-Azraq Center for Political Studies, 2013.

Lambton, A.K.S. *State and Government in Medieval Islam: An Introduction to the Study of Islamic Political Theory; the Jurists*. Reprinted. London Oriental Series 36. Oxford: Oxford University Press, 1981.

Makdisi, George. "Ashʿarī and the Ashʿarites in Islamic Religious History I." *Studia Islamica* 17 (1962): 37–80.

Marlow, Louise. "Advice and Advice Literature." *Encyclopaedia of Islam, Three*, 2007.

Marlow, Louise. "The Way of Viziers and Lamp of Commanders (Minhāj Al-Wuzarāʾ Wa Sirāj Al-Umarāʾ) of Aḥmad Al-Iṣfahbādhī and the Literary and Political Culture of Early Fourteen-Century Iran." In *Writers and Rulers: Perspectives on Their Relationship from Abbasid to Safavid Times*, edited by Beatrice Gruendler and Louise Marlow, 169–193. Literaturen Im Kontext 16. Wiesbaden: Reichert, 2004.

Al-Māwardī. *Adab al-dunyā wa-al-dīn*. Edited by Muḥammad Karīm Rājiḥ. Beirut: Dār Iqraʾ, 1985.

Al-Māwardī. *Kitāb al-aḥkām al-sulṭāniyya wa-al-wilāyāt al-dīniyya*. Edited by Aḥmad Mubārak al-Baghdādī. 2 vols. Kuwait: Dār Ibn Qutayba, 1989.

Al-Māwardī. *Qawānin al-wizāra wa-siyāsat al-mulk*. Edited by Raḍwān al-Sayyid. Beirut: Dār al-Ṭalīʿa, 1979.

Al-Māwardī. *Tashīl al-naẓar wa taʿjīl al-ẓafar fī akhlāq al-malik wa-siyāsat al-mulk*. Edited by Ḥasan al-Saʿātī and Muḥyī Hilāl al-Sarḥān. Beirut: Dār al-Nahḍa, 1981.

Mourad, Suleiman. "A Critique of the Scholarly Outlook of the Crusades: The Case for Tolerance and Coexistence." In *Syria in Crusader Times: Conflict and Coexistence*, edited by Carole Hillenbrand, 144–60. Edinburgh: Edinburgh University Press, 2020.

Peacock, A.C.S. "Advice for the Sultans of Rum: The 'Mirrors for Princes' of Early Thirteenth-Century Anatolia." In *Turkish Language, Literature, and History: Travelers' Tales, Sultans, and Scholars since the Eighth Century*, edited by Bill Hickman, Gary Leiser, and Robert Dankoff, 276–307. Routledge Studies in the History of Iran and Turkey. London: Routledge/Taylor & Francis Group, 2016.

Peacock, A.C.S. "Politics, Religion and the Occult in the Works of Kamal Al-Din Ibn Talha, a Vizier, 'Alim and Author in Thirteenth-Century Syria." In *Syria in Crusader Times: Conflict and Coexistence*, edited by Carole Hillenbrand, 34–60. Edinburgh: Edinburgh University Press, 2020.

Pouzet, Louis. *Damas au VIIᵉ–XIIIᵉ siècle: vie et structures religieuses d'une métropole islamique*. 2. ed. Recherches Nouvelle Série A, Langue arabe et pensée islamique 15. Beirut: Dār el-Machreq, 1991.

Rosenthal, Erwin I.J. *Political Thought in Medieval Islam: An Introductory Outline*. Cambridge: Cambridge University Press, 1958.

Al-Ṣafadī. *Al-Wāfī bi-al-wafayāt*. 29 vols. Beirut: Dār Iḥyāʾ al-Turāth al-ʿArabī, 2000.

Al-Ṣarrāf, Shihāb. "Mamluk Furūsīyah Literature and Its Antecedents." *Mamlūk Studies Review* 8, no. 1 (2004): 141–200.

Siddiqui, Sohaira Zahid. *Law and Politics under the Abbasids: An Intellectual Portrait of Al-Juwayni*. Cambridge Studies in Islamic Civilization. Cambridge, United Kingdom/New York, NY: Cambridge University Press, 2019.

Skinner, Quentin. "Motives, Intentions and the Interpretation of Texts." *New Literary History* 3, no. 2 (1972): 393–408.

Van Steenbergen, Jo. "The Mamluk Sultanate as a Military Patronage State: Household Politics and the Case of the Qalāwūnid bayt (1279–1382)." *Journal of the Economic and Social History of the Orient* 56, no. 2 (2013): 189–217.

Al-Subkī. *Ṭabaqāt al-Shāfiʿiyya al-kubrā*. Edited by Muṣṭafā ʿAbd al-Qādir Aḥmad ʿAṭā. 6 vols. Beirut: Dār al-Kutub al-ʿIlmiyya, 1999.

Al-Suyūṭī. *Ḥusn al-muḥāḍara fī akhbār miṣr wa-al-Qāhira*. Edited by Muḥammad Abū Faḍl Ibrāhīm. 2 vols. Cairo: Dār Iḥyāʾ al-Kutub al-ʿArabiyya, 1968.

Al-Yāfiʿī. *Mirʾāt al-jinān wa-ʿibrat al-yaqẓān fī maʿrifat mā yuʿtabar min ḥawādith al-zamān*. 4 vols. Beirut: Dār al-Kutub al-ʿIlmiyya, 1997.

Al-Yūnīnī. *Dhayl mirʾāt al-zamān*. Edited by Ḥamza Aḥmad ʿAbbās. 3 vols. Abū Dhabī: Hayʾat Abū Dhabī li-al-Thaqāfa wa-al-Turāth, al-Majmaʿ al-Thaqāfī, 2007.

Zouache, Abbès. "Une culture en partage: la *furūsiyya* à l'épreuve du temps." *Médiévales*, no. 64 (2013): 57–75.

Index

Page numbers in *italic* refer to figures and illustrations.

Abā Isḥāq al-Naṣībī 88n39
ʿAbbās I, Shāh of Persia 10
ʿAbbāsid Empire
Muslim scholars and
interaction between 16, 18
see also female scholars; al-Juwaynī, Imām al-Ḥaramayn
political power of 83, 86
see also under specific Caliphs
al-ʿAbbāssa (wife of Aḥmad b. Ḥanbal) 44
ʿAbd Allāh b. Aḥmad (b. Ismāʿīl b. ʿĪsā b. Aḥmad b. Ismāʿīl) b. Simāk al-ʿĀmilī, Abū Muḥammad 142
ʿAbd Allāh b. Aḥmad b. Qand al-Lughawī, al-Ṭayṭal, Abū Muḥammad 141
ʿAbd Allāh b. ʿAlī b. ʿAbd al-Malik b. Samajūn 138
ʿAbd Allāh b. al-Ḥasan, Ibn al-Sindī, Abū Muḥammad 140
ʿAbd Allāh b. Ibrāhīm al-ʿAṣīlī 138
ʿAbd Allāh b. Muḥammad b. al-Qāsim 138
ʿAbd Allāh b. Muḥammad al-Yūnīnī 114
ʿAbd Allāh b. Saʿīd b. ʿAbd Allāh (Muḥammad) al-Umawī, Ibn al-Shaqqāq, Abū Muḥammad 141
Abd Allāh b. ʿUmar b. Muḥammad Aqīt 56
ʿAbd al-ʿAẓīm b. Yazīd b. Yaḥyā b. Hishām al-Khawlānī 139
ʿAbd al-Ghanī b. Muḥammad b. ʿAbd al-Ghanī b. Salama b. Ḥakam al-Umawī al-Gharnāṭī 136
ʿAbd al-Ḥamīd al-Kātib 27n47, 32–33
ʿAbd al-Jabbār
Abū ʿAbdallāh al-Baṣrī and 81–82
Ashʿarism and 79
as judge (*qāḍī al-quḍāt*)
appointment of 82, 84, 87, 88–90
dating of appointment of 89n46
dismissal of 91–92
executive power and 90–91
Ibn ʿAbbād's death and 91
main responsibilities of 90
Muʿtazilism and 80–82, 87
professional mobility of
Baghdad 81
Baṣra 79–82
Hamadhān 79
inner circle of knowledge and 85–88
Iṣfahān 82
Rāmhurmuz 82
relation to power and 88–93
works of
Kitāb al-Mughnī fī abwāb al-tawḥīd wa-l-ʿadl 82
Mutashābih al-Qurʾan 81
ʿAbd al-Malik, Umayyad Caliph
in general 2
Qabīṣa b. Dhuʾayb and 19–20, 25–27, 35
on qualifications of tutor of his children 33
al-Zuhrī and 22–25, 28, 35
ʿAbd al-Raḥmān b. Ḥamdān al-Jallāb 79
ʿAbd al-Raḥmān b. Ibrāhīm b. Muḥammad, Ibn al-Sharafī 141
ʿAbd al-Raḥmān b. Muḥammad b. Aḥmad b. ʿUbayd Allāh al-Ruʿaynī, Ibn al-Mashshāṭ, Abū al-Muṭarrif 141
ʿAbd al-Raḥmān b. Muḥammad b. ʿĪsā b. Fuṭays b. Aṣbagh b. Fuṭays (ʿUthmān) b. Sulaymān 141
ʿAbd al-Raḥmān III, Caliph of Córdoba 137
ʿAbda bt. ʿAbd al-Raḥmān al-Anṣāriyya 44, 46
Abdāli Afghans 183
ʿAbdallāh b. Jaʿfar al-Iṣbahānī 79
ʿAbdallāh b. Thaʿlaba 29n58
ʿAbdolʿaẓim Shrine 197
al-Abīwardī, Abū Yaʿqūb 165–166
Abū al-ʿAbbās al-ʿUdusī 107
Abū ʿAbdallāh al-Baṣrī 80, 81–82, 86, 87, 88
Abū Aḥmad b. Salāma 80
Abū ʿAli b. Khallād 80
Abū al-Aṣbagh ʿĪsā b. Sahl 146
Abū Bakr b. Khalaf al-Anṣārī al-Faqīh, al-Mawwāq30 (al-Muwāfiq), Abū Yaḥyā 136, 137

Abū Bakr b. Muḥammad b. ʿAmr b. Ḥazm 29n57
Abū Bakr Muḥammad b. ʿAlī al-Qaffāl al-Shāshī 166
Abū Bakr Muḥammad b. Rāʾiq 83
Abū al-Faraj al-Iṣbahānī 18–19
Abū Ḥafṣ b. Salm 46
Abū al-Ḥasan ʿAlī b. Faḍl b. ʿAlī al-Majāshī 164
Abū Ḥayyān al-Tawḥīdī 86n33
Abū Ibrāhīm al-Turjumānī 43, 46
Abū Isḥāq b. ʿAyyāsh 80
Abū Isḥāq al-Isfarāʾīnī 167–168
Abū Muḥammad ʿAbdallāh b. ʿAbbās al-Rāmhurmuzī 82
Abū al-Qāsim al-Fūrānī 164, 166
Abū al-Qāsim al-Iskāf al-Isfarāʾīnī 163, 167, 168
Abū Sahl al-Muwaffaq 170
Abū Shujā 91
Abū Zaʿzaʿa 27
Abū Zurʿa 24n36
Abū-l-Ḥasan ʿAlī b. Ibrahīm b. Salāma al-Qaṭṭān 79
Adab al-dunyā wa dīn (al-Māwardī) 212
Adab al-qāḍī (al-Māwardī) 90
adab works 217, 221–222
*adab*isation 6, 207
al-ʿĀdil Kītbughā 226
ʿadl (justice) 223–224
administrative manuals 216–217
ʿAḍud al-Dawla 84
advice literature 208, 209, 211, 212–214, 218
  see also mirrors for princes
al-Afram 106, 109
Afrāsiāb (mythical king) 196
al-Aḥkām al-sulṭāniyya (al-Māwardī) 212, 215, 216–217
Aḥmad b. ʿAbd Allāh b. ʿAmīra al-Makhzūmī 139
Aḥmad b. ʿAbd Allāh b. Ghuṣn Abī Ṭālib b. Ṭālib v. Ziyād b. ʿAbd al-Ḥamīd b. al-Ṣabbāḥ b. Yazīd b. Ziyād b. Malīḥ b. Khayr al-Aṣbaḥī, Abū ʿAbd Allāh 140
Aḥmad b. Baqī b. Makhlad 137
Aḥmad b. Hanbal 159, 175–176
Aḥmad b. Ḥanbal, Muḥammad b. al-Ṣabbāḥ al-Jarajarāʾī 43
Aḥmad b. Muḥammad b. Ḥasan (al- Ḥasan) b. Muḥammad b. ʿAbd al-Raḥmān b. Saʿd b. Saʿīd b. Muḥammad al-Anṣārī al-Khazrajī al-Andalusī al-Qāḍī, Ibn al-Ghammāz, Abū al-ʿAbbās 148
Aḥmad Bābā al-Tinbuktī
  forced exile to Marrakech 55, 69
  legal responses of 69
  life and works of 54–55
  works of
    in general 67, 68, 69, 70
    Jalb al-niʿma wa-ḍafʿ al-niqma bi-mujānabat al-wulāt al-ẓalama 55, 71
    Kifāyat al-muḥtāj li-maʿrifat man laysa fī-l-Dībāj 54, 55–56, 65, 69
    Miʿrāj al-ṣuʿūd 69
    Nayl al-ibtihāj bi-taṭrīz al-Dībāj 54, 55, 65, 69
    Tuḥfat al-fuḍalāʾ bi-baʿḍ faḍāʾil al-ʿulamāʾ 55
  mention of 52
Aḥmad ibn Ḥanbal 46
Aḥmad Taymūr 82n11
Aigle, Denise 113
ajwiba (legal responses) 69
Akhbār al-quḍāt (Wakīʿ) 30
Akil, Touareg Sultan 57
Akpınar, Mehmetcan x, 7, 15–35
al-Aʿlām al-ʿaliyya (al-Bazzār) 115–116
ʿAlī b. ʿAbd Allāh al-Bunnāhī 132
ʿAlī b. b ʿAbd al-Raḥmān b. Samajūn 139
ʿAlī b. Brāhīm b. Salama al-Qazwīnī 79
ʿAlī b. Muslim al-Ṭūsī 43, 46
ʿAlī b. ʿUmar b. Muḥammad b. Musharraf b. Muḥammad b. Aḍḥā b. ʿAbd al-Laṭīf (ʿAbd Allāh) b. al-Gharīb (b. Khālid) b. Yazīd b. al-Shamir b. ʿAbd al-Shams b. al-Gharīb al-Hamadānī, Abū al-Ḥasan 141
ʿAlī l-Wāsiṭī 46
Almohad Caliphate
  spatial mobility of *qāḍīs* and 148
  vertical mobility of *qāḍīs* and 138–139, 146, 150–151
Almoravid dynasty
  spatial mobility of *qāḍīs* and 146, 147–148
  vertical mobility of *qāḍīs* and 138–139

Alp Arslān, Saljūq Sultan 172, 208
Amat al-Wāḥid 48
And-Ag-Muḥammads 56–59
Anjum, Ovamir 123
al-Anmāṭī, Abū al-Qāsim ʿUthmān b. Saʿd 166–167
Ansāb al-ashrāf (al-Balādhūrī) 19
Anushiravān 195, 198
appelations (*nisbas*) 57, 134nn20–2, 137
al-ʿĀqib b. Maḥmūd b. ʿUmar Aqīt 59, 64, 72n42
al-ʿAqīda al-Niẓāmīya (al-Juwaynī) 175
Aqīts
 in general 52–53
 And-Ag-Muḥammads and 56–59
 birth of scholarly lineage of 55–56
 "Egyptian capital" of 68
 social standing and wealth of 57–58
Arabic letters, numerical values of 210, 212
ʿArīb 2
Arjuwāsh 114
Armenia 101
artisans 133
Aṣḥāb al-ḥadīth (People of Tradition) 175
al-Ashʿarī, Abū al-Ḥasan 85, 168
Ashʿarism
 ʿAbd al-Jabbār and 79
 of Ibn Talha 214
 al-Juwaynī and 161, 164, 167–169, *169*, 177
 persecution of scholars of 160, 169–170, 176
 Sunnism and 85, 176–178
al-Ashraf, Ayyubid Sultan 208
Ashraf Hotak, Hotakid Emir
 coinage of 191–192
 decree on endowment for ʿAbdolʿaẓim Shrine 197
 edict from *see* edict from Ashraf
 legitimization of rule of 189–195, 198
 military expeditions of 185–186
 as Persianate emperor 191–192, 195–196, 199
 seals of 190–193, 197
al-Ashraf Khalīl Ibn Qalāwūn, Mamluk Sultan 218, 219, 223, 226
Askya dynasty 53, 62–63, 64, 71
Ávila, María Luisa 132
Ayyubid Empire *see under specific rulers*
Baghdad 43, 171, 172
al-Bāhilī, Abū al-Ḥasan 168
Baḥr al-fawāʾid (anon.) 212
al-Balādhūrī, Aḥmad b. Yaḥyā 19
Banū ʿAbd al-Waḥīd 147
Banū Abī ʿĪsā 135
Banū ʿAqīl 110
Banū Fatḥūn al-Anṣārī 147
Banū Furtish 147
Banū Ḥammād 138–139
Banū ʿImrān 139
Banū ʿIyāḍ 139
Banū al-Jannān 135
Banū al-Jumayyil 139
Banū al-Khaṭīb al-Tamīmī 139
Banū Makhlad 150, 151
Banū Marwān al-Hamdānī 139
Banū al-Muʾminānī 139
Banū al-Munāṣif 147, 150, 151
Banū Rushd 147
Banū al-Ṣaffār 135
Banū Samajūn 138–139
Banū Shurayḥ 147
Banū Simāk 135
Banū ʿUfayr 151
Banū Wājib 147
Banū Yakhluftān 139
Banū Zuhra 22–23
al-Bāqillānī, al-Qāḍī Abū Bakr 168–169
Barzegar, Abbas 178
al-Baṣrī, Abū ʿAbdallāh 80, 81–82, 86, 87, 88
al-Baṣrī, Ḥasan 80–81
Baybars II al-Jāshankīr, Mamluk Sultan 220, 226
al-Bayhaqī, *madrasa* of 163, 167, 169
al-Bazzār, Abū Ḥafs 99, 112, 115–116, 118–119, 121–123
Belkamel, Amal x, 8, 79–94
Berkey, Jonathan P. 4
Berriah, Mehdi x, 1–11, 98–124
bilād al-sūdān see West Africa
biographical dictionaries (*ṭabaqāt*)
 in general 1, 3, 40, 176n76, 177n81
 of Aḥmad Bābā *see* Aḥmad Bābā al-Tinbuktī
  see also Ibn al-Murtaḍā; al-Subkī, Tāqī al-Dīn
al-Birzālī 99, 114, 118

blood wit (*ʿuqūl*) 28–29
Bori, Caterina 111, 118, 121n109, 123
Bourdieu, Pierre 4
Broadbridge, Anne 4
Bughyat al-multamis fī taʾrīkh rijāl ahl al-Andalus (al-Ḍabbī) 132–133
al-Bukhārī 60
Būlāy, Ilkhanid commander 104, 105
Bulliet, Richard 3, 174
Būyid dynasty
  judicial authority and 88
  Muʿtazilism and 86
  origins of 83–85
  political power of 83, 88
  Shīʿīsm and 83–84
    see also under specific rulers

Cahen, Claude 83n21
Cairo 220
caliphates 225–226
  see also under specific Caliphates
Carocci, Sandro 2–3
Chamberlain, Michael 4
chancery/chancellery
  Hotakid *see* Hotakid Empire
  Songhay 59
  Ummayyad 27
chief judge (*qāḍī al-quḍāt*) *see* judges/judicature
coinage
  of Ashraf Hotak 191–192
  of Solṭān Ḥoseyn 187
collecting alms (*ṣadaqāt*) 28
Cooperson, Michael 40
council (*majlis*) 41–42
creed (*uṣūl al-dīn*) 121–122
Crone, Patricia 16
crusaders 107
Cyprus 107

al-Ḍabbī 132–133
Damascus
  as centre of Muslim scholarship 15
  during Mamluk-Ilkhanid War 103–105
  Umayyad court at
    Qabīṣa b. Dhuʾayb at 19–20, 25–28
    al-Zuhrī at 21–24
Darjazinians 196, 198–199
Dastur ol-Moluk (Mirzā Rafiʿā) 187–188

al-Dawʾ al-lāmiʿ li-ahl al-qarn al-tāsiʿ (al-Sakhāwī) 47, 50
al-Dawadārī, ʿAlam al-Dīn Sanjar 101, 219
deed of appointment, of judges 90
al-Dhahabī 99, 104, 117
Ḍirār b. ʿAmr 16n2
divine favour (*farr*) 192
al-Dulqundī, Ilkhanid commander 110
duties, of rulers 215–216, 222

edict from Ashraf (1138/1726)
  in general 185, 189, 198
  addressees of 194
  on Chancellery staff 196–197
  ḥadīth use in 194
  Qurʾanic passages in 193–195
  recurring theme in 194–195
  vs. Ṣafavid edicts 193
  scripts used in 194
  seal on 190–193
  translation of 199–205
education
  in general 41–42
  changes in 47
  of women *see* women
    see also teaching/training
Egypt
  al-Zuhrī's mission to 28
  Ibn Jamāʿa in 220
  Ibn Taymiyya in 121
  influence of, on *sūdānī* scholars 58–69
  judges in 30–31
  Qabīṣa's forced migration to 18–19
  sūdānī scholars traveling to 68, 70
El Cheikh, Nadia Maria x–xi, 7–8, 40–50
El Hour, Rachid 138, 139, 148
El-Merheb, Mohamad xi, 1–11, 207–227
El-Rouyaheb, Khaled 123
Empire of Mālī 60, 64
endowments (*waqf*s) 174, 189n19, 197
epistemology, political thought and 224n66
Escuela de Estudios Árabes in Granada (EEA-CSIC) 132
ethnicity
  of judges 61–62
  of *sūdānī* scholars 61, 70–71
  vertical mobility and 137
Eychenne, Mathieu 5

Faḍāʾiḥ al-bāṭiniyya wa-faḍāʾilal-Mustaẓhiriyya (al-Ghazālī) 208
Fakhr al-Dawla 84, 86, 88, 91–92
al-Fārisī, ʿAbd al-Ghāfir 162n11, 170
farr (divine favour) 192
Fāṭima bt. Aḥmad al-Sāmarriyya 48
Fāṭima l-Kurjiyya 45
fayʾ (spoils of war without fight) 110
female scholars (*muḥaddithāt*)
  in general 49–50
  creation of dynasties by 46
  in *Kitāb Tārīkh Baghdād*
    in general 40–41
    contact with scholarly world of 45
    developments in role of 48
    ḥadīth transmissions by 43–46
    teacher's certifications and 46
    teaching by 45
Fierro, Maribel 137, 138, 139–142
fiqh (jurisprudence) 81–82, 121, 164, 166, 175
Friedman, Yaron 101
friendship (*tavallā*) 193
fuqahāʾ/*faqīh* (men of understanding)
  use of term 15–16n2
    see also Muslim scholars
al-Furātī, Abū al-Faḍl Aḥmad 170
furūsiyya works 222
futūwwa movement 222

Gao 61–62, 66, 72
genealogy (*nasab*) 29
Ghaljāy Afghans 182, 183
ghanīma (spoils of war after fight) 110
al-Ghazālī 2, 48–49, 208
Ghazan, Ilkhan ruler 103, 219
Ghiyāth al-umam fī iltiyāth al-ẓulam (al-Juwaynī) 208
Gilbert, Joan E. 4
Goldziher, Ignaz 16
Griffel, Frank 161

ḥadīth
  as study subject
    of female scholars 43
    of al-Juwaynī 164
  transmissions of
    by female scholars 44–46, 49–50
    kinship networks and 43
  use in edict of Ashraf 194

al-Ḥajjāj 33
ḥalqas (councils) 41–42
Ḥamdīn b. Muḥammad b. ʿAlī b. Ḥamdīn al-Thaʿlabī, Abū Jaʿfar 143
Ḥammād b. Zayd 34
Ḥanafī legal school 82, 176
Ḥanbalī legal school 138, 176
Ḥarra, Battle of 19
al-Ḥasan b. Zayd, al-Dāʿī al-Kabīr 83
al-Ḥawwāriyya (sister of Abū Saʿīd) 44, 48
Hernández López, Adday xi–xii, 3, 8–9, 131–152
al-ḥilf bi-l-ṭalāq (oath of divorce) 112
Hinds, M. 16
Hirschler, Konrad 4–5
Hishām b. Ismāʿīl 23
Hodgson, Marshal G.S. 16, 175, 176n76, 177
horizontal mobility
  in general 7, 10
  of Ibn Jamāʿa 220, 227
  of judges in al-Andalus 139–143, 151
Hotakid Empire
  demise of 186
  establishment of 184–185, 186
  legitimization of rule of 189–195
  Ottoman diplomatic correspondence with 188, 195
  state administration during
    in general 186–187
    manuals for 187–188
    Supreme Chancellery 188, 196–197
      see also Secretariat; Supreme Records Office
  Sunnism and 192
Ḥumayḍa b. Abī Numayy al-Ḥasanī 110
Al-Ḥusayn b. Ḥayy b. ʿAbd al-Malik b. Ḥayy b. ʿAbd al-Raḥmān b. Ḥayy al-Tujībī, al-Ḥuzuqqa, Abū ʿAbd Allāh 141
Husayn b. Yūsuf b. Yaḥyā b. Aḥmad al-Ḥusaynī al-Sabtī, Abū ʿAlī 149

Ibn, as part of name 134–135
Ibn ʿAbbād al-Ṣāḥib Ismāʿīl 82, 86, 87, 88, 89, 90, 91–92
Ibn ʿAbbād al-Ṭalqānī al-Iṣfahānī *see* Ibn ʿAbbād al-Ṣāḥib Ismāʿīl
Ibn ʿAbd al-ʿAzīz, Marwān b. ʿAbd Allāh 143
Ibn ʿAbd al-Hādī 99, 112, 115
Ibn ʿAbd al-Ẓāhir 106

Ibn Abī Jaʿfar, Abū Muḥammad ʿAbd al-Raḥmān b. Jaʿfar Ibn al-Ḥājj al-Lurqī 143
Ibn ʿAsākir, ʿAlī b. al-Ḥasan 19, 176n76
Ibn al-Athīr, ʿIzz al-Dīn 169
Ibn Baṭṭūṭa 60, 102
Ibn al-Faraḍī 132
Ibn Fūrak, Abū Bakr 168
Ibn al-Ḥaddād 212
Ibn Ḥārith al-Khushanī 132
Ibn Ḥassūn, al-Ḥusayn b. al-Ḥusayn b. ʿAbd Allāh b. al-Ḥusayn al-Kalbī, Abū al-Ḥakam 143
Ibn Ḥawqal 85
Ibn ʿImad 170
Ibn Jamāʿa, Badr al-Dīn
  in general 218
  life/career of
    in general 207, 209, 227
    overview 219–220
  political thought of, professional mobility's influence on 221–227
  professional mobility of 220, 227
  on sultans/sultanate 222–225
  works of
    Mukhtaṣar ī faḍl al-jihād 221, 223–224
    Mustanadal-ajnādfī ālāt al-jihād 221–223
    Taḥrīr al-aḥkām fī tadbīr ahl al-Islām 207, 221, 224–225
Ibn al-Jawzī, Abū al-Faraj ʿAbd al-Raḥmān b. ʿAlī 170
Ibn al-Jawzī, Sibṭ 208
Ibn Juzayy 143
Ibn Kathīr 99, 102, 109, 112, 114, 117, 168, 219–220
Ibn Khallikān, Abū ʿAbbās Shams al-Dīn Aḥmad b. Muḥammad b. Abū Bakr 162n11, 170
Ibn Masʿūd 16n2
Ibn Muqla 2
Ibn al-Murtaḍā 82n11, 89n46
Ibn al-Muṭahhar al-Ḥillī 121
Ibn Qayyim al-Jawziyya 102
Ibn Saʿd, Muḥammad 21
Ibn al-Salʿūs, Shams al-Dīn 219, 223, 226
Ibn Surayj, Abū ʿAbbās 166
Ibn Talha
  Ashʿarism of 214
  life/career of
    in general 207, 209, 227
    overview 210
  al-Māwardī's influence on 215–217
  political thought of, professional mobility's influence on 212–218, 226–227
  professional mobility of 211–212, 227
  subjects studied by 210–211
  Sufism of 214, 215
  on sultans/sultanate 214–216
  works of
    al-ʿIqdal-farīd lial-malik al-saʿīd 209, 211
    Nafāʾisal-ʿanāṣirli-majālis al-Malik al-Nāṣir 211
Ibn Taymiyya
  anti-Mongol stance of 110–111
  incarcerations of 112
  influence of 123
  Mamluk power and 108, 113
  popularity of 118–120
  professional mobility of 98–117
  in general 98–100, 123–124
    advisor to Sultan al-Nāsir 109–111
    downward trend in 111–112
    Islamic sciences and 120–123
    within Mamluk army 113–117
    as official envoy 106–107
    preaching jihad 101–103
    as propagandist 101–103
    remunerations and 102–103
    spatial 99–100
    teaching positions 100–101
    vertical 117–120
    as volunteer diplomat and negotiator 103–106, 107
  pro-Nuṣayrī stance of 111
  works of
    dispersal of 121n109
    Minhāj al-Sunna 121
    Risāla al-qubruṣiyya 107
    al-Siyāsa al-sharʿiyya 111, 208
Ibn Tumart 121
Ibn al-Waḥīd 212
Ibn al-Zubayr, Caliph of Mecca 23
Ibrāhīm b. ʿAbdallāh al-Harawī 46
Ibrāhīm b. Qāriẓ 28n53
al-Idrīsī 2

ijāzas (teacher's certifications) 46
Ilkhanid dynasty
  war with Mamluks 101, 102–105, 109, 113–116, 117
    see also Mongol invasions
ʿilm ḥurūf (knowledge of letters) 210, 212
ʿImād al-Dawla 84
imāmates 223, 225
Imāmism 93
imāms 60, 62
inheritance, of slave women 22, 23
Inquisition (*miḥna*) 176
al-ʿIqdal-farīd lial-malik al-saʿīd (Ibn Talha)
  in general 209, 218
  dedication of 211
  structure of
    in general 213
    first section of 213–214
    fourth section of 217–218
    second section of 214–216
    third section of 217
  subjects covered in 212
iqṭāʿ (land grant) system 173–174
Iran
  under Hotakid rule *see* Hotakid Empire
  under Ṣafavid rule 183–184
al-Irbīlī, Tāj al-Dīn Yaḥyā 114
ʿĪsā b. Abī Bakr Muḥammad b. Saʿīd b. Muzayn (ʿĪsā b. Muzayn), Abū al-Aṣbagh 142
Iṣfahān/ Isfahanian 82, 184–187, 189–190, 194–195, 198–199, 200–201, 203
Isḥāq b. Qabīṣa b. Dhu'ayb 27
Islamic sciences
  al-Juwaynī's study of 163–164
  vertical mobility and 120–123, 133
ʿIyāḍ b. Mūsā 139

Jaʿfar b. ʿAbd Allāh b. Jaḥḥāf al-Maʿāfirī 142
al-Jāḥiẓ 208
Jalb al-niʿma wa-dafʿ al-niqma bi-mujānabat al-wulāt al-ẓalama (Aḥmad Bābā al-Tinbuktī) 55, 71
Jamshid 192
al-Jarajarāʾī 46
Jawhar (wife of al-Barāthī) 44
al-Jawhar al-nafīs fī siyāsat al-raʾīs (Ibn al-Ḥaddād) 212
Jenne 57, 61–62, 67–68, 71
jihad 101–102
journeys *see* travels
al-Jubbāʾī, Abū ʿAlī 82
al-Jubbāʾī, Abū Hāshim 80–81
Judd, S.C. 17
judges (*qāḍīs*) in al-Andalus
  horizontal mobility of 139–143
    in general 151
    as rulers 142
    state administration and 139–142, *143*
  professional *laqabs* among 134–135
  sources on 132–133
  spatial mobility of 143–149
    during Almohad rule 148
    during Almoravid rule 146, 147–148
    Berber rulers and 147
    in different periods 146–149, *147*
    emigration out of Iberian peninsula 148–149
    Maghrebi vs. Andalusī cities *149*
    other post in magistracy and 144–146
    reasons for travel and 143–144
    several posts as *qāḍī* and 146
  vertical mobility of 133–139
    during Almohad rule 138–139, 146, 150–151
    during Almoravid rule 138–139
    ethnicity and 137
    family connections and 135
    legal schools and 137–138
judges/judicature (*al-qāḍīs*/*al-qaḍāʾ*)
  in general 131–132
  in al-Andalus *see* judges (*qāḍīs*) in al-Andalus
  appointments made by 62
  appointments of
    in general 62–63
    ʿAbd al-Jabbār 82, 84, 87, 88–90
    deed of 90
    Ibn Jamāʿa 220
    political power and 132
    refusal of 131
    al-Zuhrī 29–30
  ethnicity of 61–62
  following Ḥanafī school of law 82n11
  Ibn Talha on 217
  other positions of 144–145

judges/judicature (*al-qāḍīs/al-qaḍā'*) (*cont.*)
  sources of income of 64
  of Timbuktu 56–59, 62, 64, 68
    see also judges (*qāḍīs*) in al-Andalus; *under specific names of judges*
judicial authority 88, 90
jurisprudence (*fiqh*) 81–82, 121, 164, 166, 175
juristic treatises 214–215
al-Jurjānī, Abū-l-Ḥasan ʿAlī Ibn ʿAbd al-ʿAzīz 92
al-Jushāmī 89n46
justice (*ʿadl*) 223–224
Al-Juwaini's Thought and Methodology, with A Translation and Commentary on Lumaʿ al-Adilla (Saflo) 160
al-Juwaynī, Abū Muḥammad ʿAbdullāh b. Yūsuf 162, 163, 165
al-Juwaynī, Imām al-Ḥaramayn 159–178
  in general 178–179
  Ashʿarism/ Shāfiʿism and 161, 164, 177
  birth date of 162
  intellectual genealogy of 164–168, *165*
  names of 162–163
  studies on 160–161
  subjects studied by
    Ashʿarī theological doctrine 167–169, *169*
    Islamic sciences 163–164
    Shāfiʿī legal doctrine 163, 164–167
  Sunnī doctrine and 159
  travels of
    Baghdad 171, 172
    Mecca/Medina 171–172
    Nishapur, departure from 160–161, 170–171
    Nishapur, return to 173, 174–175
  works of
    al-ʿAqīda al-Niẓāmīya 175
    Ghiyāth al-umam fī iltiyāth al-ẓulam 208
    Kitāb al-Irshād Ilā Qawaṭi' al-Adilla Fī Uṣūl al-Iʿtiqād 160
    Nīhayat al-maṭlab fī dirāyat al-madhhab 171

kalām (theology) 80, 81–82, 167–168, 175–177
Kamāl al-Dīn b. ʿAdīm 106
Kano 66
kātib al-rasā'il (chancery) 27, 59
  see also Hotakid Empire
Katsina 66
Kermān 186
al-Khabbāzī, Abū ʿAbdullāh 164
Khadīja bt. Abī Bakr 46
Khadīja bt. al-Baqqāl 45
Khadīja bt. Mūsā b. al-Baqqāl 46
Khālid al-Qasrī 29n58
Khalīl b. Isḥāq b. Mūsā b. Shuʿayb 54, 61, 67
al-Kharrāz, Abū Saʿīd Aḥmad 44
al-Khaṭīb al-Baghdādī 40, 42, 45, 79
khaṭībs (preachers) 61–62
Khodā-Bakhshi, Ḥamideh 189
Khosrow I, Sāsānid Emperor 195
Kifāyat al-muḥtāj li-maʿrifat man laysa fī-l-Dībāj (Aḥmad Bābā al-Tinbuktī) 54, 55–56, 65, 69
kinship networks 43
kinship ties 58–59
Kisrawān region 111
Kister, M.J. 32
Kitāb al-aghānī (Abū al-Faraj al-Iṣbahānī) 18–19
Kitāb akhbār quḍāt Qurṭuba (Ibn Ḥārith al-Khushanī) 132
Kitāb al-Irshād Ilā Qawaṭi' al-Adilla Fī Uṣūl al-Iʿtiqād (al-Juwaynī) 160
Kitāb al-Mughnī fī abwāb al-tawḥīd wa-l-ʿadl (ʿAbd al-Jabbār) 81n10, 82
Kitāb al-ṭabaqāt al-kabīr (Ibn Saʿd) 21
Kitāb al-taḥrīsh (Ḍirār b. ʿAmr) 16n2
Kitāb Tārīkh Baghdād (al-Khaṭīb al-Baghdādī)
  in general 40
  female scholars in
    in general 40–41
    contact with scholarly world of 45
    developments in role of 48
    ḥadīth transmissions by 43–46
    teacher's certifications and 46
    teaching by 45
Krusinski, Father 196
al-Kundurī, ʿAmīd al-Mulk, Saljūq vizier 160, 169–170
kuttāb see education

'Lā taqra'ū l-qur'āna 'alā l-muṣḥafiyyīn' (Kister) 32
Lājīn, Mamluk Sultan 101, 102
land grant (*iqṭā'*) system 173–174
Laoust, Henri 110
Lapidus, Ira M. 4
laqabs (nicknames) 134–135, 136
Law and Politics under the Abbasids: An Intellectual Portrait of al-Juwayni (Siddiqui) 160
Layth b. Sa'd 29, 34
Lecker, Michael 24n36
legal doctrine 131
legal responses (*ajwiba*) 69
legal schools (*madhhabs*) 5, 6, 137–138
  see also under specific legal schools
legal training, women's lack of 47
Little, Donald 8
Lucini, Mercedes 138

madhhabs (legal schools) 5, 6, 137–138
  see also under specific legal schools
madrasas (schools)
  establishment of 42, 174
  in Nishapur
    al-Bayhaqī 163, 167, 169
    Niẓāmīya 159, 161, 173, 175, 178
  Saljūq support for 159, 173
Maghrib, *sūdānī* scholars traveling to 65–66, 69–70, 71
al-Maḥāmilī, Qāḍī Abū 'Abdallāh al-Ḥusayn 48
Maḥmūd And-Ag-Muḥammad 56, 58
Maḥmūd b. 'Umar b. Muḥammad Aqīt 56, 59
Maḥmud Hotak, Hotakid Emir 182, 184, 185, 186–187
Maḥmūd of Ghazna, Ghaznavid Sultan 2
Majd al-Dīn al-Tūnisī 109
majlis (council) 41–42
Makdisi, George 47, 176
Makhlūf al-Balbālī 65, 70
Makkah 110
Makki, Mahmud Ali 143, 149
Mali *see* Empire of Mālī
Mālik b. Anas 16n2, 26, 61
Mālikī legal school 67, 71, 137–138, 176
Malikshāh, Saljūq Sultan 208
Mamluk Sultanate
  expeditions against population of Kisrawān by 111, 114
  Ibn Taymiyya and 108, 113
  professional mobility in *see* Ibn Taymiyya
  war with Ilkhanids 101, 102–105, 109, 113–116, 117
    see also under specific Sultans
Mamluk-Ilkhanid War 101, 102–105, 109, 113–116, 117
al-Ma'mūn, 'Abbāsid Caliph 2, 176
Mansā Mūsà, Mālian Empire ruler 67
al-Manṣūr Lājīn, Mamluk Sultan 219
al-Maqrīzī, Ṭaqī al-Dīn Aḥmad b. 'Alī 28n53, 116
Marcinkowski, Muhammad Ismail 188
Mardāwij b. Ziyār al-Jīlī 84
Marín, Manuela 133, 136n35, 137, 150
al-Marqabat al-'ulyā fī-mān yastaḥiqq al-qaḍā' wa-al-futyā ('Alī b. 'Abd Allāh al-Bunnāhī) 132
Marrakech 55, 69
Martin, Richard 176n76, 178
Martos, Juan 131n1, 138, 144
Marwān, Umayyad Caliph 20
al-Marwazī, Abū Bakr al-Qaffāl 165
al-Marwazī, Abū Isḥāq 166
al-Marwazī, Abū Zayd 166
al-Marzūbānī 33–34
al-Māwardī 90, 212, 214, 215–217
Mecca, pilgrimages to 67, 171–172
Medina
  al-Juwaynī in 171–172
  scholars in 15–17
    see also Qabīṣa b. Dhu'ayb al-Khuzā'ī, Abū Isḥāq; al-Zuhrī, Ibn Shihāb
Melchert, Christopher 175–176
men of understanding (*fuqahā'/faqīh*)
  use of term 15–16n2
    see also Muslim scholars
merchants 133
Messick, Brinkley 47
Michot, Yahya 106, 107, 113
miḥna (Inquisition) 176
Minhāj al-Sunna (Ibn Taymiyya) 121
Mi'rāj al-ṣu'ūd (Aḥmad Bābā al-Tinbuktī) 54n5, 69
mirrors for princes 111, 212–214, 218
  see also advice literature

Mirzā Rafiʿā 187–188
Miṣbāḥ al-hidāya fī ṭarīq al-imāma (anon.) 212
modernity, periodisation and 10–11
monastic complex (*zāwiya*) 41–42
Mongol invasions 99–100, 102–105, 110–111
  see also Ilkhanid dynasty
mosques, education in 41
Mu'ayyid al-Dawla 84, 86, 88, 89, 92
muḥaddithāt see female scholars
Muḥammad Aqīt 57
Muḥammad b. ʿAbd Allāh b. Yaḥyā b. Yaḥyā b. Yaḥyā al-Laythī, Ibn Abī ʿĪsā, Abū ʿAbd Allāh 140
Muḥammad b. ʿAbd al-Raḥmān al-Khazrajī al-Anṣārī al-Shāṭibī, Abū ʿAbd Allāh 148
Muḥammad b. ʿAlī b. Ḥammād, Abū ʿUbayd Allāh 139
Muḥammad b. ʿAmr b. Muḥammad b. Ayyūb b. ʿAmr al-Bakrī, Abū al-Qāsim 140
Muḥammad b. ʿĪsā b. Zawbiʿ, Abū Bakr 110, 141
Muḥammad b. Ismāʿīl b. ʿAbbād al-Lakhmī 142
Muḥammad b. Maḥmūd b. Abī Bakr Baghayogho al-Wangarī 61, 68
Muḥammad b. Maḥmūd b. ʿUmar Aqīt 59
Muḥammad b. Makhlad al-Dūrī 44, 46
Muḥammad b. ʿUmar b. Muḥammad al-Fihrī, Ibn Rashīd 149
Muḥammad b. Wahb b. Bukayr al-Kattānī, Abū ʿAbd Allāh 135
Muḥammad b. Yūsuf, Abū al-Qāsim al-ʿAbdarī, al-Mawwāq al-Gharnāṭī 149
Muḥammad b. Yūsuf b. Abī al-Qāsim b. Yūsuf al-ʿAbdarī, al-Mawwāq al-Gharnāṭī 136
Muḥammad b. Zakariyyā' b. Yaḥyā al-Tamīmī, Ibn Barṭāl, Abū ʿAbd Allāh 140
Muḥammad al-Kābarī 56, 58
Muʿizz al-Dawla 84
mujāhids (warriors) 113–116
Mu'jam al-shuʿarā' (al-Marzūbānī) 33–34
Mukhtaṣar (Khalīl b. Isḥāq) 54, 61, 67
Mukhtaṣarfī faḍl al-jihād (Ibn Jamāʿa) 221, 223–224
munāẓara 47
al-Muqaffā (al-Maqrīzī) 28n53
Murshida (Ibn Tumart) 121
Mūsā b. ʿAbd al-Raḥmān b. Ḥammād al-Ṣanhājī, Abū ʿImrān 139
Mūsā b. Muḥammad b. Ziyād b. Yazīd b. Ziyād b. Kathīr b. Yazīd b. Ḥabīb al-Judhamī, Abū al-Qāsim 140
Muṣʿab b. al-Zubayr 24n36
al-Muṣannaf (ʿAbd al-Razzāq) 26
Muslim 60
Muslim scholars (*ʿulamā'*)
  in general 1
  *adab*isation of 6, 207
  in al-Andalus *see* judges (*qāḍīs*) in al-Andalus
  in *bilād al-sūdān see sūdānī* scholars
  Būyid dynasty and *see* ʿAbd al-Jabbār
  as diplomats and negotiators
    in general 106
    Ibn Taymiyya 103–106
  emergence of 15
  female *see* female scholars
  in Imperial Songhay *see* Aqīts
  in Mamluk army 113–117
  Mamluk Sultanate and 108
    see also Ibn Taymiyya
  monopolising by 5–6
  professional mobility of *see* professional mobility
  professionalisation of 207
  as religious scholars 17
  Saljūq dynasty and *see* al-Juwaynī, Imām al-Ḥaramayn
  subjects studied by
    in general 16
    female scholars 43
    al-Juwaynī 163–169, *169*
    sūdānī scholars 60–61
  Umayyad dynasty and
    Qabīṣa b. Dhu'ayb *see* Qabīṣa b. Dhu'ayb al-Khuzāʿī, Abū Isḥāq
    al-Zuhrī, Ibn Shihāb *see* al-Zuhrī, Ibn Shihāb
      see also Umayyad dynasty
  variety of interests of 34
  wealth and 58
Muslim sinners (*fāsiq*) 81n8
Mustanadal-ajnādfī ālāt al-jihād (Ibn Jamāʿa) 221–223
Mutashābih al-Qur'an (ʿAbd al-Jabbār) 81

al-Muʿtaṣim, ʿAbbāsid Caliph 176
Muʿtazilism
ʿAbd al-Jabbār and 80–82, 87
Būyid dynasty and 86
fundamental principles of 81n8
vs. Sunnism 175–176, 177
Zaydism and 87
al-Muwaṭṭaʾ (Mālik b. Anas) 16n2, 26, 61

Naḍar b. Salama b. Walīd b. Abī Bakr b. ʿUbayd b. Balj b. ʿUbayd b. ʿAlī al-Kilābī al-Qaysī, Abū Muḥammad 140
Nāder, Shah of Iran 186, 199
Nafāʾisal-ʿanāṣirli-majālis al-Malik al-Nāṣir (Ibn Talha) 211
see also al-ʿIqdal-farīd lial-malik al-saʿīd
al-Nahj al-maslūk fī siyāsat al-mulūk (al-Shayzarī) 212
Najm al-Dīn Ayyūb al-Kurdī 116
nasab (genealogy) 29
al-Nāṣir Muḥammad, Mamluk Sultan 109–111, 116, 119, 220, 224, 226
al-Nāṣir Ṣalāḥ al-Dīn Yūsuf, Ayyubid Sultan 211
al-Nāṣir Yūsuf 106
naskh script 194
Naṣrid dynasty 146, 149
nastaʿliq script 194
Nayl al-ibtihāj bi-taṭrīz al-Dībāj (Aḥmad Bābā al-Tinbuktī) 54, 55, 65, 69
nicknames (*laqabs*) 134–135, 136
Nīhayat al-maṭlab fī dirāyat al-madhhab (al-Juwaynī) 171
nisbas (appellations) 57, 134nn20–2, 137
Nishapur
al-Juwaynī's departure from 160–161, 170–171
al-Juwaynī's return to 173, 174–175
madrasas in 159, 161, 163, 167, 169, 173, 175, 178
sectarian conflicts in 169–170
Niẓām al-Dīn Maḥmūd b. ʿAlī al-Shaybānī 104
Niẓām al-Mulk, Saljūq vizier 159, 172–175, 178–179, 208
Niẓāmīya *madrasa* (Nishapur) 159, 161, 173, 175, 178
Norris, Harry T. 57
Novo, Marta G. xi, 8, 52–73

oath of divorce (*al-ḥilf bi-l-ṭalāq*) 112
Öljeitü, Ilkhanid ruler 110
Ottomans/Ottoman Empire 184–185, 188, 190–191, 195, 197

Parsa, M.A.H. xii, 9, 182–205
Peacock, Andrew 211, 212–213
People of Tradition (*Asḥāb al-ḥadīth*) 175
Perho, Irmeli 5
periodisation, modernity and 10–11
Peter I, Tsar of Russia 184
Petry, Carl F. 4
pilgrimages 24n36, 67, 171–172
poetry 33–34
political power
of ʿAbbāsid Empire 83, 86
appointments of judges and 132
of Būyid dynasty 83, 88
political thought
epistemology and 224n66
loyalty or service to ruler and 207–208
professional mobility's influence on
in general 209
of Ibn Jamāʿa 221–227
of Ibn Talha 212–218, 226–227
pre-modern Islamic society
characteristics of 1–2
professional mobility in *see* professional mobility
professional mobility
in general 1, 5–11
of ʿAbd al-Jabbār *see* ʿAbd al-Jabbār
in *bilād al-sūdān see bilād al-sūdān*
horizontal *see* horizontal mobility
of Ibn Jamāʿa *see* Ibn Jamāʿa, Badr al-Dīn
of Ibn Talha *see* Ibn Talha
of Ibn Taymiyya *see* Ibn Taymiyya
in Islamic studies 2–5
of judges (*qāḍīs*) in al-Andalus *see* judges (*qāḍīs*) in al-Andalus
spatial *see* spatial mobility
vertical *see* vertical mobility
Prosopografía de los Ulemas de al-Andalus (PUA) 11, 132

Qabīṣa b. Dhuʾayb al-Khuzāʿī, Abū Isḥāq
forced migration of 18–19
in Medina 19
transmitters of traditions from 27

Qabīṣa b. Dhu'ayb al-Khuzāʿī (*cont.*)
at Umayyad court
ʿAbd al-Malik and 19–20, 25–27n, 35
admittance at 18–20, 35
roles of 25–28
teaching activities of 26–28
al-Zuhrī and 21–22
al-Qāḍī, Wadād 29n58
al-Qāḍī Abū ʿAlī Ḥusayn b. Muḥammad b. Aḥmad al-Marw al-Rūdhī 164
al-Qāḍī Abū ʿAlī Ḥusayn al-Marw al-Rūdhī 166
Qāḍī ʿIyāḍ 133, 142
qāḍī al-quḍāt (chief judge) *see* judges/judicature
al-Qādir, ʿAbbāsid Caliph 176
Qandahar 182, 183, 185
Qawānin al-wizāra (al-Māwardī) 216
al-Qazwīnī, Jalāl al-Dīn 109
al-Qushayrī, Abū al-Qāsim 170, 214
Quṭlūshāh, Ilkhanid commander 105

Rābiʿa al-ʿAdawiyya 2
Raff, Thomas 113
al-Raḥba 116
Rahmatallah, Maleeha 45n21
Rajā' b. Ḥaywa 27
Rāmhurmuz 82
Rasā'il (Ibn ʿAbbād) 89, 90
Rashīd al-Dīn 105
al-Rāzī, Ḥusām al-Dīn 114
refugee syndrome 100
repentance (*tawba*) 91
Risāla al-qubruṣiyya (Ibn Taymiyya) 107
Robinson, Chase 1–2
Rukn al-Dawla 84
rulers
duties of 215–216, 222
see also under specific rulers
Ruṣāfa 31–32
Russian Empire 184–185

Saʿd b. Ibrāhīm 31n68
Saʿd al-Dīn 105
ṣadaqāt (collecting alms) 28
al-Saʿdī 61–62
Ṣafavid Empire
Afghan revolt against 182, 183–186
reinstatement of 186
seals of 193, 197
Shi'ism and 187, 192–193
see also under specific rulers
Ṣafi, Ṣafavid Shah 197
Saflo, Mohammad Moslem Adel 160–161
al-Ṣāḥib Ismaʿīl b. ʿAbbād al-Ṭālaqānī 86
Saʿīd b. Abī Hind al-Aṣbāḥī al-Ṭulayṭūlī, Abū ʿUthmān 140
Saʿīd b. Muḥammad b. Maslama b. Muḥammad b. Saʿīd b. Butrī, Abū Bakr 140
Saʿīd b. Muḥsin al-Ghāsil, Abū ʿUthmān 135
Saʿīd b. al-Musayyab 22, 25, 28n53
Saʿīd b. Yaḥyā b. Qays 44
al-Saʿīd Najm al-Dīn Ghāzī, Artiqid ruler 211
al-Sakhāwī 47, 50
Ṣalāḥ al-Dīn, Ayyubid Sultan 208
Sālim Abū al-ʿĀlā' 27n47
Sālim b. ʿAbdallāh b. ʿUmar b. al-Khaṭṭāb 28n56
Saljūq dynasty
restoring social balance by 172–174
sectarian tensions under 169–170
success of 159
Sunnism and 159, 173–175
see also under specific Saljūq Sultans and viziers
Samāna bt. Ḥamdān 44
al-Ṣanʿānī, ʿAbd al-Razzāq 26
al-Sanūsī 60
Sayeed, Asma 46
Sayf al-Dīn Baktamur 103
Sayf al-Dīn Karāy 109
Sayf al-Dīn Qibshaq 101, 103, 104, 117
scholarly networks, in *bilād al-sūdān* 65, 66
schools/schooling *see* education; *madrasas*
scribes 27, 32–33
scripts 194
seals
of Ashraf Hotak 190–193, 197
of Ṣafavid Empire 193, 197
second *fitna* 19, 20, 22, 23
Secretariat (*Dār ol-Enshā'*; Hotakid Empire)
in general 182–183, 198
edict from Ashraf and 189
letters drafted by 192–196
re-establishment of 188–189
staff of 196–197
sectarian conflicts 169–170
al-Shaʿbī 33

al-Shāfiʿī, Muḥammad b. Idrīs 164
Shāfiʿī legal school 82, 163, 164, 176–177
Shāhnāmeh (Book of Kings) 196
Shams al-Dīn b. Maktūm Baʿlabakkī 113–114
Shams al-Dīn b. Quraysh 106
Shaqḥab, Battle of 115, 116
Shatzmiller, Maya 137
al-Shayzarī, Ayyubid vizier 208, 212
Shīʿism
  Būyid dynasty and 83–84
  Ṣafavid Empire and 187, 192–193
  vs. Sunnism 85–86
Shīrawayh 84
al-Shīrāzī, Abū Isḥāq 162n11
shurṭa/shurṭī 30–31
Siddiqui, Sohaira Z.M. 160, 170–171, 177n80, 224n66
Sīdī Yaḥyà 58
Sitta bt. And-Ag-Muḥammad 56, 57
Sivan, Emmanuel 100
al-Siyāsa al-sharʿiyya (Ibn Taymiyya) 111, 208
slave women 22, 23
slavery 54, 69
social mobility *see* vertical mobility
Solṭān Ḥoseyn, Ṣafavid Shah 187, 193
Songhay Empire 52–53, 59, 71
Sonni ʿAlī Ber, Songhay ruler 62, 66, 71
spatial mobility
  in general 7, 9–10
  during Almohad rule 148
  during Almoravid rule 146, 147–148
  in *bilād al-sūdān* 64–70
  of Ibn Jamāʿa 220, 227
  of Ibn Talha 211–212, 227
  of Ibn Taymiyya 99–100
  of judges in al-Andalus 143–149
spoils of war 110
students *see* teacher-student relationships
al-Subkī, Tāqī al-Dīn 119, 168, 170, 171–172, 176n76
Sudan *see* Songhay Empire; *sūdānī* scholars; West Africa
sūdānī scholars
  Aqits *see* Aqīts
  Egyptian influence on 58–69
  ethnicity of 61, 70–71
  pilgrimage to Mecca of 67
  political authorities and 66–67, 71–72
  positions held by 61–62
  professionalization of 59–64
  sources of income of 62–64
  subjects studied by 60–61
  travels of
    within *bilād al-sūdān* 66
    to Egypt 68, 70
    to the Maghrib 65–66, 69–70, 71
Sufism 214, 215
al-Sulamī, Abū ʿAbd al-Rahmān 47
Sulaymān b. Aḥmad al-Ṭabarānī 46
Sulaymān b. Ḥabīb al-Muḥārabī 30
sultans/sultanate
  Ibn Jamāʿa on 222–225
  Ibn Talha on 214–216
al-Ṣuʿlūkī, Abū Sahl 166
al-Ṣuʿlūkī, Abū Ṭayyib 166
Sunnism
  Ashʿarism and 85, 176–178
  Hotakid Empire and 192
  orthodoxy in 175–178
  Saljūq dynasty and 159, 173–175
  vs. Shīʿism 85–86
  use of term 175, 177
supreme political authority 223, 225
Supreme Records Office (*Daftarkhāneh-ye Homāyun-e Aʿlā*; Hotakid Empire)
  in general 182–183
  edict from Ashraf and 189
  fiscal administration in 197–198
  re-establishment of 188–189
Sutayta bt. al-Qāḍī b. Abī ʿAmr 45

ṭabaqāt see biographical dictionaries
al-Ṭabarānī, Sulaymān b. Aḥmad 44
Ṭāhira bt. Aḥmad al-Tanūkhiyya 44, 45, 46
Ṭahmāsb II, Ṣafavid Shah 184–186
Taḥrīr al-aḥkām fī tadbīr ahl al-Islām (Ibn Jamāʿa) 209, 224–225
al-Ṭāʾiʿ li-llāh 89
Taifa Kingdoms of Granada 146, 147
al-Tanūkhī, Abū l-Qāsim 45, 46
Tāqī al-Dīn Muḥammad b. Abī Bakr al-Ikhnāʾī 112
al-Tārīkh (Abū Zurʿa) 24n36
Tārīkh (Khalīfa b. Khayyāt) 25
Tārīkh madīnat dimashq (Ibn ʿAsākir) 19

Ta'rīkh al-sūdān (al-Saʿdī) 58, 61–62, 63
Ta'rīkh ʿulamā' al-Andalus (Ibn al-Faraḍī) 132
Tartīb al-madārik wa-taqrīb al-masālik li-maʿrifat aʿlām madhhab Mālik (Qāḍī ʿIyāḍ) 133
Tashīl al-naẓar ʿjīl al-ẓafarāq al-malikwasiyāsat al-mulk (al-Māwardī) 212, 215
tavallā (friendship) 193
tawba (repentance) 91
tax collectors 28–29
Taẕkerat ol-Moluk 188
teacher's certifications (*ijāzas*) 46
teacher-student relationships
 of al-Juwaynī 164–165, *165*, 167
 women and 48–49
teaching/training
 of caliph's children 31–32
 by female scholars 45
 by Qabīṣa b. Dhu'ayb 26–28
 of scribes 32–33
 in Timbuktu 60–61
 by al-Zuhrī 31–32
 see also education
theology (*kalām*) 80, 81–82, 167–168, 175–177
Timbuktu
 as centre
  of book trade 66
  of Islamic scholarship 53, 66
 golden age of 52
 imāms in 62
 judgeship of 57, 59
 preachers in 61
 teaching in 60–61
Timbuktu Chronicles 53, 59, 62, 64, 65–66, 67, 71
tombs, visitation of 112
training *see* teaching/training
travels
 of judges in al-Andalus 143–149
 of al-Juwaynī
  Baghdad 171, 172
  Mecca/Medina 171–172
  Nishapur, departure from 160–161, 170–171
  Nishapur, return to 173, 174–175
 of *sūdānī* scholars
  within *bilād al-sūdān* 66
  to Egypt 68, 70
  to the Maghrib 65–66, 69–70, 71
   see also spatial mobility
Tughril Beg, Saljūq Sultan 170
Tuḥfat al-fuḍalā' bi-baʿḍ faḍā'il al-ʿulamā' (Aḥmad Bābā al-Tinbuktī) 55

ʿUbaydallāh b. ʿAbdallāh b. ʿUtba 16
ʿulamā'/ʿālim see Muslim scholars
ʿUmar b. Muḥammad Aqīt 56, 57, 58
ʿUmar II, Umayyad Caliph 28n56
Umayyad Caliphate of Cordoba 142, 146, 150
Umayyad dynasty
 judiciary system of 17
 Muslim scholars and
  interaction between 16–18
  mobility of 137, 146, 150, 151
   see also Qabīṣa b. Dhu'ayb al-Khuzāʿī, Abū Isḥāq; al-Zuhrī, Ibn Shihāb
 state organisation of 15
  see also Umayyad Caliphate of Cordoba; Umayyad Emirate of Cordoba; *under specific Caliphs*
Umayyad Emirate of Cordoba 137, 146, 150, 151
Umm ʿUmar bt. Abī l-Ghuṣn Ḥassān al-Thaqafiyya 43
Umm ʿUmar bt. Ḥassān al-Thaqafiyya 44
Umm ʿUmar al-Thaqafiyya 46
ummahāt al-awlād 22
al-ʿUqūd al-durriyya (Ibn ʿAbd al-Hādī) 115
al-Urjūza al-maʿrūfa bi-Niṣf al-ʿayshfī tadbīr hādhihi al-ḥayāt (Ibn al-Waḥīd) 212
ʿUrwa b. al-Zubayr 28n53
uṣūl al-dīn (creed) 121–122
ʿUthmān b. ʿAlī b. Daʿmūq 131

vertical mobility
 in general 6–7, 10
 during Almohad rule 138–139, 146, 150–151
 during Almoravid rule 138–139
 ethnicity and 137
 of Ibn Jamāʿa 220, 227

of Ibn Talha 227
of Ibn Taymiyya 117–120
Islamic sciences and 120–123, 133
of judges in al-Andalus 133–139
of al-Juwaynī *see* al-Juwaynī, Imām al-Ḥaramayn
legal schools and 137–138
in West Africa 59–64
visitation of tombs (*ziyārat al-qubūr*) 112

Wādī al-Khāzindār, Battle of 103
Wakīʿ 30
Walāta 66–67
Walker, Paul E. 160–161
*waqf*s (endowments) 174, 189n19, 197
warriors (*mujāhids*) 113–116
Wāṣil b. ʿAṭāʾ 81n8
al-Wāthiq, ʿAbbāsid Caliph 176
Wellhausen, J. 16
West Africa (*bilād al-sūdān*)
centres of Islamic learning in 56
Islamization of 59–60, 64, 70
Muslim scholars in *see sūdānī* scholars
scholarly networks in 65, 66
spatial mobility in 64–70
vertical mobility in 59–64
see also Aqīts; Songhay Empire
Widigdo, M. Syifa A. xii, 9, 159–179
Winter, Stefan 111
women
education of
in general 41, 49–50
beyond *ḥadīth* phase 47–48
great scholars and 45
lack of legal training in 47
male relatives and 42, 43–45
subjects studied by 43
see also female scholars
*wqāf*s (endowments) 197

Yaḥyā b. ʿAbd al-Jabbār b. Yaḥyā b. Yūsuf b. Masʿūd b. Saʿīd al-Anṣārī al-Abbār, Abū Bakr 136, 137
Yaḥyā b. Bukayr 24–25n36
Yaʿīsh b. Muḥammad 142
al-Yaʿqūbī 24n36
Yāqūt al-Ḥamawī 162n11
Yazīd II, Umayyad Caliph 33
al-Yūnīnī 99
Yūnus b. Yazīd 33
Yūsuf b. ʿAbd al-Raḥmān b. Juzayy 143
Yūsuf b. Muḥammad b. ʿAlī b. Mūsā al-Anṣārī, al-Ghazzāl, Abū al-Ḥajjāj 136, 137

Ẓāhirism 138
zāwiya (monastic complex) 41–42
Zaydism 83, 87, 93
Zayn al-Dīn Abū al-Barakāt b. Munajjā 100
Zaynab bt. Sulaymān 44, 46
Ziyād b. ʿAbdallāh 46
ziyārat al-qubūr (visitation of tombs) 112
Zouber, Mahmoud 55
Zubayr b. ʿAbd al-Wāḥid al-Asadābādī 79
al-Zuhrī, Ibn Shihāb
financial hardship of 21, 22, 23
knowledge/skills of 33–34
on Qabīṣa b. Dhuʾayb 26
at Umayyad court
ʿAbd al-Malik and 22–25, 28, 35
admittance at 20–25, 35
dating of arrival at 22–24
mission in Egypt 28
Qabīṣa b. Dhuʾayb and 21–22
roles of 28–31
teaching activities of 31–32
unfinished book on genealogy 29n58
mention of 18

Printed in the United States
by Baker & Taylor Publisher Services